Economic and Social Integration

*In memory of my father*
*Wolfgang Friedrich Michael Schiek*
** 11 May 1930, Berlin*
*† 6 October 2009, Oldenburg i. O.*

# Economic and Social Integration

## The Challenge for EU Constitutional Law

Dagmar Schiek

*Chair of EU law and policy and Director, Centre of European Law and Legal Studies, University of Leeds, UK*

**Edward Elgar**

Cheltenham, UK • Northampton, MA, USA

Published by
Edward Elgar Publishing Limited
The Lypiatts
15 Lansdown Road
Cheltenham
Glos GL50 2JA
UK

Edward Elgar Publishing, Inc.
William Pratt House
9 Dewey Court
Northampton
Massachusetts 01060
USA

A catalogue record for this book
is available from the British Library

Library of Congress Control Number: 2012930563

MIX
Paper from responsible sources
FSC® C018575

ISBN 978 1 84844 542 0

Printed and bound by MPG Books Group, UK

# Contents

# Figures

# Abbreviations

(Italics indicate that this is a journal)

| | |
|---|---|
| ABGB | Allgemeines Bürgerliches Gesetzbuch (Austrian Civil Code) |
| Abs. | Absatz (German: paragraph) |
| ACT | advanced corporation tax |
| AG | Advocate General |
| API | Association de la presse international |
| ARENA | Centre for European Studies, University of Oslo |
| BBC | British Broadcasting Corporation |
| BENELUX | Belgium, the Netherlands and Luxemburg |
| *CBR WP* | *Centre for Business Research (of the University of Cambridge) Working Paper* |
| CFCs | controlled foreign companies |
| CFI | Court of First Instance (before 1 December 2009) |
| CFR | Common Frame of Reference |
| CISA | Convention Implementing the Schengen Agreement |
| CJEU | Court of Justice of the European Union (from 1 December 2009) |
| *CMLR* | *Common Market Law Review* |
| CNF | Consiglio Nazionale Forense (Italian council of lawyers) |
| COM | Commission (of the EU) |
| *ConWEB* | *Webpapers on Constitutionalism and Governance beyond the State* |
| DG | Directorate-General (of the Commission of the EU) |
| EATA | International Air Transport Association |
| EC | European Community |
| ECFIN | (DG for) Economic and Financial Affairs (of the Commission of the EU) |
| ECHR | European Convention on Human Rights |
| ECJ | European Court of Justice (before 1 December 2009) |
| ECR | European Court Reports |
| ECSC | European Coal and Steel Community |
| ECtHR | European Court of Human Rights |
| EEA | European Economic Area |
| EEC | European Economic Community |

| | |
|---|---|
| ELFAA | European Low Fare Airline Association |
| *ELJ* | *European Law Journal* |
| ELPA | Elliniki Leschi Periigiseon kai Aftokinitou (automobile and touring club of Greece) |
| ELR | *European Law Review* |
| EMS | European Monetary System |
| EMU | European Economic and Monetary Union |
| EP | European Parliament |
| ESC | Economic and Social Committee |
| EU | European Union |
| EUI | European University Institute |
| FII | franked investment income |
| FIM | Fédération Internationale de Motocyclisme (international motorcycle association) |
| FSU | Finnish Seafarer Union |
| G8 | The Group of Eight (Canada, France, Germany, Italy, Japan, Russia, the UK and the US) |
| GAEC | good agricultural and environmental conditions |
| GATT | General Agreement on Tariffs and Trade |
| GC | General Court (formerly Court of First Instance) |
| GDP | Gross Domestic Product |
| GG | Grundgesetz (German Constitution) |
| *I-CON* | *International Journal of Constitutional Law* |
| ILO | International Labour Organization |
| IR | industrial relations |
| ITF | International Transport Workers Federation |
| IZA | Institute for the Study of Labor |
| *JCMS* | *Journal of Common Market Studies* |
| MBL | Medbestemmingslagen (Swedish Labour Code) |
| MEP | Member of the European Parliament |
| MLG | multilevel governance |
| MPifG | Max Planck Institute for the Study of Societies |
| NBER | National Bureau of Economic Research |
| NF | neo-functionalism |
| NHS | National Health Service |
| nyr | not yet reported (in ECR) |
| OEEC | Organisation for European Economic Co-operation |
| OJ C | Official Journal of the European Union, C series (resolutions, recommendations, guidelines, opinions, etc.) |
| OJ L | Official Journal of the European Union, L series (legislation) |
| OMC | Open Method of Coordination |

| | |
|---|---|
| *ÖZP* | *Österreichische Zeitschrift für Politikwissenschaft* (Austrian journal of political science) |
| PPP | purchasing power parity |
| RECON | Reconstituting Democracy in Europe (research project) |
| SEA | Single European Act |
| SGEI | service of general economic interest |
| TEU | Treaty on European Union |
| TFEU | Treaty on the Functioning of the European Union |
| TGI | Technische Glaswerke Ilmenau |
| TRIPS | Agreement on Trade-Related Aspects of Intellectual Property Rights |
| UN | United Nations |
| UK | United Kingdom (of Great Britain and Northern Ireland) |
| US | United States (of America) |
| VAT | value added tax |
| WTO | World Trade Organization |
| WTO DSB | WTO Dispute Settlement Body |
| WZB | Wissenschaftszentrum Berlin (Social Science Research Center Berlin) |
| ZERP | Zentrum für Europäische Rechtspolitik (Centre of European Law and Politics, University of Bremen) |

# Acknowledgements

Following my migration from Germany to the UK in 2007, this book mirrors my intellectual journey from doctrinal to interdisciplinary approaches to the EU and its law. The journey was more meandering than originally anticipated: while the book should have been in print shortly after the coming into force of the Treaty of Lisbon, it only materialised during a renewed global economic crisis, arguably triggered by risky banking practices and a volatile housing market in the US. Its impact on the EU demonstrated impressively how solidarity between economically strong and weak Member States might be the only way for the Union to survive. Thus, the theme of economic and social integration gained unexpected currency. Developing answers to the question of what and how EU constitutional law can contribute became ever more difficult though.

While writing this book, I profited from numerous academic cooperative projects in which to reflect my ideas. These included the Blurring Boundaries Project (convened by Ruth Nielsen, Ulla Neergaard and Lynn Roseberry, Copenhagen), where I was able to discuss my first ideas for the European Social Model (2007) and the initial paper on the Social Ideal of the Court of Justice (2009), which grew into the methodology applied in analysing the EU's judicial constitution in Chapter 4. On the initiative of Dora Kostakopoulou, I was able to present my ideas on socially embedded constitutionalism to the Fifth Pan-European Conference on EU Politics in Porto (2010), and on the invitation of Ulrike Liebert I was able to present further developments on the Social Ideal to a RECON workshop in Bremen (2011). Commenting on the Antwerp expert seminar on 'Social Inclusion and Social Protection' (2011), on the invitation of Herwig Verschuren, Bea Cantillon and Paula Ploscar, I was able to reevaluate my analysis of the Treaty of Lisbon's values and objectives; and seminars of the FORMULA project (invited by Stein Evju, Oslo) and the REMARKLAB project (invited by Niklas Bruun, Helsinki, and Jonas Malmberg, Uppsala) inspired me to consider practical consequences. Last but not least, the book owes much to the multilateral research group 'EU Economic and Social Constitutionalism after the Treaty of Lisbon', which I convened at the University of Leeds, with the cooperation of Ulrike Liebert and Sandra Kroeger (Bremen), Hildegard Schneider, Sergio Carrera and Anja Wiesbrok (Maastricht), Peter Vincent-Jones, Caroline Mullen, Stephanie Fehr and Andrea Gideon (Leeds).

Andrea Gideon also provided valuable research and editorial assistance from 2010 on and particularly at the final stage of the manuscript. Without her help, good humour and perseverance all these grand ideas might not have materialised in a book. Also, Ben Booth and John Paul McDonald at Edward Elgar publishers were very supportive and never lost their patience over my numerous delays.

Finally, personal encouragement from many people helped me persevere in finishing this. I have met incredibly nice colleagues, not only at the *Centre of European Law and Legal Studies*, but at different schools at Leeds University and beyond, whose warmth, laughter and friendship created more than only a new academic home. First and foremost, I am truly and forever indebted to Ulrike Magdalena, who never ceased believing in my ideas and helped me through more than a few dark hours over this intellectual adventure, read parts and gave valuable feedback and generally makes my life worth living.

This book also commemorates Brian Bercusson and Ulrich Zachert, who both encouraged me to work comparatively and to risk academic migration. Their tireless work for imprinting EU law with more social justice is a continuing source of inspiration.

Dagmar Schiek
Leeds, 2 October 2011

# Table of cases

**Court of Justice of the European Union (numerical)**

**Court of Justice of the European Union (alphabetical)**

**General Court**

## European Court of Human Rights



## National Cases

# Introduction

This book returns to the pivotal question that stood at the cradle of the European Union: will accelerated economic integration of a number of European nation states and their societies lead to heightened degrees of social integration within those states and at a European level? And what does the European Union's law contribute to constituting the conditions of economic and social integration?

These questions are as current as ever, and possibly even more so after the Treaty of Lisbon entered into force on 1 December 2009. That date marks the end of an enhanced constitutional phase within the European integration process. The process of developing first a 'capital letter' Constitutional Treaty and then returning to the mundane process of a Reform Treaty was also accompanied by a heightened public awareness of the potential negative consequences that economic integration may exert on the social fabric of the European Union within its Member States and beyond.

There is some evidence that the negative referenda in France, the Netherlands and Ireland were at least partly influenced by fears that a further intensification of the EU integration process would damage the social models developed nationally.[1] Clearly these fears could not be backed up by the contents of the Constitutional Treaty: it did not change the EU's existing 'economic constitution', but rather added some more explicit social values. Nevertheless, the referenda demonstrated a realistic assessment of what economic integration without accompanying social policy will achieve: the demise of social integration both nationally and at EU level.

This book urges its readers to return to the original purposes of European integration, which always included enhancing the lives of the people living in Europe. If there was failure in the capital letter Constitutional phase, this failure lay in not displaying proper regard for this mission. Of course, it cannot be denied that the processes of economic and social integration in their interrelation pose a challenge both for the European Union and its constitutional law. This challenge needs to be addressed, to which goal this book seeks to contribute from a legal studies perspective. Clearly, the goal of striving towards economic and social integration cannot be achieved through law or

[1] See Schiek, 2010d, p. 162 with further references.

European legal integration exclusively. However, it has also been said that 'nearly everything the European Union touches turns into law'.[2] Even if this is an overstatement, the role of law in enabling or restricting societal processes such as economic and social integration must not be underestimated. This is especially true of constitutional law, which constitutes – whether with a capital C or not – higher law, against which other regulation is measured.

Accordingly, this book sets out to expose the extent to which EU constitutional law, in particular as developed by the EU judiciary, contributes to economic and/or social integration at EU and national levels and in how far it disembeds the economic and the social dimensions of European integration. Throughout, it engages with the influence of the EU and its constitutional law on societies in Member States and on the emerging European society. Therefore, the concern with constitutional law is from substantive – as opposed to institutional – perspectives, including the values which are supported by EU constitutional law in practice. Issues which will not be discussed include whether and how democratic legitimacy of a global polity can be secured[3] or how exactly transnational authority is capable of being legitimised.[4] The book is also not concerned with developing yet another theory of polyarchic democratic experimentalism[5] or an analysis of discourses between courts and other authorities for different entities.[6] All these questions have been covered extensively elsewhere, most recently in relation to EU constitutionalism after the Treaty of Lisbon.[7] In pursuing its aim of investigating challenges for EU constitutional law emanating from economic and social integration the book proceeds as follows.

Chapter 1 positions the legal studies perspective from which the argument departs within approaches of other social sciences to European integration and Europeanisation. It considers that the EU can neither be comprehended as a mere top-down process, through which EU policy making is 'downloaded' to Member States' spheres, nor as a bottom-up development through which

---

2 Kelemen, 2011, p. 29.

3 The question of how best to secure democracy through constitutionalism beyond states has inter alia been the theme of the 'Venice Commission' (for some documentation of its results see Nolte, 2005).

4 This is, to name only a few examples in chronological order, the focus of Schmitter, 2000, Longo, 2006, de Búrca, 2008, and Walker, 2010.

5 Developing deliberative polyarchy is the aim of Sabel, which he has pursued in cooperation with many authors, most recently – using dialogues between courts as an exemplary field – with Gerstenberg in Sabel and Gerstenberg, 2010.

6 For a cultural-critical perspective on discourses between courts see Cartabia, 2009; on the impact of EU courts' case law on Member States' prerogatives see Micklitz and de Witte, 2012.

7 On this see Schiek et al., 2011 and Wouters et al., 2009, see also Piris, 2010.

(some) Member States' perspectives are 'uploaded' to the European level.[8] Rather, the simultaneous processes of European integration governed from above and Europeanisation of national policy and societies from below influence each other and contribute to establishing European level polities and societies. Within these processes law is relied upon for justification of developments as well as for limiting political or social action, constituting an important factor of EU integration. The chapter further develops the notions of economic and social integration, identifying a number of challenges for pursuing social and economic integration in an integrated fashion. These include the impact of economic globalisation on EU discourse, the preference of (some) nation states to achieve social integration through closure rather than openness and the increasing dedication of the European integration project to purely economic principles such as competitiveness, growth and efficiency. The chapter concludes that such a mainly economic orientation risks the marginalisation of social values and along with this the alienation of large proportions of the citizenry. For the EU to regain credibility and its citizens' trust and to become an example of furthering social justice through models avoiding closure, it needs to engage with social integration.

Chapter 2 develops a notion of constitutional law beyond nation states suitable to take into perspective the interaction of law and society, corresponding to the societal notion of European integration developed in Chapter 1. It outlines the historical development of Western European national constitutionalism, demonstrating how national constitutions emerged from liberal constitutionalism and developed towards socially embedded constitutionalism. In considering two main elements of Western European constitutions, i.e. the protection of (human) rights and the establishment of spheres for democratic rule-making and collective governance, liberal constitutionalism is characterised by limiting its aspirations to narrowly defined public spheres, while socially embedded constitutionalism also strives to constitutionalise socio-economic spheres, to constrain private as well as public power and to enable women and men unable to rely on their wealth in cushioning their lives against being ruled by others to achieve true self-governance, individually or collectively. This rich concept of constitutional law at the same time is capable of meeting the challenges of social and economic integration. However, national frames of constitutionalism have become dysfunctional. While constitutional law can be developed beyond states, such constitutionalism has been more successful in relation to liberal rights than to socially embedded rights and democracy. The chapter considers how EU constitutional law could overcome these shortcomings, as a merely liberal EU constitutionalism would

---

8 The uploading/downloading metaphor is used by Börzel, 2002.

imply for the EU a failure to engender social integration. The question for the rest of the book is thus how EU constitutional law relates to the dichotomy of liberal and socially embedded constitutionalism, especially after the EU's 2004 Enlargement with its vastly increased diversity and socio-economic tensions.

Chapter 3 retraces the trajectory of EU constitutional law between those two poles up to 2004. It demonstrates that rights protection and democracy in the EU have developed on a specific trajectory that differs from those followed by European nation states. The EEC started with an economic constitution, which not only established new individual rights to access the common market beyond one's state, but also engendered embryonic social rights for free moving workers. This constitution was contradictory in that it engendered regulatory competition between Member States on the one hand and, on the other hand, created *fora* for social integration across borders. Elements of liberal constitutionalism such as effective human rights protection are relatively young at EU level, having been formalised only with the Treaty of Lisbon. Also, democracy in public spheres is of more recent origin. The interrelation between liberal and socially embedded constitutionalism at EU level was thus patchy on the eve of Eastern Enlargement and largely dependent on the Court of Justice (CJEU) for its development.

Chapter 4 analyses the development of the EU's judicial constitution, as it has been specified and reconfirmed in case law by the Court's Grand Chamber since Eastern Enlargement (2004). This chapter contains a numerical analysis of 173 out of 244 cases heard by the Grand Chamber relating to their positioning along the axes of liberal constitutionalism and socially embedded constitutionalism for the protection of rights and establishment of spheres for collective rule-making. It also offers a doctrinal and content analysis of these cases, distilling tendencies of development for the European judiciary as a key player in EU constitutionalism after Eastern Enlargement. The in-depth analysis and closer reading of cases demonstrates that the focus of CJEU case law is still on enforcing the internal market as the main element of economic integration, with an increasing tendency to support citizen's rights. This creates tensions within the EU legal order in relation to other elements of modern constitutionalism such as proactive conceptions of rights to penetrate socio-economic spheres and establishing European spheres of collective rule-making.

Chapter 5, in its first part, contrasts this factual judicial constitution with the EU's value and programmatic base as established by the Treaty of Lisbon. This part concludes that the Court of Justice will need to develop beyond today's achievements if it is to respect the recent changes, in particular in the normative notions relating to economic and social integration. However, the values now acclaimed by the EU cannot be realised by case law alone. This depends on active policy development through a range of forms of governance. The chapter's second part analyses how EU constitutional law allocates competences for the realisation of these values between Member States and the EU. It concludes that the multilevel competence regime is incomplete if only public actors are considered and that an open constitution is necessary to enable societal actors at national and EU levels to contribute to the social embedding of the predominantly economic constitution of the EU. It proposes that a constitution of social governance is read into the Treaties, which would offer the potential to meet the challenges of economic and social integration.

# 1. Economic and social integration

## I. INTRODUCTION

In relating economic and social integration to the EU and its law, it is necessary to position legal studies in the context of theories of European integration and Europeanisation, which are mainly developed by social sciences other than legal studies, such as economics, political science and sociology. This chapter first develops this theoretical frame.

Next, it will trace the notion of economic and social integration and propose an interconnected approach to these. Speaking about 'economic *and* social integration' is currently not common in European studies. This is in contrast with the original aims of the European Economic Community (EEC), which has now grown into the European Union (EU). Its Common Market (i.e. economic integration) was deemed to contribute to 'an accelerated raising of the standard of living' (Article 2 EEC), in particular among workers (Article 3(i) EEC). Accordingly, the founding Treaties pursued a dual aim of 'economic and social integration', which warrants the interrelated analysis of both concepts, as I have endeavoured to do here.

## II. TOWARDS A SOCIETAL PERSPECTIVE ON THE EU AND ITS LAW

Economic and social integration are societal phenomena. An interdisciplinary perspective on the European project is warranted to comprehend how these phenomena are related to the EU and its (constitutional) law. Economics, political science and, more recently, sociology compete with legal studies in theorising the EU. In sketching a societal perspective on the European project and its law, the first part of the chapter develops an approach adequate for this book.

### 1. Theorising the EU from State-centred Perspectives

Traditionally, the EU and its law have been approached mainly from the vantage point of states and their organisations.

This is true in particular for political science research, which is often considered the home of European integration theory.[1] Liberal intergovernmentalism[2] is a prominent example: perceiving the European integration process as a result of governmental bargaining between nation states, it explains the focus of European integration on economic issues by the Member States using the EU institutions as their functional agents; states are interested in entrusting EU institutions with (less popular) economic policies, while defending social policy as national terrain. Federalism,[3] too, is focused on states' activities. From its viewpoint, the cooperation of states will result in their amalgamation into larger federations, which may then (theoretically) take care of economic and social policies at EU levels.

International law scholars have also tended to analyse the EU as another instance of interstate cooperation. Their early EU integration studies appeared to be steeped in positivist doctrinalism paired with the excitement ignited by observing how international law could actually become a viable instrument of governance.[4] The integration through law scholarship[5] took this one step further and considered how EU law could be honed as an instrument of European integration, to create a new entity beyond states. However, even these works revealed a reluctance to relinquish a perspective on public institutions.

Similarly, economists can view the European project as an interstate endeavour. For example, Tinsbergen's definition of economic integration[6] focuses on the elimination of barriers to trade and production factors between states. It thus presupposes that national economies can function as separate units and that nation states maintain sovereignty regarding central factors of these national economies.

All these state-centred perspectives of the EU neglect the social base for attaining political, legal or economic integration and Europeanisation, and are ill-suited to the development of an approach to social and economic integration.

---

1 See, for example Wiener and Diez, 2009.

2 Moravcsik and Schimmelfennig, 2009.

3 Chryssochoou, 2009, pp. 57 et seq.

4 Arnull, 2008, pp. 416–417.

5 First Cappelletti et al., 1985, for further developments see Haltern, 2004. Political scientists' studies of integration through law rarely fully grasped the richness of legal scholarship though (see Curtin, 2006, p. 5, de Búrca, 2005, pp. 310–312 and Rehder, 2007) – with some notable exceptions (e.g. Alter, 2009).

6 Tinsbergen, 1954, more detail under section III, pp. 14–16.

## 2. Societal Perspectives on the European Project

This requires a societal perspective, in other words a view of integration as joining individuals into a coherent, although not necessarily homogeneous, society, integrating diverse individuals and groups. For the EU, the slogan 'unity in diversity' suggests such a societal perspective of blending individuals and groups from different states and regions into a multilevelled European society. Academically, societal perspectives, focusing on societal actors within states and at European level – such as trade unions, consumer associations, churches or social policy initiatives, which are not constituted by states or other public entities – have been developed from different disciplines.

In assuming that any political integration across states would require a sense of 'community and [...] practices strong enough [...] to assure [...] expectations of peaceful exchange among [the ] population',[7] Ernst Deutsch's transactionalism laid the foundations for the re-focus of international relations theory on societal actors.[8] In a similar vein, Haas's[9] vision of the European project as aiming at attaining a new political entity, in which societal actors have a central position, offered a societal perspective. His envisaged political community presupposes that 'groups and individuals show more loyalty to their central political institutions',[10] thus giving social actors an important role. Even after considerable reframing,[11] neo-functionalism maintains its focus on social actors as partly autonomous from states and supranational institutions. Multilevel governance (MLG)[12] approaches to European integration can be mentioned here also. Taking the interaction of 'institutional actors', i.e. public institutions, as a starting point, 'MLG' also considers the involvement of non-state actors at different levels of the polity, including undertakings, trade unions and other emanations of civil society.[13] Social

---

[7] Cited from Laursen, 2003, p. 4, referring to Deutsch, 1971.

[8] While some declare Transactionalism a dead theory (Wiener and Diez, 2009, p. 13), others appreciate it as the root of more current approaches (Chryssochoou, 2009, pp. 25–27), or base their theories on it (see Risse, 2010, p. 11 as well as Fligstein, 2008, pp. 8–11, Outhwaite, 2008, pp. 16–18).

[9] His neo-functionalist theory is often deemed the origin of EU integration theory (see Haas and Dinan, 2004).

[10] Ibid. at 5. See also Haas's own introduction to the re-edition at p. xiv: 'regional integration was expected to occur when societal actors in calculation of their interest decided to rely on the supranational institution rather than their own governments'.

[11] Niemann and Schmitter, 2009, pp. 45–46.

[12] Jachtenfuchs and Kohler-Koch, 2004, Chryssochoou, 2009, pp. 59–64. See also Stone Sweet and Sandelholtz, 1998 and Zürn et al., 2010.

[13] For a recent example see Littoz-Monnet, 2010, pp. 7–8.

constructivism, too,[14] in its focus on human beings and their interactions as the basis of social reality focuses on societal phenomena.[15]

Analysing European integration as a societal phenomenon is also the aim of the recently emerged sociology of European integration.[16] Departing from the traditional focus on national societies, it develops a conception of society in transnational spaces, such as Europe. Indicators of an emerging European society would include transactions between individuals at transnational levels.[17] Others would define the sociological perspective on European integration as one concerned with deeper structural changes in relation to solidarity and justice within national societies and an emerging European society.[18] Clearly, a European sociology may be different from a sociology of the European Union in that the latter not only considers national societies from a Europeanisation perspective, but also addresses the social base of European politics and law at European and national levels.[19]

Societal perspectives on the EU can also be derived from legal studies[20] if authors stress the role of law in integrating society and apply this to EU levels.[21] The notion of an 'integrative function' of national constitutions originates from the constitutional law theory of the Weimar Republic. Smend[22] first used this concept. He defined integration as unifying cooptation ('*einigender Zusammenschluss*'), considering it as one of the purposes of a (national) constitution. From a different perspective, Heller[23] demanded that any national political and legal order should strive towards establishing a type

[14] Christiansen et al., 1999, Risse, 2009. Haas saw social constructivism as the future of neo-functionalism (Haas, 2004, p. xvii: 'Our job is to see how NF [neo-functionalism] as amended by these challengers, can become part of a respectable constructivism').

[15] See Chryssochoou, 2009, pp. 110–113.

[16] Bauman, 2004, Delhey, 2004, Favell and Guiraudon, 2009 (with a literature review), the chapters in Favell and Guiraudon (eds) 2011, Münch, 2008, Fligstein, 2008, Outhwaite, 2008, Trenz, 2008. Both transactionalism and social constructivism have also been situated at the borderlines between political science and sociology (Favell and Guiraudon, 2011a, pp. 4, 8), Checkel, 1999.

[17] Outhwaite, 2008, pp. 128, 140; Delhey, 2004, p. 18; Fligstein, 2008, pp. 121, 165.

[18] Münch, 2008, p. 519.

[19] Favell and Guiraudon, 2009, pp. 559–562.

[20] 'Legal studies' are works by legal scholars integrating methods and deliberations from other social sciences such as political science, sociology and political economy (Shaw, 1995, p. 4).

[21] See Hurrelmann, 2004, p. 3; on different perspectives see Schaal, 2000, Grimm, 2005.

[22] Smend, 1968 (1928), pp. 121–186.

[23] Heller, 1971a (1930), translated to Heller, 2000.

of democracy capable of contributing to 'social equalisation'. Heller used the unfortunate term 'social homogeneity' (*soziale Homogenität*), which seemed to suggest that national unity depended on eradicating foreign elements. This was certainly not his aim. He was, rather, concerned with social antagonisms such as class antagonism. Heller feared that a weak democracy would be overthrown by a revolutionary coup of the working classes. He also recognised that 'racial conflict'[24] would form a main challenge for democracy in the 1920s. For both these reasons, Heller saw an integrated society as a precondition of any successful democratic constitution. His plea for social homogeneity aimed at achieving an equitable distribution of wealth,[25] which he again considered a prerequisite for 'social democracy' (*soziale Demokratie*).[26]

What Smend and Heller have achieved is to espouse two different concepts of society within the integrative functions of constitutions. Smend's understanding of the constitution's integrative function seems overly concerned with traditional values ('*wertkonservativ*').[27] In contrast, Heller's constitutional theory indicates a method of integration within societies that admits to and moderates conflict rather than denying it.[28] In contemporary debates these ideas have been taken up and applied to EU integration. Grimm[29] claims that any constitution should contribute towards societal integration, defining integration as the process by which citizens develop a common spirit. He maintains that constitutional values and norms can impact upon 'normatively influenced attitudes'[30] only on the basis of collective socialisation and community norms established within society. As he finds this precondition

24 Heller wrote during the German Weimar Republic, when 'racial conflict' referred to exclusion of Jews from the '*völkisch*' conception of the German 'race', among other forms of excluding those perceived as ethnically or racially different.

25 Heller, 1971b (1928) at p. 451.

26 In Heller's constitutional theory, '*soziale Demokratie*' (literally: social democracy) did not refer to the social democratic party (the traditional name of the German Labour Party), nor to a crude version of welfarist ideals that is sometimes termed 'social democracy' by Anglo-American authors (see e.g. Taylor, 2008, p. 5, Armstrong, 2010, pp. 232–235). Rather, the term is used as a contrast to '*bürgerliche Demokratie*' (literally: bourgeois democracy, although the translation quoted above in note 23 prefers 'liberal democracy'). While '*bürgerliche Demokratie*' caters to the need of the classes emergent in the nineteenth century, who could rely on their wealth for their sustenance, '*soziale Demokratie*' in Heller's vision should enable the '*besitzlosen Klassen*' (classes without wealth) to participate actively in public policy. It should also expand democracy to the work place, where the '*besitzlose Klassen*' were deprived of self-determination.

27 Schaal, 2001, at p. 228; see also Schaal, 2000.

28 Schaal refers to 'integration through conflict' as a therapeutic concept of the constitution, which he rejects (2001, reference to Rödel, Frankenberg and Dubiel).

29 Grimm, 2005.

30 Ibid., at p. 193.

lacking at the European level, he considers a European constitution useless. Schaal, by contrast, defines the constitutional aspiration to integration as enabling citizens to attain diverse concepts of the good life and self-governance. Such integration can also be realised in a pluralist polity such as the EU.[31] Preuß uses a social-constructivist concept of constitutionalism in order to define as one of the tasks of constitutions being to 'constitute union among discrete individuals', which again does not aim at assimilating these individuals into one homogenous unity.[32]

## 3. European Integration and Europeanisation

European integration theory, from the dominant political science perspective, was conceptualised to overcome the traditional schisms between international relations and comparative politics scholars.[33] This schism seems to reemerge in the divide between European integration theory[34] and theories of Europeanisation.[35] While the former focuses on the process through which individual states (and/or national societies) combine in the European Union as a new polity (and possibly society), the latter tend to offer a comparative analysis of how this process impacts on policies and societies within Member States.

The notion of European integration resonates with the notions of economic and social integration. However, this does not indicate that a 'top-down' approach to the European project is adequate for assessing these societal phenomena. European integration will never accomplish homogenisation of the many societies of Europe through a process of constructive and dialogical societal developments. Impacting on diverse societies within Member States, regional and local entities, it will engender Europeanisation, in a bottom-up perspective. In societal perspective, top-down and bottom-up processes of European integration and Europanisation occur simultaneously, and impact on one another. In order to grasp the challenges economic and social integration may pose for the EU and its law, we need to appreciate this simultaneous process rather than focusing only on one of its elements.

---

31 Schaal, 2000, pp. 70, 139, for sociological approaches see further text accompanying note 152.

32 See Preuß, 2010, p. 39.

33 Reh, 2008, and – criticising the distinction – Haas, 2004, p. xiv with note 4. Some prefer the presumably neutral notion of 'European politics', while combining an interest in non-state actors and state and international institutions (Wiener and Neyer, 2011).

34 See Wiener and Dietz, 2009 and Craig, 2011.

35 See Börzel, 2005.

## 4. The Approach of This Book

As mentioned initially, this book investigates economic and social integration from a legal studies perspective. Rather than defending any mono-disciplinary approach, this implies theorising the interrelation between economic and social integration and EU (constitutional) law from the main vantage point of legal studies, but drawing on other disciplines. The imagery of the 'tip of the iceberg' used in sociological European studies,[36] can also be applied to EU legal integration: formal law is but the tip of the iceberg of law as a social practice, and law is only one among other social practices shaping national and transnational society. The common denominator is that society lies at the base of the European project.

Without attempting to fully define society, it is assumed that society is shaped by human beings and their interaction, not only by abstract entities or notions such as 'the market', 'globalisation' or the 'laws of the economy'. Phenomena described by these terms are constituted through interactions between people – within limits posed by nature, including human nature. Even if markets, globalisation and Europeanisation appear to take on a life of their own, this is still the consequence of (past) interactions of and decisions by people. Society is governed by men and women – albeit not always by those bearing the brunt of the consequences and increasingly by interactions distanced from the location where impact is experienced.

Law in European democratic societies sets out to substitute government by men through government by law.[37] This always was an ideological construct: laws are made by men and (sometimes) women. Thus, what is achieved through 'government by law' is ideally self-government on a collective basis as opposed to a majority being governed by a minority or an individual autocrat. All such self-government through law rests on societal preconditions, e.g. a relative equilibrium of power between different factions of a society. In order to gauge these, European legal studies must take recourse to historical socio-economic conditions under which the European legal order(s) emerged. Moreover, law being just one social practice among others, it is not constituted once and for all by any positive text. Rather, it must be reconstructed hermeneutically in reference to the historical and socio-economic conditions of its emergence in order to fulfil any potential of social justice.[38] The analysis

---

36 See already Dølvik, 1999, Fligstein, 2008, p. 9, Favell and Guiraudon, 2011, p. 11.

37 See for more detail Chapter 2 II.

38 In relation to endeavours to reconstruct EU social integration as a legal mission, it is thus unconvincing to brandish 'recourse to transpositive and non-legal premises' as 'inconclusive' (as Joerges, 2011, 13, in condemning Menéndez 2011).

of EU (constitutional) law thus requires insights in its historical and socio-economic bases. From this perspective, it is also conceivable to allow for the emergence of autonomous societal law, rather than conceptualising EU (constitutional) law as a distribution of powers between public EU institutions and national public policy. A societal concept of EU legal integration, as an interrelated, simultaneous and multi-layered bottom-up and top-down Europeanisation process encompasses scope for acknowledging the legitimacy of transnational and European wide self-regulation – provided that such self-regulation is based on collective governance rather than the dominance of a few wealthy actors over the lives of many.

In methodological terms this approach encompasses the investigation of socio-economic reality as a basis for legal analysis. This is what the rest of this chapter sets out to do. The next two sub-chapters will analyse the concepts of economic and social integration from the perspective of social sciences other than law, tracing their historical development in particular in the EU polity. Any societal perspective on European integration and Europeanization theory will consider economic and social integration as interrelated processes.

To conclude: any further investigation of constitutionalisation processes needs to reflect on the phenomenon of bottom-up processes of economic and societal integration dynamics. Here, the German legal scholar Heller posed in the early twentieth century important questions as to how to achieve a social balance in societies that leave value-oriented legacies to a contemporary reading of integration dynamics across the EU.

However, separate academic discourses have developed on the issues of European economic integration and European social policy (a notion which we propose to replace by European social integration). Thus, it is useful to recapitulate these separate strands of debate before shortly considering economic and social integration processes in their interrelation.

## III. ECONOMIC INTEGRATION

In the public perception of European integration, its economic dimension is so dominant that economic integration is sometimes equated with European integration.[39] Ironically, this has led to a certain degree of under-theorising European economic integration as a process in its own right. While the Treaties provide a specific chapter on economic policy, there is little debate

[39] Daly, 2006, p. 464. This is also a typical textbook perspective, see Senior Nello, 2008, p. 123, and Craig and de Búrca, 2011, pp. 1–5.

about 'Economic Europe' or a 'European Economic Model'.[40] Despite this, economic integration is clearly one of the main pillars of the European integration process, and as such has commanded some attention in economics[41] as well as in sociology[42] and legal studies.[43]

## 1. Perspectives on Economic Integration

### a) State-centred versus societal notions

The term 'economic integration' has been defined as 'gradual elimination of economic frontiers between independent states' resulting in their 'economies [...] functioning as one entity'.[44] Such an interstate perspective has been predominant from the 1950s.[45] Following Balassa,[46] many distinguish different stages of integration: economic integration should proceed from a free trade area in which goods and possibly services would fluctuate freely towards a customs union in which a common commercial policy towards third countries would be introduced. The next stages would comprise a Common Market which would go beyond product mobility and include factor mobility, i.e. free movement of labour and capital, and progress further to an economic and monetary union and a political union. Molle added a further, and final, stage, namely the full union.[47]

Economic integration can also be analysed from within a state[48] or another entity, in which case divergence and cooperation between economic actors attain centre stage. The definition of global economic integration, developed for the World Bank, can be quoted as an example of such a societal approach. It focuses on the increasing ability of individuals and firms to undertake economic transactions with individuals and firms of other countries.[49] Whether a region or the world is economically integrated would also depend on the question of whether it is equally easy to enter into all kinds of economic

---

40 For an exception see Outhwaite, 2008, pp. 48, with reference to Alber.

41 See Baldwin and Wyplosz, 2009 on the disciplinary split of classical political economy into economics, sociology and political sciences, and for an attempt at a unified approach to European integration see Cafruny and Ryner, 2009.

42 See Outhwaite, 2008, pp. 45–71, who, of course, views economy as part of society (at p. 99).

43 See, for example, Baquero Cruz, 2002, Giubboni, 2006, and Sauter and Schepel, 2009.

44 Quoted from Molle, 2006, p. 4.

45 Tinsbergen, 1954.

46 Balassa, 1961.

47 Molle, 2006, pp. 10–11.

48 See, for example, Siebert, 1991.

49 See Begg et al., 2008, pp. 18, with reference to Brahmbhatt.

interchange from different places within the integrated entity.[50] There is a third use of the term 'integration' in economics, relating to how a single enterprise (or firm) sources, produces or markets goods or services. From the perspective of the firm, vertical integration means bringing together all these activities under single or joint ownership.[51] Microeconomic methods are utilised to decide which degree of vertical integration is suitable for specific firms and corporations. These analytical tools can also be used to discuss whether regional or global economic integration is feasible, although such applications are not very common.[52]

### b) Perspectives on global economic integration

Most economic integration theories rest on perspectives that have been developed for analysing and assessing global economic integration.[53] Predominantly, these derive from economics and partly from international political economy and sociology.[54] These perspectives constitute a background to European economic integration theory.

*(1) Orthodoxy: free trade and financial market integration* Orthodoxy's ongoing defence of the 'case for free trade' derives from the beliefs of the eighteenth and nineteenth centuries that 'comparative advantages'[55] are being multiplied by international trade. According to Ricardo's model of comparative advantage, trade liberalisation enables the rich as well as the poor national economies to capitalise on their specific comparative advantage. Comparing late eighteenth-century Portugal and Britain, Ricardo found that Portugal had a climatic advantage in producing wine and Britain a technological advantage in producing cloth, the latter based on steam-engine production, for the introduction of which Portugal was lacking in capital and engineering skills. He

---

50 Siebert, 1991, see also Fligstein, 2008, pp. 13–14.

51 See on this Williamson, 1985, pp. 85–86 with references to Kleindorfer and Knieps in note 1.

52 For applying Williamson's ideas on (EU) competition law see van den Bergh and Camesasca, 2006, pp. 31–35.

53 Global economic integration is often even equated to globalisation (see, for example, Stiglitz, 2002, p. 9 and van den Bossche, 2008, p. 4). However, global integration has cultural and even social components, for which reason the equation is not made here.

54 For references to critiques of viewing the economy in isolation Molle, 2006, p. 378.

55 Ricardo, 1817. Similar views were already defended by Smith, 1776. For accessible summaries of those theories see Hoekman and Kostecki, 2009, pp. 25–26 and Lowenfeld, 2008, pp. 4–5.

stated that both states could profit from trade liberalisation: if Portugal were to focus on producing wine and Britain on the wool, both would accumulate surpluses. In refining this model, Heckscher[56] and Ohlin[57] distinguished between national economies that were more capital intense and those that were more labour intense. Based on both these classical theories, today's conventional economists view the comparative advantages of countries of the Northern hemisphere as being able to produce goods and services requiring highly skilled labour and advanced technology, whereas the comparative advantage of countries of Eastern Asia and the Southern hemisphere is seen as their ability to trade with natural resources and produce goods and services requiring large amounts of unskilled labour.[58]

Both these classical models are vulnerable to critique. Ricardo's model neglects costs for transport, for example, and both only allow for a limited number of countries and types of products. Both models assume perfect competition and unlimited mobility of capital and labour, which are obviously unrealistic. More severely, both models neglect the social consequences of closing down such industries that do not enjoy comparative advantages and overlook the hierarchies between countries flowing from their capital endowment. Neither offers solutions for distortions resulting from these differences, the emergence of multinational enterprises and the effects of direct foreign investment.[59]

Guaranteeing free trade alone is generally not seen as sufficient to achieve global economic integration. States can also establish protectionist measures through monetary policies that obstruct financial integration. Accordingly, the second pillar of global economic integration is often seen to consist of international harmonisation of monetary policies and the establishment of an international regime for financial markets. Since the historical 'gold standard', several attempts to establish political control by states over the world financial system have been made. Immediately after World War II, the 'Bretton Woods' system established a default rule of a fixed exchange-rate system between world currencies through the 'par value system'.[60] This system relied on the ability and preparedness of the US to allow the dollar to function as lead currency by holding sufficient gold reserves to allow them to always convert dollars into gold. Its demise in 1971 is often quoted as the beginning of 'globalisation'.[61] While in hindsight the Bretton Woods regime often appears in a

---

56 Heckscher, 1919.
57 Ohlin, 1933.
58 Hoekman and Kostecki, 2009, at pp. 13–14.
59 Lowenfeld, 2008, p. 8. See also from an economist's perspective Maio, 2008.
60 See Lowenfeld, 2008, pp. 12–13, 622 et seq.
61 See for a rough overview Stiglitz, 2002, pp. 11–17.

golden light, it also had severe detriments. It limited the ability of states to devalue their currency by making devaluation above a certain threshold subject to international consensus. Thus, states which imported more than they exported could not rectify their external trade balance through monetary policies and an economic crisis could not be averted by making export goods cheaper. However, states which routinely exported more than they imported were not subject to a similar discipline. Accordingly, there was an inbuilt imbalance to the detriment of economically weak countries.[62] It is well known that other attempts to maintain the political control of exchange rates remained unsuccessful, with the result that currencies and state finances are subject to trading on global financial markets. The factual privatisation of financial markets has led to an acceleration of global financial integration, which is now ahead of trade liberalisation.[63]

*(2) Beyond orthodoxy* Recurrent global financial crises have highlighted the instability of any globally integrated market system. Accordingly, orthodoxy's optimistic views have not remained unchallenged.

'Welfare economics'[64] provided starting points for critical evaluation of classical appraisals of international trade. As a normative theory, it considers maximisation of welfare as the only legitimate parameter for organising economy (and society). On the basis of methodological individualism and utilitarian ethics, welfare is derived from individual preferences perceived as beyond change. Welfare is maximised when any change of a given entity will enhance and decrease the welfare of an equal number of persons ('Pareto optimum').[65] Applied to international trade, welfare economics identified conditions under which free trade was not preferable. For example, for states within which production was less efficient than in others, upholding tariffs may be advantageous.[66] Also the benefits of global welfare are frequently counterbalanced by increased income differentials, both within national economies and globally.[67]

Institutional economics[68] added a perspective focused on individual economic actors. Applying the transaction cost concept, they develop a model

---

62 See Lowenfeld, 2008, pp. 629 et seq.

63 See Begg et al., 2008, pp. 47–48.

64 Pigou, 1920, is often referred to as the founding volume of this. For an accessible introduction see Graaff, 1958.

65 Named after its inventor Vilfredo Pareto (Pareto, 1966).

66 See Graaff, 1958, pp. 122–139.

67 See Little, 2002, pp. 238–257.

68 Terminology is confusing here, as institutional economic approaches from the 1970s are partly referred to as 'new institutionalism' (see Levi et al., 1999, pp. 334, referring to Arrow, 1974). Williamson, whose work has been used above to explain a few ideas of welfare economics, is usually categorised as an institutionalist.

of individual economic actors who are neither fully informed nor fully rational, but rather act within 'bounded rationality', guessing their potential advantages. These individual actors are also influenced by loyalties, custom and other 'irrational factors'.[69] Institutional economics also take into account the effects of institutions on individual behaviour as well as on economic decision making.[70] From this perspective, international institutions are needed to achieve international economic integration under acceptable circumstances.[71] Also institutions will influence the conditions of economic integration once they are in place.[72]

Further critique arose from interdisciplinary approaches, such as the sociology of economics based on the works of Polanyi.[73] Polanyi observed that markets thrived on certain human characteristics, such as a drive to compete with each other and to take advantage of others, and worked to the detriment of those who relied on other values, such as cooperation and trust. Analysing the industrialisation of Britain as an example, he developed the idea that markets are only one aspect of society and are necessarily embedded within it. In his view, capitalism tended to disembed markets from society. He predicted that this would lead to re-embedding, if society were not to be destroyed. Neo-Polanyian scholars provided their own critique of orthodoxy's unwavering support for ever-increasing global economic integration, demanding the embedding of liberal international trade and monetary regimes by national policies enhancing social cohesion. For example, Ruggie's 'embedded liberalism'[74] proposed the taming of the uncontrollable beast of global economic integration through national institutions enabling the continuation of national social integration policies within an economically integrated world.

A combination of regime-oriented theories and sociological economy constitute the basis for 'varieties of capitalism' theories.[75] They assume that different national economies have established different institutions for production and exchange, which in turn favour and disfavour certain styles of economic developments. Liberal economies, which rely on free markets as

---

69 Williamson, 1985, p. 388, see also Williamson, 2010, pp. 678–679.

70 Levi, Ostrom, and Alt, 1999, p. 334.

71 Molle, 2003, see also Jones, 2005, p. xix from the perspective of welfare economics.

72 This neat summary is found in Molle, 2006, p. 13: 'Once in place, regimes matter. They create conditions and set the rules and thereby influence the behaviour of actors in such a way that they become conducive to the reaching of objectives'.

73 See Polanyi, 1957 (1944). For categorising this as economic sociology see Fligstein, 2011, pp. 102–103 with further references.

74 Ruggie, 1982. For applications to Europe with ample reference to Polanyi see Caparoso and Tarrow, 2009, and Joerges and Falke, 2010.

75 Hall and Soskice, 2001.

their main institutions, are distinguished from coordinated economies, which complement exchange on free markets by coordinative institutions such as corporations. Liberalisation of economic exchange beyond national borders will have different effects depending on the underlying style of capitalism. These theories do not offer a fundamental critique of international trade or economic integration, but rather expose the fact that comparative advantage of national economies is based on comparative advantage of individual firms, and that this comparative advantage can differ vastly in relation to the national style of capitalism. It can also be used to locate EU economic integration within the spectrum of different styles of capitalism.[76]

*(3) Critique* Economic integration as an interstate project is based on a never-ending escalation in the trade of goods and services across borders, accompanied by a steady increase in factor mobility. The preconditions for factor mobility develop unevenly though. International capital flows are provided by foreign direct investment and, increasingly, international banking activities. International mobility of labour, on the other hand, is still seriously inhibited by constraints of international migration. These curb mobility much more effectively than the often-quoted socio-cultural barriers individuals may experience.[77] On the basis of a fundamental optimism towards the effects of enhancing international trade on individuals all over the world,[78] even orthodoxy acknowledges the potential detriments of specific configurations of economic globalisation.[79] In particular, the negative effects of unrestrained mobility of venture capital on national policy choices are now widely acknowledged. Further to this, classical beliefs in self-regulating capacities of markets are increasingly questioned and competitive markets are no longer perceived as the only panacea for all societal problems.[80]

---

76 Sauter and Schepel, 2009, pp. 5–7. See also Höpner and Schäfer, 2010.

77 Boeri and Brücker, 2005. See also Freeman, 2006.

78 Hoekman and Kostecki, 2009, pp. 1–19.

79 The term of 'adjustment costs' is frequently used as an equivalent to 'collateral damage' caused in particular to developing countries by enforced economic globalisation (see Hoekman and Kostecki, 2009, pp. 19–21). Fundamental critique from orthodox economics has been prominently launched by Stiglitz, 2002; for a more moderated perspective see Molle, 2003.

80 This is for example mirrored in the fact that the 2009 Nobel Prize for economics was, inter alia, awarded to a political scientist, Elinor Ostrom. She had gathered impressive amounts of empirical evidence for the inferiority of competitive markets as governing instruments for common goods (Ostrom, 2010). Far from finding a 'tragic of the commons' (Hardin, 1968), Ostrom and her international teams established the superiority of cooperative forms of social governance for the so-called 'commons'. This approach can be used to criticise the commodification of all aspects of social life, which again resonates with the recent revival of Polanyi (see above, notes 72–73).

The case for (or against) global economic integration is overly reliant on classical economics with orthodox assumptions of methodological individualism, fixed preferences, complete information and unbounded rationality. The critique of these based on welfare economics, old and new institutional economics, sociology of economics as well as political economy is more convincing. The commonality between these diverse approaches lies in their move beyond an interstate towards a societal perspective, which also considers interactions between human beings.

## 2. European Economic Integration

This subsection considers how economic integration has developed and is conceptualised in the entity today named the 'EU', contextualising the evolving law of the EU in its political and historical context.

### a) Historical background

With the founding of the European Economic Community in 1957, economic integration became the primary imperative of European integration in practice. This was the consequence of failure to agree on political and military integration of a continent that was destroyed by two consecutive wars. The founding of the European Coal and Steel Community (1952) based on the Schuman plan was a highly political endeavour, subjecting German and French steel production to the High Authority,[81] among others for central planning. The explicit aims were to prevent future wars and to engender further political cooperation beyond the economy. However, the draft Treaty on a European Defence Union and a European Political Union were not accepted, leaving only the European Economic Community.[82] The idea that political integration would be the result of the incremental amalgamation of European (national) economies (i.e. economic integration) was, however, far from self-evident in the political climate in post World War II Europe.

This period was characterised by a shift to the left in European political life. Social justice and even socialism were widely seen as a precondition of democracy. The Western German and the Italian post-war constitutions even provided for socialisation of core industries. Communist parties gained strength due to their involvement in the anti-fascist resistance, engendering, among others, Italian euro-communism. Partly under the influence of these

---

[81] The High Authority under the ECSC Treaty was the factual predecessor of the European Commission and had as its task the guarding of the ECSC Treaty's aims.

[82] For a short overview see Baldwin and Wyplosz, 2009, pp. 15–17. See also Monnet, 1976, p. 323.

political tendencies, but also as a necessity of reviving the economy after the damage of World War II, several countries in Europe chose planification rather than market liberalism as the main economic governance principle. In the Netherlands, Tinsbergen[83] became the leader of the central bureau of planning. France entrusted Jean Monnet with the equivalent task.[84] These developments did not seem to constitute a fertile soil for the market liberal principles on which European economic integration was founded.

There were, however, countervailing tendencies. Factions of European political life were convinced that free trade and undistorted competition could serve as all-encompassing liberators. The so called ordo-liberals insisted that a certain legal framework was pivotal in order for competition and free trade to truly liberate Europe. Binding law should safeguard the 'economic order' from discretionary political 'interventions'.[85] From different perspectives, free trade between nations also acquired the status of a positive political value: historically, global economic integration as indicated by international trade had been growing from the fifteenth century and gained momentum from the early eighteenth century.[86] This momentum was interrupted by the two European wars from 1914 and 1939 respectively (now called the two World Wars), which brought increasing nationalism, fascism in a number of European countries and a decline in international trade.[87] From such accounts, free trade and more progressive forms of economic integration emerged as the alternative to the atrocities of fascism on the one hand and communism on the other hand.[88] The political impact generated by the Marshall plan contributed further to tilting the balance in favour of market liberalism: its money flows were contingent on the

---

83 Quoted above for his definition of economic integration (Tinsbergen 1954).

84 Damsgaard Hansen, 2001, pp. 237–308.

85 Not all facets of the debate on ordo-liberalism can be considered here. It certainly succeeded in reviving the credibility of economic liberalism (see Gerber, 1994, p. 83). Ordo-liberalism did not promote a laissez-faire approach to markets, but rather demanded legislation, preferably constitutionally protected against political change, to safeguard the functioning of the economy in line with rules that ordo-liberals construed as quasi-natural laws of the economy. The tendency to immunise the 'economic order' from political influence has been characterised as 'Schmittian' (see Baquero Cruz, 2002, p. 26) and was also influenced by thinking in 'specific orders' (*konkrete Ordnungen*), which again was central for national-socialist legal thought (Rüthers, 2005, pp. 277–302). The main creators of ordo-liberalism, Böhm and Eucken, were opposed to the Nazi regime as individuals though (Joerges, 2004, p. 10, Poiares Maduro, 1997, p. 63 with reference to Röpke). Classical Ordo-Liberalism was also not opposed to social policy in principle, but demanded that it only correct any undesired results of a market economy ex post. See also Schiek, 2010d, pp. 170–171.

86 See the table reproduced in Molle, 2003, p. 14, based on WTO sources.

87 Molle, ibid., pp. 22–23, Baldwin and Wyplosz, 2009, pp. 7–9.

88 See Baldwin and Wyplosz, 2009, pp. 6–7 and Ward, 2009, p. 212.

preparedness of governments to actively curb political influence of socialist or even communist parties.[89] In addition, Germany's overwhelming economic successes even early after the war[90] enhanced the credibility of ordo-liberal economic thinking, which again considered free trade a political value constituting a bulwark against a recurrence of fascism.

Such ideologies contributed to the optimism relating to European economic integration at large. As we have seen the academic critique of this optimism just emerged in the 1950s and has only quite recently gathered more support. While the EEC founders were not oblivious to potentially negative consequences of economic integration, the overall assessment that it would ultimately lead to social progress prevailed. Considering today's achievements in economic theory, some of this optimism may appear as naïve. However, while political economics have developed, the textual legal framework based on the thinking of those days has only been changed marginally. Only its teleological and renewed interpretation might ensure that the expectations of the founders can still be fulfilled.

### b) Milestones of economic integration in the EU

The post-war period under US American and liberal influences constituted a fertile soil for accepting economic integration as a political programme as well as for reestablishing the rule of law internationally,[91] on which the reorientation of European integration politics towards a primarily economic endeavour flourished.

*(1) Integration of product markets and factor mobility through law* The Common Market, as it was called in the 1957 EEC Treaty, was based on legal integration. The integration of product markets was provided for by a range of rules facilitating free movement of goods.[92] Free movement of intangible products was enabled by the freedom to provide services. Although the Treaty text stated that it was to be implemented 'incrementally' the EEC's judicial branch declared that this freedom, too, was directly applicable – twenty years

---

89 Eichengreen, 2007, pp. 64–69, Damsgaard Hansen, 2001, pp. 280–286. A contemporary account even referred to the 'education supplied by the various aspects of the Marshall plan' (Thorelli, 1958/59, p. 223). The Marshall Planners had no qualms in supporting Salazar's Portugal (Damsgaard Hansen, 2001, pp. 351–352) and the US extended aid from the OEEC to Spain under Franco as early as 1958 (ibid., 350). Western states certainly did not need to demonstrate abidance to human rights and democracy in order to receive funds.

90 Eichengreen, 2007, pp. 93–97.

91 See e.g. Damsgaard Hansen, 2001, pp. 265–269.

92 See further Chapter 3, pp. 81–82.

before the WTO even started to negotiate a General Agreement on Trade in Services in 1994.[93] The Common Market also comprised free movement of persons and capital. Thus, factor mobility complemented integration of product markets from the start, although free movement of capital was only introduced gradually: it became fully effective in 1993 (Treaty of Maastricht).

Apart from this, the Treaty provisions relating to economic integration have not been changed substantively over a number of Treaty Reforms, except for some streamlining and clarification, as well as the omission of a number of exemptions applicable during the transitional period until 1963. Their alleged character as 'economic constitution'[94] emerged from expansive judicial activity: the European Court of Justice[95] read the law of the EEC as enjoying supremacy over national law.[96] Significantly, the cases establishing this doctrine were based on free movement of goods, indicating that the practical use of direct effect and primacy would henceforth be of pivotal relevance to enforcing economic freedoms.[97]

While the founding Treaties were mainly oriented towards free markets, they also contained three counterfactual chapters, embodying other visions of the economy.[98] First, the common agricultural policy provided for extensive means for planning production, price regimes and ultimately consumption of agricultural goods. The external customs tariff was designed to protect European production and the common transport policy was meant to overcome any incentive of economically stronger Member States to disadvantage others by investing disproportionally into infrastructure. Thus, while openness inwards was constitutionalised, so was protectionism towards other, less developed regions, mainly in the field of agriculture. The acknowledgement of these policies could have grown into more fields where the European level was used in order to achieve an adequate infrastructure for the common market.[99]

---

93 ECJ 33/74 *Binsbergen* [1974] ECR 1299, paragraphs 18–27.

94 See Streit and Mussler, 1995, for a critique Baquero Cruz, 2002 (pp. 26–29).

95 The name of the Court was changed by the Treaty of Lisbon. Accordingly, case law and other activities from before 1 December 2009 will be referred to as of the 'ECJ' and relating to later developments, the new name with the abbreviation CJEU will be used.

96 See on this Chapter 2, pp. 65–68.

97 See further Chapter 3, pp. 83–90.

98 Baldwin and Wyplosz, 2009, pp. 353–379 (on agricultural policy).

99 'Within this large "home market", or common market, there must not only be free trade [...] There are other basic concepts in the treaty, like common responsibility and solidarity. Foreign trade policy, the coordination of general economic and monetary policies of member countries, social policy, policy for underdeveloped regions and, to a certain extent, agricultural policy and transport policy are based on those other basic concepts' Verloren van Themaat, 1960, p. 2.

*(2) The competition law regime* The Treaties also comprised a competition law regime, aimed at ensuring 'that competition in the common market is not distorted' (Article 3f EEC). In elaborating this principle, the Treaty prohibited cartels as well as any abuse of a dominant market position and subjected all state aid to prior approval by the Commission.[100] The EEC Treaty also contained an anti-dumping provision (Article 91 EEC), which has since vanished.

Up to the present day, it is unique for an international organisation to have its own competition law regime. While free trade and step-by-step liberalisation of factor mobility are now acknowledged principles of global economic law, a global competition law regime is not generally seen as a precondition of economic integration.[101] There is no competition law within the WTO[102] and negotiations on agreements in this field have not made much progress.[103] The mere existence of EU competition law thus proves the fact that EU economic integration transcends interstate relations, within which competition law is still seen as a mainly national affair.

In 1957, the emergence of a uniform European competition regime was a historical anomaly.[104] Competition law was very much a US tradition, into which even the United Kingdom joined only shortly after World War II.[105] US antitrust theory valued competition as the best way to decide on what is produced, in which quantities and how it is distributed. In contrast, European approaches typically only considered abuse of a dominant market position problematic, while appreciating that cooperation on markets may have positive effects.[106] Among the EEC founding states, Italy did not have any competition

---

100 More detail in Chapter 3, pp. 92–94.

101 See Molle, 2003, p. 251. Opinions differ whether this should change: US authors tend to support an international competition law regime (see, for example, Taylor, 2006), while Continental authors consider competition law an optional addition to market liberalisation (Molle, 2006, pp. 240–261).

102 van den Bossche, 2008, p. 508 points to anti-dumping provisions as a means for warding off extremely unfair competition and to the TRIPS agreement's rules targeting unfair competition through the use of geographical indicators (ibid. p. 779). Both examples are considered elements of fair trade law rather than of anti-trust law, though.

103 Ibid. p. 741. On the transnational relevance of the EU and the US competition law rules see Elhauge and Geradin, 2007, preface; Noonan, 2008.

104 Monti G., 2007, p. 1.

105 See Gerber, 1998, pp. 214–219. However, the first British competition law was less resolute than its US counterpart, in line with wider European environments (see Eichengreen, 2007, pp. 126–127).

106 This dual taxonomy (see Fox, 2008, pp. 434–438), constitutes a simplification: ideological rifts in competition law include many other issues beyond the ambit of this chapter, e.g. whether competition law can be used to create competitively large enterprises and whether and how its aims should be reconciled with social policy and regional cohesion (Monti, 2007, pp. 4–6).

law and the relevant legislation in France and the BENELUX states was focused on the abuse of dominant market positions, whose ban was merely enforced administratively.[107] A strict prohibition of cartels and concentrations, supporting a rights-based enforcement by individuals in addition to administrative control, only existed in Germany, arguably as a consequence of post-war pressure by the United States.[108]

Despite these differences in approach, the EEC competition law rules of 1957 were not only supported by Germany and the (absent) UK and Scandinavian countries, but also by the Dutch and the French government (represented by Jean Monnet).[109] The main collective motive was not promoting competition as such, but rather protecting the Common Market from anti-competitive collusions between firms, which would reintroduce barriers to interstate trade abolished by the EEC Treaty.

Today, the competition law rules are seen as the 'purest element of free market ideology' in the EU.[110] They constitute multiple challenges to national policies: Member States are restricted in encouraging a cooperative movement, in creating strong public services or social security systems or strengthening third-sector contribution to provision of welfare.[111] Unsurprisingly, Member States still resent EU competition law. While negotiating the Treaty of Lisbon, a coalition led by France achieved the omission of competition as one of the EU's objectives from Article 3(3) TFEU. However, the same notion was included in protocol No 27. As protocols have the same value as the Treaties, the omission in Article 3 TFEU was merely cosmetic.[112]

The text of the EU competition law rules has remained unchanged since 1957, except for the elimination of the anti-dumping provision. However, the approach of the European Commission and the Court of Justice towards competition law and policy has changed profoundly. While in the early years they stressed its contribution to the completion of the common market, 'economic' concepts of competition law have gained ground from the

---

107 On German, French and Belgian competition law in the 1950s see Thorelli, 1958/59; on the reluctance to accept European competition law see Gerber, 1998, pp. 342–358.

108 There remains some dispute on whether the post-war reintroduction of German anti-trust legislation owed more to US American pressure (Fox, 2008, p. 421) or to (German) ordo-liberal academic influence (Gerber, 1998). The longer tradition of US anti-trust law and the superior economic and political position of the US after World War II seems to suggest that they were more decisive than Germany though.

109 Gerber, 1998, pp. 337, 344.

110 Ward, 2009, p. 129.

111 On this see Wendt and Gideon, 2011.

112 See Piris, 2010, pp. 307–308.

mid-1990s.[113] This approach, too, rests essentially on political choices.[114] Debates on these values colour the further development of EU competition law and policy.

*(3) Economic policy and common currency (Economic and Monetary Union – EMU)* Liberalisation of product markets and enhanced factor mobility are only the first two steps towards a fully integrated regional economy, which should be followed by a common monetary system, accompanied or followed by a common economic policy.[115]

The European Union and its predecessors have followed a contradictory path, resulting in an ambiguous system: economic policy remains mainly the Member States' competence (Articles 120–126 TFEU), while monetary policy is mainly a common affair (Articles 127–135 TFEU).[116]

The process leading towards EMU, whose full exploration lies beyond the scope of this book, has been guided by a mix of motives: introducing a common currency might have served to cushion the European common market from adverse effects of global monetary instability;[117] establishing a common monetary policy may aim at pooling sovereignty in order to overcome the factual loss of autonomy resulting from the internal market;[118] and the specific shape of the EMU may also have been conditioned by self-fulfilling prophecies and economic scholarship fashions.[119]

The path towards the euro[120] began with the European currency 'snake', established immediately after the demise of the global fixed exchange rate system in 1972. The 'currency snake' soon became unstable. In 1978, it was replaced by the European Monetary System (EMS) with a fixed exchange-rate system, emulating the Bretton Woods system for the European economic space of the then nine Member States.[121] Similar to the Bretton Woods system, the EMS only subjected devaluation of national currencies to constraints, but

113 This is in parallel with US and global discourses on competition law (van den Bergh and Camesasca, 2006, p. 16 seq.) On the EU developments see Maher, 2011, pp. 728–730.

114 See Monti, 2007, pp. 74–79. Maher, 2011, seems to suggest that 'economic thinking' is decisive (p. 728), although she also gives an extensive account of individual commissioners' political scheming (pp. 729–730).

115 See above text accompanying note 47.

116 Piris, 2010, pp. 332–333 criticises the unresolved contradiction in this, while Jabko, 2011, develops a proposal for how to introduce true economic governance.

117 Lowenfeld, 2008, pp. 772 et seq.

118 Molle, 2006, pp. 265–265.

119 Cerami, 2011.

120 More detailed: Snyder, 2011.

121 Lowenfeld, 2008, pp. 772–775.

not a continuously positive external trade balance. Again, this constituted a bias to the detriment of weaker economies. From a European integration perspective, the EMS was seen as an incomplete monetary union.[122]

The Treaty of Maastricht introduced the EMU with effect from 1993. In 1999, EMU went into its third stage with the introduction of the euro and the irrevocable fixing of the exchange rates of Member States fulfilling the convergence criteria and having not negotiated an opt-out (as in Denmark and the UK). The EMU is based on the priority of price stability and budgetary discipline (Articles 126(1) and 128(1) TFEU). The budgetary discipline ordained by Article 126 TFEU is specified by a protocol annexed to the Lisbon Treaty: governments may only plan or incur deficits of 3% of their country's gross domestic product (GDP) and the government debt must not exceed 60% of the GDP.[123] Despite the finely regulated supervision of the monetary union by the European Central Bank, the Council and the Commission, there is 'considerable scope for discretion'[124] in applying these rules. Further, the protocol on the convergence criteria[125] specifies conditions, which not only determine when a country will have to introduce the euro as its currency, but also mirror ideals of economic policy: inflation must not exceed the inflation of the three best-performing Member States by 1.5%; there must not be any excessive deficit (as defined above); and exchange rates and interest rates must not deviate from the average for one and two years respectively. The Treaty does not provide explicitly for the option to refrain from the euro by the unilateral decision of any Member State, except by way of a negotiated opt-out accepted by all Member States.[126] As under the EMS system, there is still no sanction for producing a permanent export surplus. Member States with traditionally high export quotas thus maintain a means to counter-balance economic imbalance, which is not available to those with weaker exports. The recent crisis of the euro has accordingly led to the proposal that Germany leave the eurozone, in order to prevent its extreme export surplus from unbalancing the common currency.[127]

The provisions on the common currency bind the monetary and, partly, the economic policy of all Member States to political dogmas of austerity and

---

122 See Molle, 2006, pp. 271–272.

123 Protocol on the excessive deficit procedure, on its application see Council Regulation 479/2009/EC [2009] EJ L 145/1.

124 Snyder, 2011, p. 698, with references to political actors.

125 [2008] OJ C115/281, not substantively amended by the Treaty of Lisbon (see protocol 1 to the Treaty of Lisbon).

126 Athanassiou, 2009.

127 Stiglitz: Can the euro be saved? Project Syndicate 25 May 2010 (www.project-syndicate.org, accessed 17 September 2011).

conservative monetarism. They have been criticised for presupposing a high level of unemployment[128] and preventing deficit spending in particular in order to reduce unemployment.[129] The present crisis of the common currency has also spurred hopes for a more constructive approach.[130] The Treaty of Stability, Coordination and Governance, signed in March 2012 (but not yet ratified) again promotes budget discipline, however.

### c) Evaluating European economic integration

All in all, economic integration as defined by Tinsbergen is now securely anchored in the EU Treaties. Already the EEC Treaty enshrined the first two levels and the Treaty of Maastricht added the third level, stopping short of full political union. In theory, this development seems to endorse the assumptions of neo-functionalist integration theory: establishment of the common market and a competition law regime has led Member States also to adopt the next step, European Economic and Monetary Union. The question is, of course, in how far European economic integration has actually worked in practice.

The practical application of European economic integration has led to success as well as to failure. In the fields of goods and services, trade between today's EU Member States has intensified considerably since the 1960s,[131] and the convergence of prices for consumer goods seems to support this indicator of success.[132] However, factor mobility has not increased accordingly.

---

128 See Blanpain and Baker, 2004, pp. 165–189, paragraph 17 (no longer mentioned in Blanpain, 2010).

129 This contention was raised in a common newspaper campaign by the then financial ministers of France and Germany, Strauss Kahn and Lafontaine, published in *Die Zeit* (Hamburg) 14 January 1999, pp 17–18 (German) and *Le Monde* (Paris) 15 January 1999, p. 1 (French).

130 Cerami, 2011, pp. 364–365.

131 In the EEC (EU) Member States, the percentage of the GDP which can be allocated to import and export has increased from 6% (1960) to 20.7% (2010). The latter number is the same as in 2008. Data from Directorate General ECFIN 'Statistical Annex of European Economy' (Commission, Brussels 2011) tables 38 and 42.

132 According to EUROSTAT (see sub-data set 'price convergence between EU Member States', available from http://epp.eurostat.ec.europa.eu/portal/page/portal/product_details/dataset?p_product_code=TSIER020 from 1995 onwards and DG ECFIN, 1996, pp. 133 seq from 1980–1993) the purchasing power parity developed from 20 in 1980 to 24.9 in 2010. Purchasing power parity (PPP) is an index showing the difference in consumer prices, which means that a lower number indicates a higher degree of integration. The increase in disparity seems related to successive enlargements. If one only compares PPP in the 15 Member States constituting the EU from 1995, the PPP developed from 19.3 in 1995 to 14.3 in 2000 and, after remaining largely stable at around 14 from 2005 until 2009, it fell to 12.9 in 2010. Even among the 25 Member States constituting the EU from 2005, the PPP has decreased from 26.2 in 2005 to 29.9 in 2010.

The proportion of EU citizens living in other EU Member States stubbornly refuses to rise significantly above 2%.[133] This changes only in exceptional situations, such as the enlargement of the Union by more than ten new states. Significant levels of actual migration of EU citizens between EU states occurred between 2000 and 2007: an estimated 4.5 million moved from new Member States to old Member States,[134] representing only 0.5.% of the population in the old Member States, but 2.57 % of the population with respect to the Czech Republic, Estonia, Hungary, Latvia, Lithuania, Poland, Slovak Republic, Slovenia and 6.38% of the population of Romania and Bulgaria.[135] Regarding the mobility of the second decisive factor, capital, there are no figures available other than those on direct investment. These seem to show an upsurge of inner European direct investment.[136] Such overall gain in internal foreign investment corresponds to increasing inequalities within the Member States. Diversified attraction of Foreign Direct Investment frequently distorts the economic development of formerly integrated areas.[137] Accordingly, while national GDPs in the EU generally tend to equalise, differences within states tend to increase.[138] This is also true for central social indicators: income differentials have increased as a consequence of European economic integration.[139]

European economic integration's youngest branch, Economic and Monetary Union, favours export-oriented economies which can afford periods of austerity, as markets for national produce lie elsewhere. Today, it threatens to destabilise the world economy on the grounds also of the failure of the world's strongest economic regional bloc to establish an efficient common economic policy.

---

133 Databases on mobility of labour are notoriously weaker than on other economic factors. EUROSTAT tends to focus on the foreign population from other EU Member States in any given EU state, which includes economically active and non-economically active EU citizens. This percentage is measured as 2.3% in 2008, without any correction for the 2004 Enlargement (see Vasileva, 2010, p. 2). There are vast national variations, with 37% of the population consisting of EU foreigners in Luxembourg, 9.8% in Cyprus, 8.2% in Ireland, 5.1% in Spain, 3.1% in Germany and next to zero percent in Lithuania, Romania, Slovenia and Poland. Similar information is compiled in absolute numbers in the 'Eurostat Yearbooks' (see, for example, European Commission, 2010c, pp. 192–197). Due to an overhaul of statistical methods in this field (see European Commission, 2010c, pp. 187–191), the percentage of economically active EU citizens from other Member States in the EU is only available for 2006, when it was at 1.7% (see European Foundation for the Improvement of Working and Living Conditions, 2007, pp. 10–12).

134 European Integration Consortium, 2009, p. 29.

135 Ibid., p. 30.

136 Molle, 2006, p. 339.

137 Chen, 2009, Egger et al., 2006, Behrens et al., 2007.

138 See Begg et al., 2008, pp. 139–140 with reference to Saphir et al., 2004.

139 Beckfield, 2006.

### 3. Conclusion on Economic Integration

The mainstream concept of economic integration, which has been used in academic discourse from the 1950s, focuses on the amalgamation of markets formerly limited to spaces within national borders. The new, economically integrated entity would surpass national borders and encompass a larger, transnational or global economic space. The conventional perspective suggests that economic integration is best achieved by moving through a number of successive stages, starting with lowering and ultimately abolishing tariffs on foreign goods, proceeding towards a customs union and advancing further via free movement of products (including not only goods, but also services) and liberalisation of factor mobility (i.e. liberalisation of capital and labour movements) towards a monetary union with a coordinated economic policy. While global economic integration is only partly progressed, regional economic integration may be easier to achieve. The ostensible success of economic integration within the European Union is perceived as proof of this.

However, from a societal perspective on economic integration it is necessary to consider the question of whether economic actors actually engage in transborder activity, whether factor mobility is realised and whether a space without internal borders can be experienced by real people as matching their lifecycles and individual trajectories. From this perspective, European economic integration does not appear as quite so successful: labour mobility lacks behind free trade in goods and services as well as mobility of capital. Positive effects of economic integration are thus mainly experienced by a small elite of the population, while disowning effects are more widely suffered, in particular if resident in such regions from which direct investment is steered away. These distortions harbour the danger that the majority of EU citizens will experience the detriments of the internal market rather than the advantages. Thus, even where economic integration is successful, it may constitute a hindrance rather than a propeller for social integration.

## IV. SOCIAL INTEGRATION

The term social integration is less commonly used in European Studies than 'economic integration'. Preferred terms include 'European social policy',[140] 'social Europe'[141] or a 'European social space'.[142] 'Social integration' as a

---

140 Daly, 2006, p. 464.
141 Liebert, 2007.
142 Ferrera, 2009, and Freeman, 2006.

notion is preferred here[143] in order to stress that there are more dimensions to European integration from a societal perspective than just economic and political ones.[144] In defining this notion, there is less scope for relying on conventional views than in relation to economic integration, though.

## 1. Perspectives on Social Integration

### a) State-centred versus societal notions

One of the few authors using the notion of social integration in relation to the EU defines as a benchmark of its success a convergence of social trends resulting from harmonisation of laws as well as policy convergence. This could then culminate in citizens' experience of living in Europe as if in one country.[145] Interestingly, this is a societal rather than a state-centred perspective in that it focuses on citizens' experience and convergence of societies. From an inter-state perspective European social integration might aim at dissolving the national prerogatives for social policy and at the same time at creating a European social space – which might diminish the relevance of national borders to social integration. However, it is apparent that such perspectives are not currently discussed in European studies, except in the emerging sociology of Europe.

### b) Social integration within national societies in a post-national world

In contrast to the debate on economic integration, global perspectives on social integration are not yet widely discussed.[146]

*(1) What holds societies together?* Existing perspectives on social integration, initially fashioned for societies in the national age, have been characterised as being focused on the question 'what holds societies together?'[147] In this perspective, social integration occurs if social order can be maintained within a society.[148] In answering this question, typically a distinction is made

---

143 Authors who use the term in relation to the European Union include Böhnke, 2008, Borgmann-Prebil and Ross, 2010, p. 3, Delanty, 2009, p. 209, Fligstein, 2008, p. 5, Gallie and Paugam, 2002, Gerber, 1994, pp. 76, 80, 83 and Threlfall, 2003. These are listed in alphabetical order, as the degree to which the notion is defined differs starkly.

144 Similarly, Syrpis, 2007, distinguishes an economic and a social rationale for European integration (pp. 50–75). Syrpis, however, categorises the creation of the internal market not as economic, but rather as 'integrationist' (pp. 54, 12–17).

145 Threlfall, 2007, p. 273.

146 Exceptions to the rule include Alkoby, 2010 and Alexander, 2005.

147 Silver, 2010.

148 See Habermas, 1996, pp. 66–67, Trenz, 2008, p. 16.

between a Weberian and a Durkheimian (Parsonian) approach.[149] In the former, social integration is but one element of establishing legitimacy of social order and the voluntary adaptation of the normative values pursued by it.[150] Social integration is thus one of the elements contributing to a voluntary commitment to being governed. It presupposes a certain homogenisation of social opportunities and participation, though. Such notions of social integration seem to presuppose homogenous societies (or homogenisation as part of social integration). This might lead to de-recognition of different social or cultural positioning. The UN social integration programme thus proposes to reconsider such tendencies, in order to avoid disintegrating effects of a normative concept of social integration.[151]

In the Durkheimian tradition, social integration by spontaneous, voluntary appraisal of common norms and values only occurs in smaller units (communities), which are characterised by ties experienced as natural or given. This is a fertile soil for 'organic solidarity', an unquestioning commitment to common ethical and other purposes. In developed societies, which are characterised by increasing division of labour and anonymity, social integration depends on 'mechanical' solidarity. This form of solidarity can be engendered by negotiated exchange, for example. In some views, Parson's sociology builds on Durkheim and expands towards a concept of social integration based on diverse communities within a society.[152] This can be developed towards a notion of social integration combining 'unity' and 'diversity'.[153] If the nature of civilisation is to free solidarity from archaic forms of bonding, it needs to introduce a more rationally reasoned form of solidarity.

This leads to two ideal-typical perspectives on social integration: on the one hand, a homogenisation perspective would achieve social integration by injecting a community bond into society through common cultural or republican values.[154] On the other hand, a pluralist perspective would achieve social integration from the need of interaction between members of society as a result of its differentiations in modernity and beyond. Social integration would

---

149 See Habermas, 1996, pp. 66–78, Silver, 2010, Trenz, 2008, pp. 17–18.

150 Scharpf, 2009.

151 United Nations Research Institute for Social Development, 1994.

152 Silver, 2010, pp. 109, 170, Trenz, 2008, p. 17, see for a similar approach from a constitutional law perspective above pp. 10–11.

153 Trenz, 2008, uses the EU slogan 'Unity in Diversity' in criticising Durkheim/Parson (p 7).

154 I am acutely aware that there are vast differences between 'republican' homogeneity, which used to be seen as the stereotypical French way of integrating, and the culturally or even ethnically oriented type of achieving homogeneity, which has led and may again lead to erasure rather than mere exclusion of others. However, this differentiation is beyond the scope of this study.

derive from solidarity between those taking different roles in the (increasing) social division of labour or even in separately organised communities.[155] Both these perspectives converge in that they take a macro-perspective: social integration appears as an achievement of society as a whole.

They can be contrasted with micro- or individual perspectives on social integration, which perceive social integration as an achievement of the individual to fully participate in any given society.[156] From this perspective, it is also possible to define social integration as an obligation on the individual rather than a task of the polity or wider society. The concept of portraying social integration as an individual responsibility of those who may disturb homogeneity, such as non-welcomed migrants,[157] is a good illustration of the dilemmas of any homogeneity agenda of social integration. If individual integration is conceptualised as an obligation by the host state and its society to reach out to the newcomer in order to integrate her, no forced assimilation is achieved. This view would coexist better with a pluralist version of social integration, which could then be developed into a collective or truly societal responsibility. However, if individual integration is a responsibility of the migrant towards the host society, homogenisation is used to exclude those who will not assimilate.

Whether from micro- or macro-perspectives, there is as yet no uniform answer to the question of what exactly 'holds societies together', beyond the necessity to respect and promote a basic form of social justice.[158] From this perspective, social integration includes enabling individuals to participate actively in society and to fulfil their individual potential (micro-level integration) as well as balancing social tensions at the macro-level of society.[159]

Pursuing social integration from a macro-perspective can spur a variety of policies, not all of which are traditionally subsumed under social policy. For example, controlling excessive differences in income and wealth may engender social integration in the sense that no excessive cleavages are experienced by any individual citizen.[160] Beyond that, macro-level social integration can

---

155 See for a (mainly Canadian) constitutional law perspective on this Choudhry, 2008, with a review article by Meyers (Meyers, 2010).

156 See, for example, Maydell et al., 2006, pp. 74, 79 and – as an example of practical application – Kohli et al., 2009, p. 328: looking into interconnectedness as a precondition of individual social integration.

157 See for a critical appraisal, for example, Carrera, 2009, and Murphy, 2010. These authors do not link their views to wider perspectives on social integration though.

158 United Nations Research Institute for Social Development, 1994.

159 Schiek, 2001, paragraphs 75–76.

160 See Heller, 1971, p. 451, and more generally and recently Wilkinson and Picket, 2009.

be supported by institutions accessible and actually used by all. In republican countries the school system is one such institution: children of all backgrounds are educated together for basic or even secondary education,[161] depending on the degree of egalitarianism the society is committed to. Other examples for such institutions include social security institutions such as universal pension funds or health schemes. Further, the public provision of the distribution and sourcing of water, gas and electricity as well as public transport and public culture is also a necessary element in engendering social justice.[162]

Social integration at individual levels requires command over sufficient resources, the possibility of interacting with all members of society (and not just with the section one 'belongs to') as well as being able to make a sensible contribution beyond selling one's skills in the market place. De-commodification of men and women is thus another precondition of social integration.[163] With the increase of multiple social risks in the global knowledge society, enabling citizens to develop capabilities to cope with increasing insecurities becomes a precondition for individual social integration as well.[164]

*(2) Social integration and national social policy* So far, achieving social justice has been the focus of national social policy, which – as is submitted here – should aim at social integration from macro- and micro-perspectives, without pursuing an agenda of assimilating strangers, but rather of welcoming them in their difference. In contrast to economic integration, which can allegedly be achieved by removing barriers, social integration rests thus on a positive ideal (social justice) which necessitates positive policies for moving societies closer to it. Such policies have traditionally been developed at national levels and in this respect are often considered a specific legacy of European nation states.[165]

Within nation states in continental Western Europe, the institution supporting social integration as defined above has become known as 'Sozialstaat', 'Etat Sociale' or 'Estado Social'. The closest translation would be 'social state'

---

[161] See Busemeyer and Nikolai, 2010.

[162] Similarly Damjanovic and de Witte, 2009, pp. 53–54. For a narrower definition, which only includes public health care institutions, educational institutions, institutions offering social work, nursing and communal services, see Maydell et al., 2006, pp. 14–15 and (implicitly) Castles et al., 2010.

[163] Esping-Andersen, 1990, pp. 21 et seq., on the relation between de-commodification and social integration see p. 40, see also Esping-Andersen, 1999.

[164] See Browne et al., 2002; for European perspectives: Deakin, 2005. The latest offspring of this is Deakin and Supiot's *Capacitas*, 2009, now focusing on contract law. Similar, from the perspective of 'modernising' welfare states Maydell et al., 2006, pp. 73–89, Giddens, 2000 and 2006.

[165] On the European Social Model see Schiek, 2008, Falkner, 2010.

rather than 'welfare state', which may mirror a narrow notion of social policy as merely redistributive.[166] The European social state has never been limited to money transfers. Of course, redistributive measures have always been and continue to be an important element of national welfare states in Europe.[167] These payments may be made to avert risks ('social protection'), or to combat poverty (which is now often referred to as 'social inclusion').[168] However, further spectrums of norms aimed at social integration through law[169] include structural measures to socially embed the economy, inter alia, by socially imbued consumer law, labour law and co-determination structures. This is a form of active social state that does not rely on state dirigisme, but rather empowers those who are in danger of being disintegrated socially to become active in their own interest.[170] If it is to include all these traditions, European social integration requires a regulatory approach to the economy in different aspects. It will range from enabling collective relations between workers and employers as well as between landlords and tenants towards establishing a normative framework for equal access of all to education, water or land.

We can thus identify three cornerstones of social policy at national levels (focusing on EU Member States): (1) classical welfare state policies providing social protection and the combat of poverty; (2) combating domination in 'non-public' social relations, e.g. in markets for labour, housing or consumption; (3) the provision of services deemed necessary to provide full participation in society. Further, we can establish that social policy at national level can operate through three archetypical forms: redistributive payments, provision of public services exempted from market rules and the regulation of relationships on the market, which can, in part, substitute for one another. For example, comprehensive employment protection legislation may reduce the risk of becoming unemployed. As a consequence, fewer payments to unemployed persons may be necessary. Or, if there is a smoothly functioning public hospital sector, which is accessible to all, payments for obtaining adequate medical

166 A UK definition reads: 'A welfare state is a state in which the government ensures the basic social and economic necessities of its citizens by providing, through the revenues it raises from taxes and other sources, goods and services such as education, health, housing and social security' (Budge et al., 2001). This narrow vision of welfarism is also used in intergovernmentalist writings on European integration (Moravcsik, 2004, pp. 355–358).

167 Damjanovic and de Witte, 2009, and Ferrera, 2009. If only considering money transfers, the EU and the US models of welfare provision are less different than usually assumed (Alber, 2010).

168 This is particularly typical for EU policy documents, see for example European Commission, 2010a.

169 On the notion of 'Sozialstaat' in Germany see Schiek, 2001, paragraphs 1–46.

170 For a defence of the resulting 'active welfare' see Wincott, 2003, p. 549.

treatment can be lower, as they will only have to cover the cost of medical treatment outside hospitals.

*(3) Social integration beyond national borders* Since the capacity of nation states is diminishing, the question arises as to how far policies in favour of social integration can be pursued beyond national borders. The pushes and pulls of global economic integration[171] have interlinked economies and societies with each other. This has not happened without having an effect on social integration within nation states.[172] Generally, it can be assumed that increased global economic integration also leads to increased economic risks. Accordingly, protection of citizens against economic risks becomes more important and more difficult from a nation-state perspective. At the same time, global economic integration has in Europe led to higher demands for better-educated workers who are able to adapt faster to changing demands. Policies to increase or only maintain social integration at national levels will thus have to provide for higher degrees of flexibility, levels of qualification and adaptability. Finally, some data suggests that global economic integration increases inequality within nation states and may even impact negatively on tax bases and thus restrict the redistributive capacity of states.[173] In so far as mitigating inequalities belongs to the aims of social integration, this will also pose greater challenges.[174]

Whether all this can lead to developing dimensions of social integration that go beyond nation states is disputed. Mainstream discourse remains doubtful: assuming that feelings of solidarity are necessary to support social policy, and that these feelings presuppose bonds of cohesive community, it is often presumed that social policy presupposes functioning nation states.[175] However, global social movements such as those criticising globalisation,[176] but also transnational or even global cooperation between trade unionists

---

171 See above III 1. b) (pp. 15–20).

172 The exact effects are disputed though. Begg et al. (2008), conclude that economic global integration only has limited immediate effects on national welfare states and that any reduction in payments results from neo-liberal ideologies gaining currency alongside global economic integration. Glennerster (2010) equally maintains that the Western welfare states are sustainable economically, but may be threatened by increased ethnic diversity and the lack of solidarity towards migrants.

173 See Begg et al., 2008, pp. 45–47, 59.

174 See for the interrelation of global economic integration and national social policy von Maydell et al., 2006, pp. 28–45 and on social inequalities Begg et al., 2008, pp. 56–66, each with numerous further references and literature reviews.

175 See, for example, Graser, 2006, Lamping, 2010, p. 47, concluding that citizens still have a merely instrumental relation to the EU, which does not induce transnational solidarity at p. 72.

176 See de Sousa Santos, 2005.

aiming to create new social norms,[177] can be cited as counterfactual evidence of global solidarity. Despite all this, global notions of social integration are not very widespread and academic pleas to enhance potential for global social integration will usually not go beyond the demand of initiating discourses in mainly public spheres.[178]

To date, only a few initial cautious steps towards global social policy have been attempted. As a reaction to doubt as to the viability of exclusively economic globalisation,[179] the United Nations has endorsed social integration into its overall framework for advancing social development after the Copenhagen World Summit for Social Development (1995). This culminated in making 'social integration' the priority theme for the 2009–10 session of the UN Commission for Social Development.[180] In addition to related EU policy documents[181] and research informing these policy documents,[182] the theme of global social integration is also taken up in academic research.[183] However, the development of approaches proceeds more from national and even sub-national levels towards European and global levels than the other way round, as is the case for economic integration.

This mirrors a tendency to believe in the global dimension of economic integration, while the muddy waters of social policy should be left for the (increasingly powerless) nation states to deal with (or rather to neglect). Just as classical liberalism assumes that states should provide an adequate economic and political environment for individuals to lead their lives in line with their individual values, liberal international relation theory states that international law should provide an adequate frame for international cooperation between states and for international trade, but leave social policy choices to individual states.[184] As an important voice of modern liberal thought, Rawls[185] has been read as proposing a double social contract theory, which, in effect, proposes to endow international law with the capacity to establish relations between liberal states, which would remain sovereign in particular as

---

177 See Moreau, 2007, and for an early reference for one of the global collective agreements that clashed with EU constitutional law Däubler, 1997.

178 For example Alkoby, 2010.

179 See United Nations Secretary-General, 2009, pp. 17, conclusion para 71.

180 See United Nations Commission for Social Development, 2010, United Nations Secretary-General, 2009, United Nations Research Institute for Social Development, 1994.

181 Jiménez García-Herrera, 2010.

182 Begg et al., 2008.

183 See for example Alkoby, 2010, and Alexander, 2005.

184 Alkoby, 2010, pp. 47–49 (with reference to Keohane, 1990), for a critique to Keohane see Simpson, 1994.

185 Rawls, 1999.

regards distributive politics.[186] The focus of the UN policy documents described above seems rooted in this structural decoupling of international economic integration from social integration at national levels. With increasing powers at the hands of multinational enterprises and state corporations, but decreasing control of states and national non-economic actors on any policy, this results in a decrease of any policy actively supporting social integration of any society, be it at national, transnational, regional or global level.

## 2. Social Integration in the EU

European dimensions of social integration will have to be deliberated against this national and global background, but also as phenomena driven by a dynamic of their own.

### a) Historical context – social policy as a disputed mandate

When the European Communities, the predecessors of today's EU were first founded, the six founding states shared political orientations leaning more towards socialism than any programmatic preference for market liberalisation.[187] In contrast to this, they agreed on a market-liberal layout for the EEC in 1957, with severe consequences on the fate of European social integration. Yet, embracing market liberal ideology as the lode star of European integration was far from straightforward. There are even some hints that it was never fully achieved.

No account of European social integration should omit the consideration of the European Coal and Steel Community of 1952, although it expired in 2002.[188] This Treaty combined a primarily economic aim (combining French and German coal and steel production under the guidance of the High Authority) with a strong social policy approach. Realising that these ailing industries were in need of restructuring, the founding states addressed potential social repercussions of this explicitly. First, a social fund was authorised to provide sizeable payments to undertakings undergoing restructuring, in order to retrain the workforce as necessary or to provide other means for their transition to reemployment. Second, representation of management and labour was provided for in the High Authority.[189] The whole layout demonstrated a clear commitment to social regulation and active social policy. Similarly,

---

186 Alkoby, 2010, p. 51.

187 For more detail see sub III 2. a) (pp. 20–21).

188 Resulting from Articles 97, 99(2) Treaty establishing the European Coal and Steel Community (ECSC Treaty), see Decision 2002/595/EC on the consequences of the expiry of the […] [ECSC] […] OJ [2002] L 194/35.

189 See Bercusson, 2009, pp. 103–104.

Article 68 ECSC Treaty demanded intervention, should competition be distorted by irresponsibly low wages or levels of social protection in any Member State. As the ECSC, the EURATOM also provided for a social fund, inter alia used to supplement workers' income during phases of restructuring and retraining.[190]

However, when the EEC Treaty was finally concluded in 1957, the tides had changed. Influenced by the much-cited Ohlin report[191] for the ILO and the Spaak report[192] for the fledgling EEC, the founding states underwrote a minimalist social policy programme compatible with a newly fashionable liberal market ideology. Different national levels in wages and social protection were believed to mirror different strengths of national economies. This, it was assumed, would prevent any distortion of competition by those differences. A clause such as Article 68 ECSC Treaty was deemed superfluous. According to the now-dominant ideology of comparative advantage, social integration would be the natural result of unfettered markets and a regulatory environment fostering '*Leistungswettbewerb*' (performance competition).[193] The EEC itself would only need social policies directly related to the common market.

Nevertheless, social policy was enshrined in the founding Treaty. Redistributive policies were provided through the social fund and the initial agricultural policy, which largely redistributed gains from external customs to farmers, then a sizeable proportion of the populace.[194] Also, the competition law chapter initially retained a ban of social dumping.[195] Further, as a conciliation to French insistence on equalising social conditions against ordoliberal visions, provisions on equal pay for women and men and maintaining the balance of holiday regimes were introduced (Articles 119 and 120 EEC, now 157 and 158 TFEU). However, when the Commission attempted to develop these policies further and to continue social partner involvement in decision making, the Member States, which had swayed further towards market liberalism and US-style social policy did not support this course of action.[196] All that remained initially was an auxiliary social policy, designed to further the market in workers moving freely through the Community, and accompanied by a modest European Social Fund addressing some of the consequences of restructuring, based on the Treaty's normative commitment

190 Menéndez, 2011, p. 16.

191 Ohlin, 1956.

192 Comité Intergouvernemental créé par la conference de Messine, 1956.

193 See Gerber, 1994, p. 53, on the concept of 'performance competition', p. 83, explaining the ordo-liberal perspective on social integration.

194 Menéndez, as note 190. Today, agricultural payments have been reduced, but have not vanished.

195 See above section 2. b) (2) (pp. 24–26 with notes 101–114).

196 See Bercusson, 2009, pp. 105–107.

to an accelerated enhancement of working and living conditions within Member States.

The ensuing EU social policy has been described as 'scattered' and 'fitful'.[197] Nevertheless, the relentless activities of the European Commission, an economic crisis in western industrialised economies and resulting unrest of workers between 1968 and 1970 – most acutely in France and Italy[198] – allowed the first cautious steps towards an active European social policy to be spelled out by the 1974 'Social Action Programme'.[199] These were consolidated in the European Social Space pursued by then Commission President Delors in parallel with the 'Single European Market'.[200] These social policy programmes aimed at enhancing EEC legitimacy in the eyes of citizens. They addressed not only citizens in Member States, but also in states still vying for membership. Similar motives prevailed to the present day, as the comparison between a well-worn quote from 1974 and one from 2008 illustrates.

> The Community had to be seen to be more than a device to enable capitalists to exploit the Common Market, otherwise it might not be possible to persuade the peoples of the Community to continue to accept the disciplines of the market.[201]

> The geopolitical significance of EU integration will not in itself 'sell' the project to the ordinary citizen. It must also deliver improvements in their day to day well-being and quality of life – or at least not be seen as a threat to what the various populations have already achieved.[202]

### b) Milestones of social integration in the EU

The 'European Social Model' in all its national diversity was thus sufficiently strong to necessitate a minimum commitment of the European polity in the social field.[203] Slowly but surely the EU engaged in the normative project of society building alongside market building.[204] The ensuing milestones of EU

---

197 See Daly, 2008, pp. 1, 2.

198 On the relevance of this see Sanders, 1985, p. 3, stressing the impact of the British public's reaction, and in particular its Labour party, on expanding social policy in the EEC (p. 4).

199 OJ [1974] C 13/1.

200 EC Bull 2/1986, 2. See, for the general 'French' commitment to the image of a European Social Space, Vandamme, 1983.

201 Shanks, 1977, p. 378.

202 From Alber et al., p. 1. Similarly, Paul Taylor suggests intensifying social policy to boost citizens' identification with the EU (Taylor, 2008, pp. 158–162).

203 Falkner, 2010, pp. 298–300, observes a factual supranationalisation of social policy, although it still falls short of the demands of some (e.g. Ferrera 2009, Scharpf, 2010). Others recommend reverting the political integration process towards a confederation, in particular in the field of social policy (Majone, 2005, pp. 207–210).

204 Trenz, 2008, pp. 28–30.

social integration differ markedly from the three cornerstones of social integration at national level identified earlier (social protection and inclusion, combating domination in market societies, providing public services), as they followed the initial focus of the EEC on economic integration.

*(1) Market-annexed social policy at EU level* As a result, EU social policy first developed as an annex to creating the Common Market.

This was most pronounced in relation to the guarantee of free movement of workers. It was mainly aimed at accelerating mobility of labour as an economic factor, which hardly qualified as a social policy aim.[205] It could even be said to contradict the time-honoured phrase 'labour is not a commodity'.[206]

However, acceleration of factor mobility involved movement of real people with lives beyond work, including families and other needs. The Community responded by coordinating national social security systems, making acquired entitlements to pensions, health care and unemployment benefits exportable.[207] The underlying ideal was the 'cosmopolitan worker' who should be able to carry her social entitlement to different EU Member States. This became the lodestar for developing transnational social rights for EU citizens more generally. Also, from a purely market-liberal approach to economic integration, equal treatment of goods and services would fully suffice to establish an Internal Market, while persons are best left to compete against each other.[208] The EEC has not followed this path. Rather, the cosmopolitan worker was to derive an upward movement from her migration effort, among others by the right to be treated equally with other workers in the host state.[209] Thus, free movement of workers as a market-annexed right was equipped with a social edge in order to avoid downward competition.

Avoiding downward competition was the initial impetus of the other class of market-annexed social policy, as embodied in the principle of equal pay for equal work irrespective of gender (now Article 157 TFEU), and the obligation of Member States to maintain the equilibrium of rights to annual leave, which

---

205 See also Bercusson, 2009, p. 32.

206 This is the first principle of the International Labour Organisation, laid down in the declaration of Philadelphia in 1944 (Constitution of the International Labour Organisation, Geneva 1992, annex I a)).

207 On the principle of coordination see Damjanovic and de Witte, 2009, pp. 60–62, 68–73.

208 See for the defence of such a view Magnette, 2007, p. 672: 'To equalise the salaries of workers meant depriving migrant workers from their main economic advantage, their lower costs'.

209 See for a good defence of this view Davies, 1997, p. 588.

was deemed to be in existence when the EEC was founded (now Article 158 TFEU). The European judiciary qualified the equal pay principle as another cornerstone of EU social policy in the 1970s, as part of the Defrenne series of case law.[210]

Both free movement of workers and equal pay for women and men, in aiming at preventing distortions of competition, also led to developing legislation aiming at a floor for (minimum) employment rights.

*(2) From a floor for employment rights to 'flexicure' employment conditions* Such enhancement of working and living conditions was first pursued in fields where downward spiralling seemed a real danger, such as restructuring of industries in response to the enhanced opportunities of the larger market.

The risks for social integration inherent in this were illustrated by the restructuring of the transnational AZKO group during the 1970s crisis in the chemical sector. Due to losses in its Netherlands and German branches, the group initially planned to dismiss 5000 German and Dutch workers. However, German and Dutch employment protection legislation was efficient, due to a statutory obligation of employers to negotiate compensation in Germany and a requirement to lodge any dismissal with a court in the Netherlands. Hence, the group decided to dismiss 5000 Belgian workers instead, although the Belgian plant remained the most efficient one throughout the crisis.[211] This practical example of downward spiralling resulting from regulatory competition motivated adoption of a group of directives on employees' rights on the transfer of undertakings,[212] on collective redundancies[213] and on their employer's insolvency.[214] These did not impinge on entrepreneurial decisions to restructure, transfer or give up an undertaking, but required Member States to provide for mitigating legislation. Still, they were based on a principle of regulation from times gone by, in that they create a floor for rights, which cannot be undercut.[215]

More flexible concepts of employment rights were first introduced in the field of health and safety with directives implementing the new concept of a

---

210 ECJ 43/75 *Defrenne* [1976] ECR 455, paragraphs 9–10. More detail on this in Chapter 3.

211 See Hinrichs, 2001, p. 23.

212 Originally Directive 77/187/EEC, now Directive 2001/23/EC OJ [2001] L 82/16.

213 Originally Directive 75/129/EEC, now Directive 98/59/EC OJ [1998] L 225/16.

214 Originally Directive 80/987/EEC, now Directive 2008/94/EC OJ [2008] L 283/36.

215 On the limited effects of this if implemented into diverse national employment legislation see Sciarra, 2001, O'Leary, 2002.

safe 'working environment'. In contrast to preceding legislation, which – for example – established maximum thresholds for exposure to harmful substances, the 'Framework Directive'[216] refrained from detailing any standards.[217] Instead, it relied on procedures aimed at preventing occupational risks as the primary measure to protect health and safety. The Working Time Directive[218] established relatively modest rules on limiting daily and weekly working times and also avoiding the worst negative effects of night work, alongside a minimum guarantee of four weeks' annual leave.

A further group of directives protecting employees in precarious forms of employment, such as on part-time[219] and fixed-term contracts[220] and in temporary agency work,[221] combined a floor of rights with a guarantee of equal treatment for employees on precarious contracts with those on regular contracts. Equal treatment did not cover the precariousness defining the specific type of employment. Thus, for example, fixed-term employees were not granted the right to demand the same level of employment protection as the employee on an unlimited contract. The directives thus establish the acceptance of a diversity of employment standards, which also includes choice by Member States. All these aspects point towards flexible employment regulation[222] and thus beyond reliable floors for employment rights.

*(3) Equal treatment and non-discrimination as social integration factors*
The initial foundation of equality and non-discrimination in the Treaty provisions on equal pay and free movement of workers soon gained relevance in a number of ways decisive for European social integration and European impact on social integration within Member States.

From 1974, the Community legislated in favour of equality between women and men, issuing directives on equal pay and equal treatment in employment and in social security systems.[223] This was seen as a strategy for

---

216 Directive 89/381/EEC on health and safety OJ [1989] L 181/44.

217 This was in line with the 'new approach to technical harmonisation and standards' introduced for free movement of goods by Council Resolution of 7 May 1985 (OJ [1985] C 136/1).

218 Today Directive 2003/88/EC OJ [2003] L 299/9 (originally 93/104/EEC).

219 Directive 97/81/EC (OJ [1998] L 14/9), expanded to the UK by Directive 98/23/EC (OJ [1998] L 131/10), following the adoption of the provisions originally contained in the 1993 social policy agreement as regular Treaty norms with the Treaty of Amsterdam.

220 Directive 1999/70/EC OJ [1999] L 175/43.

221 Directive 2008/104/EC OJ [2008] L 327/9.

222 This has sprouted various theoretical approaches (e.g. Rogowski (ed.), 2008).

223 Directives 75/117/EEC OJ [1975] L 45/19 and 76/207/EEC OJ [1976] L 39/40 have been consolidated by the 'Recast' Directive 2006/54/EC OJ [2006] L 204/23. Directive 79/7/EEC OJ [1979] L 6/24 has not been updated yet.

the Community to take social policy forward in a field where most Member States did not have a strong tradition: equality law rarely extended beyond the relevant constitutional clauses.[224] In practice, legislative endeavours had been supported by a considerable amount of lobbying, including a cunning litigation strategy.[225] From 1999, the EU also embraced non-discrimination on grounds of racial and ethnic origin, religion and belief, disability, sexual orientation, age and sex (today Article 19 TFEU). This provision moved EU equality law beyond the gender nexus[226] and also beyond social policy. The combat of discrimination is regarded as a general human rights issue. However, relating it first and foremost to the market place, it also serves to combat social exclusion and is thus part of EU social policy.

The principle of equal treatment for migrant workers had likewise been expanded upon by secondary law[227] and a wide array of case law. Mainly, these principles supported an ideal of a European lifestyle of free movers, relying on equal treatment throughout the EU, to which as of now only a minority of citizens adheres.[228] The creation of EU citizenship expanded upon this development, aided by case law expanding rights of non-economically active citizens.[229] The resulting expansion of rights of migrants to participate in higher education and welfare payments can be seen as strengthening social integration in the EU. However, it has also been regarded as disrupting social integration at national level.[230]

Equality and non-discrimination are not, however, necessarily aimed at enhancing social integration: equality can also be achieved by withdrawing social benefits for all. Accordingly, they may contribute to disturbing nationally achieved models of spatially restricted social integration by downgrading social advantages and thus diminishing social integration overall.

*(4) European collective workers' representation* Finally, the employment-related European social policy also strengthened European dimensions of collective labour relations. Consultation of workers' representatives was an important element of the directives on restructuring of enterprises, which

224 Streeck, 1995, p. 400.

225 On socio-political backgrounds Hoskyns, 1996, p. 60, on litigation strategies Alter and Vargas, 2000.

226 See on this Schiek, 2010a, Schiek et al., 2007, Schiek and Chege, 2009, and Schiek and Lawson, 2011.

227 Regulation 1612/68 and 1408/71, now both replaced by Directive 2004/38/EC, Regulation 492/2011 and Regulation 833/2004/EC.

228 See above section III 2. c) (pp. 28–29) on actual mobility of persons.

229 More detail on this in Chapter 3, p. 98 and Chapter 4, pp. 156–162, 213.

230 Trenz, 2008, p. 17.

forced some Member States to establish such representatives.[231] Further, the directive on European Works Councils[232] established European representatives for undertakings with branches in several Member States, albeit in a very flexible system, leaving Member States to choose from a wide 'menu' of possible forms and an agreement between management and labour at enterprise level. The principle of negotiated representation was carried over to the creation of a workers' representation in European Companies.[233] Minimum requirements for information and consultation of employees have subsequently been established for all employers.[234] The role of collective agreements as well as employee representatives at national level is also strengthened by directives which, as for example in the Working Time Directive, allow a greater degree of flexibility by collective agreement than otherwise. At the European level, collective labour relations were bolstered by the participatory rights of social partners in Community legislation and the competence to issue social partner agreements (Article 154, 155 TFEU).[235] The relevance of establishing European institutions of social dialogue such as European Works Councils and European social partner negotiations lies also in establishing procedures of engagement between management and labour beyond national borders. These may prove to be arenas for the development of social integration through interaction at European levels.

*(5) Traditional welfare state tasks* The predominance of employment-related social policy at EU level seems to contrast with the predominance of traditional core sectors of social policy at national level.

Initially, the impact of European integration in this field was indirect. EU legislation in social security tried to balance claims of migrating workers with the protection of national welfare institutions. Yet, case law on free movement of workers and citizens expanded individual rights beyond these compromises, creating migrants' claims to healthcare[236] and other social benefits, forcing Member States to open up formerly closed national systems. As Maurizio Ferrera puts it, European integration confronts the 'logic of closure' guiding national welfare states with the 'logic of opening, aimed at fostering

---

231 ECJ C-383/92 *COM v UK* [1994] ECR I-1479.

232 Directive 94/45/EC, now replaced Directive 2009/38/EC OJ [2009] L 122/28.

233 Directive 2001/86/EC OJ [2001] L 294/22, finalising regulatory attempts initiated as early as 1972.

234 Directive 2002/14/EC OJ [2002] L 80/29.

235 More detail on this in Chapter 3, pp. 109–111. See Ales et al., 2006, and Ales, 2009, who also demand further Community legislation to support these activities.

236 See on the field of health care Mossialos, Permanand, Baeten and Hervey, 2010.

free movement [...] and non-discrimination by [...] tearing apart those spatial demarcations [...] that nation states have [...] built around (and often within) themselves'.[237] In response to growing national concerns about this, the Treaty of Lisbon establishes the opportunity for Member States to refer new legislation in this field to the European Council (Article 48 TFEU) and explicitly safeguards the Member States' competence to maintain non-economic services of general interest (Protocol No 26 Article 2).

More recently, a truly European dimension of classical welfare policy has been developed via the Open Method of Coordination (OMC). This has been initiated by the Treaty of Amsterdam's addition of an Employment Chapter (now Articles 145–150 TFEU). It aims at establishing conditions for higher employment levels. As with the economic policy chapter,[238] it is not aimed at hard legislation, but rather at initiating a process of mutual learning by Member States from one another. This 'new' mode of governance enabled the EU to become actively engaged in policy fields of the classical welfare state, although this was the province of Member States. The 'Lisbon Strategy' of 2000,[239] aiming to change the EU into the world's most dynamic and competitive knowledge economy, also covered the modernisation of the European social model by furthering social inclusion and eradication of poverty and a sustainable economy. It was said to reconcile the equal pursuit of economic and social aims at European level.[240] Since its reform in 2005, the Lisbon Strategy no longer nurtured the three policy goals 'jobs', 'competition' and 'social inclusion' at equal levels, but mainly focused on growth and jobs.[241] Social policy under the Lisbon Strategy thus became more market orientated than before.[242] After its expiry in 2010, the Lisbon Strategy was succeeded by the Europe 2020 strategy.[243] Its three strategic key-points are smart growth, sustainable growth and inclusive growth. Inclusive growth seems closest to any social policy aspiration, comprising the 'flagship initiatives', 'new skills

---

[237] Ferrera, 2009, p. 220.

[238] On this see above, pp. 26–28.

[239] Presidency Conclusions, Lisbon European Council, 23 and 24 March 2000, 'Putting Decisions into Practice: a more coherent and systematic approach', paragraphs 5 and 24, the latter mentioning that the modernisation of the social model refers to combating unemployment, social exclusion and poverty.

[240] See for a positive view on this reconciliation, based on the 2000 Lisbon Strategy, Wincott, 2003.

[241] See European Commission, 2005, p. 12, Armstrong, 2010, pp. 106–114.

[242] See Daly, 2008, p. 7, see also explicitly Magnusson, who considers that the mid-term review 'focused on competitiveness at the expense of social and environmental issues' (Magnusson, 2010, p. 18).

[243] European Commission, 2010b, adopted by the Council on 17 June 2010 (European Council Conclusions EUCO13/10 CO EUR 9 CONCL 2, 17 June 2010).

and jobs' and 'a European Platform against Poverty'. The strategy is, inter alia, accused of subordinating anything that could be achieved within the OMC on Social Policy and Social Inclusion to budget stabilisation prioritised by the Stability and Growth Pact.[244]

Despite these shortcomings of the Lisbon Strategy and its follow-up, they map out a sustained engagement of the EU with traditional welfare policy, social protection and social inclusion, potentially contributing to European social integration. However, in the framework of the Lisbon process and Europe 2020, these policies are bound up with an economic policy aiming to enhance competitiveness, indicating that economic integration is still a factor overshadowing any EU level social integration efforts.

### c) Evaluating European social integration

The practical effects of European-level social policy on actual EU social integration are less well established than in the field of economic integration. If social integration is enhanced through interaction of citizens beyond their national environments, policies encouraging temporal migration, for example during phases of higher education, might be more important to establish social integration than explicit social policies. From within social policy, the emergence of European levels of employee participation and social partner dialogue also offers concrete experiences of European social integration. Empirical research indicates that social integration by establishing new social networks and practices is successful only within higher status groups from the European middle classes,[245] while poorer sections of the populace experience European integration as a threat to their individual social integration.[246]

If social integration is indicated by reduced income differentials, developed states of industrial relations and wide coverage by institutions such as social security,[247] the evaluation might appear even less positive. From this perspective, the EU's 'Eastern Enlargement' from 2004 onwards has reduced the opportunities for social integration within the European Union through increasing divergence between Member States.

---

244 Barbier, 2010.
245 Andreotti and Le Galès, 2011.
246 Fligstein, 2008, pp. 250–251.
247 Liebert, 2007, p. 267.

## 3. Conclusion on Social Integration

The notion of social integration oscillates between a descriptive and a normative notion. As a descriptive notion, social integration within nation states has been defined as a condition for stabilising societies by creating bonds between citizens, and an acceptance of the polity and its rules. As a normative notion for the era of the nation state, social integration meant overcoming the crudest detriments of capitalism, i.e. the commodification of people just emerged from serfdom and creating the pre-conditions for democracy inclusive of all sectors of society. In Western Europe, social integration at national levels was pursued through national social states, evolving around the three policy fields of social protection and combatting of poverty, overcoming domination in market societies, and establishing social institutions, and in three different modes of policy making: (re)distributing resources, regulating markets and establishing and maintaining institutions.

Beyond nation states, the descriptive notion of social integration must be expanded to encompass transnational interactions between citizens and the establishment of transnational or even European institutions as a basis for transnational solidarity. For the EU, such instances of transnational interaction have emerged not only as exchange within the internal market, but also through participation in higher education in other Member States or transnational involvement in civic associations. Policies aiming at wider access to such concrete emanations of European social integration[248] would contribute to promoting social integration nested globally as well as regionally.

As a normative notion, social integration beyond the nation state requires new approaches to social policy. Whether these can be developed for the global sphere is beyond the scope of this book. Within the EU, social policy has only developed in a somewhat timid fashion. Frequently, redistributive policies are seen as not having a sufficient basis for legitimacy at European levels,[249] although the European Communities has always involved redistributive policies, notably through the agricultural policy and its social funds.[250] Based on this misconception, redistributive policies are relegated to Member States only. Regarding the regulatory modus of social policy, the

248 Fligstein, 2008, pp. 165–169 in particular; see also Calhoun, 2005, p. 279, referring to the need to develop concrete instances of actual possibilities of organisation of solidarity.

249 See, e.g., Moravcsik, 2002, Majone, 2006, see also Graser, 2006, Lamping, 2010, p. 47, p. 72.

250 See above, p. 39 with note 194.

EU is seen as legitimately complementing national activities if there is a need to correct markets under competitive pressures.[251] This would imply that any EU activity intended to enhance social integration remains firmly tied to the paradigm of *marketisation*,[252] and has to forgo the emancipatory potential of social policy, e.g. through securing decommodification of human beings, for EU levels. Cosmopolitan visions for European integration can support a demand for widening the integration paradigm in the direction of a 'European Model of Society',[253] but these proposals have not yet been specified.

## V. INTERCONNECTION OF ECONOMIC AND SOCIAL INTEGRATION

The separate accounts of economic and social integration were partially based on an artificial perspective. After all, 'the economy' is but one aspect of society and society would hardly function without an economic base. Accordingly, any process of Europeanisation would always impact on economic and social integration within nation states. At the same time, any successful economic integration at European level would also lead to social repercussions at national or European level, whether these are integrative or disintegrative. It is thus necessary to consider how economic and social integration are interrelated within the European integration project.

In the classical ordo-liberal perspective,[254] markets are viewed as the sole legitimate and efficient source of social integration, possibly supported by distribution of welfare payments.[255] Accordingly, economic integration would qualify as socio-economic integration, without any need for a specific social policy at EU level. It is easy to see how one could consider the basic rules of the Common Market as an embodiment of the demands of these policies.[256] In contrast to the European tradition of more elaborate welfare states, social policy should not go beyond distributing welfare payments, which is again best left to national politics. Whether this model of socio-economic integration by reliance on 'natural' market forces has been successful in the case of European integration is of course notoriously disputed.

---

251 See Graser, 2006, pp. 281–287.
252 Somek, 2006.
253 Delanty, 2009, p. 211, contradicting Habermas.
254 See above pp. 21–22.
255 See Gerber, 1994, p. 83.
256 See More, 1999.

One critical perspective maintains that under such models European socio-economic integration is non-existent. Rather economic integration and social policy are perceived as 'decoupled':[257] while the European Union and its predecessors took excellent care of economic integration, social integration was left to nation states and at best complemented by 'cheap talk about the "social dimension" of European integration'.[258] The critical approaches to varieties of capitalism proceed from this assumption and conclude that, while different forms of capitalism have been sustainable under the pressure of European economic integration in the past, the integration process in its constitutionalised form has now become more aggressive and is set to destroy social market economies.[259]

Today there is much demand for the retention of full competences of nation states in social policy within the EU. These demands are particularly brought forward by those supporting and defending a specific European social model.[260] While this is an understandable reaction to case law by the Court of Justice, increasingly experienced as impinging on Member States' social policy choices, it also coincides with the classical liberal and ordoliberal positions sketched above.[261] This perspective, in preserving social policies as a national reservation, shows a limited understanding of the interrelation of economic integration and social policy.

In the practice of European integration, social policy and economic integration have never been fully separated. As demonstrated above, constituting free movement of workers through the principle of non-discrimination and equal treatment promotes factor mobility and at the same time creates instances of social integration.[262] The so-called 'market-correcting' early European social policy[263] can also be seen as aiming at socio-economic integration. The OMC is generally seen as a further attempt to infuse market integration with social aims.[264] Partly, this is the reason for critique

---

257 Scharpf, 2002, p. 646. This image has been taken up by too many authors to recount here.

258 Scharpf, 2010, p. 211.

259 Höpner and Schäfer, 2010 and Scharpf, 2010.

260 See, for example, Syrpis, 2007.

261 For the former position see, for example, Joerges, 2007. The German Constitutional Court, in its Lisbon judgment, also demanded that the EU refrain from interfering with national social policies (Judgment on 30 June 2009 – 2 BvE 2/08 et al., available from http://www.bundesverfassungsgericht.de/entscheidungen/es20090630_2bve000208en.html, pararaphs 256–259), the latter view is supported by Giubonni, 2010, p. 254.

262 See above pp. 41–45.

263 Barnard, 2010, pp. 6 et seq.

264 See, for example, Wincott, 2003.

of the 'Social OMC', as the Lisbon Strategy which formed the base of the 'Social OMC', was not primarily aimed at social policy, but rather at structural change of the Member States' economies which should enhance competitiveness of the EU economy as a whole.[265] Accordingly, the EU has taken a number of steps towards actively interrelating social and economic integration, although arguably there remains scope for more steps towards this direction.

## VI. CONCLUSION

This chapter has developed notions of economic and social integration and their interrelation. It has identified a number of challenges for pursuing both social and economic integration within the European integration project. These include the subjection of the European integration project to the pressures of economic globalisation, the tendency of nation states to achieve social integration by national closure (i.e. excluding non-nationals from the social state) rather than through openness and the increasing dedication of the European integration project to capitalistic or neo-liberal principles such as competitiveness, growth and efficiency. Such a mainly economic orientation risks the marginalisation of social values, and along with this the alienation of large proportions of the citizenry from any realistic perspective of social integration. This will at best lead to their increasing distance from or indifference towards Europe, but at worst to 'generalised xenophobia'.[266]

Engaging positively with EU social integration, the EU could regain credibility and identification of the citizenry, and become an example of how to achieve social justice through other models than closure within national boundaries. The EU's ultimate success may well depend on such a better-balanced interaction between its economic and social dimensions. For the period up to 2007, there is some evidence that it is mainly the economic and social elite who develop a European identity, while the economically less fortunate continue to derive their identity from and focus their perspectives on the national levels.[267] This perception is based on the predominance of EU-derived rights for economically successful citizens and a lack of any social dimension in the European project. With increasing Europeanisation of societies a situation could emerge where large sections of the population

---

[265] Begg et al., 2008, p. 73, Daly, 2008, 2006; 'Europe 2020 strategy' above pp. 46–47.

[266] See Outhwaite, 2008, p. 97.

[267] Fligstein, 2008, pp. 206–207 (conclusion).

not only disengage with the European project, but also experience Europeanization as further threatening their already volatile social position. Such a situation would ultimately threaten the acceptance of the European project in democratic societies. It is in this sense that economic and social integration poses a challenge to the EU and its constitutional law.

# 2. EU constitutional law

## I. INTRODUCTION

Before considering whether and how EU constitutional law addresses any challenges posed by economic and social integration, it will be necessary to clarify the notion of EU constitutional law. The EU has come a long way from constitutionalisation through case law by its Court of Justice, and towards establishing constitutionalism in a multilevel polity. With the rejection of the Constitutional Treaty, any capital letter 'EU Constitution' has been committed to history for the time being.[1] Against this background, the notion of 'constitutional law' has been chosen deliberately: while it abandons the concept of a constitution, it maintains that there can still be constitutional law.

In developing a societal notion of EU constitutional law,[2] this chapter first considers national constitutions and constitutional law beyond the state, contrasting merely liberal traditions of constitutionalism with moves towards socially embedded constitutionalism and relates these types of constitutionalism to social and economic integration. It will then outline the elements of EU constitutional law. This will be the basis for identifying parameters suitable to gauge whether and how EU constitutional law meets the challenges posed by economic and social integration, especially after Eastern Enlargement and under the new constitutional framework provided by the Treaty of Lisbon.

## II. NATIONAL CONSTITUTIONS

European constitutions were offshoots of modernity, the Enlightenment and the subsequent establishment of nation states,[3] emerging either from a

---

[1] For an article regretting this see Tsebelis, 2008; for a more recent overview see Menéndez, 2010.

[2] Usually, European and global constitutionalism is discussed from national and international (public) law perspectives instead, as, for example, by Dunoff and Trachtman, 2009b, Dobner and Loughlin, 2010, Bodgandy and Bast, 2010, and Weiler and Wind, 2003, Krisch, 2010, and Everson and Eisner, 2007.

[3] See Grimm, 2010, pp. 5–13, Preuß, 2010, pp. 23–33.

revolutionary moment or through incremental evolution.[4] The French constitution as the European archetype of the first kind replaced traditional rule with a single constitutional text outlining the principles of self-governance, human rights and the rule of law. It envisaged constituting society, not (only) the state.[5] This process most likely contributed to fashioning a common identity of the population of a nation state. Such 'constitutional patriotism' has even been viewed as a step towards replacing primordial bounds based on blood relations and their refined ideological form in the notion of ethnicity by true republicanism.[6] The evolutionary constitution, by contrast, shares some common ground with 'ancient constitutionalism',[7] with its incremental development and partly its lack of written documentation and definite constitutional moment(s). This has the advantage that constitutions can be interpreted in line with social reality, which again enables judicial activism and progressive adaptation to change.[8] The notion of 'constitutionalisation' captures this incremental process by which a given entity achieves autonomy and through which its law will fulfil constitutional functions.

Both types of constitutions eventually served needs emerging at the dawn of modernity, with enlightenment as the new philosophical coin of the day and the emergence of new forms of organising economy and society, known as capitalism. In this sense, national constitutions fulfilled functions which were ultimately and at least partly societal rather than merely aimed at constituting new forms of state organisation.

A brief narrative of constitutionalism's birth and early stages in Europe could be presented as follows: when Western-style constitutionalism first emerged, the main constitutional functions consisted in creating, perceiving and identifying an entity whose organisational and regulatory authority is acknowledged as legitimate.[9] Before the Enlightenment, the monarch's power and authority was perceived as vested by God himself[10] or conditioned by an imaginary social contract ending a supposedly destructive state of nature.[11] The Enlightenment led to a new philosophical appreciation of humankind.

---

4 For references to this popular distinction see Möllers, 2010, pp. 170–177 and Besselink, 2009.

5 Preuß, 2010, pp. 23–25, quoting Article 16 of the French declaration of the rights of man ('a society in which the separation of powers is not assured and the guarantee of rights is not established has no constitution').

6 See Habermas, 1996, pp. 499–500.

7 Loughlin, 2010, pp. 48–49.

8 Möllers, 2010, p. 175. Möllers is rather critical towards this 'restricted normativity' though.

9 See for example Tagourias, 2007, pp. 3, 4.

10 See Grimm, 2010, p. 6.

11 On the latter see Grimm, 2010, pp. 7–8.

Instead of being tied to given social structures, human beings were now perceived as enlightened by their own rationality and capable of relating with the world from a purely individualist position. They emerged as imaginary rulers of their own, individual destiny. Consequently, any outer rule was in need of being traced back to a decision by the individual consenting to it. This was achieved by constituting institutions which made this possible; mainly through parliamentary democracy, complemented by elements of direct democracy. Modern constitutions also guaranteed individual rights to political participation, such as rights to vote and to assemble in public. The latter would become an important means to lobby for certain politics or embody individual freedom of expression. Combined, all this constitutionalised a novel form of democratically legitimised authority.

At the same time, scientific progress and the invention of mechanically enhanced production created a new class of economically independent individuals, craving for liberty to exploit their wealth by producing ever more commodities. They were not in need of any absolutist protection against a purportedly aggressive state of nature. Their economic success rather necessitated the creation of a class of labourers willing to engage in untraditional work, rooted in neither land nor guild. While the willingness at times was created by driving peasants away from the land,[12] the idea of individual rights also supported the transformation from being a farmer or craftsman, embedded into an intractable web of socio-economic obligations and bonds, to being an individualised, anonymous and exchangeable worker, driven by equally anonymous powers of economic necessity.[13] In this context, modern constitutionalism arose to guarantee human rights, mainly as individual liberties.[14] These rights protected property of non-gentry and non-land-bound economic actors against arbitrary intervention from the monarch and its successor, the democratic state, and liberated labour from traditional restrictions.

Modern national constitutions were thus first based on classical liberal constitutionalism. Human rights only addressed state authorities and democratic institutions merely established accountable government for public spheres, leaving private spheres (among others the emerging capitalist economy) as a field for private autonomy, where dominance and rule based on ownership could flourish. The philosophical foundations of modern democracy as established by Rousseau, Locke and Montesquieu only conceptualised liberal democracy and failed to conceive of democracy as self-governance for all.[15]

---

12 Polanyi, 1957 (1944), pp. 34–38.

13 Weber, 1980 (1922), pp. 497 et seq.

14 On the origins of inalienable human rights in those times see Mahoney, 2007, pp. 21 et seq. in particular.

15 See Stein, 2001, pp. 4–6 (paragraphs 1–3).

After expanding their electoral base towards non-possessing classes and women, modern national constitutions depended on public consensus and needed to respond to social inequality. In Brunkhorst's words, they 'transform[ed] [...] the elitist bourgeois parliamentarianism of the nineteenth century into egalitarian mass democracy'.[16] Brunkhorst focuses on the ability of constitutionalism at state level to pacify an emerging class conflict, one of the achievements necessary to enable Western societies to flourish. Alternative contemporary perspectives stress the need to add a social element to democracy, in order not only to safeguard the emancipation of the bourgeoisie, but also to enable the emancipation of the working class.[17] Classical liberal constitutions, which guaranteed rights and established democratic rules merely for narrowly defined public spheres, could not accommodate these demands.

Reforming constitutions to enhance social inclusion first required a more expansive conception of human rights. If rights were to support and not to suppress social inclusion, they needed to go beyond hollow formulas and were to be interpreted in ways that would extend their promise to the majority of the population. Guaranteeing human rights in ways that are significant in the reality of many (rather than protecting the privileges of a few) is therefore a common endeavour of modern national constitutions and the courts supervising them. Guaranteeing socio-economic rights explicitly[18] is only one way to achieve this aim. In many European countries, social state principles inform the content of human rights, even if these are phrased in traditional liberal ways.[19] With the evolution of social state principles, rights are increasingly interpreted as enabling rather than merely liberating.[20] At the same time, human rights must be reconceptualised from protecting individuals conceived as group-detached entities to becoming relevant for socio-economic reality, which is characterised by social interaction. Producers and traders need to interact in order to profit from their products or their trading skills, relying on the cooperation of their employees in the process. It is not sufficient for rights to only *liberate* individuals. They must also *enable* individuals to relate to each other, to activate their interconnectedness.[21] This

---

16 Brunkhorst, 2010, p. 183.

17 Heller, 1971, see also Chapter 1, pp. 9–10.

18 The South African constitution is one of the more prominent examples for this (see Davis, 2008).

19 See for an English language overview Koutnatzis, 2005; for the German constitution see Schiek, 2001.

20 Möller, 2009.

21 On this see also Cartabia, 2009, pp. 18–19, quoting the Italian Constitution as considering 'each human being [...] both as an individual and within the intermediate social bodies'.

has led to demands to develop positive obligations flowing from human rights.[22]

Secondly, democracy needed to go beyond the narrow confines of the public sphere as well. Democratisation of society, and also the economy, seemed necessary. The concept of economic democracy (*Wirtschafts-demokratie*) achieved constitutional rank in the Weimar Constitution,[23] based on works by Heller as well as Neumann,[24] and was complemented by the social constitution.[25] Arguably economic democracy continues to be one of the principles enshrined in the social state principle of today's German constitution.[26] Similar ideas had been developed in the UK and elsewhere[27] and were also embraced by the first democratic constitutions of Spain and Portugal.[28] Among others based on such traditions, the European social state was never a merely redistributive welfare state. It has always included regulatory elements.[29] In establishing rights to social self-governance of societal spheres, it is closely related to social democracy as opposed to bourgeois democracy.[30] Workers' rights to combine in order to force enhancement of working conditions and to take industrial action, if necessary, are only the best-known examples of such rights. The human right of freedom of association, which originally was conceived for the state-centred public political sphere, eventually came to encompass these rights to ward off private rule in

---

22 On this see Fredman, 2008.

23 Schiek, 2001, pp. 6–7, paragraph 7 with further references.

24 Heller, 1971a, first printed in 1930, and Neumann, *Koalitionsfreiheit und Reichsverfassung* (1932), reprinted in Neumann, 1967, pp. 7 et seq.

25 On this see Hänninen, 2010.

26 Schiek, 2001, pp. 76–77.

27 For the UK see Dukes, 2008, pp. 342–343, for an international overview see Creighton, 2010.

28 Article 2 of the post-Salazar Portuguese Constitution (1976) read 'The Portuguese Republic is a democratic State based on the rule of law [...]; its aim is to achieve economic, social, and cultural democracy and to push participatory democracy further.' After the 1982/1989 reforms, partly motivated by Portugal's accession to the EU (Baquero Cruz, 2002, p. 33), only the notion of 'economic, social and cultural democracy' remained (today's Portuguese constitution in English: http://www.tribunal-constitucional.pt/tc/conteudo/files/constituicaoingles.pdf). The Spanish constitution guarantees the right of workers and professionals to establish organisations defending economic and social interests provided that their structure is democratic (Article 7 and 59) – an endorsement of the 'social and democratic state' established by the Constitution (Article 1), which also demands a 'fair economic and social order' and an 'advanced democratic society' (English translation retrieved from http://www.senado.es/constitu_i/index.html).

29 See also Brunkhorst, 2010, p. 183 and Chapter 1, pp. 34–36.

30 See Chapter 1, pp. 9–11, 33–34.

non-public economic realms.[31] However, there are more (potential) emanations of the principle of social self-governance ranging from providing a legal status for non-commercial cooperative societies over creating national health and other social services and towards allowing collective ownership of land or other means of production.

All these more developed forms of national constitutionalism, originally referred to as 'social democracy',[32] strive to constitutionalise socio-economic spheres. They endeavour to legitimise private rule through horizontally effective human rights and democratic governance, thus offering ways to negotiate societal conflicts. Relations between citizens are no longer individualised, and conflicts of interest not merely referred to the supposedly neutral 'laws of the market'. Western democracies did not, however, succumb to state planning of economy either.[33] In parts, public authority countered injustices on markets, for example, through providing services of general interest as public service. There may even be a third way, which would provide alternatives to the 'rule of the market', that are not based on well-developed bureaucracies. Such alternatives would include governing resources collectively rather than competitively, as proposed for 'the commons' in the works by Ostrom.[34] Beyond these specific models, a multitude of ways exist to provide for collective regulation within socio-economic realms, relying on cooperation and negotiation. Examples for this include the constitutional guarantee for municipal autonomy[35] and the provision of a more stable legal base (although not in the form of a constitutional guarantee) for a sector called the 'économie sociale' in France.[36]

All these emanations of social democracy differ from liberal democracy in that they aim at self-governance within society, while liberal democracy is content with providing justification of governmental rule in public spheres through public discourse.

These modern developments of constitutionalism can be characterised as a 'social re-embedding' of national constitutionalism: while constitutions at the

---

[31] On the European history of workers' freedom of association Jacobs, 2009.

[32] Heller, 1971, first published 1934.

[33] See, however, on the long tradition of planification in France, van der Eyden, 2003, pp. 206–222.

[34] See on this Chapter 1, p. 19, note 80.

[35] Municipal autonomy has been addressed at European level by the European Charter of Local Self Government. Article 28 GG (German Constitution) can serve as a national example, which goes beyond mere devolution of governmental tasks under the paradigm of liberal constitutionalism (see Tettinger, 2010, para 133) in that municipalities also command over local social policy. Similar concepts are also pursued in France and Sweden (see Wollmann, 2010, pp. 334–339).

[36] See on this Fraisse, 2005.

start of capitalism mainly served to support rights suitable for use by those endowed with sufficient wealth to participate in the new market-driven economy successfully, the tendency of 'society [to] protect [...] itself against the perils inherent in a self-regulating market system'[37] led to democratisation and the ensuing need to protect rights and capacity to participate for the less affluent sections of the populace as well. Accordingly, the term *socially embedded constitutionalism* shall be used to characterise this combination of social state principles, positive duties to effectuate human rights, horizontal protection of human rights and constitutional rights towards collective self-governance on imbalanced markets.

To conclude, constitutions at national level fulfilled a variety of functions, only some of which are common to all constitutions. First of all, a constitution must be able to constitute order in state and society. It thus needs to be regarded as higher law or authoritative text. Second, they contain public authority. Third, they legitimise authority through democratic procedures. Fourth, they protect individual rights and (fifth) social values. In Europe, a move from classical liberal constitutionalism towards socially embedded constitutionalism ensued from expanding rights to vote to the entire populace. Classical liberal constitutionalism focused on spheres traditionally classified as public, i.e. any activity emanating from the nation state and its agents. Public authority is contained and legitimated through parliamentary democracy and individual rights are protected against encroachment by public authority. Spheres traditionally classified as private, such as the economy or the family, are protected as spheres for personal rule without state interference. The historical function of the classical liberal constitution was to liberate the new class of economically independent bourgeois from absolutist rule. Accordingly, it focused on protecting rights to property and to engage in a profession or trade, thus contributing to economic integration through the new capitalist methods of production.

In societies where wealth and opportunities are distributed unevenly and where equal recognition is withheld – for example, depending on a person's sex, alleged race or physical abilities – liberal constitutionalism tends to result in purely nominal autonomy and self-governance for large sections of the populace. Expanding the vote to all sections of the populace thus necessitated the social embedding of constitutionalism. Socially embedded constitutionalism endeavoured to expand legitimacy of authority beyond public spheres and to contain private power. In order to guarantee rights in meaningful ways for all through substantive rather than only through formal rights, constitutions satisfying the demands of 'social democracy' as formulated by

---

[37] Polanyi, 1957 (1944), p. 80.

Heller[38] endeavour to constitutionalize socio-economic spheres and to contribute to social inclusion. They safeguard the actual enjoyment of human rights by the less affluent factions of the populace and provide scope for democratisation of the economy and other social spheres. This active contribution to social integration can be seen as a move to socially embedded constitutionalism after the establishment of wider markets, supported inter alia by liberal constitutionalism, had run its course.

## III. BEYOND STATES: FROM CONSTITUTIONS TO CONSTITUTIONAL LAW

Given that constitutions first emerged with the nation state, it has been questioned whether constitutionalism beyond their borders is conceivable.[39] Two elements of national constitutions appear to prevent this. First, the states constituted by national constitutions are tied to territorial boundaries. The constitution's authority presupposes not only formal, but also substantive autonomy of the nation state within its geographical borders.[40] Second, national constitutions have successfully created consensus in society to accept the rule of law, rather than of man. Sceptics doubt whether this consensus can be achieved beyond close communities within the nation.[41]

The case for constitutional law beyond nation states is based on challenges to these main elements. First, the territoriality of authority is shattered by the fact that, if they are to maintain any order at all, nation states must recognise that they are vastly interdependent on each other. Thus, national constitutional ordering may become dysfunctional and is in need of being complemented. National constitutions need to interlink, which presupposes constitutional law beyond national borders. Of course, nation states continue to wield power. Constitutional law beyond the nation state will thus have to compete with national constitutions and to compensate for their dysfunctionality,[42] leaving some form of constitutional pluralism[43] or plurality[44] as

---

[38] See above p. 57 with note 24.

[39] Grimm, 2010, and Krisch, 2010, pp. 27–68 (Chapter 2) reject this possibility.

[40] See on this aspect Benhabib, 2006, p. 33.

[41] See Bellamy, 2006, and Lamping, 2010, p. 47.

[42] Peters, 2006.

[43] The concept of constitutional pluralism is usually attributed to MacCormick, who developed it as a concept for the EU (MacCormick, 1995, and MacCormick, 1993) and is said to have given it up later. It was then developed into a general notion for global law (see Walker, 2010a and Rosenfeld, 2008).

[44] Krisch conceives of plurality as an alternative to post-national constitutional-

the only alternative.[45] Second, constitutional authority can be conceptualised as a discursive phenomenon (rather than rule by command and obeisance). Such civil constitutional authority is better suited to civil societies and also to the complex reality of transnational and multileveled socio-economic processes.[46] Finally, private ordering has increased immensely[47] and multinational companies are certainly not restricted by national borders in their ordering activities.[48] Constitutional law thus needs to develop beyond the nation state (as well as beyond the strictly public realm) if its authority is to be maintained.[49] Accordingly, constitutionalism beyond nation states is widely accepted.[50] It provides nation states with a means to counterbalance the loss of practical governmental power in the age of globalisation.[51]

However, one element of national constitutionalism seems difficult to reproduce beyond states: the common identity of citizens within states, which drives constitutional moments resulting in a 'revolutionary' constitution[52] and is also the basis for the incremental development of evolutionary constitutions.[53] The collective entity of states cannot substitute for the collective identity of citizens (if that ever existed beyond a mere ideological construct). This does not, however, prevent international organisations from developing constitutional law, a notion comprising any legal rule serving functions fulfilled by constitutions in territorial nation states.[54] This refocussing on functions puts constitutions into perspective, unmasking their roots in specific historical and economic circumstances, allowing us to identify subsets of constitutional functions which also enable a nuanced assessment of the potential of constitutionalism beyond nation states,[55] rather than predicting its doom along with nation states.[56]

---

ism and finds plurality the ultimately superior concept (see in particular 2010, pp. 302–307 (conclusion)).

45 For European perspectives on constitutional pluralism see Wind, 2003, Mayer, 2010, and Walker, 2010.

46 Preuß, 2010, pp. 29–30; on the latter aspect see also Schepel, 2005, p. 403.

47 See Cutler, 2003, as well as the edited collections by Peters, Koechlin, Förster and Zinkernagel, 2009 and Dilling, Herberg and Winter, 2008.

48 See e.g. Cutler, 2003, Teubner, 2010.

49 See on different versions of societal constitutionalism Schepel, 2005, and Teubner, 2010.

50 See for example the recent contributions referenced in note 2.

51 Remarkably, the Czech Constitutional Court has accepted this necessity of states to restrict their sovereignty in order to maintain it (see Komárek, 2009, and Bříza, 2009).

52 See above p. 54 with notes 4 to 6.

53 See above p. 54 with notes 7 to 8.

54 On a functional approach to constitutionalisation see Loughlin, 2010.

55 For this reason Dunhoff and Trachtman, 2009, advocate a functional approach to constitutionalism.

56 The latter is advocated by Grimm, 2010, p. 22.

We have identified above the functions required to constitute order by providing higher law, to safeguard individual liberties against encroachment by public authorities as well as by private powers, and to constitute institutions for democratic rule in public realms as well as to enable collective self-governance in socio-economic realms. It seems plausible that law created at transnational or even global level can serve these functions – although possibly in different ways from national constitutions in the age of nation states.

The basic formal function of any constitution – to provide higher law – is fulfilled by any international or transnational organisation capable of asserting its law's autonomy coherently beyond mere political discourse.[57] This is easily conceivable. Also, the safeguarding of individual liberty against encroachment by public authority is feasible as witnessed by international and regional human rights regimes, while democracy beyond nation states is seen as notoriously difficult due to its perceived territoriality.[58] However, the connection between those bound by laws in one country and those who create those laws in another country is not beyond conceptualisation for the public sphere.[59] Given the fact that legislation created in countries encompassing powerful economies has vast repercussions throughout the world, such legislation seems necessary, if only from a liberal perspective: even if democratic legitimacy within those countries were to work perfectly, the rules would not fulfil the requirement of having been legitimised by all to whom they apply. Constituting transnational fields for democratic rule-making beyond nation states may be more demanding than from within them. However, it is a precondition for upholding principles of democracy in an increasingly interconnected world.

This leaves the functions associated with socially embedded constitutionalism, i.e. the protection of liberties against encroachment by market actors and the promotion of those liberties by ensuring that they can actually be enjoyed by all as well as constituting collective self-governance in socio-economic realms.

In practice, international constitutional law remains wedded to public spheres: international human rights regimes focus on states and any international organisation can be seen as merely complementing democracy in public spheres. Where international law transcends public spheres, this is mainly based on transnational economic integration and is not aimed at socially embedding any rights. Transnational agreements creating rights-based market regimens such as the EU, but also the WTO, empower multinational enterprises from the Western hemisphere to pursue the rights to conduct their business unhindered by state legislation before courts that are created without a

---

57 See for this last view Bogdandy, 2010, pp. 14, 18.

58 Kohler-Koch, 2010, p. 101.

59 See de Búrca, 2008.

direct foundation in a national democracy. The same treaties do not tend to emphasise those rights that enable people without possessions to actually enjoy individual or collective autonomy. Rather than furthering socially embedded constitutionalism, transnational economic liberties protected by 'new constitutionalism' empower transnational economic actors[60] to use courts in their endeavour to delegitimize social compromises achieved at national levels. Constitutionalism beyond national borders has thus been likened to imperialism in more modern forms.[61]

At national level, pressure by the populace led to socially embedded constitutionalism. International organisations, their courts and international arbitrators are more remote from social unrest engendered by their decisions than are national legislators and courts. However, exerting direct pressure beyond nation states is not impossible. As global outrage against a succession of G8 meetings has demonstrated, economic globalisation can be characterised as 'a site of struggle between hegemonic and counter-hegemonic forces'.[62] Recent manifestations against austerity politics demanded by the International Monetary Fund from Greece and Spain are evidence of ongoing public discourse.[63] Accordingly, counter-hegemonic notions of constitutionalism beyond states are possible. Such counter-hegemonic notions would, for example, focus on social inclusion from a subaltern cosmopolitan angle, complementing individual rights by solidarity entitlements and potential for sustained political mobilisation.[64] Such transnational constitutionalism would go beyond protecting rights of the world's most powerful economic actors and progress to endow those exploited by them with countervailing rights.

In the practice of constitutionalism beyond the nation state the ideas underpinning socially embedded constitutionalism have not been at the forefront so far. This is closely linked to widespread doubts relating to the possibility to provide for social integration beyond such close community bonds as those created in nation states.[65] Accordingly, the question of whether constitutionalism in all its facets, and with the potential to support counter-hegemonic moves, can be used beyond nation states, still awaits answers from a practical perspective.

---

60 See in particular Gill, 1995, see also Harvey, 2005; from an EU perspective see Parker, 2008.

61 Tully, 2007.

62 Anderson, 2005, referring to rights constitutionalism.

63 See, for example, BBC News 'Greece austerity: PM Papandreou tries to persuade MPs' http://www.bbc.co.uk/news/world-13877932 and BBC News 'IMF says Spain's economy still facing major risks' http://www.bbc.co.uk/news/business-13867158.

64 See de Sousa Santos and Rodriguez-Garavito, 2005, pp. 14–16.

65 See on this Chapter 1, pp. 36–38.

## IV. EU CONSTITUTIONAL LAW

What is difficult globally may be less complex regionally, however, and especially in the EU with its relatively long history of regional integration relying partly on integration through law. Potentially, the fact that the EU is a territorially limited entity also eases the task of developing a notion of constitutional law suitable to respond to the challenges of economic and social integration.

This does not necessarily require a formal EU constitution, which would have to transform the EU into a federation. This specific path for the EU's future is now foreclosed by the national identities, which have recently been reasserted by the Treaty of Lisbon (Article 6(3) EU),[66] of its Member States. The failure of the EU's Constitutional Treaty can be interpreted as the result of attempting the impossible: the Laeken process, which could only end in a constitution with a capital C and thus a definitely state-like EU, has failed.[67] However, if international organisations and transnational cooperation between states can have constitutional laws, so can the EU.

Constitutional law has been defined above as law fulfilling three basic functions, of which two are framed differently under the respective paradigms of liberal and socially embedded constitutionalism: [68] asserting authority, safeguarding liberties and equality rights against public authority and private power, and constituting democracy in public spheres and legitimate collective self-governance in socio-economic realms. The latter function would at the same time help to maintain modes of governing society (provided there is already a European society)[69] beyond the blind trust in the 'laws of the market'. This would contribute to de-commodification of social spheres by enabling non-market modes of governance, for example through charitable organisations, mutual societies and other institutions constituting an 'économie sociale'.

While international organisations will have to come a long way to fulfil the socially embedded aspects of these functions, this may be easier for the EU. Granted, there is neither a constitutional document derived from a revolutionary moment nor an evolutionary constitutional consensus.[70] However, engendered by the process of Europeanisation, there are today not only binding Treaty norms that can formally be qualified as constitutional, but also an increasing number of general principles of EU law, in addition to an incre-

---

66 See also Fossum, 2010, pp. 44–48, with more detail and Griller, 2008, pp. 40–42.

67 See Menéndez, 2010, pp. 80–85.

68 See text subsequent to note 54 and accompanying notes 55–10.

69 On this see Chapter 1, p. 9 with notes 16–19.

70 Fossum and Menéndez, 2010.

mentally evolved *acquis communautaire* serving as backdrop for evolving constitutional law. Thus, the EU has more norms to draw on for fulfilling constitutional functions than international organisations.

## 1. EU law and its Constitutional Authority

The EU is well advanced in asserting constitutional authority of its law through doctrines established by the Court of Justice in a series of foundational cases. This process commenced with two pivotal judgments from the 1960s. In *van Gend*,[71] the Court found that any citizen could rely on directly enforceable EU law against his or her own Member State, stating:

> The objective of the EEC Treaty [...] to establish a Common Market [...] implies that this Treaty is more than an agreement which merely creates mutual obligations between the contracting states. This view is confirmed by the preamble [...] which refers not only to governments but to peoples [and ...] the establishment of institutions endowed with sovereign rights, the exercise of which affects Member States and also their citizens. Furthermore, [...] the nationals of the states [...] are called upon to cooperate in the functioning of this Community through the intermediary of the European parliament and the Economic and Social Committee. [...] The task assigned to the Court [...] to secure uniform interpretation of the Treaty [...] confirms that [...] Community law has an authority which can be invoked by [...] nationals before [national] courts and tribunals. The conclusion [...] is that the Community constitutes a new legal order of international law for the benefit of which the states have limited their sovereign rights, albeit within limited fields, and the subjects of which comprise not only Member States but also their nationals. [...]'[72]

Significantly, even before emphasising its own role, the Court stressed the importance of citizens' cooperation in European institutions such as the European Parliament and the Economic and Social Committee (ESC). This implied that – in the Court's view – the EU would share the task of integrating society with its Member States.

In *Costa*[73] the Court asserted that the EEC Treaty enjoyed primacy over national law. The main reasons are summarised in head note 3 of the judgment:

> By contrast with ordinary international treaties, the EEC Treaty has created its own legal system which, on the entry into force of the Treaty, became an integral part of the legal systems of the Member States and which their courts are bound to apply. By creating a Community of unlimited duration, having its own institutions, its own personality, its own legal capacity and capacity of representation on the

71 ECJ 26/62 *van Gend* [1963] ECR 1.

72 Ibid., p. 12.

73 ECJ 6/64 *Costa* [1964] ECR 585.

> international plane and, more particularly, real powers stemming from a limitation of sovereignty or a transfer of powers from the states to the Community, the Member States have [...] thus created a body of law which binds both their nationals and themselves. [...] The law stemming from the Treaty, an independent source of law, could not, because of its special and original nature, be overridden by domestic legal provisions, however framed [...]

This ruling asserted the autonomy of EU law, imagining the Treaty as an independent source of law. Only in 1986[74] did the Court first baptise the founding Treaties a constitutional charter of the then European Economic Community, at the same time placing it among the constitutional democracies providing for judicial review of actions of its institutions: '[...the EEC] is a Community based on the rule of law, inasmuch as neither its Member States nor its institutions can avoid a review of the question whether the measures adopted by them are in conformity with the basic constitutional charter, the Treaty.'[75]

The two initial rulings have been subject to much academic debate.[76] Most commentators agree that they constituted a courageous step based on little textual material,[77] but favoured by a pro-integration consensus among European elites.[78] The remoteness of the actual facts[79] from any contentious area of social life within the Member States may also have eased acceptance.[80]

The Court's assertion of EU (constitutional) law's autonomy remained a one-sided affair. Courts and legislators in EU Member States have subsequently engaged with the concepts of primacy and direct effect, but not a single national constitutional instance has ever accepted the autonomy of EU law, i.e. the Court's assertion that primacy and direct effect are flowing from

---

74 ECJ 294/83 *Les Verts* [1986] ECR 1339. This assessment was reaffirmed in the Court's first opinion on the EEA (ECJ Opinion 1/91 [1991] ECR I-6079, paragraph 21).

75 ECJ 294/83 ibid., paragraph 23.

76 See Alter, 2009, Vauchez, 2010, and Münch, 2008, pp. 535–528 for interdisciplinary perspectives; for a recent defence see Baquero Cruz, 2008.

77 For example, Hartley maintains that the invention of supremacy and 'autonomy' of Community law constituted blatant judicial lawmaking (Hartley, 2004, p. 150) and Münch, 2008, p. 527 states that primacy of EU law is 'owed to an offensive interpretation of the Treaties'. Joerges has long demanded to move beyond the doctrine of supremacy by devising a heterarchical relation of EU and national law based on traditional conflicts of law teaching (Joerges, 2007, Joerges, 2010).

78 This is the main point of Alter, 2009.

79 *van Gend* concerned a customs levy for a chemical substance, which should not have been increased after the Treaty came into force. In *Costa*, the claimant denied payment of a relatively modest bill for electricity because he was not content that the company had been nationalised.

80 See Scharpf, 2010, pp. 216–217.

EU law as an independent source of law.[81] Most courts explicitly refer to their own constitutions as the source of limiting national sovereignty in favour of the EU, while accepting the higher authority of EU law in practice. The position of the Spanish Constitutional Court demonstrates that a pragmatic acknowledgement of EU law's primacy is possible, while maintaining that the source of this is national sovereignty.[82] The closest the Union has come to settle this issue explicitly is Declaration number 17 attached to the Treaty of Lisbon, according to which 'The Conference recalls that in accordance with well-settled case law of the Court of Justice of the European Union, the Treaties and the Law adopted by the Union on the basis of the Treaties have primacy over the law of Member States, under the conditions laid down by said case law'.

A declaration, in contrast to a protocol, however, has no legally binding effect, but only establishes a guide to interpreting the Treaties.[83] Accordingly, the relationship between national and EU law is not agreed explicitly on the terms the ECJ stated in the early 1960s. Rather, there are different, 'equally legitimate'[84] perspectives of courts of highest authority. This state of affairs is the basis for the contention that the EU is constitutionalised on the base of some form of pluralism,[85] an overlapping consensus[86] or on principles of constitutional tolerance[87] or heterarchy.[88] These views have come to replace the conception of the EU (or its predecessors) as a federation of states[89] and as a mere international-law type union of independent states.[90]

In conclusion, the primacy and direct effect of EU law independently of specific implementation of each of its norms has been widely accepted, but its inherent autonomy has not. Rather, there is now a regime of coexistent legal authorities within the EU, in which constitutions of Member States and EU

---

81 See on acceptance by the Member States Witte, 2011; in particular on the states having acceded after 2000, see Sadurski, 2008.

82 See Declaración Del Pleno Del Tribunal Constitucional 1/2004, de 13 de diciembre de 2004, requerimiento 6603-2004; for an English summary see Castillo de la Torre, 2005.

83 See Piris, 2010, pp. 81–82 with a reproduction of the Council Legal Service's assessment regarding the declaration.

84 See de Witte, 1991, p. 22.

85 See Walker, 2010a, Poiares Maduro, 2009.

86 Sabel and Gerstenberg, 2010.

87 Weiler, 2003, pp. 15–23.

88 Halberstamm, 2009.

89 Eric Stein famously drew this conclusion from the case law referred to above ('[...] the Court of Justice of the European Communities has fashioned a constitutional framework for a federal-type structure in Europe' – Stein, 1981, p. 1).

90 Kirchhof (2010, pp. 745–746, stressing the primacy of national law) still maintains this view.

constitutional law cooperate more or less peacefully. EU constitutional law does not, after all, presuppose the creation of an EU federation. It rather constitutes a multilevel entity.

## 2. Multilevel Character of EU Constitutional Law

The multilevel character of the EU has repercussions on its constitutional law.

Creation, interpretation and specification of EU constitutional law is based on concepts derived from and developed in national legal cultures and above all the interaction of these legal cultures with EU law and, through this medium, with each other. The interaction between national and EU law is perhaps most apparent in legislative endeavours of the EU: comparative reports are routinely requested by the EU Commission through the various networks of legal experts established for various fields and, for more important legislative projects, research funding for serious comparative reports is granted.[91] Any serious analysis of secondary EU law will uncover some or several national models on which a legislative proposal was based and also consider in how far the result is actually a mix of different national concepts with EU concepts and whether any 'transplantation'[92] of such concepts into all the legal orders of the EU would encounter any barriers in the difference of legal cultures.

Interactions between national and EU levels are also relevant for the creation of general principles of law. The European Courts, inter alia, rely on constitutional traditions common to the Member States to create these principles, in other words using a certain kind of comparative methodology.[93] Also, much EU case law originates before national courts, as the reference procedure (Article 267 TFEU) is the main source of EU case law today.[94] In these

---

[91] See for example the 'Joint Network on European Private Law', funded under the EU Commission's 6th Framework Programme (http://www.copecl.org/), whose proposal of a 'Common Frame of Reference' (CFR) for European contract law' (Bar, Clive and Schulte-Nölke, 2009) was referred to in the Commission's legislative proposals (http://ec.europa.eu/justice/policies/civil/policies_civil_contract_en.htm#cfr). For an academic critique see Mattei and Nicola, 2007, pp. 20–25. Similar structures operate in the field of consumer law (for a critique see Reich and Micklitz, 2009) and non-discrimination law (for a critique see Schiek, 2007 and Schiek, 2010b).

[92] On legal transplants see Graziadei, 2006.

[93] Lennaerts, 2003.

[94] See Court of Justice, 2011, p. 102. The table including all new cases from 1953–2010 shows that initially direct actions were the main source of new cases. Only between 1975 and 1977 and in 1991 did preliminary rulings slightly outnumber them. This has changed profoundly: from 1994 preliminary rulings became the main type of cases until today, with a dip in 2003. In 2010, there were even more than twice as many references for preliminary rulings than direct actions.

cases, the interrelation between national and EU law cannot be overlooked. But also if the Commission or a Member State initiate proceedings before the Court under Articles 258–259 TFEU, these cases originate from national developments, which may be perceived as violating the Treaty and the case law-based *acquis communautaire*. In turn, national courts engage with the verdicts given by the European judiciary. In extreme cases they may refuse respect, but more frequently they accept the Court's rulings grudgingly, at times signalling potential limits of their patience.[95] The EU's judicial constitution is thus not engendered in any EU vacuum, but always related to legal (and political) cultures within the Member States – even though there may be an emergent specific character of EU (constitutional) law.[96]

Treaty norms obviously require consensus of all the Member States, which again presupposes that national legacies can be reconciled with each other. Even for values common to the EU and the Member States, as expressed in the Lisbon Treaty, it is often possible to discern influences by discrete national models or by their amalgamation with some academic or political concept of the day.

Accordingly, a dialogical process between national and EU law concepts, integrating those capable of influencing case law, legislation or even Treaty amendments, is often decisive for EU constitutional law. Its interpretation will be more accurate if all these *formants* are reflected upon, including not only case law and positive legislation, but also academic opinion and socio-political influences (as far as is discernible).[97] However, the national level is no longer exclusively determinative for developing concepts and reflection of EU constitutional law. There is an emerging scholarship, doctrine and, last but not least, civil society movement (even if partly motivated by attracting EU Commission funds) which generates a discourse of its own, influencing and shaping EU constitutional law inter alia.

## 3. Elements of EU Constitutional Law

Within the multi-level constitutionality it is possible to identify the elements of EU constitutional law.

Our account of the assertion of EU constitutional law's primacy, if not its autonomy, has already demonstrated the pivotal role of case law produced by

---

95 The German Constitutional Court's Lisbon ruling has been read in this vein by Doukas, 2009.

96 See Zeno-Zencovich and Vardi, 2008.

97 The concept of 'formants' developed within the structuralist approach to comparative law. It encompasses legislative, judicial and scholarly resources and invites reflection on their socio-cultural and socio-political context (Sacco, 1991).

the EU judiciary. It has established not only primacy of EU law, but also its direct effect, thus transforming individual citizens and other economic actors[98] into prosecutors of EU law.[99] Having defined its own role as adjudicator providing a pivotal element to the constitutional character of EU law, the Court had ample opportunity to subject an ever-greater number of fields of national law to its judicial scrutiny, going beyond what founding Member States may have intended. Accordingly, the European Courts have successfully established their constitutional role[100] and their case law must be considered as one of the strongest elements of EU constitutional law.

Partly as a result of these judicial activities, the Treaties are considered as another main element of EU constitutional law. Obviously, however, not each and every Treaty norm is constitutional. EU constitutional law emerges where the Treaties created European spheres of democratic rule-making or maintained socio-economic fields of democratisation. Presently, this emerges more frequently where the Treaties vest economic actors with individual rights (fundamental freedoms and competition norms) that can be enforced against their Member States and the EU itself, and where they endow citizens (even if not powerful economic actors) with rights to equal treatment, citizenship rights and more recently human rights. These constitutional Treaty norms also contribute to such economic and social integration that as has already been achieved.[101] Due to their primacy over national law these concepts also fulfil constitutional functions.

These norms are in turn based on certain values, which remained largely unwritten at the time when the EEC was founded. With only six Member States whose socio-economic traditions were comparatively similar, the EEC could base itself implicitly on the values common to its Member States. With every expansion, this common base became more fragile. When the EU was founded after the fall of the Berlin wall, it equipped itself with principles (Article 6 EU pre Lisbon). The Treaty of Lisbon transformed these into values (Article 2 TEU), covering the span from liberty and rule of law as emanations of liberal constitutionalism to solidarity and social justice as emanations of socially embedded constitutionalism. In addition, the EU is governed by its objectives (Article 3 TEU), which started life as tasks in the EEC Treaty (Article 2). Values and objectives on which the Treaties base the EU and its Member States constitute the second element of EU constitutional law.

---

98 'Economic actors' not only comprise human beings, but also corporations, whose interests may only loosely link to any natural person.

99 This is even referred to as 'extending constitutional rights of citizens' (Petersmann, 2008, p. 776).

100 On their political role see Alter, 2009.

101 See Chapter 1, IV, pp. 22–26, 41–44.

Given the EU's multilevel character, interrelations between different levels of rule-making and governance are an important element of its constitutional law. The Treaties constitute a regime of legislative competences, reserving some fields for exclusive competences of the EU (Article 2(1) and 3 TFEU), providing shared competences of the EU and national levels for most fields (Article 2(2) and 4 TFEU), restricting EU legislation to complementing and coordinating national lawmaking in other fields (Article 2(5) and 6 TFEU) and implicitly reserving all other fields for national rule-making (Article 4(1, 2) TFEU). The division of competences only appears clear-cut if one considers traditional top-down governance as the only way of engendering Europeanisation of policy fields. This is not the case, since it has long been complemented by a wide array of governance styles, including 'soft' modes of governance that seem to offer further perspectives in particular for transnational and European spheres embracing diverse levels.[102] While it seems exaggerated to characterise policy coordination as a new form of enabling law,[103] it is correct that new forms of governance offer a way for the EU to respond to challenges of globalisation:[104] where neither the EU nor its Member States command sufficient authority to regulate, they may still be able to influence processes by deliberation.

EU constitutional law, in conclusion, thus consists of principles established in EU case law and directly effective Treaty articles, which have recently been complemented by a legally binding human rights catalogue. The common value base of these constitutional norms, though shared between the EU and its Member States, is also an element of constitutional law. Furthermore, the EU is a multi-level polity, which is, inter alia, constituted by the regime for division of competences between the EU and its Member States. This competence regime, too, is an important element of EU constitutional law.

## 4. The EU and Judicial Constitutionalism

The dominant role of the Court in developing EU constitutional law reinforces the character of the EU as a constitutional democracy, with a tendency to judicial rule-making complementing legislation through other routes.

This resonates with the fact that the majority of EU Member States are also constitutional democracies. Their common features include judicial control of government and legislator by a strong constitutional court on the basis of a bill

[102] On the relevance of those for principles of European constitutional law see Wiener, 2005; on their relevance for furthering social integration see Armstrong, 2010 and Dawson, 2009; see also Chapter 1, pp. 46–47.

[103] See Velluti, 2010, p. 79.

[104] Velluti, 2010, pp. 56–64.

of rights which cannot be amended by a simple majority in parliament. Constitutional democracy is entrenched in European national constitutions: it was first motivated by the atrocities of the Holocaust and later by the perceived human rights deficiencies of Soviet-style democracy.[105]

Constitutional democracy, and in particular judicial control of parliament, is often criticised for its potential to de-politicize fundamental decisions about values and engendering 'juristocracy'.[106] It has even been ridiculed as the 'Constitutional Protection of Capitalism'.[107] Clearly, in constitutional democracies courts compete with parliaments to a certain degree. However, this control can also be viewed as a precondition for democracy[108] on grounds of the danger inherent in majoritarian rule to infringe positions of structural minorities.[109] In order to be defendable, judicial review of democratic legislators must be firmly rooted in a value base derived from the common humanity of all people. Such a value base should presuppose the fundamentally equal claim of all humans to lead a human life.[110] It proceeds from the assumption that there is one essence of humanity that calls for protection against abuse – whether by states, other public actors or by powerful economic entities. Human rights and their enforcement through courts have a legitimate role in ensuring such protection.

In a minority of EU Member States, comprising the UK and the Scandinavian states, majoritarian democracy prevails. In this model, constitutions provide a framework for justifying rule through parliamentary democracy and – in the case of the Scandinavian countries – leaving important social realms to self-governance by societal institutions.[111] As judicial redress against unwelcome policy developments is not a dominant feature in these countries, their citizens also tend to litigate less frequently before the EU courts.[112]

At the EU level, there are more arguments in favour of constitutional democracy. In contrast to its composite states, the EU does not exercise

---

105 Stone Sweet, 2011, pp. 122, 125–126.

106 Hirschl, 2004, pp. 38–49.

107 Nicol, 2010.

108 Stone Sweet, 2011, p. 125.

109 The classical treatise on this (from a US perspective) is Ely, 1980.

110 Sen and Nussbaum, 1993, Nussbaum, 2001.

111 See on the difference between majoritarian and constitutional democracies Dworkin, 1996, pp. 1–38, and Ginsburg, 2003, pp. 1–19, juxtaposing the British majoritarian principle of parliamentary supremacy with the US idea of constitutional democracy. For European voices see Petersmann, 2006, contrasting rights-based constitutions such as the German and South African with process-based ones, such as the US or unwritten UK one, and Nergelius, 2008, on the Scandinavian variety.

112 See on this aspect Wind et al., 2009.

command over a dense web of social relations that could mitigate exclusionary and autocratic tendencies. Judicial control thus becomes ever more important in such an endeavour. Increasing transnationalisation of societies also entails the juridification of many aspects of daily lives.[113] At a more practical level, the availability of judicial review also enables individuals to make use of court procedures in order to lobby for political change. Again, this is particularly important in larger entities, where direct pressure on political actors may be more difficult to organise.[114] Accordingly, the EU is necessarily characterised by judicial constitutionalism. This is not necessarily detrimental for developing socially embedded as opposed to liberal constitutionalism though. While practices of collective self-governance through functioning industrial relations – which are one way of socially embedding democracy – are best established in the Scandinavian countries, strong judicial protection of collective bargaining and collective action has also been developed in constitutional democracies, as has judicial protection of rights derived from social citizenship. A strong judiciary can be an asset as well as a curse in terms of developing socially embedded constitutionalism.

## 5. EU Constitutional Law – a Societal Notion

In order to assess whether and in how far EU constitutional law restrains or enables economic and/or social integration,[115] a societal view of EU constitutional law is necessary. From such a perspective, constitutional law constitutes society and not only an authority in a public sphere, which must in turn remain distinct from society.

Such a view of EU constitutional law is supported by its specific characteristics: in contrast to some national constitutions, EU constitutional law is based on an openly substantive mission. The EEC aimed at enhancing the standard of living of the peoples of Europe, initially only through establishing a common market. Today's EU also pursues this aim by enhancing solidarity and social justice as well as protecting human rights. These links between the life of the people and EU constitutional law presuppose a societal notion of EU constitutional law.

---

113 Kelemen, 2011, p. 11.

114 This aspect is stressed by Alter, 2006, on participation through adjudication see Cichowski, 2007, and Conant, 2006.

115 From a formal perspective, constitutions fulfil enabling and restraining functions (Dunhoff and Trachtman, 2009a, pp. 10–13). Enabling functions are served by rules defining lawmaking and adjudication within the constituted entities and restraining functions by rules limiting government, protecting individual rights and counterbalancing majoritarian rule by judicial protection.

Such a notion of EU constitutional law perceives of law as a social practice[116] and of constitutional law as a framework for embedding legal relationships into society. It presupposes an interrelation between law and society, without, of course, making a naïve assumption that values expressed in constitutions would translate immediately into social reality. Rather, it considers the narratives supported by constitutional law in its many emanations, ranging from case law, constitutional values and constituted processes of democratic and collective rule-making. These narratives necessarily relate to society (including its economic base) within the EU's Member States. At the same time, they contribute to engendering European socio-economic spheres. Given its authoritative character, law as a social practice not only mirrors but also shapes balances of power within societies.

From this perspective, an adequate response to social and economic integration becomes a challenge to be taken up by constitutional law.

## V. ECONOMIC AND SOCIAL INTEGRATION AND EU CONSTITUTIONAL LAW

The factual challenges for furthering economic and social EU integration have already been identified in Chapter 1. Its summary[117] concluded that the EU integration project is increasingly under pressure from, on the one hand, the global economic integration process and, on the other hand, the insistence of Member States on remaining the sole governors of any social integration. National policies for social integration, however, tend to rely on national closure, rather than on openness, and thus have the potential to undermine EU integration. For this reason, they frequently conflict with EU constitutional law. The friction between the global pressures to increase economic integration at EU level and national claims to social integration has only partly been addressed. The increasing dedication of the EU integration project to merely liberal principles, such as competitiveness, growth and efficiency, enhances the response to global pressures and minimises the opportunities for social integration at any level. This again drives competition between Member States and their social models.

As we have seen, the Court has recognised early on that primacy and direct effect of EU constitutional law should be derived from engagement of national citizens with each other. This again seems to depend on a minimal degree of

116 Schiek, 2010b, pp. 70–71, with further references.

117 See Chapter 1, VI, pp. 51–52.

social integration – across and not only within Member States.[118] Successful economic and social integration have thus been acknowledged by the European judiciary as preconditions for successful constitutionalisation of the EU. Consequently, a harmonious interrelation between economic and social integration is also necessary. Such interrelation or a holistic approach to integration is attempted by the EU institutions and increasingly so since the inauguration of the Lisbon Strategy in 2000.[119]

Eastern Enlargement (2004/2007) has made any progress in this direction more difficult. This most comprehensive and significant territorial expansion of the EU since the EEC's foundation in 1957 multiplied inequalities between Member States.[120] Any economic or social indicator is affected, including average wages, unemployment rates, productivity, foreign direct investment or exports. Furthermore, Eastern Enlargement has effects within all Member States. An exodus of qualified workers and the intelligentsia from new Member States (the so-called 'brain drain') limits resources and capacities dearly needed for successful reorientation of society and economy.[121] In the old Member States, Eastern Enlargement was largely perceived as creating 'opportunities for low-cost competition nearby'.[122] At the same time, Eastern Enlargement meant the bringing together of governments and EU office holders, including EU judges, who did not share the social democratic consensus characteristic of the EU of the 1990s. They rather tended to support neo-liberal values in distancing themselves from former socialist economies, which were perceived as having failed. As a consequence, establishing consensus for EU legislation has become more difficult. This again enhances the relevance of case law and Treaty norms as mediums to assess how EU constitutional law responds to the increased challenges of economic and social integration. All in all, Eastern Enlargement constitutes a turning point for any factual opportunity of economic and social integration beyond national borders within the EU and at the same time any constitutional orientation. Accordingly, the analysis of European constitutional law, which will be the subject of the next chapters, is going to focus on the post-2004 period.

---

118 See Münch, 2008.

119 See Chapter 1, V, pp. 49–51.

120 See Vaughan-Whitehead, 2003, but see also Heidenreich and Wunder, 2008, with evidence for an incremental reduction of inequalities between and a parallel increase of inequalities within Member States. For empirical data on the social situation in the post-Enlargement EU, see Alber et al., 2008.

121 On the exodus of intelligentsia see Mayes and Mustaffa, 2010, p. 8.

122 Visser, 2008, p. 175.

## VI. CONCLUSION AND OUTLOOK

The next chapters will investigate the EU's judicial constitution (Chapters 3 and 4) and its value base and competence regime (Chapter 5), in order to answer the question of how each of the elements of EU constitutional law responds to the challenges of economic and social integration in an increasingly diverse EU. As has been shown, liberal constitutionalism can be assumed to be better able to further economic integration, while socially embedded constitutionalism should be more adequate to further social integration. Socially embedded constitutionalism as the most recent development in modern Western national constitutionalism can also be expected to be a greater challenge for EU constitutional law than its more traditional liberal counterpart. The investigation focuses on the substantive constitutional law of the EU, leaving to one side the assertion of authority which the EU has so successfully achieved.[123]

In order to assess how far liberal and socially embedded constitutionalism are determinative for the EU, it is useful to distinguish between the two core constitutional functions of rights protection and enabling democratic governance and collective rule-making (partly as opposed to 'spontaneous' market rule) in relation to these two paradigms. Under the paradigm of liberal constitutionalism, constitutions must fulfil the function of protecting (human) rights in public spheres and of establishing public spheres of democratic rule-making. Under the paradigm of socially embedded constitutionalism, protecting (human) rights must proceed towards market and other horizontal relations and it must include consideration for the actual enjoyment of rights.[124] Such constitutionalisation of socio-economic spheres from democratic perspectives[125] aims at true self-determination of all citizens. Among others, this requires alternatives to the free rein of 'laws of the market'. On the one hand, this can be achieved by subjecting markets to public governance. On the other hand, this can be achieved by creating alternatives to markets, the decommodification of relations between citizens in welfare state institutions and the 'économie sociale'. The enabling of truly democratic collective regulation beyond public spheres is another element of these more recent elements of constitutional law.

Further, scope for democratic rule-making must be established for socioeconomic spheres, thus transcending the traditional separation of public and private and politics and markets. If contributing to such developments, EU

---

123 See above pp. 65–68.
124 See above pp. 56–60.
125 See above pp. 59–60.

constitutional law may also enhance citizens' interaction. Any mode of enabling citizens to engage with each other across borders – in processes of rule-making or through enforcing rights – will potentially enable constituency building at European levels[126] and thus further European economic and social integration. All this can be visualised in a four-cornered chart, Figure 2.1, across which citizens' interaction can be considered as well:

| **EU constitutional law – relating to EU and national levels** | | |
|---|---|---|
| Citizens' interaction | Protecting rights | European spheres of democratic/collective rule-making |
| Liberal constitutionalism: Guaranteeing rights and democracy in 'public spheres', safeguarding spheres where private rule prevails (economic life and families) | Member States and the EU institutions should not infringe<br>• Individual liberties<br>• Rights to equality and non-discrimination<br>• Economic freedoms | European public spheres to be governed by principles of<br>• Parliamentary democracy<br>• Direct democracy<br>• Transparency |
| Constitutionalising Socio-economic spheres – guaranteeing rights in social reality, expanding principles of democracy into traditional spheres of private autocratic rule | • Protecting human rights (including rights to equality and non-discrimination) horizontally<br>• Creating preconditions for actual enjoyment of human rights (including rights to equality and non-discrimination)<br>• Guaranteeing economic freedoms and social rights in markets | • Constitutionalising social antagonism (e.g. industrial relations)<br>• Empowering civil society in socio-economic realms<br>• Allowing public and collective regulation of markets and non-market structures to provide important services |

*Figure 2.1 EU constitutional law under liberal and socially embedded perspectives*

The chart shown in Figure 2.1 provides the structure for the argument in the chapters following. The analysis therein is premised on the expectation that each of the four fields of the chart will relate to economic and social integration

126 See also Fossum and Trenz, 2006, p. 61.

differently. Sometimes, rights protection and enabling of collective governance will reinforce each other, but at times rights protection under liberal paradigms will also clash with collective rule-making under socially embedded paradigms. Gauging the extent to which EU constitutional law enables any equilibrium between liberal and socially embedded constitutionalism, which may then constitute an adequate response to the challenges of economic and social integration, promises to become a complex affair.

# 3. The trajectory of EU constitutional law

## I. INTRODUCTION

This chapter will retrace the trajectory of EU constitutional law as it has developed through case law and Treaty reforms, using the chart in Figure 2.1. As EU constitutional law emerged incrementally rather than in one constitutional moment, it can best be understood in its historical development.[1] For the purposes of this book, it is important to understand how layer upon layer of the different phases of European integration have added to liberal and socially embedded constitutionalism EU style – especially up until 2004, that magical turning point for rights protection and democratic life respectively as a consequence of Eastern Enlargement.[2] Thus, the focus will be on developments up until that year, including changes made by the Treaty of Lisbon except for the restatements of the EU's value and programmatic base, which are the subject of Chapter 5.

The initial purpose of the EEC was economic integration, and EU constitutional law first developed an 'economic constitution'.[3] A 'political constitution',[4] institutionalising democracy under liberal paradigms, only emerged later, through a series of Treaty reforms from 1987 up to the Treaty of Lisbon in 2009.[5] It was accompanied by the 'civic constitution', offering judicial protection for the economic constitution, but also citizens' and human rights. Whether a 'social constitution' ever emerged is contested: while some view this as the neglected aspect of European constitutionalism,[6] others have maintained that democracy and citizenship have developed as a 'converse inverted pyramid', in that social rights (and implicitly social constitutionalism) emerged even before political and liberal rights.[7]

---

1 Tuori, 2010, p. 14.

2 On the relevance of this see Chapter 2, V, pp. 74–75.

3 See also Tuori, 2010 and the presentation in Chapter 1, pp. 22–28 with notes 91–130.

4 The constitutional categories rely on Tuori, 2010, except for the civic constitution, which he termed the judicial constitution.

5 Academic writing on EU democracy and its deficit is too voluminous to be fully referenced, see, for example, Lord, 1998, Hix et al., 2007, Eriksen, 2009.

6 See Tuori, 2010, p. 24, branding it as the 'constitutional underdog'.

7 Fitzpatrick, 2000.

This brief highlight already indicates that EU constitutional law has developed on a specific trajectory that differs from its national equivalent. This may even make it seem dubious whether the categories of liberal constitutionalism and socially embedded constitutionalism as developed above are adequate for assessing its current state. In tracing the trajectory of EU constitutional law, this chapter also sets out to demonstrate that this is indeed possible, and to show analytically how the different layers of EU constitutional law are positioned between these two poles. It recounts the development of EU constitutional law first for rights protection and then for developing democratic institutions and procedures for legitimate collective regulation, relating both fields to the paradigms of liberal and socially embedded constitutionalism.

## II. RIGHTS PROTECTION AND TYPES OF CONSTITUTIONALISM

Protection of rights, in particular human rights, is a central element of any written[8] European constitution and decisive for constitutional democracies. However, the founding Treaties of today's EU did not provide for any explicit human rights regime.[9] Instead, they protected a number of economic freedoms and competition law rules, which created the basis of EU constitutionalism, facilitating European integration through economic integration.[10] In parallel with expanding judicial protection for economic rights, the European judiciary also established constitutional dimensions for equality rights, in particular the right of equal pay irrespective of sex. From the late 1970s political demands for complementing EU rights with classical human rights emerged.[11] However, these only succeeded with the Treaty of Lisbon.

---

8 The unwritten constitution of the UK did not contain a human rights catalogue traditionally – an interesting contrast to the UK's leading role in establishing the European Convention on Human Rights (ECHR) and promoting the incorporation of human rights into the constitutions of its former colonies (Hirschl, 2004, p. 7). The Human Rights Act 1998, which aimed to incorporate the ECHR into UK law, has been seen to create a new model of human rights protection which does not actually give judicial protection against public infringements of fundamental rights (Hiebert, 2010).

9 For an interesting overview of alternatives debated before the six founding states settled for the focus on economic integration see de Búrca, 2011.

10 See Chapter 1, p. 23.

11 European Parliament (EP), Council and Commission jointly declared in 1977 that they were henceforth bound by human rights (see Joint Declaration by the European Parliament, the Council and the Commission 'Concerning the protection of fundamental rights and the European Convention for the protection of Human rights and fundamental freedoms' OJ [1977] C 103/01).

Thus, the trajectory of development of EU rights constitutionalism moved from the economic constitution, proceeding from its more social emanations in the fields of equality, citizens' and workers' rights, to embracing human rights protection eventually in 2009.

## 1. The 'Economic Constitution'

Possibly dictated by the positioning of the European Economic Community as one of the pivotal steps towards International Economic Law after World War II,[12] EU rights constitutionalism first emerged in relation to the economic freedoms and competition rules. Direct effect and primacy initially emerged in the field of free movement of goods, and they apply without any doubt to free movement of services, persons and (since 1993) capital, as well as to competition rules.[13] Thus, the Court effectively introduced a new set of individual liberties available to transnational economic actors,[14] whether corporations or human beings, creating an economic constitution before any civic rights protection.[15] The economic freedoms and EU competition law constitute the main pillars of this judge-made economic constitution. First established by the founding Treaties in 1957, their texts have not been changed substantively yet. Accordingly, any development of their contents has been left to the judges, which will not have to fear 'intervention' by other EU institutions. Having interpreted these norms as sources of individual rights early on, the Court could expect a steady stream of cases brought by powerful economic actors wishing to shake off limitations of their transnational economic activities. It will thus remain to be able to govern European integration in this field.

The notion of economic freedoms is used here to comprise the four freedoms,[16] also referred to as fundamental freedoms,[17] which are at the heart of the internal market: free movement of goods (mainly Articles 34 and 35

---

12 Petersmann, 2008.

13 See on the relevance of these for economic integration Chapter 1, section III, pp. 22–26.

14 See Petersmann, 2008, pp. 776–777, praising the citizen-driven case law on fundamental freedoms, which practically elevated those to human rights supporting any transnational economic activity.

15 The notion of economic constitution has been utilised from the 1960s (Poiares Maduro, 1998), and is also defended in more recent academic writing, predominantly from Germany (Hatje, 2010); see also Kingreen, 2010, on the constitutional relevance of the fundamental freedoms and Drexl, 2010, on the constitutional relevance of EU competition law.

16 This is the common term in UK academic writing (e.g. Barnard, 2010b, which has the subtitle 'The Four Freedoms').

17 This term is mainly used by German scholars of EU law, see for an overview and a defence of this notion Kingreen, 2010, pp. 515–519.

TFEU),[18] services (Article 56 TFEU), workers and self-employed persons (Articles 45, 49 TFEU) and capital (Article 63 TFEU), all geared towards creating the internal market as a space without frontiers (Article 26(2) TFEU). The Court maintained the link to the internal market by making involvement in a more than minor economic activity with a transborder element a precondition for claiming rights under the economic freedoms. Economic liberty in a wider sense is also protected by competition law rules (Articles 101–106 TFEU), which, in the EU legal order, include the prohibition of state aid (Articles 107–110 TFEU). Ideologically, competition law can be read as protecting the individual freedom to engage in markets,[19] and in this libertarian vision it constitutes a source of economic liberty.

The economic freedoms and competition rules were not devised to serve business interests, but rather to support the creation of the internal market, which was meant to further European integration at large. This aim served higher goals such as the conquest of petty parochialism beyond the market,[20] or, in the words of the Court, the 'economic and social interpenetration' of the European Union.[21]

## 2. Economic Freedoms

### a) Constitutionalising the internal market for public spheres: direct effect and expansive reading

Direct effect was the first step towards developing the economic freedoms into pillars of a powerful economic constitution. After acknowledging direct effect of the customs regime and subsequently the free movement of goods rules in the 1960s,[22] direct effect of the free movement of persons and services was recognised only in the following decade, due to some obscure wording of the predecessors of Articles 45, 49 and 56 TFEU.[23] Free movement of capital only

[18] Free movement of goods is also supported by the abolition of custom tariffs between Member States (Article 30 TFEU) and the prohibition of protective and discriminatory taxation (Article 110 TFEU).

[19] See Chapter 1, III, pp. 21, 24–26.

[20] This is the contention of Weiler in devising his 'constitutional Sonderweg' (Weiler, 2003).

[21] This expression has first been used in *Reyners* (case 2/74 [1974] ECR 631, paragraph 21) and is a standing phrase in the Court's case law on freedom of establishment to the present day (see, for example, case C-97/09 *Schmelz* 26 October 2010 (nyr), paragraph 37).

[22] Cases 26/62 *van Gend* [1963] ECR 1 and 6/64 *Costa v E.N.E.L.* [1964] ECR 614.

[23] Cases 2/74 *Reyners* note 21 paragraphs 24–31 (freedom of establishment),

became directly effective after the Treaty of Maastricht, which removed the provisional nature of that fundamental freedom.[24]

The next step was the substantive expansion of the economic freedoms from mere prohibitions of discrimination on grounds of nationality to general defences against any minor hindrance to expanding economic activity across national borders. As in the case of direct effect, this doctrinal development started in the field of free movement of goods. In the seminal case *Cassis de Dijon*,[25] the Court first established that free movement of goods went far beyond a mere prohibition to explicitly discriminate against goods imported from other Member States. It established that Member States could in principle establish rules to restrict trade in goods for public policy reasons, but that these rules, even if they were not discriminatory, would be scrutinised by the Court for any adverse effects on trade ('principle of mutual recognition').[26] Before *Cassis*, the fundamental freedoms could have been read as merely targeting discriminatory barriers to trade, which Member States would need to justify before the Court. *Cassis* established that any non-discriminatory 'barrier' could now be questioned and brought before the Court for justification by European standards, rather than by criteria developed nationally.[27]

---

33/74 *Van Binsbergen* [1974] ECR 1299, paragraphs 24–26 (freedom to provide services) and 167/73 *French Merchant Seamen* [1974] ECR 359, paragraph 41 (free movement of workers).

24 Case C-222/97 *Trumner and Mayer* [1999] ECR I-1661 was one of the first cases brought under the new rules and led to judicial appraisal of direct effect of Article 56 EC (now 63 TFEU).

25 Case 120/78 *Rewe Zentrale AG* (*Cassis de Dijon*) [1979] ECR 649.

26 The Court found 'no valid reason why, provided that they have been lawfully produced and marketed in one of the Member States, alcoholic beverages should not be introduced into any other Member State'. The Commission tried to derive a principle of mutual recognition from this line, according to which all Member States must accept any good lawfully produced in or imported into any other Member State (Communication from the Commission concerning the consequences of the judgment given by the Court of Justice on 20 February 1979 in Case 120/78 ('Cassis de Dijon') OJ [1980] C 256/2, see also COM/99/0299 final, which seeks to expand the argument to services). However, the Council disagreed, considering that legislation was necessary (Regulation No 764/2008/EC OJ [2008] L 218/21, repealing Commission Decision 3052/95/EC, for free movement of goods). Attempts to endorse the principle for free movement of services as well failed (Directive 2006/123/EC is fundamentally different from the Commission's original proposal of the Services Directive (see Neergard et al., 2008)).

27 See for a textbook assessment (Barnard, 2010b, pp. 21–22, 93–95). Specific criticism has been raised by numerous writers. Maduro accused the Court of crossing the line between 'securing the access to the market for further market integration and securing access to the market to enhance economic freedom', conceding that it is a thin line (Poiares Maduro, 1999, p. 451).

In contrast to free movement of goods, the Court initially considered free movement of workers, freedom of establishment and freedom to provide services merely as prohibitions to discriminate. Thus, Member States could apply their national law to migrating workers, self-employed persons and service providers, as long as they did not treat them differently from nationals (host state rule). The reinterpretation of these provisions as rules easing access to foreign markets first emerged in relation to the freedom to provide services (Article 56 TFEU). In 1974,[28] the Court held that this freedom entailed the right of a Belgian attorney not only to be treated equally with Dutch attorneys, but also to be given an effectively equal status economically. The Court became more explicit in the *Saeger* case of 1991,[29] holding that a host state must not subject foreign service providers to each and every one of its rules, since this would force them to comply with two rather than one legal regime. In 1995, the Court expanded this principle to extend to freedom of establishment, declaring that today's Article 49 TFEU is violated if a national measure is 'liable to hinder or make less attractive the exercise of fundamental freedoms guaranteed by the Treaty,'[30] and to free movement of workers.[31] From 2000, the Court used a uniform phrase for all free movement rights, according to which 'provisions relating to the freedom of movement of persons [...] preclude measures which might place Community nationals at a disadvantage when they wish to pursue an economic activity in the territory of another Member State'.[32] All this meant that territoriality, which had been a common principle of legislation affecting natural persons, could be fundamentally challenged by relying on free movement rights.

In theory, the economic freedoms apply to the EU and its Member States equally, as the Court established in 1984.[33] In practice, the judicial review on economic freedoms impacts mainly on Member States' legislation and policies. These principles thus had the potential to subject any national rule to the scrutiny of the European judiciary upon claims brought by economic actors before national courts and referred to the Court or infringement procedures brought by the Commission.

---

28 Case 33/74 *van Binsbergen*, note 23.

29 Case C-6/90 *Saeger* [1991] ECR I-4421, paragraph 12.

30 Case C-55/94 *Gebhard* [1995] ECR I-4165, paragraph 37.

31 Case C-415/93 *Bosman* [1995] ECR I-4921. Here the Court stated that national rules which 'preclude or deter a national of a Member State from leaving his country of origin in order to exercise his right to freedom of movement therefore constitute an obstacle to that freedom even if they apply without regard to the nationality of the workers concerned' (paragraph 96).

32 Case C-233/01 *van Lent* [2003] ECR I-11525, paragraph 15.

33 Case 15/83 *Denkavit Nederland* [1984] ECR 2171, headnote 1.

### b) Mitigating negative integration

This wide-ranging potential of the economic freedoms has been mitigated in two ways.

First, the economic freedoms only apply to transnational situations. Legislation not affecting market access from abroad only comes into their scope of application if they discriminate against foreign products or economic actors. For free movement of goods, the *Keck* case[34] differentiated between 'certain selling arrangements',[35] which were deemed to not impinge on freedom to import and other national legislation. The much-criticised[36] categories were refined subsequently,[37] but with no substantive change. The *Keck* formula has never been applied to the other freedoms,[38] but similar principles ensure that all of them only apply to rules inhibiting access to foreign markets.[39] Recently, this has been classified as a residual element of non-discrimination.[40] However, the 'obstacles approach'[41] differs from a non-discrimination regime in that it suffices for any measure to be liable to make the transnational exercise of economic freedoms less attractive. This requirement can be fulfilled even if rules apply equally to internal and foreign economic actors, while under a non-discrimination approach, different treatment of internal and foreign economic actors in equal situations, or equal treatment in unequal situations, must be established.

Second, Member States and the EU itself can rely on a wide, and in principle unlimited, range of justifications to uphold rules inhibiting market access in non-discriminatory ways, as long as the justification satisfies the principle of proportionality.[42] The Court first introduced the category of 'overriding issues of the general interest' in its 'Cassis' jurisprudence.[43] The reason given was that transnational market integration does not generally exclude differences between the national legal orders. The rationale goes much further, though: if the Court had only allowed justifications of non-discriminatory

---

34 Case C-267/91 *Keck & Mithouard* [1993] ECR I-6097.

35 Case C-267/91 ibid., paragraphs 16 and 17.

36 Reich, 1994, Wilsher, 2008, Barnard, 2009, Barnard, 2010b, pp. 103–108.

37 See, for example, case C-405/98 *Gourmet* [2001] ECR I-1795, for younger developments see Chapter 4.

38 Explicitly rejected for free movement of workers in case C-190/98 *Graf* [2000] ECR I-493, paragraphs 18–25.

39 See, e.g., for free movement of workers case C-415/93 *Bosman*, note 31, paragraph 103.

40 AG Maduro in his opinion on case C-446/03 *Marks & Spencer v Halsey* [2005] ECR I-10837, paragraph 28.

41 Banks, 2008, p. 493.

42 All this was first developed in *Cassis de Dijon* (see above p. 83). For a textbook coverage see Barnard, 2010b, pp. 171–187.

43 See note 25.

restrictions under explicit Treaty rules, most differences between national legal orders would have been ruled out. Accordingly, the expansion in scope of the economic freedoms led to an expansion in justifications available to the Member States. This also established the principle that public interests must be safeguarded in the internal market and that Member States had a prerogative for this safeguarding in the absence of EU legislation.[44] For a long time, the Court has, as a consequence, only accepted the general interest justification in cases where Member States' legislation was not discriminatory. However, from the late 1990s, cases both occurred where discriminatory restrictions were justified by general interests and where the Court only allowed justifications made explicit in the Treaty for non-discriminatory restrictions.[45] This of course corrupted the inherent legitimacy of expanding justification grounds along with the reach of economic freedoms and it introduced an element of arbitrariness.[46]

### c) Regulatory competition and general freedom to conduct one's business

Notwithstanding these mitigating principles, the expansive reading of free movement rights has led to establishing a new form of competition in the internal market: the national regimes of ordering any affair within the scope of economic freedoms are pitched against each other (competition between legal orders or regime competition). In its innocent form, competition between legal orders occurs each time that a person moves to another country. A worker may find employment more easily across a border or she may be attracted by higher levels of maternity leave and public childcare in a country other than one in which she was born. However, due to the fact that real people move with less ease than capital,[47] regulatory competition rarely is this innocent. As companies and capital use economic freedoms with more ease, and much more frequently than do workers, they will benefit more.

Regime competition clearly has the potential to disrupt national legal orders. As these are at the same time the main location of any social policy, it is prone to disrupt social integration at national levels.[48] The cross-relation of

---

44 See more detail on this Schiek, 2008a, pp. 45–47.

45 See for further references Barnard, 2010b, pp. 165–166.

46 Spaventa, 2000, and Nic Shuibhne, 2002. Consequently, the distinction between distinctly and indistinctly applicable measures is still defended (e.g. Gormley, 2009, paragraphs 11.93–11.97). Others argue that the distinction is best abolished and the mandatory requirements read into Article 36 TFEU (Craig and de Búrca, 2011), pp. 677–679.

47 See Chapter 1, pp. 28–29.

48 See on this already Chapter 1, pp. 49–50.

competence distribution and interaction between European economic and social integration is the subject of a separate chapter. However, competition between legal orders is also one of the main mechanisms established by substantial constitutional law of the EU.

From a critical perspective, these effects have been termed 'regulatory competition'[49] or even 'law shopping'.[50] The notion of regulatory competition invites critical assessment of the functionality of such competition, posing the question of whether the complexity of information needed to assess legal orders does not make 'information costs' prohibitive at least for small and medium enterprises. The 'law shopping' metaphor invites a more fundamental critique engaging with the potential of upholding the rule of law on a free market for legal orders. The notion of 'competitive federalism' is the basis for a more conciliatory perspective, according to which the active choice of suitable legal environments will not necessarily lead to a preference for such legal environments as are focused on business interest as opposed to the interest of labour and any public interest in social integration.[51]

Two developments further enhanced the effectiveness of this aspect of the EU's economic constitution: the radicalisation of free movement of companies and the blurring of boundaries between freedom of establishment and freedom to provide services.

Originally, the Court had been reluctant to let companies choose their legal environment. In 1988[52] the investment company owning the *Daily Mail* challenged the requirement imposed by the UK Inland Revenue to liquidate a sizeable proportion of its assets before moving its fiscal residence to the Netherlands, because this rendered the move to a country with considerably lower corporate tax less profitable. The Court held that in the absence of EU harmonisation of national company law, the UK retained the right to subject a split corporate domicile (a tax domicile in the Netherlands and a corporate domicile in the UK) to specific conditions.[53] Eleven years later,[54] the Court's position had changed. It held that Denmark could not enforce its rules on minimum capitalisation of companies against a Danish couple who first established a company in the UK (where capital requirements are minimal) and subsequently established a branch in Denmark where they had always intended to conduct their main business. The Court held that the choice of a legal environment best suited to business purposes was inherent in the right to freely

49 Deakin, 2006.
50 Supiot, 2010, pp. 155–158.
51 Barnard, 2010, pp. 25–30.
52 Case 81/87 *Ex parte Daily Mail* [1988] ECR 5483.
53 Paragraph 24 of the judgment.
54 Case C-212/97 *Centros* [1999] ECR I-1459.

move one's companies across the internal market, and that taking advantage of more lenient regimes in other countries did not amount to abuse.[55]

This case seemed to jeopardise a certain set of national rules establishing the link of a company with its domicile. European states operate two different regimes: the '*siège réel*' and the incorporation regime. Under the first, a company's legal personality depends on it having its true domicile ('*siège réel*') within the respective nation state. This prevents companies from maintaining 'letter box offices' in different states and thus ensures that stakeholders such as employees or creditors can rely on national law being applicable to those companies conducting their main business in any state. Countries following the incorporation theory, such as Denmark, but also the UK and the Netherlands, only require a company to incorporate under their law for it to have national legal personality. This allows companies to enjoy the protection of their home legal order should they expand their main business, for example, to colonies. These models have come to be associated with Continental and Anglo-Saxon varieties of capitalism respectively.[56] The *Centros* and subsequent cases meant that the '*siège réel*' states could not prevent companies from establishing secondary seats in other states and subsequently transferring their main business activities to these states,[57] which has been criticised as facilitating 'law shopping'.[58]

Further, the Court approximated the economic freedom to a business right to unfettered economic activity by blurring the boundaries between freedom of establishment and freedom to provide services. Until 2003, the Court had carefully distinguished between these two,[59] based on the principle that those establishing themselves abroad can be expected to integrate into the host society, which again justifies them being subjected to national rules. Service providers, by contrast, were thought to provide services only temporarily,[60] which also reflected the residual character of the freedom to provide services (see Article 57 TFEU). Thus, provision of services was seen not to mandate a permanent integration into another Member State, for which reason service providers should not be expected to comply with the full set of national rules of their host state. The distinction between the two freedoms is still upheld in central pieces of secondary legislation, such as the Directive on recognition of

---

55 Paragraphs 26–28.

56 See Biermeyer, 2011, pp. 152–158 with further references.

57 Cases C-208/00 *Überseering* [2002] ECR I-9919, C-167/01 *Inspire Art* [2003] ECR I-10155, on the combined impact of these and *Centros* see Höpner and Schäfer, 2010.

58 Supiot, 2010, pp. 155–157.

59 Case C-55/94 *Gebhard* [1995] ECR I-4421.

60 Case 6/90 *Saeger* [1991] ECR I-4425, paragraph 12, confirming Case 205/84 *Commission* v *Germany* [1986] ECR 3755, paragraph 21.

professional qualifications[61] and the Directive on services in the internal market ('Services Directive').[62]

In the age of cyber-communication and ever more efficient means of transport, the opportunities of being active internationally without establishing a company across a border have increased immensely. Service providers can often send their services through the internet and, if a customer needs specialist support abroad, this certainly does not require an established settlement at the customer's location. Since the choice of a place of establishment is less constrained by physical proximity to markets than before, business can consider other factors in that choice, such as the availability of cheap labour, low taxes and a legal order perceived as cost-efficient – or, conversely, availability of well-educated labour and/or environmental, cultural and educational surroundings suitable for attracting high-profile personnel. If establishment in any state becomes too burdensome, businesses can choose to provide services from more convenient locations instead.

As if to ease such a choice, the Court started to blur the boundary between services and establishment in two ways. First, it held that providing services for a period of more than seven years was still temporary.[63] This decision formally maintained the temporary character of service provision, but seemed to cast doubt on the residual nature of the freedom to provide services.[64] As a result, the reference to a maximum period of 16 weeks for any service provision was eliminated from the draft for Directive 2005/36/EC.[65] Second, the Court acknowledged that a single rule can violate both freedoms at the same time.[66] Contrary to what could have been expected,[67] the Court did not reconsider justification standards, but rather allowed business to rely on the lighter regulatory touch Member States had to apply to service providers generally, irrespective of the duration of their presence within their borders. Since 2004, free movement of capital was added to the medley: if an establishment is listed on a regulated (stock) market, its shares constitute capital, and any restriction

61 Directive 2005/36/EC OJ 2005 L 255/22, Article 5 (last amendment by Regulation 213/2011/EU, consolidated version available from http://eur-lex.europa.eu).

62 Directive 2006/123/EC OJ 2006 L 376/27, providing for a special, and stricter, regime for service providers seeking to establish themselves in another Member State in Articles 9–13.

63 Case C-215/01 *Schnitzer* [2003] ECR I-14847.

64 See O'Leary, 2011, p. 533.

65 Article 12 Regulation 883/2004/EC maintains an upper limit of 24 months for service provision though.

66 Case C-243/01 *Gambelli* [2003] ECR I-13031, paragraph 59, against AG Alber's thorough opinion.

67 O'Leary, 2011, p. 533.

on trading shares may impinge upon free movement of that capital. From a business perspective, these freedoms merge into a general right to pursue business transnationally with as few inhibitions as possible.

As a result of all these changes, the economic freedoms already resembled a constitution of business to choose the friendliest regulatory environment in the internal market. This corresponded to the perspective of liberal constitutionalism, as it was based on the liberty of businesses to act as they choose.

#### d) Economic freedoms in society – socially embedded rights?

The mainly judicial economic constitution also entailed elements of socially embedded constitutionalism. For one, the Court acknowledged horizontal effects of economic freedoms. This case law emerged from the mid-1970s and was based on the 'effet utile' of the free movement rights. The Court stated that 'abolition [...] of obstacles to freedom of movement for persons and to freedom to provide services, which are fundamental objectives of the Community [...], would be compromised if [it] could be neutralized by obstacles resulting from the exercise of their legal autonomy by associations or organizations which do not come under public law'.[68] In the first of these cases, individual sportsmen or their team members attacked rules established by sports associations as autonomous private entities, which discriminated against participants from other Member States. From the mid-1990s, numerous cases concerning sports associations emerged. The Court took the opportunity to clarify that it had always meant for any obstacle emerging from unilateral rules made by private associations to come within the economic freedoms' scope of application.[69] In 2000, the Court added that nationality discrimination in individual employment contracts also infringed economic freedoms.[70] This reasoning already indicated that the Court would hold agreements between trade unions and employers bound by these economic freedoms as well – and this was explicitly confirmed by the end of the 1990s.[71]

Horizontal effects of economic freedoms are criticised by academic writers pointing to the need to protect private autonomy against any public intervention.[72] Partly, this critique was spurred by the fact that the Court never acknowledged horizontal effect of free movement of goods because any restrictions of inter-EU trade by private economic actors was addressed by the

---

68 Case 36/74 *Walrave* [1974] ECR 1405, paragraph 18.

69 Case C-415/93 *Bosman*, note 31, paragraphs 82–84.

70 Case C-281/98 *Angonese* [2000] ECR I-4139, paragraph 34.

71 Case C-435/97 *Fernandéz de Bobadilla* [1999] ECR I-4773, paragraphs 18–21.

72 Marenco, 1987, Kingreen, 2010.

competition rules.[73] Also, the Court's doctrine that Member States are under an obligation to prevent private parties from compromising free movement of goods[74] seemed to imply that such indirect horizontal effects could be sufficient to safeguard effectiveness of the economic freedoms.[75]

However, the counter-arguments had some weaknesses. First, the indirect horizontal effects developed in only two key cases arose from direct action by civil society organisations.[76] Even if the Court were to declare such actions invalid, this would have little effect without positive steps being taken by Member States to deter civil society from continuing the condemned action. If there is a piece of 'private legislation', then declaring it invalid in law could well substitute for other positive action.

The second counter-argument is somewhat stronger, as the competition rules enshrined in Articles 101 and 102 TFEU do not only apply to cases where free movement of goods is at stake. Certainly, the Court had pronounced in the 1990s that neither employees nor their associations are undertakings under Articles 101, 102 TFEU.[77] This seemed to imply that the Court stood by one of the founding principles of the ILO ('Labour is not a commodity'). However, later on the Court held that collective agreements between trade unions and employers' associations could still fall under Articles 101, 102 TFEU.[78] Although the Court considered in *Albany* that the specific collective agreement was outside the scope of Article 101, 102 TFEU, the reason for this was not that the trade union, as one of the partners to the collective agreement, was not an undertaking. Rather, the Court derived the competition law immunity of this agreement from its aim to improve working and employment conditions.[79] Subsequently, the EU Commission has classified decisions by sports associations involving conditions on using labour as potentially anti-competitive.[80] The slogan 'labour is not a commodity'

---

[73] Case 65/86 *Bayer* [1987] 3801, paragraphs 17 et seq., thus overruling case 58/80 *Dansk Supermarket* [1981] ECR 181.

[74] Case C-265/95 *COM v France* (tomatoes and strawberries) [1997] ECR I-6959, Case C-112/00 *Schmidberger* [2003] ECR I-5659.

[75] Kingreen, 2010, pp. 547–548 with further references.

[76] Case C-265/95 concerned direct action by a French farmers' association who, over a period of ten years, destroyed Spanish tomatoes and strawberries in order to neutralise the climatic advantage of Spanish farmers. Case C-112/00 concerned a 36-hour blockade of the Brenner pass by an environmental organisation in protest of overuse of the Alps by motor traffic.

[77] Case C-22/98 *Becu* [1999] ECR I-5457, paragraph 26.

[78] Case C-67/96 *Albany* [1999] ECR I-5751, paragraphs 60–64, recently confirmed by a decision of the Court's first chamber (Case C-437/09 *AG2R Prévoyance v Beaudort Père et fils*, 03 March 2011, nyr).

[79] Ibid., paragraph 59.

[80] See EU Commission White Paper on Sport COM(2007) 391 final, under 4.3.

apparently has little value in the internal market. Agreements and unilateral decisions by associations of undertakings concerning service provision can be captured by EU competition law if they focus on the 'product quality' of services,[81] and this also applies to rules restricting establishment.[82] Thus, competition rules may partly apply in markets for employment, services and establishment. However, there will also be cases when they do not apply, and in these cases the Court rightly scrutinises discriminatory effects of individual contracts. In cases of unilateral regimes established by associations more powerful than their potential contract partners, its scrutiny should also consider mere non-discriminatory obstacles to the economic freedoms.

In principle, such case law could even support a socially embedded constitutionalisation of the EU. The Court could proclaim that standard contracts issued by associations of banks, mobile telephone providers and insurance companies, which subject anyone using the relevant services from across a border to exorbitant additional fees, are invalid as this might serve to deter them from transborder economic activity. So far, the case law has only been used to check collective labour agreements though, leaving the multiple obstacles for migrating citizens untouched. This may well be a consequence of the fact that consistent doctrinal coverage of restrictions of the economic freedoms by private associations and other non-state actors still awaits development.

## 3. Competition Rules

Competition law has always had a prominent position within the EU constitutional order.[83] The prohibitions of cartels (Article 101 TFEU) and of abuses of dominant market powers (Article 102 TFEU), as well as the principled prohibition of state aid (Article 107 et seq. TFEU), are among the oldest legally binding Treaty norms. They are substantively constitutional in character, as they ordain competitive markets as a principle for organising society. They protect as well as restrict economic liberties and these functions are enforced by the EU Commission as the EU's competition authority.

---

[81] See, e.g., case C-41/90 *Höfner and Elser* [1991] ECR I-1979 – a prohibition of private employment services violates free movement of services and competition rules at the same time.

[82] See case C-309/99 *Wouters* [2002] ECR I-1577. The Court held the rule of the Dutch bar prohibiting multidisciplinary practices between advocates and chartered accountants was to be not in conflict with EU competition law on the grounds that any resulting restriction of competition did not go over and above what was necessary to achieve an aim (the integrity of advocates) unrelated to competition (paragraph 109).

[83] See Chapter 1, II, pp. 24–26.

The prohibition of cartels and the abuse of a dominant market position are mainly aimed at horizontal relations between economic actors, safeguarding the internal market and a system of undistorted competition against distortion by anti-competitive actions and agreements.[84] However, from the 1980s[85] the Court held Member States bound by Articles 101 and 102 TFEU in exceptional cases. This case law relied on the general obligations of Member States not to distort the EU's objectives (now Article 4(3) TEU, ex Article 10 EC).[86] The Court held that this principle prevents Member States from taking measures rendering the competition law rules ineffective.[87] In particular, legislation should not encourage cartels or abuse of dominant market positions by private actors. Initially, the Court held that this excluded any delegation to regulate economic affairs to private associations or to any business association, even if incorporated as a public body.[88] However, more recently, Member States have been given some room for manœuvre: if they retain ultimate responsibility for the specific rules, this does not constitute violation.[89] Member States also must refrain from creating legislation that will lead an undertaking to abuse a dominant market position, although granting exclusive rights to undertakings is not in principle in violation of Article 102.[90] Thus,

84 On the purposes of competition law see Monti, 2007, pp. 1 et seq.

85 The principle was first established in a case concerning French legislation on uniform book prices (case 229/83 *Leclerc* [1985] ECR 1, paragraph 14) ('Member States are [...] obliged under [Article 4 (2) TEU] not to detract by means of national legislation, from the full and uniform application of [EU] law or from the effectiveness of its implementing measures, nor may they introduce or maintain in force measures, even of a legislative nature, which may render ineffective the competition rules applicable to undertakings'). In this case, the Court held that due to the limited extent of EU legislation in the field of book trading, the Member States remained free to legislate in the matter and investigated the case exclusively under free movement of goods. As a result, any national legislation on book prices extending to transborder trade is considered as conflicting with EU law (see case C-531/07 *Fachverband der Buch- und Medienwirtschaft* [2009] ECR I-3717).

86 Baquero Cruz (2002, pp. 155–159) considers this as an illegitimate intrusion into democratically legitimated national policies.

87 First held in the case 311/85 *Vlaamse Reisbureaus* [1987] ECR 3801, paragraph 31, confirmed in C-96/94 *Centro Servizi Spediporto* [1995] ECR I-2883, paragraph 20. In both cases, legislation establishing price regimes in reliance on agreements between (competing) economic actors.

88 ECJ C-185/91 *Reiff* [1993] ECR I-5801. Note that in this specific case the fixing of transport tariffs by a tariff board composed of business representatives was held not to violate Article 85 EEC in combination with Article 5 EEC (now Articles 101 TFEU and 4(3) TEU). For a critical view see (Schepel, 2005, pp. 327–328), with references to contemporary criticism.

89 Case C-35/99 *Arduino* [2002] ECR I-1529, on setting lawyers' fees.

90 Case C-41/90 *Höfner and Elser* above, note 81.

economic actors can derive rights to protect their freedom to conduct their business against Member States' legislation from competition rules in principle, although these were originally conceived to protect competitors against each other. The doctrine of binding Member States in this way has been criticised on the grounds that the limited scope of defences available under competition law rules is not adequately respecting the political responsibility of states.[91]

Provisions on state aid (now Articles 107–109 TFEU) are directed against Member States, as they aim to prevent distortion of the internal markets by national aid. These rules can also be relied upon by economic actors (and other parties affected), which can demand that state aid to a competitor is frozen or reclaimed.[92] While this does not constitute horizontal effects, the state aid provisions can thus have repercussions in horizontal relations.

## 4. Embedding Economic Rights – Equality Rights and Free Movement

Rights protection before the Court has never been limited to the economic freedoms.

For one, the European judiciary has been an active promoter of equality rights, starting with equality between women and men.[93] Clearly, this particular development of judicial constitutionalism was initially based on campaigns not initiated by the EU, and this strategy has been expanded to further 'discrimination grounds', with the explicit motivation of repeating the success story of gender equality.[94] Equality law is, however, also a field where the Court of Justice has developed constitutional law from a rather scarce Treaty base. Initially, equality between women and men only had a Treaty base in Article 119 EEC (today paragraphs 1 and 2 of Article 157 TFEU). Article 119 originally stated that 'Each Member State shall during the first stage ensure and subsequently maintain the application of the principle that men and women should receive equal pay for equal work'.[95] This wording did not seem to fulfil the criteria for direct effect of any Treaty norm as developed in *van*

---

[91] Baquero Cruz, 2002, pp. 155–162.

[92] The recent case C-199/06 *CELF* ECR [2008] I-469 originated from such a constellation when it was first brought before the EU courts.

[93] On the role of judicial campaigning in this field see also Chapter 1 p. 44 with notes 225–226 (with reference to Hoskyns, 1996 and Alter and Vargas, 2000).

[94] See Schiek, 2010a, pp. 472, 483.

[95] Paragraph 2 of the original provision is maintained in Article 157 paragraph 2 TFEU, while paragraph 1 now reads 'Each Member State shall ensure that the principle of equal pay for male and female workers for equal work or work of equal value is applied'.

*Gend*,[96] and in particular it seemed to lack sufficient clarity to be applied by national courts without further implementation. It rather suggested that specific measures at national level were needed, which could even subject the principle to unspecified exceptions.

The Court still acknowledged not only direct effect, but also horizontal effects of the provision, in the second *Defrenne* case (1976).[97] As with horizontal effects of economic freedoms, the reasoning was teleological, referring to the effectiveness of Community law. Also, the Court rejected the defence of safeguarding private autonomy or the autonomy of collective agreements.[98] After the Court held in the ensuing third *Defrenne*[99] case that, while sex equality constitutes a fundamental principle of EU law, it is not directly applicable beyond Article 119 EEC.[100] The Court has since expanded the reach of the equal pay clause: while it was initially only held to be directly effective when direct discrimination occurred, the Court soon established the prohibition of indirect sex discrimination long before its legislative definition.[101] It extended the application of equal pay to equal rights to occupational pensions[102] and time off for maternity[103] and training for employee representation,[104] as well as in specifying equal pay for work of equal value.[105] The Court also continued to stress the constitutional character of the right of women and men to equal treatment irrespective of sex, for example when banning pregnancy-related discrimination as sex discrimination.[106] This last case, which started a whole line of other cases, also demonstrated how EU equality law went further than US equality law conceptually. While in the US, courts had severe difficulties acknowledging that discrimination on grounds of pregnancy was sex discrimination although no woman could name a pregnant man as a comparator, the ECJ had no problems in appreciating that only women can become

---

96 See above Chapter 2, pp. 65–67.

97 Case 43/75 *Defrenne II* [1976] ECR 455.

98 Paragraph 38.

99 Case 149/77 *Defrenne III* [1978] ECR I-1365.

100 Paragraphs 19/23.

101 See Tobler, 2005.

102 ECJ 170/84 *Bilka* [1984] ECR 1607.

103 Cases C-342/93 *Gillespie* [1996] ECR I-3101, C-147/02 *Alabaster* [2004] ECR I-3101.

104 Cases C-360/90 *Bötel* [1992] ECR I-3589, C-457/93 *Lewark* [1996] ECR I-260, C-278/93 *Freers* [1996] ECR I-1165.

105 ECJ 237/83 *Rummler* [1986] ECR 2101, ECJ C-127/92 *Enderby* [1993] ECR 5535, ECJ C-400/93 *Royal Copenhagen* [1995] ECR I-1275.

106 Case 177/88 *Dekker* [1990] ECR I-3941. This case related to Directive 76/207/EEC, now replaced by Directive 2006/54/EC OJ [2006] L 204/23, but nevertheless referred to the fundamental rights quality of banning sex discrimination.

pregnant and concluding from this that discrimination on grounds of pregnancy is sex discrimination, without the need to find a pregnant male comparator.[107]

The field of gender equality was the first in which the Court relied on the legitimising force of human rights rhetoric in order to reinforce rights granted to citizens by the then EEC. Although the predecessor of Article 157 TFEU had clearly been introduced for economic reasons,[108] the Advocates General in *Defrenne II* and *Defrenne III* referred repeatedly to the human rights quality of equal treatment between women and men.[109] The Court, however, preferred to rely on the dichotomy of economic versus social aims of the equal pay principle,[110] thus indicating that human rights protection fell within the sphere of social policy.[111] Obviously, given the predominance of liberal constitutionalism in the Member States at that time (the 1970s), this was a rather far-sighted parallel. The Court repeated the formula that the equal pay clause served economic and social aims in later case law, until it held in 2000,[112] that, given the increased relevance of human rights, the social aims of the equal pay clause now outweighed its economic motives. Accordingly, an employer, having violated the equal pay clause over a period of more than 20 years, to the detriment of its female employees, could not rely on competitive disadvantage caused by the obligation to make good past discrimination in its occupational pension schemes.

Equally, free movement of persons has been treated as a right with social aspects. Legislation actively promoted preconditions for workers to actually enjoy their rights to free movement from the 1960s. These went well beyond formal equal treatment rights, for example providing for derived rights of workers' family members to reside and work in the host state[113] and to receive

---

[107] See More, 1992; for a comparison with UK law see Wallace, 2000, p. 131.

[108] See Chapter 1, pp. 39, 41–44.

[109] See opinion of AG Trabucchi in case 43/75 *Defrenne II,* note 97, pp. 490 et seq., and of AG Capotorti in case 149/77 *Defrenne III*, note 99, pp. 1384 et seq. The Court had recognised the prohibition of sex discrimination as human rights and general principle of Community law earlier in two staff cases (cases 20/71 *Sabbatini* [1972] ECR 345, 21/74 *Airola* [1975] ECR 221) and reaffirmed this in *Defrenne III* (paragraph 27).

[110] Stressing that Article 119 EEC aimed at avoiding competitive disadvantage for undertakings in Member States prohibiting pay discrimination, but also pursued social objectives while striving to enhance working and living conditions (*Defrenne II*, paragraphs 9–10).

[111] Stating that 'the principle of equal pay forms part of the foundations of the Community' (*Defrenne II*, paragraph 12), thus indicating that the AG's human rights rhetoric was not lost on the Court.

[112] ECJ C-270/97 *Sievers & Schrage* [2000] ECJ I-929, paragraphs 53–57.

[113] Originally Articles 10, 11 Regulation 1612/68/EEC OJ [1968] L 257/2, now

education for their children, and equal access for workers and their families to social advantages,[114] and coordinating national social security systems to ensure that entitlements accrued in different Member States can be combined.[115] The Court reinforced Member States' obligations to make free movement rights effective in socio-economic reality. In the *Sotgiu* case of 1974, the Court relied on the 'effective working of one of the fundamental principles' of the EU when finding that free movement of workers required equal treatment of workers in fact and in law and thus also prohibited indirect discrimination.[116] Further, the Court interpreted the legislation quoted above expansively, stressing that these rights were also based on Article 45 TFEU and expanding them to self-employed workers.

Since 2000, the Court has stressed the human rights character of non-discrimination law, whether in the field of gender equality or the 'other equalities' (relating to race and ethnic origin, religion and belief, age, disability and sexual orientation).[117] Recently, this has led to a line of case law that resulted in giving non-discrimination clauses – if in Directives implementing equality principles into national law – horizontal direct effect,[118] another example of how human rights can be utilised to expand the reach of EU law obligations within Member States. However, equality law retains its position as a market-motivated right, with strong horizontal effects. Its expansion towards a socially embedded right is closely linked to the pivotal role of non-discrimination rights in establishing an internal market as well as the lack of comprehensive jurisprudence on equality and non-discrimination in horizontal relations in the vast majority of Member States.[119]

---

replaced and expanded by Articles 7(2), 9, 11 and 12 Directive 2004/38/EC OJ [2004] L 158/77.

114 Article 7 Regulation 1612/68, superseded by Articles 7, 9, 10 Regulation 492/2011/EU OJ [2011] L 141/1 as of 15 June 2011.

115 Regulation 1408/71/EEC, superseded by Regulation 883/2004/EC OJ [2004] L 166/1 and 987/2009/EC OJ [2009] L 284/1 as of May 2010. Originally, the legislation only provided that entitlement to pensions and unemployment benefits add up for migrating workers (see also Chapter 1, p. 41). The new rules expand some of these rights to economically inactive citizens (for an overview see White, 2010).

116 Case 152/73 *Sotgiu* [1974] ECR 153 (on allowances for working away from home, which differentiated between residence in Germany and abroad).

117 On the Commission's tendency to separate these into two different socio-legal fields and the Court's only partial reluctance to accept this, see Schiek, 2010a; on a proposal to organise the different equalities in a non-hierarchical way see Schiek, 2011.

118 Case C-144/04 *Mangold* [2005] ECR I-9981 started this (Chapter 4, II, p. 179).

119 Streeck (1995, p. 400), see Chapter 1, p. 44. Somek (2011) has recently revived Streeck's opinion that non-discrimination law is the only form of social policy compatible with the EU's agenda of competitiveness and neo-liberalism.

From relatively early on, free movement of persons has been used to establish citizens' rights.[120] From the Treaty of Maastricht, free movement of EU citizens for economic purposes has been complemented by free movement rights of EU citizens irrespective of any economic purpose (Article 21 TFEU) and embryonic free movement rights for non-EU nationals could be developed from new competences to create secondary law under what is today Title V TFEU (area of freedom, security and justice).

EU citizenship as a Treaty right has, similar to the economic freedoms and equal pay, developed into a judicially enforceable right far beyond the relatively timid text of the Treaty (now Articles 18, 20–25 TFEU).[121] Case law concerning welfare rights of students[122] and unemployed citizens[123] has required Member States to provide a 'certain degree of financial solidarity'[124] towards citizens from other EU Member States. 'Citizenship matters'[125] and it matters not least as a constitutionalised concept.

So far, the Court has only decided cases on Member States' relations to EU citizens, more recently also in relation to their own nationals as EU citizens. Neither the Court nor the legislator have expanded citizenship rights horizontally. However, from 2004 the Court has sometimes required Member States to positively ensure that citizens can actually enjoy their rights, thus taking first steps towards socially embedding citizenship rights.[126]

## 5. Human Rights Protection

### a) From the civic constitution to the Charter of Fundamental Rights

Human rights protection in the EU was originally a product of the Court. The judicial acknowledgement of EU law's constitutional authority through the doctrines of primacy and direct effect[127] made conflicts with national guarantees

---

[120] However, Nic Shuibhne maintains that citizenship rights remain wedded to the internal market (2010).

[121] See also Chapter 1, IV, p. 44.

[122] ECJ C-184/99 *Grzelczyk* [2001] ECR I-6193 (confirming a French student's potential claim to social assistance in Belgium), ECJ C-209/03 *Bidar* [2005] ECR I-2119 (concerning whether a French student resident in the UK from primary school age was 'sufficiently integrated' to qualify for a Local Educational Authority grant towards his study fees). Recently, this case law has been partly reverted, though (see below Chapter 4, II, pp. 160–162.

[123] For example ECJ C-456/02 *Trojani v CPAS* [2004] ECR I-7573.

[124] ECJ *Grzelczyk*, note 122 above, paragraph 44.

[125] Kostakopoulou, 2008, p. 293.

[126] More detail in Chapter 4, in particular pp. 162–169.

[127] See Chapter 2, IV, pp. 65–68

of human rights inevitable.[128] Positive constitutional law in the founding states provided for the protection of property and personal liberty, in line with the ECHR, to which all founding Members were signatories. Thus, clashes between market regulation (and particularly the planification of Community agricultural policy) and those constitutional rights were predictable.[129] Confronted with those clashes, the Court derived the principles of human rights protection against Community (now EU) acts from general principles of law, relying on the Court's competence to 'ensure that in interpretation and application of the Treaties the law is observed' (Article 19 TEU, ex Article 220 EC).[130] This case law has been seen as combating the EEC's legitimacy deficit stemming from the lack of a fundamental rights catalogue.[131]

For the content of the unwritten human rights catalogue, the Court was 'inspired by' common constitutional traditions of the Member States and took 'guidance from' international agreements to which all or most of the Member States were signatories.[132] This partly comparative method of judicial lawmaking[133] effectively maintained the Court's own autonomy: while taking inspiration and guidance, the Court remained free of any obligations to defer to other courts specifically tasked with enforcing human rights treaties, such as the European Court of Human Rights (ECtHR) or national constitutional courts.[134]

The character of human rights EU style did not change fundamentally when the Treaty of Maastricht (1993) first included them into Treaty law. Article 6 EU (now Article 6(3) TEU) required the EU to 'respect' fundamental rights, and referred to the ECHR[135] as well as to the constitutional tradi-

128 However, some authors purport that such conflict was not foreseen by the Treaty makers (see Sabel and Gerstenberg, 2010, p. 514).

129 Unsurprisingly, national human rights and EU law first clashed in the field of agriculture: the *Hauer* (44/79 [1979 ] ECR 3727) and *Internationale Handelsgesellschaft* (11/70 [1970] ECR 1125) cases, both having been dealt with in parallel by the German constitutional Court, concerned clashes of property rights and quota planification regime under the Common Agricultural Policy.

130 See cases 29/69 *Stauder* [1969] ECR 419 at 425, ECJ 11/70 *Internationale Handelsgesellschaft* note 129 at 1134, ECJ 4/73 *Nold* [1974] ECR 491 at 507, ECJ 44/79 *Hauer* [1979 ] ECR 3727 at 3732.

131 Weiler and Lockhart, 1995, p. 581.

132 See, for example, case C-299/95 *Kremzow* [1997] ECR I-2629 paragraph 14 – when inspiration was first mentioned. The formula established in this case is now consistently repeated.

133 See Lennaerts, 2003.

134 Douglas-Scott, 2006, and Harpaz, 2009.

135 This contrasts with the case law of the Court, which also refers to other human rights instruments. The Court has not been deterred from using other human rights instruments though. See, for example, case C-438/05 *International Transport Workers*

tions common to Member States. By qualifying fundamental rights as general principles of EU Law, the Treaty of Maastricht reaffirmed the Court's autonomy in interpreting these principles.

Only the Treaty of Lisbon changed this. The Charter of Fundamental Rights in the EU (Charter)[136] is now legally binding (Article 6(1) TEU), adding a positive catalogue of human rights to the Court's own inspiration. For the first time, the EU institutions are bound explicitly to respect human rights when issuing legislation and in their administrative activities. Members of the EU judiciary seem to express in interviews that they are prepared to grasp the opportunity of enhancing rights protection[137] and, as we will see in Chapter 4, the very first cases now exist where EU legislation is invalidated on grounds of human rights violation. Also, the EU's accession to the ECHR (Article 6(2) TEU) will eventually bring the Court within the jurisdiction of a specialist human rights court. However, the process of accession is predicted to be a protracted one, precisely because of the prospect for the CJEU of losing some of its prerogatives over the field.[138] Even once the accession is in place, there is reason to believe that human rights aspects of the internal market will remain the prerogative of the Court, precisely because the ECtHR accords state parties a wide margin of discretion in the implementation of human rights in their specific cultures. Accordingly, human rights under the name of fundamental rights as general principles of EU law (Article 6(3) TEU) remain an important source of EU human rights law for the time being.

The trajectory of developing EU human rights law differs in interesting ways from the development of economic freedoms, equality law and EU citizenship, both in relation to liberal constitutionalism and socially embedded constitutionalism.

### b) Liberal constitutionalism

As far as liberal constitutionalism is concerned, human rights are meant to protect citizens from intrusions by public authority. The main function of EU human rights would thus be to limit EU government activities. However, a number of case law analyses[139] have demonstrated that this potential had little

---

*Federation (Viking)* ECR [2007] I-10779, paragraph 43 (reference to the ESC and ILO Conventions). For a critical assessment of the ECJ's reluctance to refer to UN conventions see Ahmed and de Jesus Butler, 2006.

136 OJ [2010] C 83/381.

137 Morano-Foadi and Andreadakis, 2011.

138 See Jacqué, 2011. It is interesting to note that the Court's own discussion paper on the accession stresses over more than two pages that the Court alone has the power to declare an act of the Union invalid (Court of Justice of the European Union, 2010, pp. 3–4).

139 See recently Cartabia, 2009.

practical effect, as in most cases the Court held that EU legislation or administrative activities did not violate human rights.[140] The field of competition law quickly became the exception to the rule, as powerful economic actors partly successfully defended their procedural rights to fair process against a sometimes overactive Commission as European competition authority.[141] Only within the period scrutinised in more detail in Chapter 4 has the Court invalidated EU legislation on the grounds of human rights violations.

Member States' activities, by contrast, have increasingly been subjected to human rights control EU style. In some cases Member States were held responsible for ensuring human rights conformity of EU legislation when the EU institutions had not adequately respected human rights.[142] While it is legitimate to oblige Member States to use any discretion left for implementing directives in order to safeguard fundamental rights, it seems counterintuitive if the Court responds to a question on human rights compatibility of EU legislation by stating that Member States are under an obligation to iron out the EU legislator's lack of consideration for human rights issues. Rather than laying all the responsibility at the door of the Member States, the Court might be expected to hold to account the EU institutions which created the legislation.

In another group of cases, the Court expanded the reach of EU human rights to bind Member States even when legislating internally, in particular if relying on any exceptions from economic freedoms contained in the Treaties. In relation to these cases the ECJ has been accused of taking an instrumental

---

[140] This is the thrust of the classical critique by Coppel and O'Neill, 1992, who coined the term of 'offensive use' of human rights, when the ECJ only announces them 'in order to extend its jurisdiction into areas previously reserved to Member States' courts and to expand the influence of the EU over the activities of the Member States'. For a counter-critique see Weiler and Lockhart, 1995. More recent studies still find a tendency of the ECJ to not find fault in the EU as such (see Harpaz, 2009, at p. 116 with further references in note 73).

[141] Douglas-Scott states laconically 'It was not until 28 years later [than Hauer] in Baustahlgewebe [C-185/95 [1998] ECR I-8417] that the ECJ actually found an EU institution to have violated fundamental rights.'(2006, p. 633).

[142] The 1980s saw the first case in this regard, where Germany was obliged to change the wording of a regulation upon implementation to ensure that no infringement of the right to property ensued (case 5/88 *Wachauf* [1989] ECR 2609). Another case on those lines, also relating to the common policy on agriculture and fisheries rights, but relating to a directive, was decided in 2003 (joined cases C-20/00, C-64/00 *Booker Aquaculture and Hydro Seafoods v Scottish Ministers* [2003] ECR I-7411). In the same year, the Court rejected the EP's application to declare the directive on family reunification of third-country nationals void on grounds of human rights violation – stating that Member States were to ensure that implementation of that directive did not violate Article 8 ECHR (case C-540/03 *EP v Council* [2006] ECR I-5769, paragraph 33).

approach to human rights, using them to expand its authority over Member States rather than obliging institutions to respect, protect and promote human rights.[143] The pivotal case relates to a municipal television station in Greece which violated an exclusive broadcasting licence held by a larger radio and television company. This rule was held to fall within the scope of application of EU law, inter alia, because it restricted the freedom to provide services. Accordingly, Greece was obliged to observe the human right to freedom of information and opinion (Article 10 ECHR) when restricting that freedom. This seems to suggest that the Greek constitution cannot be trusted to provide a sufficient standard of protection in this purely internal Greek case, where there is no relation whatsoever to any human rights risk created by EU activities.[144]

However, there is arguably legitimate scope for the Court to prompt Member States to respect the human rights of EU citizens if they are citizens of other Member States. Not all Member States grant equal protection of human rights for their own citizens and for foreigners.[145] Even if the protection is formally equal, some additional support for the rights of strangers may well be adequate. In a number of cases the Court has required Member States to safeguard human rights of freely moving citizens of other Member States when restricting their economic freedoms. In this vein, the Court has acknowledged the right to freedom of expression in the public sphere in favour of economic actors importing goods to other Member States,[146] or the right of a migrant self-employed health worker to use his name in the correct spelling for business purposes.[147] While these cases – just as the *ERT* case – concerned Member States policies, there is a difference between the ECJ deciding on an entirely internal conflict and protecting rights of foreign citizens in other Member States.

Liberal dimensions of human rights in the EU have received a boost from the Charter becoming legally binding with the Treaty of Lisbon. The main civil and political rights as guaranteed in the Charter are also referred to as 'rights', which again means that they are judicially enforceable. This can be

---

143 See again Coppel and O'Neill, 1992.

144 Case C-260/89 *ERT v DEP* [1991] ECR I-2925, paragraphs 41–45, a similar constellation was at stake in Case C-368/95 *Familapress* [1997] ECR I-3689.

145 For example, the German constitution only grants to Germans freedom to choose one's profession and to engage in any profession one likes as well as freedom of association. Obviously, these are human rights which are quite relevant to self-employed or employed migrants from other EU Member States.

146 Cases C-368/95 *Familapress* note 144, C-71/02 *Karner v Troostwijk* [2004] ECR I-3025.

147 Case C-168/91 *Konstantinidis* [1993] ECR I-1191.

derived from Article 52(5), which states that principles are only 'judicially cognisable' to a limited extent. By *conclusio e contrario* this implies that there are no limits of judicial enforcement of rights. A question mark may be placed on this under Article 52(2) of the Charter, according to which the rights are only recognised within the limits defined by the Treaties. This may in due course be interpreted as meaning that human rights continue to play second fiddle to economic freedoms.[148] Thus, the Charter itself may contain some undue limitations of human rights after all. However, Article 52(3) clarifies that any rights guaranteed in the ECHR must be interpreted in line with the ECtHR jurisprudence. This again means that rights can only be limited in so far as it is proportionate, a principle also confirmed in Article 52(1) Charter. What is more important is that some liberal rights cannot be limited at all, e.g. the prohibition of torture or the right to life. It remains to be seen as to how this enhanced human rights protection against acts of public authority will be developed in practice though.

### c) Socially embedded constitutionalism

As far as socially embedded constitutionalism is concerned, human rights should include a responsibility for public bodies to create the conditions for their actual enjoyment. Also, horizontal effects of human rights as well as rights to social self-defence (e.g. freedom of association in industrial relations) should be acknowledged. EU human rights law has taken the first cautious steps towards socially embedded constitutionalism (with, as stated above, equality law being a little further progressed), without offering the same level of protection as for rights acknowledged under the paradigm of liberalism.

Horizontal protection of human rights has become relevant in one of the key human rights cases before the Court, the *Schmidberger*[149] case of 2003, which, together with the *Omega*[150] case, is usually referred to as support for the heightened sensitivity of the Court towards human rights protection. In both cases, human rights were relied upon as a defence for Member States against claims that their legislation allegedly conflicted with economic freedoms. In *Schmidberger*, Austrian authorities allowed a manifestation (freedom of assembly and speech) although it impinged for a short time on the free movement of goods transported on roads, and in *Omega*, German authorities prohibited the use of a computer-animated war game in order to protect human dignity.

148 The pivotal cases *Schmidberger* and *Omega* will be discussed below, on grounds of their relevance for horizontal relations (pp. 103–105).

149 C-112/00 [2003] ECR I-5659.

150 Case C-36/02 *Omega Spielhallen- und Automatenaufstellungs GmbH* [2004] ECR I-9609.

These cases thus concern national activities promoting, rather than only respecting, human rights. Positive obligations to ensure the actual enjoyment of human rights have been associated with socially embedded constitutionalism above.[151] Thus, the Court's position may become decisive for socially embedded constitutionalism at national level.

In *Schmidberger,* the Court famously stated that, when human rights are concerned, 'the interests involved must be weighed having regard to all the circumstances of the case in order to determine whether a fair balance was struck.'[152] The Court also annnounced that Member States have a 'wide margin of discretion' for this assessment.[153] While some authors now believe that human rights receive the same legal appreciation as economic freedoms,[154] others stress that human rights only became relevant at the stage of justifying a perceived infringement of economic freedoms.[155] This indicates their inferior position to economic freedoms, in favour of which human rights can be restricted without any justification under EU law. The reasoning in *Omega* is a good example: without paying much attention to the human rights base of dignity, the Court stressed that any justification for a derogation from 'the fundamental principle of the freedom to provide services' must be interpreted strictly,[156] and that even human rights can only justify a restriction of that freedom if this objective cannot be achieved by less intrusive means.[157] The Court does not mention any necessity of weighing diverging interests derived from economic freedoms and human rights.

The *Schmidberger* case, on closer inspection, represented a horizontal human rights conflict: the interests of eco-activists blocking a street and of a transport entrepreneur wanting to use this street clashed. Instead of choosing to frame his rights in the language of the internal market, Schmidberger could also have chosen to rely on a constitutional right to conduct his business. Accordingly, the clash appears as a horizontal human rights conflict. Such horizontal effects of human rights do not feature large in ECJ case law. In the *Defrenne III* case, the Court even rejected explicitly that human rights as

---

[151] Chapter 2, II, pp. 56–60.

[152] Paragraph 81 of the *Schmidberger* case. Paragraphs 79 and 80 of the judgment stress that economic freedoms as well as the human rights in question, as guaranteed by the ECHR, can be restricted.

[153] Paragraph 82.

[154] See Sabel and Gerstenberg, 2010, pp. 515–516.

[155] For example Morijn, 2006. For some cautious development beyond this restricted view see Chapter 4, II. 3. d) (2), on case C-271/08 *COM v Germany – 'Riester Rente'*, note 465.

[156] Case C-36/02 (above note 150) paragraph 30.

[157] Paragraph 36.

general principles could have horizontal effects.[158] In *Schmidberger* the horizontal dimension of human rights was not considered at all.

Thus, while the Court has made some progress towards socially embedded constitutionalism in relation to equality rights and had promoted horizontal effects of economic freedoms, the case law on human rights seems to lack any such development up until 2004.

Whether the Charter will change anything in this regard is open to doubt. First, the Charter is not generous with rights for societal self-organisation, providing only for a right to association (including trade union freedom) in line with traditional human rights law. Citizens' rights (Articles 39–46) are restricted to rights to vote and stand for elections. Furthermore, the Charter contains a title on solidarity (Article 27–37), comprising rights to collective bargaining and action as well as workers' information and consultation, consumer rights, rights to health care and access to services of general interest. Beyond that, Titles II and III also contain some guarantees going beyond mere liberties, including an objective guarantee of media pluralism (Article 11(2)), a right to education (Article 14(1) and (2)), a right to work (Article 15) and an objective guarantee of cultural, religious and linguistic diversity. Because some rights more akin to socially embedded constitutionalism are contained in these titles, the Charter has been characterised as not compartmentalising civil and political rights and so-called economic and social rights.[159] However, the concluding provisions of the Charter raise doubts to whether rights and guarantees relating to socially embedded constitutionalism are truly placed at the same level: they draw a distinction between rights and principles (Article 51, 52 Charter), which has even been enhanced following the Treaty of Lisbon. According to Article 51, rights shall be protected, while principles shall only be respected. This is spelled out more precisely in Article 52, according to whose paragraph 5 principles are only 'judicially cognisable' in so far as the interpretation of acts implementing the principles is concerned. This effectively means that the EU and Member States' institutions may also refrain from implementing principles in order to avoid that they become enforceable before courts. Unfortunately, the Charter does not clearly spell out what is a right and what is a principle. However, the wording of Articles 27–37 is such that it has supported the interpretation of these rights as mere principles.[160]

---

[158] Case 149/77 note 99, paragraphs 26–33.

[159] Kenner, 2003, p. 4.

[160] See, for example, the official explanations relating to the charter, OJ [2007] C 303/17, which qualify Articles 25 (rights of the elderly), 26 (integration of disabled persons) and 37 (environmental protection) as principles.

# III. EUROPEAN FIELDS OF COLLECTIVE AND DEMOCRATIC RULE-MAKING

Turning to the democratic function of EU constitutional law, this part addresses the question of whether EU constitutional law enables the establishment of European fields of democratic and collective rule-making, again both in relation to public spheres (based on the paradigm of liberal constitutionalism) and to socio-economic spheres (based on the paradigm of socially embedded constitutionalism).

According to liberal constitutionalism, democracy in public spheres secures the justification of governmental rule by public deliberation.[161] The division between public and private spheres risks despotism or economic egotism becoming decisive for non-public spheres, such as the economy or family, rather than democratic deliberation.

Democratisation of socio-economic spheres under the paradigm of socially embedded constitutionalism appears more challenging and complex, because it aims at establishing substantive self-governance in socio-economic spheres. In principle, this can be achieved in two different ways: on the one hand, spheres can be moved from the 'private' to the public, e.g. by creating public undertakings. On the other hand, elements of democratic governance can be introduced into 'private spheres' such as the economy or the family. This latter route is closely related to modernising human rights law: as threats for the actual enjoyment of human rights increasingly emanate from private power rather than from public authority, individuals will need rights to defend their autonomy within society. Such rights have only partly been included in human rights instruments. Freedom of association is one example, as it includes the right of workers to combine in trade unions and to engage in collective action in order to achieve collective agreements. Such human rights rarely reach beyond the field of industrial relations, although this is theoretically possible. If one were to conceptualise all socio-economic spheres as a basis for such rights, these could be termed 'status social activus'.[162]

The common theme of these two dimensions of democratisation lies in the challenge of overcoming collective action problems and, at the same time, avoiding disenfranchising citizens either in spheres considered as public traditionally or in socio-economic spheres.

In contrast to rights protection, the democratic function of EU constitutional law was not primarily developed by the EU judiciary, but rather by practices of other EU institutions that partly were endorsed in Treaty reforms.

---

161 See Chapter 2, p. 55 after note 14.

162 Schiek, 2012, pp. 121–122.

## 1. Liberal Constitutionalism

As regards liberal constitutionalism, the EU has been repeatedly criticised for its democratic deficit,[163] partly because it has not reproduced parliamentarianism national-style.[164] The initial EEC and ECSC Treaties only provided for a 'parliamentary assembly', consisting of members elected or delegated by national parliaments. Direct election for the EP was introduced in 1979, but only 30 years *after* the foundational Treaties was this reform included in the EEC Treaty (1987, SEA). However, the Parliament was slow to progress from an advisory to a legislative body.[165] Only the Treaty of Amsterdam introduced true co-legislation[166] for the Council and the Parliament, giving the EP the power to reject a Commission proposal against the vote in the Council. This legislative procedure applies today to about 70% of the competence norms (Article 14, 16 TEU, 294 TFEU in conjunction with the specific legislative competences). However, the right to propose legislation still rests exclusively with the Commission (Article 17 EU, 294 TFEU). As the main thrust for EU legislation thus lies with the Council and the Commission, the European public tends to participate in EU legislation through national publicity.[167] In other words, EU constitutional law contributes little to establishing EU public spheres through parliamentary democracy.[168]

The EU institutions have long attempted to balance this perceived deficit by establishing elements of direct democracy by integrating factions of European society in their decision making. Institutionally, the Social and Economic Committee is designed to provide representation of employers' and

---

163 Scharpf, 1999.

164 Craig, 2011, pp. 31–33. See for a critical account Dehousse, 2003; for an interesting historical parallel between today's critique of EU parliamentarianism with the parallel critique during the Deutsche Reich see Oeter, 2010, pp. 72–75.

165 Thirty years does not seem a long time to everyone. Hix et al. state: 'In a rather short space of time, a matter of decades rather than centuries, the European Parliament has developed from an unelected consultative body to one of the most powerful elected assemblies in the world' (Hix et al., 2007, p. 3).

166 The Treaty of Maastricht was the first to use the term co-legislation. However, the EP could not prevent a legislative procedure from being passed if the Council and the Commission agreed on a measure. This only changed with the Treaty of Amsterdam.

167 This result of many decisions being taken in the Council has been questioned in the last ten years relying on empirical evidence from media analysis (see, for example Trenz and Eder, 2004).

168 This has led more conservative authors to maintain the argument that democracy at EU level is not possible in principle, see, e.g., von Bogdandy, 2010, pp. 49, 52–53.

employees' associations and other groups representative of civil society in EU political and legislative processes (see Articles 300, 304 TFEU).

Since the late 1990, the Commission has required itself through procedural rules to consult relevant sections of society. The Treaty of Lisbon has constitutionalised this practice by including these rules into the Treaty (Article 11 EU).[169] Even on the basis of informal procedures encouraging civil society building, there have been examples of concerted action of certain EU-wide lobby groups that have successfully achieved legislation that again empowers individuals, and through them their organisations, to contribute to judicial enforcement of these new rules.[170] However, the establishment of European 'civil society' by EU Commission activities has also provoked critique, in that the Commission tends to sponsor those whom they consult in their legislative proposals.[171]

The most prominent element of direct democracy introduced by the Treaty of Lisbon is the 'citizens' initiative' (Articles 11(4) TEU, 24 TFEU): from April 2012[172] one million citizens from at least seven Member States can demand that a legislative proposal on a specific issue is tabled. However, the citizens' initiative is directed at the European Commission, which retains the right to formulate a legislative proposal. Also, the regulation effectively prevents any citizenship initiative from proposing a specific piece of legislation by limiting the number of words for any initiative to about one thousand.

Further, the EU institutions have attempted to make their policies seem more legitimate by combating the image of secret decisions taken behind closed doors. Transparency and accessibility have become elements of the Commission's campaign for good governance. With the Treaty of Lisbon, the principle of transparency has become a general principle of EU democracy (Article 11(3) TEU) in addition to a merely administrative principle (Article 15 TFEU = ex Article 255 EC), and access to documents has been elevated to a fundamental right of EU citizens (Article 42).

All in all, the EU has made considerable progress in establishing democracy for its public spheres under the paradigm of liberal constitutionalism.

---

169 On the effects of consulting civil society organisation generally see Ruzza and Sala, 2007; specifically on civil society integration in the process of establishing the draft Constitutional Treaty see Trenz et al., 2009.

170 Evans Case and Givens, 2010; see from the perspective of the relevant umbrella organisation Dummet, 1994; for the potential of judicial proceedings to empower civil society see Cichowski, 2006.

171 Bell, 2008, pp. 190 et seq. for the field of anti-discrimination law.

172 Regulation 211/2011/EU OJ [2011] L 65/1 11, Article 23.

## 2. Socially Embedded Constitutionalism

Turning to socially embedded constitutionalism, we need to consider elements for collective rule-making in socio-economic spheres as well as the relation of EU constitutional law to alternatives to the market.

Regarding the socio-economic spheres, the Treaty entails some elements of industrial democracy: Article 155 TFEU, first introduced with the Treaty of Amsterdam (ex Article 138 EC), provides for a right to initiate legislation for a common initiative of the 'European Social Partners': they can conclude a social partner agreement and ask the Commission to make it legally binding by issuing a directive to that effect (Article 155 TFEU). Under the Treaty of Lisbon, the EP shall be informed of such endeavours, but it still has no active role to play. In effect this means that the European Social Partners can do what is still denied to the EP: submit a fully fledged legislative text for adoption by the EU institutions, in this case the Commission and the Council. This was developed immediately after the Treaty of Amsterdam and it remains slightly dominant today: 11 out of 20 EU social partner agreements have been implemented by Council decision.[173] This is a practical consequence of the corporatist background of Article 155 TFEU, which can be comprehended against the background of corporatist practices in many Member States.[174] The Tripartite Social Summit for Growth and Employment, which arguably strengthens the corporate dimension of EU-level industrial relations, has been given a Treaty basis with the Treaty of Lisbon (Article 152 TFEU second sentence).

However, in many Member States, most pronounced in the Scandinavian countries, agreements between management and labour are considered as an autonomous affair and not a preparation of legislation. This autonomy tradition of collective labour relations is also mirrored in the new clause introduced by the Treaty of Lisbon according to which the EU recognises and promotes the role of the 'social partners' at EU level and respects their autonomy (Article 152 TFEU first sentence). From this perspective, one would assume that the social partners cannot only propose legislation communally, but can also create agreements which they implement autonomously. The wording of Article 155 TFEU would support such an assumption, as it states that agreements concluded at EU level 'shall be implemented [...] in accordance with the procedures and practices specific to management and labour and the Member

---

[173] See 'Social Dialogue texts database' (http://ec.europa.eu/social/main.jsp?catId=521&langId=en) and http://www.eurofound.europa.eu/areas/industrialrelations/dictionary/definitions/autonomousagreement.htm.

[174] See for a comparison of European collective labour law regimes Jacobs, 2009, and Schiek, 2005; on the reality of new corporatism in the EU see Avdagic et al., 2011.

States' in the first alternative. However, there is no consensus on whether this actually is a basis for autonomous collective labour agreements at EU level.[175] Despite this insecurity, the autonomous implementation of social partner agreements has recently been used increasingly, and by now nine out of 20 EU social partner agreements are implemented in this way.

So far, there is limited support for socio-economic democratic rule-making at EU level. As in most Member States, democracy in society is only formalised in the field of industrial relations, neglecting power imbalances in relation to consumption, primary food production and education. Even in regard to industrial relations, EU constitutional law is incomplete: while the Charter guarantees the right to association, collective bargaining and collective action (Article 12, 27 and 28 Charter), the Union has no competences in creating legislation in this respect (Article 153 (5) TFEU).

Undeterred by the lack of a clear Treaty base, the Court has ruled implicitly on industrial relations and collective agreements since the 1970s, when it first held that free movement rights are binding upon the parties to collective agreements.[176] From the 1990s it explicitly announced that collective agreements are just another element of public regulation of the employment relationship.[177] By contrast, collective agreements were exempted from the scope of application of competition law if they remained within certain limits.[178]

The second dimension of socially embedded constitutionalism may be most difficult to achieve in a polity originating from the primacy of an economic constitution that aims at introducing market rule over as many factions of society as possible. If one is to establish ownership of governance by those affected in any societal pocket, one would also aim at establishing alternatives to 'market rule' at European or at least at national level. This can be achieved by maintaining or creating public sectors or, alternatively, by maintaining or creating sectors not governed by competition. In the Treaties, there has long been a foothold for respecting the 'économie sociale' (now: Article 106 TFEU). This provision, which was already included in the EEC Treaty, exempts public undertakings or undertakings entrusted with a service of general economic interest (SGEIs) from the scope of application of economic freedoms and EU competition law. While this provision does not

---

175 For an argument deriving an autonomous right of European-level trade unions and employer associations to conclude EU-level collective agreements see Schiek, 2005, and 2008b; for a critique of this (demanding an EU regulation), see Ales et al., 2006, and Ales, 2009.

176 Case 36/74 *Walrave* [1974] ECR 1405.

177 See cases C-184/89 *Nimz* [1991] ECR I-297, paragraphs 17–20, C-33/89 *Kowalska* [1990] ECR I-2591, paragraphs 118–120, C-196/02 *Nikoloudi* [2005] ECR I-1789.

178 Cases C-67/96 *Albany*, C-437/09 *AG2R Prévoyance*, above, note 78.

allow any non-market associations at EU level, the rule certainly respects such associations at national level. It thus enables Member States to maintain certain elements of socially embedded constitutionalism. However, it also requires that any such elements are specifically justified. They are thus more the exception than the rule. In addition to this, the Treaty of Amsterdam had first introduced a provision asserting that the EU accepted SGEIs (Article 16 EC, now Article 14 TFEU). The Treaty of Lisbon for the first time added a legislative competence (Article 14 TFEU last sentence), which empowers the EU to establish principles and conditions enabling SGEIs to fulfil their mission. It may thus be used to provide legislation directed at Member States. However, the use of this competence in favour of EU-level SGEIs,[179] which may encompass social services of general interest, is not excluded. This certainly has the potential to establish another semi-public field of consensus building as a basis for lawmaking at EU levels.

## IV. CONCLUSION

Considering the categories of liberal constitutionalism and socially embedded constitutionalism, the European Union has followed a trajectory different from any national counterpart. Within Member States, liberal constitutionalism emerged first and horizontal effects of human rights as well as elements of socially embedded constitutionalism, such as positive duties providing for the actual enjoyment of human rights, developed more recently. In contrast, the European Union guaranteed some rights horizontally from the start, but only recently took responsibility for protecting its citizens against violations of human rights by the Union itself.

Further, our overview has demonstrated that the trajectory of EU constitutional law differed in different fields within EU constitutional law.

In the ‘economic constitution’, progress through case law towards socially embedded rights has been more substantial than in relation to human rights, except for equality rights. As regards democracy – both from the perspectives of liberal constitutionalism and socially embedded constitutionalism – the judicial constitution is less pronounced. EU-positive constitutional law has only recently progressed towards enhancing democracy in the liberal sense.[180] For socially embedded constitutionalism, only limited progress has been

179 The EU Economic and Social Council promotes using this clause for establishing EU-level services of general interest as a contribution to European integration (EESC Social Services of General Interest, own initiative opinion, OJ [2010] C 218/65).

180 Possibly with a deliberative turn, see Eriksen and Fossum, 2011.

made, e.g. through mentioning social partners' capacity to propose legislation and conclude agreements and the EU's obligation to remain in dialogue with churches and other civil society organisations. The EU economic constitution, while leaving some scope for Member States to maintain a public sector or establish services of general economic interest, contributes little to non-market dominated spheres at EU level.

Any progress in enhancing the democratic functions of EU constitutional law has been achieved by Treaty change rather than case law. Treaty reforms have successively enhanced the EP role, lately acknowledged a role for national parliaments, created legislative capacity for EU social partners and, also lately, mentioned other civil society realms, such as churches, with the Treaty of Lisbon. The elements of institutional democracy under liberal constitutionalism paradigms are more developed today than elements of socially embedded democracy, which would aim at democratising the economy, maintaining or establishing alternatives to market rule and empowering collective self-regulation by those subjected to non-legitimated rule in socio-economic realms. As there is little Treaty base in the latter aspect, it will be interesting to explore whether case law contributes to or inhibits the development of socially embedded EU democracy.

# 4. The EU's judicial constitution after Enlargement

## I. INTRODUCTION AND METHODOLOGICAL APPROACH

This chapter considers the judicial constitution, focusing on its specification by the Court's Grand Chamber since the EU's Eastern Enlargement from 2004.[1] The analysis starts from the results of its rulings, gauging how many of them support or inhibit rights and democracy as demanded by liberal constitutionalism and socially embedded constitutionalism respectively, proceeding to a content analysis and tracing any doctrinal (in)consistency that may expose a bias towards one or other form of constitutionalism and thus a positioning between social and economic integration.

Case law is considered as a mirror of constitutional conflict. As processes of constitutionalisation and even ordinary legislation become more and more complex and long-winded, the resulting norms (e.g. in the EU Treaties) must remain sufficiently open to allow adaptation by interpretation.[2] Such adaptation is needed increasingly due to rapidly changing global socio-economic realities and ever-shifting spheres of conflict creating new challenges for the law's task, which is to provide normative order. Interpreting is the task of an arbiter, as distinct from the norm-creator – this is a task of the judiciary (among others). Within the European Union, it is up to the EU courts and national courts to specify the meaning of EU constitutional law. Such specifications can never be exclusively dictated by the norms themselves. Accordingly, judicial interpretation at any level always entails rule-making, partly by specification, partly by filling lacunae. This activity is of essentially political character. Judicial interpretation also has to follow the rules of legal discourse if it is to command credibility and authority. In this sense, it is of the utmost importance that the Court (as any constitutional court) refrains from

[1] On the impact of Enlargement on the conditions for European economic and social integration see above Chapter 2, V, p. 75.

[2] On the tasks of the Court in dealing with open norms see Bell, 2010.

putting itself into the position of a legislator.[3] Judicial lawmaking first must assure that the law has not (yet) been made by the competent legislator and, further, that there are overarching legal principles to draw a judicial solution from. In order to assure accountability of judicial lawmaking it is important that the value base of any such lawmaking is exposed, rather than being shrouded in secrecy. All this only confirms that CJEU case law is but one contribution to the political development of constitutional law, although endowed with judicial authority. Its analysis must acknowledge this inherently political character as well as its special form of argumentation, which is based on the principles of syllogism and consistency.

The double aim pursued in this chapter is derived from these deliberations. On the one hand, it endeavours to show where the European judiciary is positioned on a continuum bordered by liberal constitutionalism and socially embedded constitutionalism in the fields of rights protection and establishing spheres of collective (democratic) rule-making. On the other hand, it provides an analysis of the judicial discourse that led to such positioning, isolating the strictly doctrinal discourse from the exposure of values that go beyond the texts of the Treaty or established legal principle. Both aims are pursued retrospectively: the first one by evaluating the results of case law (or its outcome, legitimacy), the second one by analysing its content.

From both these perspectives, analysing only particularly contentious cases – while attractive to the legal researcher – is not sufficient, as such an approach may deliver a distorted picture of positioning of the Court.[4] Accordingly, a systematic evaluation of case law, nearly emulating an empirical approach,[5] is needed here. This analysis should establish whether there are any discernible trends towards stressing or neglecting certain fields of the scheme condensed in Figure 2.1. Such an approach to CJEU case law is not, however, without difficulties. The Court sits in four different configurations,[6] among which the

---

3 See Grimmel, 2010, pp. 15, 22–24.

4 Weiler and Lockhart, 1995.

5 Empirical approaches to case law are not always sufficiently differentiated to mirror the complexities of court activities. US political science research on courts frequently focuses on categorising cases by their results into binary camps representing the major political parties in the US (for an example see Carruba et al., 2008, for an overview see Macaulay, 2008, and Nourse and Shaffer, 2010, both contributing to 'New Legal Realism'). Slightly more nuanced, European political scientists have started to evaluate CJEU case law numerically by, e.g. relevance of a number of social policy issues (Leibfried, 2010, pp. 265–68) or the results in a limited number of fields (Conant, 2006) – each without doctrinal analysis, though.

6 Articles 16 Statute of the Court of Justice (Protocol No 3 to the Treaty of Lisbon, OJ [2008] C 115/210) and Article 9 Rules of procedure of the Court of Justice (consolidated version in OJ [2010] C 177/1).

composition of the chambers of three and five judges changes most frequently (every three years).[7] Thus, any analysis of their case law would not allow for identifying the positioning of the Court over a longer period of time. Given the large number of judges (13) in any Grand Chamber composition, more continuity and perhaps even coherence should be expected, and this should apply even more to decisions by the Full Court. Thus, an analysis of their case law is more likely to uncover any specific positioning. For a study of the substantive constitutional law of the EU, Grand Chamber decisions are also particularly suitable because the Grand Chamber usually hears cases of specific importance or complexity.[8] Of course, such an analysis cannot uncover the role of litigants:[9] due to the Member States' and EU institutions' prerogative to request having cases involving them heard by the Grand Chamber,[10] cases brought by citizens will be underrepresented among those cases. However, this does not impact on the aims of this study.

As established above, Eastern Enlargement constituted a turning point for the EU, and not least in relation to economic and social integration. This will be mirrored in the European judiciary, which can be expected to be confronted with more of these challenges than before Enlargement. At the same time, the European judiciary has changed decisively and rapidly through the addition of ten, and ultimately 12, new judges from new jurisdictions and also a number of Advocate Generals from those jurisdictions. This seems to suggest that the CJEU's doctrines were prone to change after Enlargement. The choice of cases thus started with any case submitted in 2004. The first of these Grand Chamber cases was decided in July 2004,[11] and the cut-off point was May 2011, which allows a period of nearly seven years for analysis.

With all these restrictions, 244 cases on a wide variety of issues remained for analysis. Not all of these are of relevance to an evaluation of EU-substantive constitutional law with a view to challenges of economic and social integration. All in all, 71 cases were disregarded, either because they only finished substantive disputes closed long ago – related to procedural issues or competence conflicts rather than substantive constitutional law – or because they focused on the interpretation of specific terms of secondary law without constitutional relevance, related to the EU's international competence or in vertical relations between the EU institutions and their national counterparts or to internal conflicts between EU institutions and individual functionaries.[12]

---

7 Article 9 Rules of procedure.

8 Article 44(3) Rules of procedure.

9 On the role of litigants before the Court see Cichowski, 2007, see also Alter, 2009, pp. 63–90 and pp. 188–203.

10 Article 9 Rules of procedure (above note 6).

11 Case C-27/04 *Commission v Council* [2004] ECR I-6649.

12 See Appendix, Table A.3 (pp. 288–295), for detail.

The numerical analysis of the remaining cases shows that cases on the economic freedoms dominate (93 out of 173). The second-largest group of cases consisted of claims regarding violation of human rights (43 cases) against the EU and (implicitly) the Member States as well as in one horizontal situation, followed by cases concerning equal treatment and non-discrimination (23 cases), market regulation by national and EU institutions (17 cases) and industrial relations (9 cases). A sizeable number of all these can be categorised as 'citizenship cases', supporting individuals rather than corporate actors (altogether 49 cases out of 121 cases concerning rights protection). Among those 121 cases concerning rights protection, the majority concerned conflicts between economic actors or citizens and Member States, with the exception of the field 'equality and non-discrimination'. Rulings relating to (EU-wide) spheres of democratic rule-making were less frequent overall (35 cases overall), some of which were also relevant for rights protection. Here, the majority of cases related to market regulation and industrial relations – i.e. to the democratisation of societal spheres, which was associated with socially embedded constitutionalism above.

In isolation, this numerical analysis does not say very much. The remainder of the chapter will provide a doctrinal and content analysis of case law. This analysis will take the distinction between protecting rights and democratic rule-making as the main divisor and relate to the categories of liberal and socially embedded constitutionalism in turn. An interim evaluation will close each sub-part to prepare the overall conclusion of the chapter due to the large amount of case law.

## II. RIGHTS PROTECTION POST EASTERN ENLARGEMENT

Considering the Grand Chamber's case law on rights protection, the analysis will follow the trajectory along which rights protection under EU law developed:[13] starting with the economic constitution and proceeding towards equality rights and human rights protection and moving from liberal constitutionalism towards socially embedded constitutionalism in each field.

This means that not all rights rhetoric used in case law will be captured. Corresponding to the pivotal contribution of citizens as advocates of EU law,[14] at times any provision of any directive is presented as an individual right for

13 See above Chapter 3, II, pp. 80–105.
14 See above Chapter 2, III, p. 73.

the Court to enforce.[15] While this vocabulary is not incorrect, it is not particularly helpful in a constitutional context. Rights granted by legislation may or may not protect or promote economic freedoms or liberty, equality and non-discrimination or other human rights. Thus, this chapter only considers such rights enshrined in secondary legislation that reinforce those rights mentioned above and have been recognised as such by the Court. This includes directives on equality and discrimination, which are mostly dedicated to make those rights relevant in horizontal relations or on citizenship rights, which often constitute codification of former case law. Consumer rights are only considered where there is a clear relation to free movement of goods and services. Otherwise, secondary law is not covered.

## 1. The EU Economic Constitution before the Grand Chamber since 2004

### a) Notion and reach

Rights derived from the EU's economic constitution are mainly rooted in the economic freedoms and competition rules, which pursue the common aim of establishing 'an area without frontiers in which the free movement of goods, persons, services and capital is ensured', i.e. the internal market (Article 26(2) TFEU). Partly, these rights are reinforced by secondary law and in so far as the Court itself categorises its case law on directives and regulations by notions such as 'freedom to provide services'[16] and 'rights of undertakings',[17] it is also covered in this sub-chapter.

Further, EU citizenship has increasingly developed in the direction of a 'fifth freedom'.[18] While the conception of EU citizenship, especially since the Treaty of Lisbon, also has a close affinity to democratic rights, the European judiciary is mainly confronted with claims challenging unequal treatment or restrictions of the rights to move freely. As these rights are also at the heart of the economic freedoms, case law on citizenship rights has its rightful place in this sub-chapter.

### b) Numerical overview

Overall, the largest portion of Grand Chamber cases (93 out of 173 cases) in the reference period originates in this field. Within these, the perspective of liberal constitutionalism prevails: 77 out of 93 cases relate to protection of rights

---

[15] A good example of such rhetoric is to be found in Trstenjak and Beysen, 2011, where any entitlement of consumers is considered a 'right'.

[16] This applies, for example, to any case law on public procurement.

[17] This applies to rules on taxation, which often impinge on freedom of establishment, even if the matter at stake is regulated by directives, for example, on VAT.

[18] See Wollenschläger, 2011.

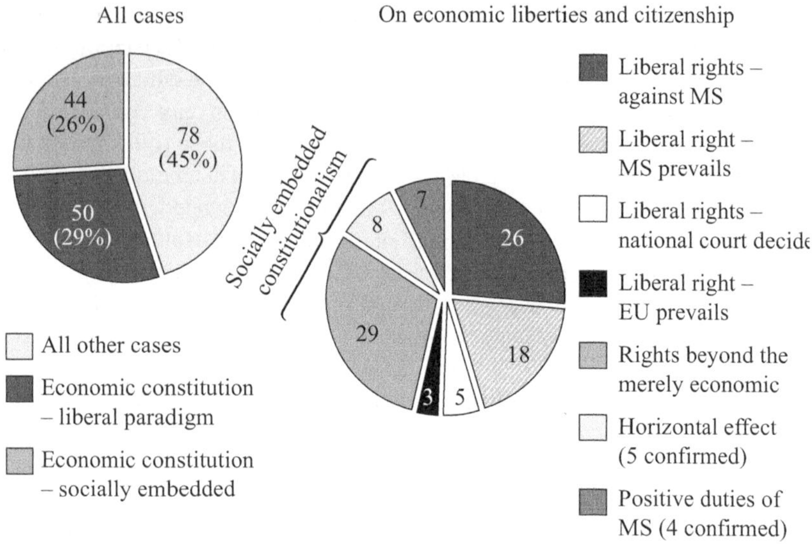


*Figure 4.1 Economic liberties and citizenship*

against public authorities. However, out of these, 29 cases were launched by individual citizens rather than business corporations. These rulings typically developed rights beyond the perspectives envisaged by liberal constitutionalism and went beyond a merely economic constitution as well. There were also 16 cases demanding rights directly associated with socially embedded constitutionalism, such as positive duties (eight cases) and horizontal rights protection (eight cases). Most frequently, rights were claimed against Member States (82 cases) and 54 times Member States lost. The EU itself never had to change its action in the three cases here. Accordingly, the prevalence of values informing liberal constitutionalism curbs Member States' actions more frequently than do EU policies. (See Figure 4.1, economic liberties and citizenship.)

**c) The perspective of liberal constitutionalism**

From liberal perspectives, economic freedoms should mainly be protected against intrusion by 'the public', i.e. against Member States and the EU.

*(1) Competition law rules* The practical relevance of competition rules in enforcing economic liberties against Member States has been limited further, as the Grand Chamber has reaffirmed the state action doctrine[19] for the

19 See Chapter 3, II, pp. 93–94.

prohibition of cartels[20] in the joined cases *Cipolla* and *Cipodarte*,[21] on setting of lawyers' fees. Under Italian law, a fixed scale of fees was established by the national council of lawyers (CNF), which became legally binding upon confirmation by the Ministry of Justice. The Court reaffirmed the principle that Member States infringe Articles 4(3) EU, 101 TFEU if they encourage anti-competitive agreements or reaffirm their effects. However, it categorised the ministerial confirmation of the scale as an independent act, thus further reducing the practical relevance of the state action doctrine. The Court ruled substantively on freedom to provide services instead.[22]

Conversely, the MOTOE case[23] expanded the state action doctrine for the abuse of a dominant market position (Article 102 TFEU),[24] under which Member States may confer exclusive rights on undertakings, but this must not lead the undertaking to abuse the resulting dominant market position. MOTOE, a non-profit organisation holding motor bike races, challenged Greek rules on authorisation of such races, which required the prior consent by the Automobile and Touring Club of Greece (ELPA), another non-profit organisation representing the International Motorcycling Federation (FIM) in Greece. ELPA, which also commercially exploits races, did not respond to one of MOTOE's applications, thus preventing it from holding some of its races. The Court held in favour of MOTOE that this legislation encouraged abuse and thus infringed Articles 102, 106(1) TFEU. The practical impact of this case will be felt by any non-profit organisation because the Court also confirmed a second chamber ruling[25] establishing that non-profit organisations are undertakings under Articles 101, 102 TFEU if their activities have the potential to impinge on markets. Accordingly, the 'third sector' continues to be under the scrutiny of the EU competition authorities.[26]

*(2) Free movement of goods* Free movement of goods is by now a fairly established field attracting little attention from the Grand Chamber. The six cases decided in 2004 included an action by the Natural Health Alliance and

---

20 See Chapter 3, II, p. 93 note 69.

21 C-96 and 202/04 *Cipolla* [2006] ECR I-11421.

22 See below p. 147 with note 191.

23 Case C-49/07 MOTOE [2008] ECR I-4863

24 See Chapter 3, II, pp. 93–94 for more explanation.

25 Case C-222/04 *Cassa di Risparmio de Firence* [2006] ECR I-289 paragraphs 122–123. A banking foundation mainly engaged in not-for-profit social and cultural work could be in competition with undertakings offering research, education, art or health.

26 On further aspects of the third sector's role under EU competition law see Wendt and Gideon, 2011.

the Association of Health Food Stores[27] challenging the legality of Directive 2002/46/EC under freedom to import (Article 34 TFEU). The directive prohibited trade with any food supplement not listed in its annex or contained in a list composed in a specific procedure. The main argument before the national court was that there is no proof for the banned substances being detrimental to human health and also that economic actors have no opportunity to prove that a certain substance is indeed harmless. The Court first confirmed that Article 34, although explicitly only addressed to the Member States, also binds the EU itself. However, it granted the EU legislator 'broad discretion' to assess the proportionality of a piece of EU legislation, deeming it sufficient that the EU legislator could 'reasonably take the view' that the restriction in trade was necessary to protect human health,[28] finding it 'not evident that the prohibition (was) inappropriate'.[29]

Two more cases from the field of food and stimulants concerned the traditional Swedish state monopoly on trade with alcohol (the Systembolaget). The *Rosengreen* case[30] concerned the prohibition for consumers to order wine directly from foreign vineyards. The Court reiterated[31] that Member States' prerogative to maintain commercial state monopolies (Article 37 TFEU) must be read narrowly, as it constitutes an exception from free movement of goods, a 'fundamental principle' of EU Law.[32] Accordingly any legislative provision safeguarding the exclusive rights of the state monopoly, but not directly related to it, is to be assessed under Article 34 rather than 37 TFEU.[33] The Court found that, because the Systembolaget can refuse to import precisely what a private person wishes to consume, the prohibition of private imports constituted a quantitative restriction. Considering justifications under Article 36, the Court duly stated that 'health and life of human beings rank foremost'.[34] This did not help Sweden in defending the legislation, as the Court applied the principle of proportionality extremely strictly. The Court held that the Systembolaget would usually satisfy all demand (contradicting its former statement that it would also refuse applications). Thus, the monopoly system

---

27 Case C-154 and 155/04 *Alliance for Natural Health and Association of Health Stores* [2005] ECR I-6451.

28 Paragraphs 52, 68.

29 Paragraph 129.

30 Case C-170/04 *Rosengreen* [2007] ECR I-4071, see also Case C-196/05 *COM v Sweden* [2007] ECR I-129 (only published in summary, as this case did not add much to the legal reasoning after *Rosengreen*).

31 Case C-189/95 *Franzen* [1997] ECR I-5909.

32 *Rosengreen* paragraph 31.

33 Paragraphs 21–27.

34 Paragraph 39.

was held not suitable for the purpose of curbing alcoholism.[35] The second case was brought by the Commission, who found that Sweden had infringed the prohibition of protective taxation (now Article 110 TFEU) by lowering taxes levied on beer after its accession to the EU, in order to mitigate the influx of Danish beer onto the Swedish market. The Court upheld the rule: after assuming that beer can substitute wine, it found the tax component of the end price too insignificant to influence consumer choice.[36]

Two cases on national consumer protection legislation also turned on free movement of goods – with diverging results. One[37] concerned Belgian consumer legislation prohibiting the demand of 'a deposit of any form of payment' before expiry of the seven days' withdrawal period required by Article 6 Directive 97/7/EC for the conclusion of distance contracts. Belgian courts had established that this prevented providers from asking consumers to register their credit card number at purchase. Belgium relied on Article 14 of the directive, which allows for Member States to introduce or maintain provisions ensuring a higher level of consumer protection. The Court stated that the directive only specified the freedom to export (Article 35 TFEU), which remained the main point of reference. It argued that maintaining this specific rule would adversely influence exports from Belgium to other Member States because foreigners usually paid by credit card, and early disclosure of credit card numbers is an easier way to secure payment than suing for payment in foreign lands. From this broad notion of restriction, the Court went on to consider justifications, again applying an extremely strict standard of scrutiny. While the measure was suitable to achieve the aim to protect consumers, it was held to go over and above what was necessary to achieve that aim, as criminal liability of the vendor, although 'not truly and entirely effective', constituted a less intrusive method of protecting consumers than prohibiting credit card disclosure.

This case contrasted with *COM v Italy*,[38] concerning a prohibition in Italian law to tow a trailer behind a motorcycle, challenged as a breach of freedom to import (Article 34 TFEU). The Court again applied an extremely broad notion of an infringement. Assuming that the owner of a motorcycle will not buy a trailer if forbidden by law to use it, the Court concluded that the legislation would 'hinder access to the Italian market for trailers that are specially designed for motorcycles and are lawfully produced and marketed in (other) Member States'.[39] The Court did not discuss whether market access of foreign producers was affected more detrimentally than market access of Italian

---

35 Paragraph 47.
36 Case C-167/05 *COM v Sweden* [2008] ECR I-2127.
37 C-205/07 *Gysbrecht* [2008] ECR I-9947.
38 C 110/05 *COM v Italy (Trailers)* [2009] ECR I-519.
39 Paragraph 58.

producers. This has been criticised as giving up any requirement of inter-state trade.[40] As if to compensate for this, the Court adopted a medium standard of scrutiny for justifications of the measure, finding that Member States do not have to choose the least intrusive measures to achieve road safety for the legislation to be proportionate.[41]

Overall, these recent cases seem to demonstrate that the Court accords free movement of goods a wide scope of application. Justifying the infringement is thus the decisive element in any free movement of goods case. Most of the time, Member States' legislation is subjected to strict scrutiny here under the proportionality test. Only the safeguarding of road security in Italy seems sufficiently important to lower the level of scrutiny to an intermediate one. By contrast, the EU legislator was awarded a 'broad discretion' in the one case concerning the legality of EU legislation.

*(3) Freedom of establishment* Freedom of establishment has occupied the Grand Chamber in no fewer than 18 cases during the reference period, mainly focused on the position of the professions, the health care sector and free movement of companies.

(a) THE PROFESSIONS AND THE ECONOMIC FREEDOMS Cases on freedom of establishment for the professions also relied on secondary law promoting this freedom.[42]

Free movement of 'European lawyers', i.e lawyers practising in another Member State from the one in which they qualified, was unduly restricted by Luxembourg in contravention of Directive 98/5/EC and Article 49 TFEU,[43] mainly through a rigid interpretation of the directive. Excessive requirements to re-register, reproduce documents and undergo multiple language tests were held to infringe EU law in two cases, thus substantively defending the freedom of establishment against intrusive national legislation. Conversely, the Court did not offer an expansive interpretation of Directive 89/48/EEC on the recognition of diplomas (including professional qualifications)[44] in support of the application by a Greek national qualified in the UK to join the profession of 'environmental engineer' in Greece. The claimant wished her work as

---

[40] Barnard, C., 2010b.

[41] Paragraph 67.

[42] See above pp. 116–117 with notes 14 and 15 on secondary law with a constitutional character.

[43] Case C-193/05 *COM v Luxembourg* [2006] ECR I-8673, C-506/04 *Wilson* [2006] ECR I-8613.

[44] The directive has now been replaced by Directive 2005/36/EC (OJ [2005] L 255/22, which only covers access to regulated professions and no longer the recognition of diplomas generally.

researcher to be recognised as professional experience. While the Court found that she could rely on the directive itself, it also stressed that the requirement of two years' full-time professional work cannot be interpreted flexibly.

The first case on the Services Directive[45] also concerned the professions: a French accountancy firm challenged the statutory prohibition of canvassing, relying on Article 24 Directive 2006/113/EC, according to which any total prohibition on commercial communications must be repealed. Member States may only maintain or establish rules on such communications if justified by overriding reasons relating to the public interest. This provision limits the scope for national legislation further than Article 56 TFEU: under this provision a prohibition of commercial communication for certain sectors is not beyond justification. For that reason, AG Ruiz-Jarobo Colomer had proposed to interpret the directive restrictively and not to curb the national pursuit of public interests further. The Court, however, found that Member States can no longer justify any prohibition of canvassing by members of a regulated profession.

A group of six infringement actions initiated by the Commission concerned the access to the profession of civil law notaries.[46] The Member States had restricted access to that profession to their own nationals, relying on Article 51 TFEU to justify this derogation from the freedom of individual citizens to establish themselves abroad (Article 49 TFEU). The principal task of civil law notaries is to establish authentic documents, and partly their contribution is mandatory, in particular in relation to conveying real estate or to inheritance. Documents drawn up by notaries are good evidence in court and are enforceable nationally. AG Cruz Villalón had proposed to apply the exception from freedom of establishment provided under Article 51 TFEU on a sliding scale, rather than drawing a clear distinction between persons who exercised public authority and those who did not.[47] The Court did not follow this doctrinal innovation, but rather relied on its old case law according to which Article 51 TFEU as an exception to freedom of establishment must be read narrowly.[48] It then qualified the activities of notaries as not exercising official state authority,[49] thus enforcing the freedom of establishment against these civil law Member States, mainly in the interest of access to the profession from common law Member States.

---

45 Case C-119/09 *Société fiduciaire nationale d'expertise comptable* 11 April 2011 (nyr).

46 Cases C-47/08 *COM v Belgium*, C-50/08 *COM v France*, C-51/08 *COM v Luxembourg*, C-53/08 *COM v Austria*, C-54/08 *COM v Germany*, C-61/08 *COM v Greece* all 24 May 2011 (nyr).

47 Paragraphs 80–82 of the AG's opinion.

48 Paragraphs 83–84 of the judgment in case C-47/08 *COM v Belgium*. As all cases were reasoned identically, only this judgment is referred to here.

49 Paragraphs 90–94 of the judgment.

All in all, this case law mostly supports the freedom of establishment by migrating businesses against the Member States, without leaving much scope for relying on general interests nationally. Again, a restriction of actual free movement by Directive 89/48/EC was found to be unproblematic.

(b) FREEDOM OF ESTABLISHMENT AND THE HEALTH CARE SECTOR Four cases concerned freedom of establishment in the health care sector. This sector can be seen as imbued with general interest, especially after the Treaty of Lisbon which emphasises the relevance of the protection of public health (Article 4(2) k and 168 TFEU). Also, case law on freedom of establishment tends to relate to the business aspects of health care,[50] which are also seen as the source of the rising costs of public health in the EU.[51]

The *Hartlauer* case[52] concerned the right of a German company to establish an independent outpatient dental clinic in Vienna. The Austrian authorities rejected the relevant application in line with the *Krankenanstaltengesetz* (Act on Health Institutions) and statutory instruments, because there was no need to establish an additional clinic. The assessment of 'need' was stricter for commercial providers than for individual medical doctors and collectives of those ('group practices'), because the latter were bound by a professional code rather than driven by purely commercial interest. The Court accepted in principle the Member State's prerogative to require authorisation of new outpatient clinics. It acknowledged that public health care systems which provide health care in kind through contracted doctors and hospitals need to plan for adequate provision for all, and across the whole country, and that such planning may legitimately aim at avoiding unlimited increase in supply in particularly affluent parts of the country.[53] However, the Court stated that the distinction between professional and commercial health care was not justified, as it was arbitrary,[54] expressing a preference for commercial provision of health care as more efficient.[55]

Two cases decided on the same day concerned German[56] and Italian[57] legislation on licensing pharmacies, also based on a preference for the

---

50 The consumer aspects will be considered under socially embedded constitutionalism, see below, pp. 156–159.

51 The Court acknowledged this in its case law on recipients of healthcare, see, for example case C-173/09 *Elchinov* 5 October 2010 (nyr), paragraph 43.

52 Case C-169/07 *Hartlauer* [2009] ECR I-1721.

53 See paragraphs 43 (for the submission of Austria) and 50–53 of the judgment.

54 Paragraphs 58–61.

55 Paragraph 62.

56 Case C-171 and 172/07 *Apothekerkammer des Saarlandes* [2009] ECR I-4171.

57 Case C-531/06 *COM v Italy (Pharmacies)* [2009] ECR I-4103.

professions over commercial providers. German law prescribed that a pharmacy must be operated by a pharmacist and not by a commercial company such as DocMorris domiciled in the Netherlands.[58] Italian legislation challenged by the Commission restricted the operation of pharmacies to pharmacists alone, either individually, in partnerships or in the form of cooperative societies, excluding commercial companies.

In both cases the Court found the legislative preference for professional over commercial ownership of pharmacies to constitute a non-discriminatory obstacle to Article 46 TFEU and, in the Italian case, also to free movement of capital, as limiting the acquisition of stakes in a cooperative pharmacy would deter investors from other Member States. The Court found a restriction, although there was no indication whatsoever that foreign pharmacists were prevented from operating pharmacies in Germany or Italy (provided that their qualifications were acknowledged in accordance with relevant EU legislation). Relying on the *Hartlauer* decision, DocMorris and the EU Commission argued that the distinction between pharmacists and commercial providers was inconsistent. However, the Court stressed the heightened importance of protecting public health and held that it was within the 'discretion' allowed to the Member States to consider professionally independent pharmacists less liable to neglect health care over profit interests.[59]

The *Blanco Pérez* case[60] concerned Spanish legislation which may seem even more restrictive: it established a planning system for pharmacies, which only allowed new pharmacies if a minimum distance of 250 metres between pharmacies was maintained and no fewer than 2800 citizens were served by one pharmacy, with some flexibility for rural areas. It also devolved adaptation to geography and population density to the autonomous provinces. On this basis, Asturias had issued guidelines establishing a preference for applicants with experience in Asturias. Supported by a Spanish public interest group on liberal establishment of pharmacies, two Spanish citizens challenged the refusal of their application to open a pharmacy in Asturias. Again, the Court considered that this general restriction of freedom to conduct one's business also restricted the EU freedom of establishment, although there was limited transborder activity in this case. Unsurprisingly, the rule in favour of regional pharmacists did not satisfy the Court because this could be to the detriment of

58 This commercial chain of pharmacies had already achieved a small victory over German pharmacists by having its internet sales of non-prescription medicines protected against public intervention (Case C-322/01 *Deutscher Apothekerverband v DocMorris NV* [2003] ECR I-14887). It now sought to access the market for prescriptions by establishing branches in Germany.

59 Case C-531/06 paragraph 84, case C-171/07 paragraph 54.

60 Case C-570, 571/07 *Blanco Pérez, Chao Gómez* [2010] ECR I-4629.

foreign applicants as well. Beyond that, the Court accepted that the legislation was justified, after assessing in detail the benefits of preventing an overly dense network of pharmacies while achieving sufficient access to pharmacies everywhere.

This case law seems contradictory in its assessment of professional versus commercial provision. However, it reconfirms the trend emerging from the free movement of goods cases: fundamental freedoms increasingly mutate towards rights to pursue one's business, with limited recourse to any cross-border element.

(c) FREE MOVEMENT OF COMPANIES In 2008,[61] the Court revisited the *'siège réel'* principle, questioning whether Hungarian law may prevent Cartesio, a Hungarian company, from transferring its headquarters to Italy, but maintaining its incorporation in Hungary. This clashed with Hungarian company law, under which each Hungarian company must maintain its headquarters in Hungary. Returning to its approach from the *Daily Mail*, the Court held that Member States, in the absence of EU harmonisation of national company laws, remain free to choose any system for domiciling companies. Thus, Hungary could maintain legislation based on the *'siège réel'* doctrine.[62] However, the past case law[63] suggests that this is not sufficient to justify restrictions on the establishment of secondary seats.[64]

'Golden share rules' constitute another set of national legislation that in practice may limit free movement of companies or their capital. These rules reserve certain rights to public shareholders, frequently after privatisation of public undertakings.[65] From 2000, the Commission launched a number of infringement procedures against such rules.[66] The obvious defence for

61 Case C-210/06 *Cartesio* [2008] ECR I- 9641 (see also Case C-411/03 *SEVIC* [2005] ECR I-10805, on German legislation preventing a German company from merging with a Luxembourg one – this was held to infringe freedom of establishment). The Cartesio court also asked questions relating to the reference procedure, which are not considered here (paragraphs 54–98 of the judgment).

62 AG Maduro proposed to invalidate the Hungarian legislation (paragraphs 31–34 of his opinion)

63 See Chapter 3, II, pp. 87–88 with notes 52–57.

64 Barnard, C., 2010b, pp. 320–322 stating that this may still erode the *'siège réel'* principle (page 332).

65 Some authors use the term 'golden shares' only in relation to post-privatisation scenarios. See, for example, Borlotti and Siniscalo, 2004, p. 21 ('the existence of golden share mechanisms (the special rights retained by governments after privatisation)').

66 Case C-367/98 *COM v Portugal* [2002] ECR I-4731 and further confirmation in case C-42/01 *COM v Portugal* [2004] ECR I-6079 (on these see Schiek, 2010b, pp. 89–90), cases C-463/00 *Com v Spain* [2003] ECR I-4581 and C-98/01 *COM v UK* [2003] ECR I-4641.

Member States, that according to Article 345 TFEU the Treaty does not affect rules on property, was not accepted, as this provision would not 'exempt Member States' systems of property ownership from the fundamental rules of the Treaty'. The Court found that 'golden share rules' infringe free movement of capital (Article 63 TFEU) by curbing investment of foreigners, although Article 65(2) TFEU, according to which any rule justifiable under freedom of establishment does not infringe Article 63 TFEU, would suggest that freedom of establishment enjoys priority.[67] The Court's finding that 'golden shares' must be justified in each individual case, would probably not have been different under Article 49 TFEU, though. The Court hypothetically accepted provision of services in the public interest and policies maintaining strategic industries as justifications, but has so far invalidated all 'golden share rules' before it.

The final ruling in this line concerned the Volkswagen Act (VW Act 1960).[68] It originated in post-war Germany, when the workers continued to run the Volkswagen factory, although it was left ownerless after withdrawal of the allied forces.[69] Soon, Volkswagen workers, trade unions, a large number of small shareholders, as well as the newly founded Federal Republic of Germany and the federal state of Lower Saxony, claimed stakes in the factory. The VW Act 1960[70] aimed at securing the company's future as a company by shareholding. Among other rules, it capped the maximum amount of capital to be held by a single shareholder to 20% and granted the federal government and the state of Lower Saxony privileges in controlling the company board. It also required 80% rather than the usual 75% for restructuring decisions of the assembly of shareholders, which meant that any public shareholder retaining 20% of the shares had a blocking minority. The intention was to prevent any shareholder from gaining excessive influence. The Court found that this was 'liable to deter investors from other Member States',[71] and thus constituted an obstacle to free movement of capital – although there was ample evidence for Volkswagen shares being much sought after around the globe. Turning to justifications, the Grand Chamber demonstrated its disaffection with 'Rhenish capitalism' by questioning whether the aim of maintaining the company by making about 20% of its employment available in an economically weak region as such could ever be in the general public interest.[72] The Court held

67 AG Ruiz-Jarobo Colomer (opinion on case C-463/00, paragraph 36).

68 Case C-112/05 *Commission v Germany* [2007] ECR I-8995.

69 See on this AG Ruiz-Jarobo Colomer, opinion on C-112/05, 29 et seq.

70 Following the judgment, the legislation was adapted (see VW Act 1960, last changed by Act of 30 July 2009, (BGBl. I 2479), also available from http://www.gesetze-im-internet.de/vwgmbh_g/index.html).

71 Paragraph 52 of the judgment in Case C-112105.

72 Paragraph 80.

that the provisions preventing shareholder dominance were not necessary in order to achieve this aim, and that also the protection of workers' and minority shareholders' interests against being dominated by large shareholders could have been achieved by less intrusive means.[73] It is worthy of note that the Court considered whether to investigate the legislation under freedom of establishment.[74] Under this heading, the Court seems determined to supervise Member States' company law in great detail, which may well go beyond its judicial competences in the future.[75]

These two cases confirm the CJEU's tendency to allow business maximum choice of the legal system under which they wish to operate, thus enhancing regime competition.

(d) MISCELLANEOUS CASES Among the two miscellaneous cases, the *ČEZ* case[76] is worthy of note.[77] It concerned the question of whether Austrian landowners could prevent the operation of a nuclear power plant situated in Temelin in the Czech Republic. The claimant relied on injunctive relief against the neighbours' activities impacting negatively on their land without being approved by the relevant planning authority under Article 364(2) ABGB (Austrian Civil Code). Had the incriminating use of land been officially approved, the neighbours would only be able to claim damages. The highest civil court interpreted Article 364(2) ABGB as requiring approval by Austrian authorities. Accordingly, ČEZ could not rely on its valid authorisation by the Czech administration to ward off discontinuation of its plant by paying damages. While this case clearly related to freedom of establishment,[78] the Court decided under the EAEC Treaty as *lex specialis*. That Treaty neither guarantees freedom of establishment nor prohibits nationality discrimination. Relying on a general principle of EU law derived from Article 18 TFEU, the Court held that preventing foreign economic actors from relying on the exception provided in Article 364(2) ABGB constituted nationality discrimination, violating EU law. The Court then engaged in an extensive consideration of whether this different treatment could be 'justified by objective considerations unrelated to nationality'. Thus, although applying a discrimination test, the

---

73 Paragraphs 74–79.

74 Paragraph 13–16. The result would not have been different though – see opinion Ruiz-Jarobo Colomer, paragraphs 57–60.

75 Ringe, 2010.

76 Case C-115/08 *Land Oberösterreich v ČEZ* [2009] ECR I-10265.

77 The other case concerned an aviation agreement between the Netherlands and the US on air fares and computerised reservation systems excluding companies whose main capital was held outside the Netherlands from its benefits (Case C-523/04 *COM v Netherlands* [2007] ECR I-3267).

78 See the opinion of AG Poiares Maduro paragraph 7.

Court also allowed for a wide array of justifications. Although no such justification was found, this is an example of abandoning the distinction of discriminatory and non-discriminatory restrictions.[79] If the Court were to continue this line of argument, Member States' might well gain more opportunities to justify discriminatory rules under the EU Treaties as well.

*(4) Freedom to provide services* In line with the increasing relevance of the service industry, the freedom to provide services has gained in practical relevance. From 2004, the Grand Chamber decided nine cases under this freedom, with some degree of focus on taxation, the territoriality of labour law and public procurement.

The recent judgment in the *Neukirchinger*, as in the *ČEZ* ruling, approximates non-discrimination and market access rationales in establishing Treaty violations.[80] The claimant wished to offer commercial balloon flights in Austria from his establishment in Germany, avoiding the need to apply for a new Austrian licence in addition to the German one and to establish a residence in Austria as a precondition for acquiring such a licence. While this is clearly a services case, the Court considered that balloon flights are covered by the chapter on transport policy (now 100(2) TFEU), which prevails as *lex specialis* over Article 56 TFEU. The Court stated that air transport policy should also strive for the internal market and that Neukirchinger's activities were accordingly within the scope of the application of the Treaty. Accordingly, he could rely on the prohibition of discrimination on grounds of nationality (Article 18 TFEU). Unsurprisingly, the residence requirement was qualified as inadmissible discrimination. In assessing the requirement to obtain a licence, the Court in effect merged 'non-discrimination' and 'obstacle'. While originally the requirement to comply with national legislation was only qualified as a non-discriminatory obstacle, the Court now argues that requiring a licence from someone who has obtained a licence in her state of origin is also indirectly discriminatory, as it operates to the detriment of foreign service providers.[81] This indirect discrimination could be justified by public interests such as health and safety of air space only in so far as the conditions an applicant had already fulfilled for a licence in his home state do not satisfy those interests already. Thus, Austria could rely on air security as justification for a new licence, but had to assess whether the licence regime in Germany covered all the security requirements deemed important in Austria. By implication, as in the *ČEZ* case, Member States can generally justify discrimination by reference to public interest requirements.

---

79 On the necessity of this distinction see Chapter 3, II, pp. 85–86 with notes 40–43.

80 Case C-382/08 *Neukirchinger* 28 January 2011 (nyr).

81 Paragraph 39 of the judgment.

(a) INDIVIDUAL TAXATION AND FREEDOM TO PROVIDE SERVICES

Taxation cases constitute a sizeable proportion of the Grand Chamber cases analysed, 12 cases altogether, of which nine related to company and shareholder taxation.[82] The EU has no competence on taxation except for harmonising indirect taxation (Article 113 TFEU). Accordingly, the Court regularly confirms as a starting position that 'direct taxation does not as such fall within the purview of the [EU]', only to add that 'powers retained by the Member States must nevertheless be exercised consistently with [EU] law'[83] – a classical intonation of the 'spill over principle'[84] in the crude language of legal doctrine.[85]

As far as individual taxation beyond shareholder taxation is concerned, the freedom to provide services (Article 56 TFEU) is the main reference point. Article 56 TFEU was violated by a German tax rule requiring that anyone receiving services from a provider not ordinarily resident in Germany retain any taxes owed by the service provider in Germany at source,[86] which was meant to avoid risks associated with enforcing tax payments abroad. The Court first stated that if such retention is required, the service recipient must at least be allowed to deduct the service provider's business expenses.[87] Beyond this the Court held that the principle of the legislation was justified by the necessity to 'ensure the proper functioning of the procedure for taxation'.[88] It also held that third-country nationals cannot rely on the freedom to provide services, even if their business is established in a Member State.[89]

Italian legislation levying a specific tax in Sardinia on stopovers by aircraft or recreational vessels whose tax domicile lies outside of this Italian region also infringed Article 56 TFEU.[90] Interestingly, the Court considered whether such a rule was within the scope of application of Article 56 TFEU at all, as providers resident in Sardinia may be in a different situation from others.[91] This argument was rejected, but the Court considered the 'cohesion of the tax

---

82 These will be covered below (text following note 148), as they often concern a combination of economic freedoms. Tax exemptions are also relevant in cases of free movement of persons and will be discussed in this context (below note 212).

83 Case C-290/04 *FKP Scorpio* [2006] ECR I-9461, paragraph 30, for example, referring back to the *Schumacker* case of 1995 (case C-279/93 [1995] ECR I-225, paragraph 21).

84 Further on Neofunctionalism see Chapter 1, II, p. 8 with notes 9–11.

85 For a critical assessment see Menéndez, 2009.

86 Above note 83.

87 *FKP Scorpio* paragraph 49, see also case C-234/01 *Gerritse* [2003 ECR I-5933.

88 *FKP Scorpio* paragraphs 59–61.

89 Paragraph 68, see also Case C-452/04 *Fidium Finanz* [2006] ECR I-9521.

90 Case C-169/08 *Regione Sardegna* [2009] ECR I-10821.

91 Paragraphs 35–39.

system' as a possible justification, although this was a discrimination case and this justification is not contained in Article 52 TFEU. The Court did not accept justification of the rule, because it constituted state aid in favour of the regional tourism sector.[92]

A final case questioned whether the EU VAT Directive infringed freedom to provide services.[93] A German citizen let holiday accommodation on a small scale in Austria and, as a non-resident, could not profit from an exemption on turnover tax in favour of small and medium enterprises. This rule, derived from the VAT Directive, was held to constitute a discriminatory restriction of the freedom to provide services. The Court found that this discriminatory restriction was justified by general reasons of the public interest. Member States are usually not allowed to use general interests as justifications for discriminatory restrictions of economic freedoms – this is the privilege of the EU. In this case, the Court accepted the aim to protect the tax revenue as justification.

In two out of three cases, tax regimes that were discriminatory or at least detrimental to foreign service providers were accepted as justified under Article 56 TFEU.

(b) FREEDOM TO PROVIDE SERVICES AND THE TERRITORIALITY OF LABOUR LAW

Business frequently experiences national employment legislation as burdensome and seeks legal redress against its application. EU service providers posting workers to other Member States have successfully relied on Article 56 TFEU in this regard. From 1990, the Court had established the principle that workers posted to another Member State cannot rely on the non-discrimination clause inherent in free movement of workers (Article 45 TFEU), because they have not moved of their own volition[94] and do not strive for integration into the labour market in the host state.[95] Subsequently, service providers from Member States with wages below the EU average wage argued that they would only temporarily post their employees to a host state and should not be subjected to local employment or social security law, nor to local wage regimes. The Court agreed in principle that such policies constituted a restriction of Article 56 TFEU, because being subjected to two legal orders is burdensome.[96] However, it also accepted that host states could justify imposing on foreign service providers those employment rules that referred to

92 Paragraphs 46–50; on state aid, 51–66.

93 Case 97/09 *Schmelz* 26 October 2010 (nyr).

94 Case C-43/93 *Vander Elst* [1994] ECR I-3803 paragraph 21–22.

95 Case C-113/89 *Rush Portuguesa* [1990] ECR I-1417 paragraph 15.

96 Case *Saeger*, C-6/90, see Chapter 3, p. 84 with note 29.

protection of workers.[97] This restriction would only be proportionate if legislation or collective agreements in the country of origin would not provide comparable protection.[98] Encouraged by this case law and dreading the impact of Eastern Enlargement, high-wage Member States lobbied successfully for the Posted Workers Directive (Directive 96/71/EC), which steered an ambiguous course between furthering the internal market and protecting national employment law regimes.[99] It coordinated the diverging national employment law regimes for the posting of workers in the construction industry, requiring Member States to ensure that national minimum wages and a number of further employment rules were applied to them, without guaranteeing equal treatment with national employees in other fields. These rules deviated from the conflict of law rules under the Rome Convention,[100] according to which a temporary posting into another Member State did not impact on the relevant employment law regime.

During the reference period, the Grand Chamber decided the contentious *Laval*[101] case on freedom to provide the service of hiring out workers, and also the *Koelzsch* case[102] on the employment law regime applicable to having workers deliver their services in other Member States under the conflict of law regulations. Thus, the underlying contradictions were further illuminated.

The *Laval* case will be revisited under the topics of human rights and industrial relations as a sub-section of socially embedded democracy. Here, the right of foreign employers to rely on freedom to provide services against national legislation is of interest. The legislation under attack, Articles 41 and 42 Medbestemmingslagen (MBL, Swedish Labour Code), is directly related to the traditional territoriality of labour law.[103] Swedish working conditions are

---

97 This was first established in the *Vander Elst* case (paragraph 22) and confirmed for minimum wages in cases C-369/96 *Arblade & Leloup* [1999] ECR I-8453, C-164/99 *Portuguaia Construcões* [2002] I-787, for social security payments to achieve special payments when works stop due to winter weather (case C-272/94 *Guiot* [1996] ECR I-1905) or to secure annual holiday pay (case C-490/04 *COM v Germany* [2007] ECR I-6095) and for the requirement to provide surety for workers' wages (case C-60/03 *Wolff & Müller* [2004] ECR I-9553).

98 This idea was first generated in case C-165/98 *Mazzoleni* [2001] ECR I-2198, see also Case C-49/98 *Finalarte* [2001] ECR I-7831.

99 Davies, 1997.

100 Convention on the law applicable to contractual obligations, opened for signature in Rome on 19 June 1980 (OJ 1980 L 266/1). This convention has been replaced by the 'Rome I Regulation' (Regulation 593/2008 on the law applicable to contractual obligations OJ 2008 L 177/6).

101 Case C-341/05 *Laval* [2007] I-11767.

102 Case C-29/10 *Koelzsch* 15 March 2011 (nyr).

103 Territoriality lies at the base of the '*lex loci laboris*' principle which is used in many national conflicts of law regimes to determine the law governing a contract of

traditionally regulated by collective agreements with a minimum of state intervention. The autonomy of the collective bargaining process is, inter alia, ensured through constitutional rights to collective industrial action, which include the right to sympathy or solidarity action. Thus, Swedish trade unions may call for strike or boycott in order to support the collective action initiated by another trade union in another industry in order to enhance working conditions there, and conversely employers may take collective action in solidarity with other employers. The positive regulatory function of collective agreements, on the other hand, is protected by imposing a statutory social truce on parties to any collective agreement (Article 41 MBL), but – corresponding to the right to solidarity action – also on anyone else (Article 42 MBL).[104] This means that a Swedish employer need not fear being subjected to strike action or boycotting as long as she is bound by a collective agreement. In 1989, the Arbedsdomstolen (Swedish Labour Court) was called upon during a strike concerning seafarers' wages and held[105] that the statutory social truce also protected foreign collective agreements. This decision abandoned the traditional territoriality of labour law and hindered Swedish trade unions from taking collective action in order to defend uniform wage levels in Sweden against being undercut by foreign employers whose workers receive lower wages and have weaker rights to strike. The Swedish legislator revised Article 42 MBL, clarifying that the industrial truce only extended to collective agreements governed by Swedish law, i.e. predominantly collective agreements between Swedish trade unions and employers.[106]

The *Laval* case concerned hiring out of labour[107] as a service provided by

---

employment (Franzen, 2010, pp. 229–231), but it is also a political principle of organising labour law generally (see on the territoriality of labour even under conditions of global competition Hepple, 2005, p. 223; on the resulting territoriality of labour law even in the European Union see Mundlak, 2002; for alternatives to territoriality of labour law see Mundlak, 2009).

[104] For a short summary of these principles see Edström, 2008, pp. 177–180.

[105] Case no 120/1989, reported in the Laval decision under paragraph 14.

[106] Under the conflict of law rules on collective agreements (van Hoek, 2007, pp. 460–463 with further references) it is possible for a foreign employer to conclude a collective agreement with a Swedish trade union governed by Swedish law. It is just not a very common practice.

[107] This was not a straightforward posting case, as most Member States define posting as a situation where a company contracts to carry out work in another Member State and sends employees working under their direction into that Member State. In Laval, a Swedish company delivered construction work in Sweden, relying on its Latvian parent company to make available Latvian workers receiving Latvian wages. The service provided transnationally thus consisted in making workers available to work under the direction of the Swedish company on the basis of employment contracts under Latvian law. This is usually classified as hiring out employees and constitutes the main business of temporary works agencies. The definition of posted workers used in

the Latvian company Laval to its Swedish subsidiary Baltic Bygg, which had won a tender to build a school in the Swedish town of Vaxholm, to start in May 2004, just after Latvia gained EU membership. In June 2004, the Swedish trade union for the building sector (BYGGNADS) started negotiations with Laval, aiming to conclude a collective agreement under Swedish law. On 14 September and 20 October respectively, Laval concluded collective agreements with a Latvian trade union.[108] The timing suggests that this was a strategic decision to evade coverage by Swedish collective agreements.[109] By mid-October 2004, BYGNADDS notified Laval of their intention to commence industrial action, as no progress had been made in the negotiations.

*Inter alia*, the Court had to decide whether Article 42 MBL, restricting the social truce to the parties of collective agreements governed by Swedish law, constituted a restriction of the freedom to provide services. For its answer, the Court relied on a non-discrimination test,[110] stating that foreign companies would be treated less favourably than Swedish companies, because they had to comply with Swedish collective agreements rather than with collective agreements from their home state in order to profit from any social truce obligation. This was in contrast to earlier case law, which established that applying national law or collective agreements to posted workers was a non-discriminatory obstacle to freedom to provide services.[111] Because the Court had classified the legislation as a discriminatory obstacle, it considered that Sweden was restricted to justifications under Article 52 TFEU. The Court stated that the principle that employment relations in Sweden should be governed by Swedish law, including Swedish collective agreements,[112] could not be considered as public policy under this provision.

Territoriality of labour law is also decisive in conflict of law situations, characteristic for thoroughly transnational employment relations such as that of Mr Koelzsch,[113] who worked as a lorry driver for a Luxembourg company

---

Directive 96/71/EEC is sufficiently wide to cover hiring out of workers (see also *COM v Germany* C-490/04 [2007] ECR I-6059, paragraphs 85–87, by the first Chamber). Some authors doubt whether this particular case of provision of labour within one multinational group of companies had any transnational dimension at all (Deakin, 2007–2008, pp. 587–590).

108 See paragraph 27–29 of the *Laval* ruling.

109 See Woolfson and Sommers, 2006, p. 54. The funding of this legal action by the Swedish employers' associations (ibid., p. 61; Malmberg, 2010) may even suggest a carefully orchestrated action to regain the validity of the Swedish Labour Court judgment of 1989, exploiting the EU's Eastern Enlargement.

110 Paragraphs 114 to 115 of the *Laval* judgment.

111 This was the common core of all the cases reported above (pp. 131–132, with notes 94 to 100).

112 Paragraph 118 of the *Laval* judgment.

113 Case C-29/10, above note 102.

(Gasa), transporting flowers from Denmark to Germany using lorries stationed in Germany. When a restructuring of Gasa was announced, the drivers operating from Germany constituted a works council under German law and elected Mr Koelzsch as alternate member. After a takeover by a Danish company, Gasa dismissed Koelzsch, who challenged that dismissal relying on German law. The Luxembourg labour court dismissed the claim, relying on less protective Luxembourg legislation. Mr Koelzsch challenged this decision, relying on the Rome Convention.[114] According to its Article 6(1), any choice of law clause in an employment contract must not deprive the employee of a higher level of protection than would be applicable but for the choice of law clause. In the absence of a choice of law clause, the employment law of the state where the employee's contractual obligations are habitually discharged applies (Article 6(2)). Koelzsch argued that the stationing of the lorries and the fact that he returned to his home in Germany after each tour meant that his contractual obligations were mainly carried out in Germany and that German law governed the contract of employment but for the choice of law clause. The Luxembourg court of first instance considered that the employer's corporate domicile and the location of the logistics office in Luxembourg were decisive. The Court was asked to decide between those views. Leaving the final decision to the national court, the Court found that the stationing of the lorries, the countries touched by the tours, and the end point of the tours were the main relevant connecting factors in this employment relationship. All this pointed to Germany. In the Court's interpretation, the conflict of law rules (now confirmed by secondary EU law) do not support employers' 'law shopping' as practised in *Laval*. Rather, the territoriality of labour law prevailed. Had Gasa established subsidiaries in Germany and Denmark and declared that its workers were posted to these countries, it would possibly have been in a better position.

The clash between the two cases could not be more pronounced. If the employer relies on freedom to provide services, the territoriality of labour law emerged as unjustifiable discrimination against them. If an employee relies on the conflict of law rules, territoriality of labour law prevails, without any argument being wasted on the question of whether this might constitute an obstacle to the employer's transnational service provision.

(c) OBLIGATION TO TENDER FOR CONTRACTS BY PUBLIC AUTHORITIES (PUBLIC PROCUREMENT) Five Grand Chamber rulings on the award of public contracts also concern freedom to provide services. The directives on public

---

114 See above, note 100.

procurement[115] aim at securing that freedom, mainly through the requirement to publicly tender for all public services, works and supply throughout the EU and to conduct the tendering in the most transparent and open way possible. The Court held that Italy[116] violated these directives by awarding all supply contracts for a certain type of helicopter for army use to one traditional supplier, thus supporting economic freedoms of potential competitors. On referral by a Greek court, the Court had to consider a national rule excluding all owners of media companies from all public works contracts in order to ensure that the press remained independent from the government (*Michaniki*).[117] The Court found that, although the relevant directive specified grounds for exclusion referring to professional qualifications in an exhaustive list, Member States could still establish other exclusion grounds unrelated to this field, if and in so far as these additional exclusions aimed at safeguarding equality and transparency in a proportionate manner.[118] The Court found the Greek rule to go over and above what was necessary to achieve its aim in establishing an irrebuttable presumption that any owner, main shareholder or executive manager of a media company was not fit to perform services under a public contract. Again, the economic interests of potential foreign and domestic competitors were protected, at the expense of the constitutional argument that the media should be independent from payments by the state.

Two further cases concern waste treatment in Germany. The Commission[119] challenged a contract between different municipalities according to which they would use a large communally built waste incineration facility, rather than each tendering for having their waste incinerated commercially. The case turned on the question of whether the incineration of waste affected free movement of services. The Court held that it did not, because the municipalities had to provide waste removal as a public service. Accordingly, in this case the Court did not derive an obligation to commercialise public services from the economic freedoms. In the Wall case,[120] the Grand Chamber had to pass judgment on the operation of 11 public toilets in Frankfurt. Here the Court established that the obligation to conduct transparent tendering processes flows directly from Article 56 TFEU[121] – in a case where two

---

115 Directives 77/62/EEC (OJ [1977] L13/1) and 93/36/EEC (OJ [1993] L 199/1) on public supply contracts, Directives 92/50/EEC (OJ [1992] L 209/1) and 2004/18/EC (OJ [2004] L 134/114) on public service contracts, see on their aims Case C-213/07 *Michaniki* [2008] ECR I-9999, paragraph 39.

116 Case C-337/05 *Com v Italy* [2008] ECR I-2173.

117 Above, note 115.

118 Paragraph 47 of the judgment.

119 Case C-480/06 *COM v Germany (waste treatment)* [2009] ECR I-4747.

120 Case C-91/08 *Wall AG* [2010] ECR I-2815.

121 Paragraph 33 of the judgment.

German companies competed for a contract with a German city. In substance, the decision was left to the national court though.

Finally, the Commission brought an infringement action against Germany[122] because several cities had established schemes under which employees could surrender a proportion of their collectively agreed wages for contributions to an additional pension (*Riester Rente*) by collective agreement rather than through a tendering procedure. The collective agreement specified the pension providers as public bodies, local authority insurance companies or the *Sparkassen* group (public savings institutes). Rationales behind this choice included the fact that the designated pension schemes provided for worker representation in their organisations,[123] would not engage in discriminatory premium calculation,[124] were barred from squandering contributions on volatile financial markets and, beyond that, were protected by public guarantees.[125] The Court first stated that, while the right to bargain collectively was a general principle of EU law,[126] it was not without limitations.[127] Next it confirmed that, as the public procurement directives are emanations of economic freedoms as protected by the Treaty,[128] any deviation from the directives constituted an obstacle to freedom to provide services, which needed justification. The Court found that a collective agreement may be suitable as justification in principle if it aims at enhancing social protection. It also found that the collective agreement in question did just that, but that the same aims could also have been achieved through public tendering. Thus, using the collective agreement to choose certain service providers was disproportionate.[129] Clearly this case warrants a more elaborate discussion under the topic of protecting human rights against economic freedoms.[130] What is relevant here is that the Court did not allow justifying a restriction of freedom to provide services by social interests pursued through collective bargaining.

The case law on freedom to provide services, too, seems contradictory. The Court sometimes accepts justification of discriminatory rules by reference to general public interests that are not included in Article 52 TFEU, and sometimes insists on using only the three grounds established there. Also, the Court has sometimes accepted justifications brought forward by Member States on the basis of a lenient proportionality test and has even succumbed to territoriality,

---

122 Case C-271/08 *COM v Germany* ('*Riester Rente*') [2010] ECR I-7087.
123 See paragraph 54 of the judgment.
124 See paragraph 57 of the judgment.
125 See paragraph 59 of the judgment.
126 Paragraphs 36–39.
127 Paragraph 43.
128 Paragraph 44.
129 Paragraph 44.
130 See below II. 3. d) (2) (p. 199) and III. 4 (p. 208).

while using a strict proportionality test at other times. As a result, national tax rules, the EU directives on VAT and the regulation on conflict of laws retain the upper hand against freedom to provide services, while Member States have had to accept foreign planning approval decisions as if they were national, are obliged to relinquish a constitutional principle of press independence, and trade unions are prevented from protecting wages and pensions in order to safeguard employers' freedom to provide services.

*(5) EU freedom to conduct business – services, establishment and capital*
The incremental merger of freedom of establishment, freedom to provide services and lately also free movement of capital towards a general freedom to conduct business[131] in the internal market was evident since 2004 in that the Grand Chamber decided no fewer than 30 cases on the basis of more than one economic freedom. These are mostly related to the fields of gambling and betting, corporate and shareholder taxation and some miscellaneous cases.

(a) GAMBLING AND BETTING Traditionally,[132] the Court has shown some leniency towards national legislation regulating or even prohibiting gambling for public policy reasons. However, even an activity which is criminal under the national law of several Member States can be a service under the Treaty if provided for remuneration because 'it is not for the Court to substitute its assessment for that of the legislatures of any Member States where that activity is practised legally'.[133] While this seems to express respect for national regulation, this rule means that under EU law any national decision that a certain activity is illegal or should not be provided on the market must be disregarded.

The rules at stake in five post-2004 cases before the Grand Chamber did not prohibit gambling and betting but merely restricted them, and were mostly linked to the tradition of providing lotteries through public monopolies. This system has aimed at raising revenue for social and other public interest projects, as well as channelling into controlled and safe environments the propensity of humans to gamble.[134]

Italian law[135] imposed a licence on all gambling and betting businesses,

[131] See Chapter 3, II, pp. 86–90.

[132] Case C-275/92 *Schindler* [1994] ECR I-1095.

[133] Ibid, paragraph 32 with reference to case C-159/90 *SPUC* [1991] ECR I-4685 paragraph 20.

[134] Paragraph 38 to the *Gambelli* case [2003] ECR I-13031 (see also Chapter 3, note 66).

[135] Case C-338/04 *Placanica* [2007] ECR I-1891. Swedish restrictions of gambling and betting through requiring a licence under national law and banning any advertisement for foreign gambling and betting services (including those provided

requiring companies to disclose all their owners in order to obtain a licence. This rule is comprehensible, given the strength of the position of clandestine societies ('Mafia'), but it also effectively closed the market for companies listed on the London Stock Exchange. In order to prevent circumvention, the use of agents for gambling and betting was also banned. The Court repeated that these rules infringed both freedom of establishment and freedom to provide services.[136] This means that Member States must apply equal standards to both service providers and actors wishing to establish themselves, which hinders Member States from requiring the latter to integrate into the social fabric of their societies. The Court also held that excluding companies that operated on regulated markets could never be justifiable, but left it to the national court to decide whether a licensing system is justifiable by channelling gambling into safe environments. In slight contradiction, the Court held three years later in the *Markus Stoß* litigation[137] that the conclusion of a commercial contract with an intermediary is a form of using one's freedom of establishment.[138] Allowing for restrictions adequate for companies wishing to establish themselves, the Court explained that Member States had a 'margin of discretion' as to whether granting a monopoly to a public body is more efficient than other legal instruments, even if these may be less intrusive.[139]

The *Portuguese Football League* case[140] addressed an exclusive right to operate and license betting held and enforced by a religious charity originating from the sixteenth century. A company domiciled in Gibraltar offering sports bets via the internet was fined for violating the law, and relied on its freedom to provide services in challenging this. The religious motives behind the Portuguese system were disregarded: granting exclusive rights to La Casa also served to justify the sinful activity of gambling and betting by the charitable use of its proceeds.[141] For justifying its legislation, Portugal only relied on the aim of preventing the exploitation by dubious and even criminal providers of the human propensity to gamble, together with the need for consumer protection. In this case on freedom to provide services, the Court refrained from requiring Portugal to assess whether Gibraltar legislation

online) not possessing such a licence have formed the background of a Grand Chamber case which, however, mainly referred to the principle of judicial protection (Case C-432/05 *Unibet* [2007] ECR I-2271).

136 Case C-243/01 *Gambelli* [2003] ECR I-13031.

137 Case C-316/07 *Markus Stoß et al.* 8 September 2010 (nyr).

138 Paragraph 58.

139 *Markus Stoß* ruling, paragraph 81.

140 Case C-42/07 *Liga Portuguese de Futebol Profissional* [2009] ECR I-7633.

141 Interestingly, AG Bot partly endorsed this logic, stating that 'it is not without relevance that lotteries make a significant contribution to the financing of benevolent or public interest activities' (paragraph 26 of his opinion). This reasoning is not taken up by the Court though.

already achieved these aims.[142] Rather, it granted the Member States some discretion in deciding whether their rules were proportionate.[143]

Two German cases also concerned challenges to monopolies on lotteries and bets. The 'Winner Wetten' case[144] must be seen as a strategic reference by a first instance court aimed at a ruling by the German Constitutional Court that allowed for an interim period to revise legislation restricting business freedom in order to give Parliament time to debate new legislation. As an infringement of Articles 56 and 49 TFEU was stipulated, the Court did not decide on any substantial problems here. The claimant in the *Carmen Media*[145] case challenged regional legislation in the German state Schleswig Holstein in order to defend its business practice of targeting that state with internet betting from its corporate domicile in Gibraltar. The referring court was not at ease with the fact that the legislation privileged certain games, such as horse betting, by exempting them from the absolute monopoly. The Court, however, held that such inconsistency may well be justifiable and that even transitory measures do not necessarily render legislation disproportionate.[146]

Overall, this is a contradictory set of rulings. On the one hand, Member States cannot protect any type of activity from being subjected to market forces; even if it – as gambling – is traditionally reserved for a charity at national level, commercial providers from other Member States must not be barred from competing in principle.[147] However, there is some improvement in relation to justification. While the Court based its 2007 ruling on a general economic freedom to conduct business transnationally (which was conducive to strict requirements in justifying any restrictions) and – in line with this – held in 2009 that a general social policy aim, such as utilising the human propensity to gambling for generating revenue in favour of charitable activities, cannot justify a monopoly, nevertheless in 2010 the decision whether justifications are adequate was left to the national courts, stressing explicitly Member States' 'margin of appreciation'.

(b) COMPANY AND SHAREHOLDER TAXATION As mentioned above,[148] taxation has been of increasing importance in case before the Grand Chamber. The nine cases on company and shareholder taxation mostly were heard under a combination of economic freedoms.

---

142 Paragraphs 68–69 – in stark contrast to case law referring to posting of workers (above pp. 131–135).

143 Paragraphs 70–72.

144 Case C-409/06 *Winner Wetten GmbH* 8 September 2010 (nyr).

147 Case C-46/08 *Carmen Media* 8 September 2010 (nyr).

146 The *Markus Stoß* case had a similar result (above note 137).

147 Case C-42/07 *Portuguesa Futebol* [2009] ECR I-7633.

148 See above p. 130 with note 82.

Most of these involved national legislation aimed at preventing tax evasion by multinational companies, which responded to an OECD strategy, first devised in 1998,[149] to avoid harmful tax competition. Despite the OECD's efforts, there is as yet no international agreement on how best to devise national tax law. One pair of competing principles consists of capital export neutrality and capital import neutrality. The first principle requires that any income by a resident, whether from home or abroad, should be taxed equally, whereas the second principle requires that all economic activity within one country bears the same tax burden. Capital export neutrality is said to reduce the relevance of national tax to localisation decisions, while import neutrality is preferred by corporate managers.[150] Considering the problem of how tax revenue should be distributed between countries, the OECD model is based on the principle that the resident country of foreign investors (i.e. typically a capital-intense country) should tax investment, whereas the source country (i.e. a country which attracts foreign investment) should tax corporate gains.[151] The OECD recommendation tries to find a complex balance between different forms of tax neutrality and at the same time aims at preventing tax avoidance typically sought by multinational companies.

From the perspective of economic freedoms, efficient rules to combat tax evasion may conflict with freedom of establishment and free movement of capital, because establishing subsidiaries and moving capital to subsidiaries in low tax countries will often be targeted. More fundamentally, one might ask whether it is conducive to any internal market to maintain different national tax regimes without even coordinating them. However, the EU has no competences in tax legislation, which means that the regime beyond indirect taxes is one of independent states. Considering the tensions between economic and social integration, reducing the tax base threatens redistributive social integration, while allowing maximum choice between tax regimes may be seen as furthering economic integration. How did the Court steer between these two poles?

First, in the *Cadbury* case,[152] it ruled on UK legislation aiming to prevent tax evasion through moving corporate gains to a subsidiary in a low-tax country, which Cadbury had tried to achieve by establishing two subsidiaries in Ireland (with a corporate tax of 10% at the time), and to tax part of its profits in Ireland. UK tax law demanded special taxation rules for 'controlled foreign

---

[149] See OECD, 1998, which also includes the relevant recommendation and OECD, 2006.

[150] Graetz and Warren, 2007, p. 1582.

[151] Ibid., p. 1587.

[152] Case C-196/04 *Cadbury* [2006] ECR I-7995.

companies' (CFCs), i.e. companies not resident in the UK in which a UK company owned more than 50%. In contrast to other profits of subsidiaries, profits of CFCs established in a country with less than three-quarters of the UK's corporate tax rate were taxed at source in principle. The parent company could be exempted from this rule upon proof that there was a genuinely economic motive, other than tax evasion, for establishing a subsidiary. The ECJ held that freedom of establishment for a company includes the right to establish any subsidiary in any Member State of its choice, and also stated that treating subsidiaries in different Member States differently constituted an obstacle to freedom of establishment (and not discrimination), thus opening the way for the UK to justify its legislation relying on general interests. However, the aim of avoiding tax evasion was not accepted as suitable to justify this, because any company should be free to seek advantages of all legal environments within the EU.[153] Only 'wholly artificial arrangements' could legitimately be targeted. The assessment of whether the Cadbury arrangement was wholly artificial was left to the national court. This critical position in regard to national legislation protecting the tax base inspired three group litigations on related UK rules.

The *ACT Group Litigation*[154] challenged rules on advanced corporation tax (ACT), which UK companies had to pay for any dividend paid to subsidiaries in principle. However, payments to shareholders resident in the UK or in a country covered by a double taxation agreement with the UK attracted a tax credit. This privilege was challenged under freedom of establishment. Here, the Court did not even consider whether the rules would present an obstacle for establishing a subsidiary in a non-privileged Member State, but relied on a non-discrimination approach instead.[155] Stressing the autonomy of Member States in taxation issues, the Court found that different taxation of residents and non-residents was not generally prohibited, because residents and non-residents were not generally in comparable situations.[156] Thus, Member States had to treat dividends paid by resident and non-resident companies equally if paid to resident tax payers,[157] but not if paid to residents and non-residents. In line with classical taxation theory,[158] this judgment implied that Member States are under no obligation to avoid economic double taxation of income from corporate profits and dividend shares.

153 See also Chapter 3 II, pp. 87–88.

154 Case C-374/04 *Test Claimants in the ACT Group Litigation* [2006] ECR I-11673.

155 Paragraph 43.

156 Paragraphs 46, 52, 57, 74.

157 Paragraph 55 of the ruling.

158 Graetz and Warren, 2007, p. 1597.

The *FII Litigation*,[159] launched by the company group British American Tobacco, challenged UK tax on dividends paid to UK companies. In principle, the law classified those dividends as 'franked investment income' (FII), which attracted a tax credit in order to avoid the dividend being taxed as income for the subsidiary and the parent. However, dividends received from foreign subsidiaries did not constitute FII. Accordingly, the UK parent company was liable to pay taxes on those dividends – again, with modifications corresponding to any double-taxation agreements. This led to differences in company taxation depending on the corporate domicile of susidiaries. The Court again relied on a non-discrimination approach to freedom of establishment.[160] It also held that different treatment of different forms of investing capital constituted an obstacle to free movement of capital if it would discourage companies from investing capital abroad.[161] Under both freedoms, some parts of the UK legislation were held to be in violation of the Treaty, as the aim of preventing tax avoidance was not suitable as justification.

The *Thin Cap Group Litigation*[162] challenged rules aimed at preventing 'tax planning'[163] by multinational companies through 'thin capitalisation' (thin cap), i.e. financing a company by credit rather than by capital (equity). If national legislation allows setting off interest payments from taxable income, multinational groups of companies can use intra-group loans in order to move revenue from high- to low-tax countries. To counteract such strategies, UK law treated interests paid on loans by a foreign parent to a UK company as dividends, thus privileging loans by resident parent companies. The Court considered this rule only under freedom of establishment and relied again on a non-discrimination approach. AG Geelhoed had proposed a specific variety of this: as in the absence of any EU competence on direct taxation, differences between national tax laws were bound to prevail and mere consequences of such diversity should be treated as 'quasi restrictions', which did not infringe freedom of establishment.[164] The Court did not refer directly to this. It found that Member States may, as a default rule, tax interest on loans from non-resident parents as dividends, but that they must allow companies to justify their contractual arrangement as commercially reasonable. If such reasonableness can be proved, the interest would be comparable to an interest payment

159 Case C-446/04 *Test Claimants in the FII Group Litigation* [2006] ECR I-11753.

160 Paragraph 40.

161 Paragraphs 63–64.

162 Case C-524/04 *Test Claimants in the Thin Cap Group Litigation* [2007] ECR I-2107.

163 This notion is used by Graetz and Warren, 2007, pp. 1587–1589.

164 Paragraph 40 of his opinion on case C-524/04.

between resident companies and would have to be treated equally (i.e. under the UK system exempted from corporate tax). As this was decided only under freedom of establishment, companies with their corporate domicile outside the EU could not profit from the partial invalidation of UK law.[165]

The *Oy AA* case[166] on Finnish corporation tax seemed to leave more scope for national law: Finnish legislation in principle granted a tax credit for financial transfers within groups of companies, but the tax authorities did not apply this rule to international transfers between UK and Finnish group members. The Court found that internal and European inner-group transfers were comparable, because any different treatment would discourage establishing a subsidiary outside Finland. This argument seems imprecise. It relied on a non-discrimination approach and an obstacles approach simultaneously: the concept of comparability is only relevant for non-discrimination and the question whether a rule discourages establishment through a subsidiary relates to an obstacles approach. It also contradicted the *ACT* ruling, delivered only six months earlier. However, after finding an infringement of freedom of establishment, the Court accepted 'the need to safeguard the balanced allocation of power to impose taxes between the Member States'[167] as a justification for the privilege granted to inner Finnish transfers. Similarly, in the *Skatteverket* case,[168] a justification relating to securing the Swedish tax base was accepted, upon being challenged by a Swiss company relying on free movement of capital.[169] The complex rules on tax exemptions for dividends allowed tax credits only if the parent company distributed all its gains in proportion to the shares held by its daughter companies. This system was held to be a restriction of free movement of capital, which was justified by the difficulty of obtaining information on the structure and exact dividend payment by foreign companies.

As regards taxation of dividend payments to individual shareholders, the *Meilicke* ruling[170] held that German legislation infringed free movement of capital by providing tax credits for shareholders receiving dividends from companies subject to German corporation tax, but not from companies subject to foreign tax regimes. The Court said this constituted an obstacle to free movement of capital, as investors may be deterred from investing abroad. In stark contrast to the *Oy AA* case, any justification relating to cohesion of the

---

165 This resulted from the principle reiterated in the *Fidium Finanz* case (see above note 89).

166 Case C-231/05 *Oy AA* [2007] ECR I-6373.

167 Paragraph 51 of the ruling with further references.

168 Case C-101/05 *Skatteverket* [2007] ECR I-11531.

169 See again the principle reiterated in *Fidium Finanz* (note 89).

170 Case C-292/04 *Meilicke* [2007] ECR I-1835.

tax base was rejected though. The *Kerckhaerdt* case[171] concerned the tax burden of two Belgian individuals receiving dividends on shares in a French company. The claimants before the national courts requested that dividends paid to them by French companies were taxed differently from dividends received by Belgian companies, because the equal treatment of both types of income resulted in a higher tax on French dividends. The Court found no violation, as any difference resulting from equal treatment of both incomes was a consequence of 'the exercise in parallel by two Member States of their fiscal sovereignty'.[172] The Court thus relied on the natural territoriality of the tax regime, as proposed by AG Geelhoed in the *Thin Cap Group Litigation* case discussed above.

Finally, the *Orange European Smallcap Fund* case[173] concerned Dutch legislation exempting fiscal investment enterprises from taxes: if they distributed their entire profits to their shareholders, the fiscal investment enterprises' profits were taxed at a rate of 0%. Any dividends received by a fiscal investment enterprise were usually taxed at source. For payments from other companies with their corporate residence in the Netherlands, the legislation provided for a tax refund, to maintain the principle of zero taxation. However, this did not apply for dividends received from companies domiciled outside the Netherlands. In addition, recipients of dividends of collective fiscal enterprises could claim a tax concession if taxed in the Netherlands. The Court reaffirmed that Member States were not under any obligation to avoid or mitigate economic double taxation on dividends and company profits resulting from the parallel existence of several territorially based tax systems.[174] Following *Meilicke*, the Commission had argued that the Netherlands should offset any domestic tax burden on dividends originating from other Member States. The Court did not accept this argument,[175] finding the legislation admissible, except for the tax concession for recipients of dividends.

This contradictory set of rulings has attracted some academic critique. One line of critique focuses on the difference between EU and international tax law.[176] Such criticism could be rejected, as the EU establishes an internal market, where territoriality should not be a consideration, while in international economic law territoriality is decisive. However, due to the lack of EU competence for a comprehensive tax system there is some doubt whether

171 Case C-513/04 *Kerckhaerdt* [2006] ECR 10967.
172 Paragraph 20 of the judgment.
173 Case C-194/06 *Smallcap Fund* [2008] ECR I-3747.
174 Paragraph 31 of the judgment, see also paragraph 20 of the *Kerckhaerdt* judgment.
175 Paragraph 39 of the *Smallcamp Fund* judgment.
176 This is the main point made by Graetz and Warren, 2007.

internal market principles should govern tax law. In fact, any common logic behind the corporation tax cases seems based on territoriality. This would explain why the Court seems to base some rulings on a non-discrimination rather than an obstacle-based logic.[177] Banks argue that it would be unconvincing if tax legislation were to be treated with more leniency than other fields. By contrast, Snell finds good reasons for such different treatment in that tax legislation is concerned with distributing wealth rather than regulating the economy.[178] Both criticisms seem to hint at the territorial character of tax legislation even within the internal market. This seems to mirror what the Court is doing in fact. There is a remaining discrepancy, as the Court in some cases even rejects the existence of a restriction based on arguments relating to territoriality,[179] while in other cases the territorial base of the taxation system informs the justification.[180] While most of these cases emerge from 2004 and later, it is difficult to predict how the case law will develop. So far, the common denominator is that protecting the territoriality of the tax base justifies even discriminatory restrictions.

(c) MISCELLANEOUS CASES The combination of establishment and services was also used in two rulings originating from infringement procedures against Italy. One[181] targeted a statutory obligation to a contract imposed on any insurance company authorised to provide third-party motor vehicle liability insurance. Details on premiums calculation were also prescribed and regional premium differentiation prohibited. Further, all owners of motor vehicles were under a statutory obligation to obtain third-party liability insurance. All this served a social function, aiming to ensure that all victims of road accidents could claim compensation from an insurance company, and that taking out such insurance was affordable for all sections of the populace and in all regions of Italy, despite a general reluctance of insurers to contract with younger men resident in Sicily. The Court held that the diversity of different national laws as such does not constitute a restriction of the combined freedom of establishment and freedom to provide services,[182] and also stated that any 'substantial interference into the freedom of contract which economic operators, in principle enjoy',[183] creating the necessity for foreign providers to 'rethink their business policy and strategy',[184] would constitute a restriction.

177 This is the main point of Banks, 2008.
178 Snell, 2007.
179 The *Kerckhaerdt* case (note 171) is an example for this.
180 Here, the *Oy AA* case (note 166) may serve as an example.
181 Case C-518/06 *COM v Italy (motor insurance)* [2009] ECR I-3491.
182 Paragraphs 62–64, again with references.
183 Paragraph 66 without any reference, as this is new.
184 Paragraph 69, again without references.

One wonders which differences between national laws will fail to qualify as restrictions.[185] However, the Court returned to the diversity of national legal orders when considering justifications:[186] Member States have some discretion if public interests differ from one Member State to another.[187] If accidents amass in certain regions, the Member State may thus prohibit regional risk categories in motor insurance.[188] The Court explicitly rejected the argument that social objectives such as victim protection should be achieved through a public guarantee fund rather than through compulsory contracting,[189] which corresponded to the ordo-liberal principle of refraining from 'intrusion' in market mechanisms at all costs, and burdening the tax payer rather than business. In an internal market, such orthodoxy would condemn Italian taxpayers to put up with irresponsible behaviour by insurance businesses from all over Europe in not providing insurance to men under 30 in Sicily. Although the Court offered no substantive argument on this, there is always hope that similar insights may inform future case law of the Court.

The second action against Italy[190] concerned maximum tariffs for lawyers. Following the *Cipolla* ruling,[191] legislation on lawyers' fees had been reviewed and the minimum fees repealed in order to allow lawyers to waive fees when they lost a case. The Commission challenged the remaining ceiling for fees as it would discourage lawyers from other Member States from establishing themselves in or providing services to Italy. Here, the Court stated that the mere fact that national rules are stricter than in other Member States is not sufficient for a statutory rule constituting a restriction of the combined two economic freedoms. Thus, the Commission should have adduced specific evidence to demonstrate that the market access of lawyers from other Member States was actually inhibited. The Court rejected the Commission's claim on this basis, in slight contrast to the part of the Cipolla ruling on Article 56 TFEU: there, the Court had held that minimum fees constituted a barrier to market access, leaving it for the national court to decide whether this restriction was justified by protecting consumer interest and standards of services.

Taken together, these cases seem to demonstrate a certain arbitrariness in deciding similar issues, together with a preparedness of the Court to derive a

---

[185] Barnard, 2010b, concludes from the use of expressions such as 'serious' or 'substantial' that a remote impediment to market access is not sufficient to trigger the economic freedoms (at 258 note 259).

[186] Paragraph 85 of the judgment.

[187] Paragraph 84 of the judgment, referring to case C-110/05 *COM v Italy* in relation to trailers (note 38).

[188] Paragraphs 88–89.

[189] Paragraphs 79–82.

[190] Case C-565/08 *COM v Italy* 29 March 2011 (nyr).

[191] C-96, 202/04, discussed above, p. 119 with note 21.

general freedom of contract from the combined economic freedoms, nearly relinquishing any requirement of transnational business activity for its application.

*(6) The EU economic constitution and consumer rights* One ruling illustrates how opportunities to utilise the EU economic constitution in favour of market citizens are being missed: as any EU consumer knows, mobile phone companies exploit borders between Member States by charging exorbitant 'roaming fees' for any phone call crossing them. The Commission could have initiated proceedings as competition authority with consumer welfare in mind. Also, judicial campaigners could have tested the horizontal effects of economic freedoms when used against big business rather than against workers or their trade unions.[192] Instead, the Commission issued Regulation 717/2007/EC, which capped the wholesale and retail charges for roaming, thus underwriting unilaterally imposed rulebooks making it less attractive to receive mobile phone services across borders. Vodafone challenged this regulation before UK courts, relying on its economic freedoms to provide services across a border – without success, as the Court found the regulation to be within the EU competence and also not disproportionate in relation to the economic freedoms of service providers.[193]

**d) The perspective of socially embedded constitutionalism**

The question remains in how far the Grand Chamber supports the paradigm of socially embedded constitutionalism in relation to the EU economic constitution. Positive public duties towards ensuring the actual enjoyment of rights for all as well as the extension of constitutional rights towards horizontal relations have been identified as decisive elements of socially embedded constitutionalism.[194] As regards the EU economic constitution, free movement rights have nurtured approaches to rights just below the threshold of establishing explicit positive duties or acknowledging horizontal rights of weaker parties. This may nevertheless constitute a first step towards a socially embedded constitutionalism. These will be considered as 'rights beyond the merely economic', and analysis of the few cases establishing explicit positive duties and horizontal effects will conclude this part chapter.

*(1) Workers' and citizens' rights beyond the merely economic* Free movement of workers, freedom of establishment and freedom to receive services,

192 On this see below, pp. 164–169.
193 Case C-58/08 *Vodafone Ltd et al.* [2010] ECR I-4999.
194 See above Chapter 2, II, pp. 56–62.

acknowledged from the 1980s,[195] are not merely business freedoms, but have also supported rights of less affluent migrants. They have thus been seen as a forerunner of EU citizenship proper.[196] The related judgments seem to acknowledge that free movers are not only commodities,[197] even though only those pursuing an economic activity enjoy unconditional free movement and equal treatment rights.[198] However, they often generate social rights which can contribute to the actual integration of free movers into their host society. From 2004 the Grand Chamber has repeatedly ruled on rights to social advantages and social security (social rights), rights to migrate or remain in a country (also for family members) and, finally, rights to access institutions providing social services of general interest, such as health care and education.

(a) SOCIAL RIGHTS Social rights for free movers have traditionally been derived from Article 45 TFEU, which not only guarantees equal treatment of migrant workers, but also demands the removal of any obstacles to actually taking advantage of employment opportunities abroad.[199] Secondary law guaranteeing equal treatment in relation to tax benefits and social advantages and coordinating different social security systems[200] is ultimately rooted in these Treaty rights, which have partly been expanded to EU citizens via equal treatment rights.[201] Some of the eight recent Grand Chamber rulings on benefits and tax advantages for workers and former workers contain some interesting expansions of this.

One of the benefits in question was the child-raising allowance under German law. Funded from the general tax revenue, it was provided for one parent per child who was either on parental leave or had reduced her[202] working hours in order to have more time for childcare. It had long been held to qualify as a social advantage under Article 7(2) Regulation 1612/68.[203] The *Geven* case[204] challenged the fact that frontier workers had to fulfil the additional

---

195 Cases 286/82 and 26/83 *Luisi and Carbone* [1984] ECR 377, 186/87 *Cowan* [1989] ECR 195.

196 See, for example, Plender, 1976, p. 40 and Evans, 1982.

197 O'Leary, 2011, pp. 506–507.

198 Wollenschläger, 2011.

199 As first held in the *Bosman* case, above Chapter 3, p. 84.

200 See above Chapter 3, pp. 96–97.

201 See above Chapter 3, p. 98.

202 There was an insignificant percentage of men taking advantage of child raising allowance (3%). This allowance has since been replaced by significantly higher parental benefits, where 20% of the recipients are male (Statistisches Bundesamt, 2011, p. 6)

203 Case C-85/95 *Martinez Sala* [1998] ECR I-2691 paragraphs 25 et seq.

204 Case C-213/05 *Wendy Geven* [2007] ECR I-6347.

requirement of working for a minimum of 15 hours a week. This rule also applied to German nationals working abroad and did not discriminate directly against foreign workers. However, in order to avoid a verdict of indirect discrimination, Germany needed to justify the rule as it affected foreign workers more frequently. The Court found that the allowance was a measure of 'national family policy intended to encourage the birth-rate',[205] thus belonging to a field of social policy where Member States have 'wide discretion'.[206] Therefore, Member States could lawfully require beneficiaries to have a 'close connection with [their] society',[207] and thus deny the benefit to non-residents not sufficiently integrated on fractional employment contracts only.

The *Hartmann* case[208] concerned the right of a male German frontier worker residing in Austria for his non-working wife to receive child-raising benefit. The Court found that denying the benefit on the basis that Mrs Hartmann resided in Austria in the family home and had never worked in Germany would pose an obstacle for Mr Hartmann to maintain his occupation in Germany. Interestingly, Hartmann could derive rights from Article 45 TFEU although he had not moved in order to gain employment in another Member State. Rather he had maintained his employment in his Member State of origin and had moved over the border into Austria for undisclosed reasons.[209] AG van Gerven had stressed that for the purposes of Article 45 a migrant worker could not be 'dissociate(d) [...] from what he represents in economic terms'.[210] The Court rejected this view without further comment. Its judgment is based on the deliberation that Mr Hartmann as a full-time worker is at least as integrated as a 15-hrs/week part-time worker and must not be denied the benefit for that reason.[211]

The related *Bosmann* case[212] concerned the question of whether a frontier worker may claim child benefits as tax allowance in her country of residence. This ruling was made under Regulation 1408/71/EEC entirely, which explicitly states that only one social regime applies to each person. Contrary to established case law, the Court held that this does not exclude the voluntary expansion of benefits by another Member State.[213] While this improves the

---

205 Paragraph 21.

206 Paragraph 27.

207 Paragraph 28.

208 Case C-212/05 [2007] ECR I-6303.

209 Probably Mrs Hartmann could draw on more non-market resources such as unpaid services by relatives for raising their common children and providing a home in her native Austria.

210 Paragraph 41 of his opinion.

211 Paragraph 34, 37.

212 Case C-352/06 *Brigitte Bosmann* [2008] ECR I-3827.

213 This specific rule is maintained in Article 11 of Regulation 883/2004/EC, thus, the judgment will remain relevant. See on this van der Mei and Essers, 2009.

workers' position, one wonders why the loss of a benefit for the claiming single mother would not deter her from seeking work over a border, while the loss of his wife's benefit is deemed to deter a full-time working father from moving freely.

The *Hendrix* case[214] concerned a non-contributory benefit for disabled young people under Netherlands legislation (the 'Wajong'), which was discontinued after Mr Hendrix moved from the Netherlands to Belgium as a frontier worker. The Court confirmed the position that a worker moving to another Member State for non-economic reasons while maintaining his employment in the Member State of origin can benefit from Article 45 TFEU. The 'Wajong' as wage complement was seen as a social advantage under Article 7(2) Regulation 1612/68/EEC, but also as a non-contributory benefit under Regulation 1408/71/EEC. Regulation 1408/71/EEC explicitly allowed subjecting non-contributory benefits to residence requirements. Reconciling these contradictory rules, the Court stated that the principle of equal treatment, as protected by Article 45(2) TFEU, prevailed, meaning that the residence requirement allowed, but not required, by Regulation 1408/71/EEC needed to be justified to avoid a verdict of indirect discrimination. As in the *Geven* case, the Court found the benefit in question to be closely linked to the national socio-economic situation. However, it gave Mr Hendrix a slightly stronger position, stating that even a justified residence requirement must not be applied if the ensuing infringement of rights went over and above what is required to achieve the legislation's aim. The final judgment was left to the national Court.

Three cases on former workers concerned the portability of social benefits, i.e. the right to continue claiming a benefit after moving away from one's country of origin. Portability is regulated in detail in Regulation 993/2004/EC, then 1408/71/EEC.

In the *Perez Naranjo* case[215] on the portability of a supplementary allowance to old-age pensioners under French law, the Court relied exclusively on the regulation. Accordingly, the question of whether a Spaniard returning to his home country for retirement could claim the allowance on top of the pension depended on the question of whether this allowance was non-contributory or not. The decision on this rather technical question was left to the national court, without any hint of the fundamental social rights quality of the issue.

In the *Habelt et al.* cases[216] on portability of old-age pensions under German law derived from payments made from the territory of Nazi Germany,

214 Case C-287/05 [2007] ECR I-6909.
215 Case C-265/05 [2007] ECR I-347.
216 Cases C-396/05, 419/05 and 450/05 [2007] ECR I-11895.

Regulation 1408/71/EEC was not sufficient, because the Regulation contained exceptions allowing Germany to withhold portability of these pensions. The Court thus had to decide on the legality of the regulation. Germany defended the exception arguing that pensions to persons having been employed in territories no longer belonging to Germany after World War II were only granted in order to facilitate integration of refugees into German society and that the migration of these refugees to other Member States would frustrate this aim. However, the Court did not accept this, relying on the regulation's purpose to give effect to free movement of workers.[217] This purpose did not allow including obstacles for free movement. This reasoning seems to resonate with the idea that integration into one Member State is not complete without granting its citizens the right to free movement throughout the European Union.

The *Cuyper* case[218] concerned the portability of unemployment benefits to older long-term unemployed persons who – like Mr Cuyper – were exempted from the obligation to seek work. Regulation 1408/71/EEC provided for portability of unemployment benefits only for those still actively seeking work. Mr Cuyper, who had moved from Belgium to France, was denied his Belgian unemployment benefit and tried to rely on his Treaty rights. The Court decided the case on the basis of his free movement rights as a non-economically active EU citizen (Article 21 TFEU). Spectacularly, the Court established that an EU citizen's right to reside in a country other than that of his origin must not be infringed in principle,[219] thus recognising the potential of citizenship to protect against non-discriminatory restrictions[220] and potentially approximating citizenship rights to those rights derived from economic freedoms. This did not help Mr Cuyper, because the Court maintained the doctrine of conditionality of free movement rights under EU citizenship. Accordingly, the need to 'monitor the employment and family situation of unemployed persons' justified the restriction of Mr Cuyper's free movement.[221]

Lastly, the Court also found that tax credits for pension fund contributions constituted a social advantage. Thus, Denmark infringed the Treaty by only granting credit for contributions to institutions domiciled in Denmark:[222] the Court found that withholding the advantage from employees who had

---

217 Paragraph 78 of the judgment.

218 Case C-406/04 *De Cuyper* [2006] ECR I-6947.

219 Paragraphs 35–36 of the judgment; more explicitly paragraphs 104–111 of AG Geelhoed's opinion. This was first developed in the *Pusa* case, decided by the 5th Chamber (case C-224/04 *Pusa* [2004] ECR I-5763), building on the *D'Hoop* case, decided prior to the creation of EU citizenship (Case C-224/98 *D'Hoop* [2002] ECR I-4509).

220 Barnard C., 2010, pp. 449–452.

221 Paragraphs 41–47 of the *De Cuyper* judgment.

222 Case C-150/04 [2007] ECR I-1163.

migrated and wished to maintain their former pension fund might deter citizens from moving freely. It also held that the rule could not be justified by prevention of tax avoidance and the coherence of the tax system.

This case law is based on a preference for former workers as pensioners over unemployed workers,[223] who are in a better position than free movers who are not economically active. The case law on family benefits seems to arbitrarily distinguish between working mothers and fathers and also the distinction between the Wajong and a tax credit for children's maintenance does not seem convincing. Protection of social rights for free movers is thus only granted in an incoherent fashion.

(b) RESIDENCE AND MIGRATION RIGHTS Social integration of free movers into a host state first and foremost requires secure residence rights and rights to access the employment markets. Accordingly, migration rights have always been an important element of free movement of workers, leading to seven Grand Chamber rulings since 2004.

In five of these the Court expanded the migration rights of workers' or citizens' family members from non-EU member states. The *Jia* case[224] challenged Swedish immigration law: Mrs Jia, the Chinese mother-in-law of a German migrant establishing herself in Denmark, applied for permanent residence while on a visitor visa because of the financial hardship she was experiencing in China. The Court expanded its former case law[225] in holding that the moral obligation towards a family member in financial hardship is sufficient to establish derived residence rights even in the absence of any legal obligation to support the family member, and in confirming that it is sufficient for a migrant to be legally in the host country (rather than residing legally) when she applies for residence. This rather formal logic was complemented by more substantive arguments in the *Eind* case,[226] concerning derived residence rights of Mr Eind's daughter of Surinamese nationality after his re-migration from the UK to his native country, the Netherlands. The Dutch authorities wanted to expel Ms Eind, because her father was unable to work for health reasons and could not provide for her. The Court relied on a combination of Mr Eind's right to move freely as a non-economically active EU citizen (now Article 21 TFEU) and his former worker status, stressing that the prospect of being unable to re-migrate might deter a worker from migrating and thus

223 As long as they do not actively seek work, see Case C-292/89 *Antonissen* [1991] ECR I-745, paragraph 21.

224 Case C-1/05 *Jia* [2007] ECR I-1.

225 Case C-109/01 *Akrich* [2003] ECR I-9607, C-459/99 *MRAX* [2002] ECR I-6591.

226 Case C-291/05 *Eind* [2007] ECR I-10719.

infringe Article 45 TFEU. This further strengthened migrant workers' rights to a functional family life.[227] The *Metock* case[228] continued this line of case law, now explicitly rejecting the 'prior lawful residence requirement'.[229] The four claimants were all third-country nationals whose application for asylum in Ireland had been rejected and who had married migrant EU citizens. As asylum applicants they had not been lawfully resident, but only had a right to remain. All but one of the EU citizens were workers. The Court argued that 'if Union citizens were not allowed to lead a normal family life in the host Member State the exercise of the freedoms they are guaranteed by the Treaty would be seriously obstructed',[230] adding that this contributes to realising the internal market.[231] This suggests that even rights of non-economically active EU citizens are ultimately derived from economic objectives.

Two cases on inner-EU migrants[232] finally confirmed that parents may derive rights from their children's residence rights under EU law and that migrant workers' children must be granted the right to continue their education after following their parent, even after that parent has left the country or ceased to care for his child. Again, the rationale behind this was that the prospect of detriment to their children's education in the host country would give workers 'far less incentive' to exercise their rights to migrate to other countries.[233] The Court carefully distinguished rights of parents to remain with underage children in education, which derived from their former workers' status, from rights of non-economically active parents under Directive 2004/38,[234] thus indicating that 'mere' citizenship rights are weaker.

Finally, two rulings confirmed conditional residence rights of citizens who were threatened by extradition under European arrest warrants. The *Kozlowski* case[235] concerned a Polish citizen living in Germany for a period of a little more than two years, when a Polish court issued a European arrest warrant for the enforcement of five months' imprisonment. Mr Kozlowski, who had earned his living from a mixture of building work and petty crime while in Germany, was in a German prison at the time, where he would have preferred to remain. One of the questions before the Court was whether EU citizens' right to equal treatment (Article 18 TFEU) requires Member States to allow

---

227 See also case *MRAX*, above, note 225.
228 Case C-127/08 *Metock et al.* [2008] ECR I-6241.
229 Paragraph 58.
230 Paragraph 62.
231 Paragraph 68.
232 Cases C-480/08 *Teixeira* [2010] ECR I-1107, C-310/08 *Ibrahim* [2010] ECR I-1065. See on those O'Brien, 2011.
233 Paragraphs 40, 44.
234 Paragraphs 46, 52.
235 Case C-66/08 *Kozlowski* [2008] ECR I-6041.

foreign EU nationals to choose whether to be extradited, if their own citizens have that choice. In substance, the case turned on the interpretation of the term 'staying' in the European Arrest Warrant Framework Decision. While the Court acknowledged the right to equal treatment, it did not interpret the term progressively in the light of this, finding that Mr Kozlowski was not staying in Germany and not entitled to equal treatment. Mr Wolzenburg,[236] a German citizen residing in the Netherlands, was more successful in a similar situation. When Germany required his extradition in order to serve a sentence, he had already been legally resident in the Netherlands for five years and had applied for naturalisation, but had omitted to apply for a permanent residence permit. Dutch rules would only have given him the option to resist extradition (and serve the sentence in the Netherlands) had he been permanently resident. Here, the Court held that the claimant was resident in the Netherlands, which again was a result of him making use of his right to free movement under Article 21 TFEU. Accordingly he could rely on Article 18 TFEU in order to be treated equally with Netherlands nationals as regarded extradition.

(c) ACCESS TO INSTITUTIONS OFFERING SOCIAL SERVICES Social integration of citizens across the EU is also aided by gaining access to institutions offering services such as social security, education and health care. No fewer than ten cases related to this, based on free movement of workers, freedom to receive services and citizenship rights respectively.

(i) Free movement of workers A seemingly internal Belgian case concerned access to a Flemish public care insurance scheme, which was compulsory for persons residing in the Flemish-speaking regions of Belgium, voluntary for persons residing in the bilingual region of Brussels and did not admit persons residing in the French-speaking regions. While the Court conceded that this legislation would only have limited transborder effects, it found that it was 'not inconceivable, given such factors as the ageing of the population, that the prospect of being able or unable to receive dependency benefits [...] should be taken into consideration by the persons [...] exercising their freedom of movement'.[237] Accordingly, the Court applied an extremely wide notion of transnational effects of this Belgian legislation. Once it was stated that access to this scheme was imperative to the realisation of free movement rights, it was held that the exclusion of residents in some regions of Belgium infringed EU law.

236 Case C-123/08 *Wolzenburg* [2009] ECR I-9621.

237 Case C-212/06 *Gouvernement de la Communauté française and gouvernement wallon* [2008] ECR I-1683, Paragraph 53.

(ii) Recipients of services Recipients of services have been covered by freedom to provide services from the 1980s,[238] thus converting Article 56 TFEU into a potential charter for consumer rights.[239] The Court's tendency to declare public services as provided for remuneration also meant that it confirmed rights of access of citizens to these public services relying on economic freedoms, here Article 56 TFEU.

This has long been apparent in the health care sector, where a long line of cases established that health care services, although provided through public insurance, constituted commercial services under Article 56 TFEU and that Member States must fund treatment of their citizens covered by any public health scheme abroad in principle, even beyond the provisions of Regulation 1408/71.[240] The Court had also accepted a number of justifications to restrict cross-border reception of services, including the need to maintain a balanced medical and hospital service open to all.[241] Four Grand Chamber rulings expanded and consolidated this case law.

The *Elchinov* case[242] revisited, against a drastic factual background, the question to what extent EU citizens can rely on having the best-available treatment at EU level reimbursed: Mr Elchinov, covered by the Bulgarian compulsory public health scheme, suffered from a malignoma in the right eye. In Bulgaria, only radical treatment by removing the eye was available. His doctor recommended restorative treatment by proton therapy in a specialist hospital in Berlin, which would retain the eye. While his application for treatment in Germany was pending, Mr Elchinov's condition deteriorated to such a degree that he was immediately admitted to and treated in the specialist hospital after travelling to Berlin, as the doctors found that any further waiting would jeopardize the treatment's success. The Bulgarian health fund rejected reimbursement of the treatment on the grounds that adequate treatment was available in Bulgaria and that reimbursement without advance authorisation of the

---

238 See above p. 148 with note 195.

239 Early cases concerned going abroad for acquiring privately funded health care (joined cases 286/82 and 26/83 *Luisi* [1984] ECR 377), travelling on the Paris Metro (C-186/87 *Cowan* [1989] ECR 195) and being a tourist (C-348/97 *Calfa* [1999] ECR I-11, C-215/03 *Oulane* [2005] ECR I-1215).

240 On the successor of this regulation see Chapter 3, II, p. 97, note 115.

241 Relevant earlier case law included case C-158/96 *Kohll* [1998] ECR I-1931, C-368/98 *Vanbraekel* [2001] ECR I-5363, C-157/99 *Smits and Peerbooms* [2001] ECR I-5473 and C-385/99 *Müller-Faure* and *Riet* [2003] ECR I-4509, see further Baquero Cruz, 2011.

242 Case C-173/09 *Elchinov* 5 October 2010 (nyr); this was the only case on a conflict between a new Member State and one of its citizens in the field of economic freedoms. The Court also answered some questions on the reference procedure (paragraphs 26–32), which are not of interest here.

treatment was not an option. The Court held that excluding reimbursement categorically in cases such as Elchinov's was a disproportionate restriction of freedom to receive services, but decided on the extent to which reimbursement must be made available on the basis of Regulation 1408/71 exclusively, aided by proportionality. It held that radical treatment was not adequate in this situation as restorative treatment was available, avoiding the need to base its decision on Article 56 TFEU[243] or the right to preventive health care (Article 35 Charter of Fundamental Rights for the EU) in addition. The case, as well, thus confirmed rights to public healthcare abroad in transborder cases involving the poorest and the richest EU Member States.

The *Watts* case[244] concerned hospital treatment under the English National Health Service (NHS): Yvonne Watts was told initially to wait for 12 months (until October 2003) for a hip replacement to cure her arthritis and then, subsequently, 'only' until May 2003. Following deterioration of her health and exhausted by constant pain, she had a hip replacement in France in March 2003 and applied to the NHS for reimbursement of about £3900. Judicial review of the refusal to reimburse led to a referral to the Court of Justice.

One question concerned whether the Court would expand the reach of the freedom to receive services in the direction of an entirely public health care system, although only services provided for remuneration (Article 57 TFEU) are within its scope of application. So far, the Court had addressed systems where patients paid for their health care up front and claimed reimbursement[245] and where healthcare was provided in kind on the basis of contracts between independent hospitals and doctors and health insurance providers financed by employees' contributions.[246] When *Watts* was referred to the Court, there was no contractual element in the provision of health under the NHS system, which was entirely public.[247] This suggested that Mrs Watts' case was beyond the reach of Article 56, 57 TFEU – in the same way as public education.[248] However, the Court focused on the relationship between Mrs Watts and the French hospital, which was contractual and seemed to involve

243 AG Cruz Villalon proposed to base the judgment on Article 56, which would preclude a narrow interpretation of Regulation 1408/71 (paragraph 44).

244 Case C-372/04 *Watts* [2006] ECR I-4325.

245 As under the Belgian and French system, see case *Kohll* above, note 241.

246 Case *Vanbraekel*, above note 241. Such triangular situations, where the party receiving the service is not the one paying for it, have long been held to be within the scope of application of Article 56 TFEU (first in case 52/79 *Debauve* [1980] ECR 833, 62/79); explicit for the health care sector in case *Smits & Peerbooms*, above note 241, paragraph 56).

247 See on the subsequent contractualisation of the English NHS Vincent-Jones and Hughes, 2008.

248 Case 263/86 *Humbel* [1988] ECR 5365, paragraphs 18, 19.

the exchange of a service against remuneration. The Court disregarded the fact that Mrs Watts would have been unable to obtain reimbursement for private hospital treatment on a contractual base in the UK as well. Thus, the Court should have explained why the situation changes because private hospital treatment takes place in France.[249] Without any explanation, the NHS was classed as offering services in return for remuneration, and the Court confirmed this qualification in relation to the Spanish health care system as well, under which the constitutional right to health care is also fulfilled in a fully state run system.[250]

The next question was whether the NHS's refusal to reimburse Mrs Watts' private treatment abroad qualified as a restriction of freedom to provide services. The Court repeated that Article 56 TFEU 'precluded the application of any national rules which have the effect of making the provision of services between Member States more difficult than the provision of services purely within a Member State'.[251] Interestingly, the service recipient Mrs Watts vanished from the picture, to be replaced by health care providers.[252] On this basis, the refusal to reimburse private treatment abroad was classed as a restriction. The NHS prevailed on justification of its refusal: it was able to rely on the objectives of mitigating the risk of seriously undermining the financial balance of a social security system, and of maintaining a balanced medical and hospital service open to all and of retaining sufficient treatment capacity and medical competence on national territory,[253] subject to proportionality, of course. In principle, hospital treatment abroad – as well as treatment outside hospitals with major medical equipment[254] – can be subjected to a requirement of prior authorisation, as long as it is based on objective, non-discriminatory criteria known in advance and the individual disposition of each patient is taken into account. The final decision in *Watts* was left to the national court.

In the subsequent case *COM v Spain*,[255] the Court seemed to retrace its

---

249 For a critical assessment see Baquero Cruz, 2011, pp. 88–89 and Spaventa, 2007, pp. 56–58 and AG Stix-Hackl, Opinion *in Gootjes-Schwartz* (below note 258), paragraph 39, stressing that this approach would effectively oblige Member States to commercialize all public services. AG Geelhoed had defended the equation of a public health care system with health care provided by private hospitals by stating that it should be unwise to create different categories of health services in the internal market.

250 Case C-211/08 *COM v Spain* [2010] ECR I-2947.

251 Case *Watts* paragraph 94 with further references to other health cases.

252 In the *Elchinov* case (above note 242), the Court clarified that freedom to provide and receive services protects both patients and service providers (paragraph 44).

253 Paragraphs 103–105 of the judgment.

254 See case C-512/08 *COM v France* 5 October 2010 (nyr).

255 *COM v Spain* note 250.

steps slightly. A French migrant worker resident in Spain and covered by the public health care system there underwent unplanned hospital treatment while temporarily in France, instead of returning to Spain and his local hospital. According to Spanish law and Regulation 1408/71, in non-urgent cases the patient should be in the same situation as if he were resident in France, which meant that he had to pay a 'ticket modérateur' of less than 300 €. Here, the Court found no infringement of freedom to provide and receive services, because such unplanned treatment was not foreseeable and the lack of full reimbursement would not deter anyone from seeking treatment abroad.[256]

The Court has now also extended the freedom to receive services to charity-run primary schools, thus distinguishing them from public education institutions.[257] Two cases decided on the same day referred to German tax credits for school fees. The *Grootjes-Schwartz* case[258] concerned a married couple living comfortably off their wealth in Germany, whose children attended an expensive Scottish school that specialised in educating above-average intelligence children. The parents claimed a tax credit of about 5000 € annually per child, which corresponded to the full school fees. However, the tax credit for school fees presupposed that the schools were approved by German authorities and it was capped at 30% of the fees actually paid. The Court qualified the charity education as a service provided for remuneration, because it was neither predominantly funded by the state nor offered as part of the public education system.[259] The disadvantage for parents wishing to have their children educated in private schools abroad was held to constitute a restriction of the freedom to receive transborder services. In the parallel judgment in an infringement procedure against Germany,[260] the Court also considered freedom of establishment and free movement of workers in this respect, but did not apply Articles 20–21 TFEU, as the economic freedoms take precedence as *lex specialis*.[261] In order to justify its legislation, Germany relied on republican principles for school education: while allowing and funding private schools in order to cater for a variety of religious and ethical orientations of parents, legislation should ensure that children were not fully segregated according to their parents' wealth in (primary) schools. This was pursued by subjecting all schools to public accreditation, and by requiring private schools

256 See for a similar logic cases C-69/88 *Kranz* [1990] ECR I-582 (paragraph 11) and C-190/98 *Graf* [2000] ECR I-493 (paragraphs 24–25), on free movement of goods and workers respectively.

257 See above, note 248.

258 Case C-76/05 *Schwartz & Grootjes-Schwartz* [2007] ECR I-7001.

259 Paragraphs 30, 40–42.

260 Case C-318/05 *COM v Germany* (non-state schools) [2007] ECR I-6957.

261 Paragraph 32, this was held against the claim made by the EU Commission.

to offer a minimum number of subsidised places and not to exceed a maximum fee. Tax credit for school fees was seen as part of the state subsidy, which should only be granted to accredited schools bound by these rules. The Court, in rejecting this justification,[262] maintained that such values were unsuitable for justifying any restriction of economic freedoms, although they are related to educational, cultural and also to social policies where EU competences are minimal.

(iii) Citizenship rights By contrast to public health care and charity schools, higher education is still framed as a state service, to which access can mainly be claimed on the basis of citizenship right, as confirmed by three Grand Chamber rulings.

The *Förster* case[263] closed a string of cases involving migrant students claiming a student-related benefit from or in Member States other than their country of origin. The Court had established that a 'certain degree of solidarity'[264] is due to citizens of other Member States, although this could be limited by requiring a certain degree of integration in the host state, on a case-by-case assessment.[265] In the *Förster* case, a German student at a Dutch university, who had settled in the Netherlands and married a Dutchman, and whose employment had been terminated due to the tight labour market, challenged the refusal of the Netherlands to refund her study fees, as had been the case while she was still employed. The Netherlands provides refunds of study fees and an income-related grant as a combined student support system. This is paid to other EU citizens if qualifying as workers or workers' dependants, but only to economically inactive EU citizens after they had been lawfully resident for five years. This schematic criterion was now, against the opinion of AG Mazak, held to be justified. Questions can be raised as to why the receipt of education was not a service, just as the receipt of health care, and why, as a worker who had recently been dismissed, Ms Förster was not classed as a worker under Article 45 TFEU. Had she been within the reach of an economic freedom, her unequal treatment with Dutch students would have been more difficult to justify.

In the *Morgan and Bucher* case,[266] two German citizens pursued their rights to obtain the German study grants for studying abroad, having enrolled in courses not offered by German universities in the Netherlands and the UK respectively. The German student allowance only covers studying abroad

262 Paragraphs 75–82, see further Chapter 1, p. 34.

263 Case C-158/07 *Förster* [2008] ECR I-8507.

264 See Chapter 3, note 124.

265 Case *Bidar* Chapter 3, note 122.

266 Case C-11/06 *Morgan and Bucher* [2007] ECR I-9161.

under certain conditions, which the two claimants did not meet. As in the portability cases, the students made a claim against their own Member State, trying to rely on the free movement aspects of citizenship. The Court held that the restrictions were likely to deter German citizens from studying abroad, which would constitute a restriction of free movement rights under Article 21 TFEU. The Court also went on to consider whether this restriction was justified 'based on objective considerations of the public interest independent of the nationality of the persons concerned', which also required the restriction to be proportionate to the aim pursued. The Court allowed Member States to rely on the need to avoid 'studies in (other Member States) from becoming an unreasonable burden',[267] but in this case the Court found that less intrusive measures than those chosen were possible.

The *Bressol*[268] case concerned a combination of access to university and protection of public health and was also decided on the basis of EU citizenship. Due to the principle of free access to university education in the French-speaking parts of Belgium, which contrasts with high entry thresholds in France, Belgian universities found themselves swamped with French students in medical and paramedical subjects.[269] To remedy this, the government of the French-speaking region of Belgium required universities to limit the number of non-resident students in medical and paramedical subjects. The claimants, students and lecturers alike, challenged the validity of the decree before the Belgian Constitutional Court which referred questions to the Court of Justice. As regards EU citizens' rights to free movement and equal treatment (Articles 21 and 18 TFEU), the Court found the residence requirement central to the decree to be indirectly discriminatory, if not justified by a legitimate objective for the achievement of which the policy is appropriate and proportionate. The Court mainly discussed justifications, relying on the specific objective of 'maintaining a balanced high-quality medical service open to all',[270] thus evading any consideration of maintaining a viable public higher education sector in general. The final decision and the evaluation of this evidence, was, however, left to the national court.

The case law based on reception of services obliges Member States not only to open social institutions to citizens of other Member States, as in the Wallonian case, but also to enable citizens to use social services abroad, as in the health care and primary school case, effectively requiring Member States

---

267 Paragraphs 42, 35–39 of the judgment.

268 Case C-73/08 *Bressol et al.* [2010] ECR I-2735.

269 See opinion of AG Sharpstone paragraphs 22–24. A similar problem between Germany and Austria has led to infringement proceedings, which Austria lost (Case C-147/03 *COM v Austria* [2005] ECR I-5969).

270 Paragraph 62.

to provide a certain form of social integration. These rights are attractive to the European cosmopolitan citizen, who uses services abroad and perhaps engages in a bit of social tourism. While these principles can have negative effects on social budgets nationally,[271] they certainly add a social leg to economic freedoms, which convert into rights to participate in (or profit from) social institutions provided in other Member States. Partly, similar rights can be derived from EU citizenship, although rights to support for study fees proved weaker here.

(2) *Explicit positive duties* The case law above has already demonstrated that the Court, in protecting free movement rights of workers, service recipients and citizens, is not content with only defending their rights against infringements by Member States by preventing Member States from interfering positively. The cases on residence rights of workers and former workers lend themselves to implying positive duties of Member States to aid actual enjoyment of free movement rights. In three cases on citizenship the Court went further in establishing positive duties to further the actual enjoyment of citizenship rights, and in two cases social rights were hinted at.

In the *Grunkin-Paul* case,[272] the Court in effect required Germany to provide conditions for integrating a child with a multinational identity, without explicitly spelling out positive rights. The German child Leonard was born to two Germans residing in Denmark and registered under a name combining the names of both his parents in Copenhagen as Leonard Grunkin-Paul. In Germany, a child can only be registered with one of its parents' names. Accordingly, Leonard would have been registered under a different name in Germany than in Denmark. While not finding this discriminatory, the Court considered that having to use two surnames would be an inconvenience for young Leonard, sufficiently severe to qualify as an obstacle to his free movement within the EU.

The Court quoted its *Rottmann* ruling[273] as first establishing an obligation for Member States to safeguard the 'genuine enjoyment of the substance of rights conferred by' EU citizenship.[274] This case concerned the question whether Germany was barred from withdrawing German citizenship from Mr Rottmann because he had fraudulently concealed a serious criminal conviction when acquiring German citizenship after migrating from Austria, which German authorities only learned about from a European Arrest Warrant issued

---

[271] Deftly summarised in the heading '*Killing national health and insurance systems but healing patients?*' (Hatzopoulos, 2002).

[272] Case C-353/06 [2008] ECR I-7639.

[273] Case C-135/08 *Rottmann* [2010] ECR I-1449.

[274] Case C-34/09 *Ruiz Zambrano* 8 March 2011 (nyr) paragraph 42.

by Austria. As Rottmann had lost his Austrian citizenship upon naturalisation, the withdrawal would have left him stateless and without EU citizenship as well. A German court referred the question of whether this consequence was commensurate with EU citizenship. The Court held that the matter fell within the scope of application of EU law and that a Member State had to observe the principle of proportionality under EU law, leaving the final decision to the national court.

The youngest citizenship case[275] concerned residence rights of Colombian citizens in Belgium, whose children had Belgian nationality. The parents had come to Belgium as applicants for asylum and refugee status in 1999 and 2000 respectively. Upon rejecting their applications, Belgium was barred from expelling them because of the insecure situation in Colombia. After settling in Schaerbeek, the Zambrano parents had two more children, born in 2003 and 2005, who acquired Belgian citizenship. Mr Ruiz Zambrano was subsequently issued with a deportation order because he was working without a work permit and was claiming unemployment benefits. A Belgian court referred a number of questions to the Court of Justice, mainly concerning derived residence rights for parents whose young children were EU citizens, based on Articles 18, 20 and 21 TFEU and 21, 24 and 34 of the Charter of Fundamental Rights. In a remarkably brief decision, the Grand Chamber held that the children could rely on citizenship rights, although they had never moved away from Belgium and were unlikely to do so in the near future, being aged 6 and 4 respectively when the case was referred to the Court of Justice. The Court derived from Article 20 TFEU that, while it institutes EU citizenship as the fundamental status of nationals of the EU Member States, it 'precludes measures which have the effect of depriving citizens [...] of the genuine enjoyment of the substance of' citizenship rights.[276] Here, the Court has certainly established a positive duty of Member States to not only grant the children's parents residence, but also to grant their father a work permit in order to allow him to provide for them.

The general idea that Member States are under a positive duty to ensure the enjoyment of rights surely lends itself to a much wider array of rights being granted. Here, two EU citizens who were not yet economically active and had never used their free movement rights profited from it.

The Court has also occasionally supported positive obligations of Member States to support and protect original social rights. In the *Adelener* case[277] this concerned rights relating to fixed-term employment contracts (Directive

---

275 Case C-34/09 *Ruiz Zambrano* 8 March 2011 (nyr).

276 Paragraph 41, with reference to the *Rottmann* case.

277 Case C-212/04 *Adeneler et al.* [2006] ECR I-6037 (usually discussed for effects of directives, though).

1999/70). The Court derived the social right to an indefinite employment contract from the aims of the directive and from general principles of EU law, from which deviations could only be made in exceptional circumstances. Similarly, in the *Schultz Hoff* case,[278] on the interpretation of provisions relating to annual leave contained in Directive 2003/88, the Court derived a social right of workers to leisure from Article 32 of the Charter of Fundamental Rights for the European Union and ILO convention number 132. These two cases are cautious steps towards obliging Member States to safeguard social rights in the economic sphere, with potential effects on horizontal relationships such as the employment relationship.

*(3) Horizontal direct effect* Cases on horizontal effects of rights could support a socially embedded notion of constitutionalism in so far as rights protection is expanded beyond the state–citizenship relationship. However, this would only be the case if horizontal rights protection were actually to contribute to enhanced enjoyment of rights.

(a) ECONOMIC FREEDOMS As regards horizontal effects of economic freedoms, this is not necessarily the case. It may well protect parties that are able to impose their preferences in a horizontal relationship due to their socio-economic superiority and may thus not need the protection of the law or the courts in order to actually enjoy their rights. If they can still use courts to further enhance their position, the effect may rather disturb the social embedding of constitutionalism, which should enable the inferior party actually to enjoy their rights in reality. While in the cases referenced for this above,[279] horizontal effects of economic freedoms worked to the advantage of the inferior party, this is not always the case. For example, during the reference period, two particularly contentious cases relating to industrial action resulted in protecting employers against workers and their trade unions. The two other cases concerning horizontal relations originated from the application of competition law rules on two competing not-for-profit associations and from applying free movement of workers in the unbalanced relationship between an individual sportsman and his employer governed by unilaterally decreed rules of sports associations.

The first cases decided in the reference period in the same month were the particularly contentious cases *Laval* and *Viking*.[280] Both cases involved

278 Case C-350, 520/06 *Schultz-Hoff et al.* [2009] ECR I-179.

279 Chapter 3, II, pp. 90–92.

280 Cases C-341/05 *Laval* [2007] I-11767 and C-438/05 *International Transport Workers Federation v Viking* (hereafter referred to as *Viking*) [2007] I-10779. Cases

employers relying on economic freedoms to provide services (*Laval*) or to choose the wage regime most suitable to them via freedom of establishment (*Viking*) against activities of trade unions.

As may be recalled,[281] the *Laval* case evolved around the hiring out of Latvian workers by the Latvian company Laval to its Swedish subsidiary and the industrial conflict resulting from the refusal of Laval to negotiate wages with Swedish trade unions. As regards horizontal effects of economic freedoms, the case turned around the question whether the collective sympathy action taken by the Swedish electricians' union in support of the building workers' union infringed Laval's freedom to provide services. This case is difficult to comprehend due to the relevance of Directive 96/71/EEC on posting of workers alongside freedom to provide services (Article 56 TFEU). As the Court has repeatedly rejected horizontal effects of directives,[282] any horizontal effects could only be relevant in the framework of Article 56 TFEU. AG Mengozzi was acutely aware of this, and relied on Article 56 TFEU being directly applicable in this case (paragraph 155). While the Court did not waste any argument on this, Mengozzi stressed that Directive 96/71 constitutes only an interpretation of Article 56 TFEU (paragraph 145), which of course meant that the Treaty norm continues to apply to situations governed by Directive 96/71 alongside the directive. Accordingly, the doctrine of horizontal effects of economic freedoms could be applied to the *Laval* case.

The *Viking* case was less complex in that no directive was involved. It concerned a company (Viking) owning several ferries that wished to reflag a vessel named Rosella from Finland to Estonia. The main purpose was to enable Viking to negotiate collective agreements with Estonian trade unions under Estonian law, which typically have lower wages than collective agreements with Finnish trade unions under Finnish law. Before Estonia became an EU member, the following actions occurred: on request by the Finnish Seafarer Union (FSU), who did not agree with the policy of lowering wages on board the vessel, the International Transport Workers Federation (ITF) sent out a circular by e-mail to all its members, stating that no one (including the Estonian seafarer union) should enter into collective bargaining with Viking over the Rosella crew. As this circular was complied with and the FSU threatened strike action, Viking gave an undertaking to refrain from reflagging until

C-346/06 *Rüffert* [2008] ECR I- and C-319/06 *COM v Luxembourg* [2008] ECR I-4323, which are frequently analysed in context with those, as they also illustrate the Court's misinformation on collective labour law and industrial action, were not decided by the Grand Chamber and are thus beyond the scope of this chapter.

281 For an extended report of the facts see above pp. 133–134.

282 This was first established in the case 152/84 *Marshall* [1986] ECR 723, confirmed in case C-91/92 *Faccini Dori* [1994] ECR I-3325 and has been maintained ever since. For a summary of academic critique see Witte, 2011, pp. 335–336.

the end of February 2005. The FSU had initially opposed the reflagging as such, but settled in the course of negotiations for the demand that the employer should continue to conclude collective agreements with them. The employer had given in to the demand of the trade union to not reduce staff levels below a certain threshold for security reasons. Once Estonia had joined the EU, the employer again pursued the reflagging agenda because the Rosella also still ran at a loss. Rather than waiting to see whether the FSU would again take recourse to collective action, the employer took the industrial conflicts to the courts. On 18 August 2004, three months after Estonia's accession to the EU, Viking sought declaratory and injunctive relief against the ITF, domiciled in London, before the Commercial Court in London. The application required ITF to withdraw the circular and the FSU to refrain from collective industrial action over future reflagging. The Court of Appeal referred the case to the Court of Justice, seeking clarification, amongst other things, on whether freedom of establishment applied to reflagging of vessels and was horizontally effective between trade unions and employers, and whether the action by the ITF and FSU would represent an unjustifiable restriction of that freedom.

Thus, a common element of both cases was the question of whether horizontal effects of economic freedoms encompassed actions by trade unions aiming at achieving collective agreements. This required some further development of the doctrine. As explained above,[283] horizontal effects of economic freedoms were so far only accorded to either contractual or unilateral regulatory frameworks, while state obligations to protect the *effet utile* of free movement of goods were relevant for disruptive activities by non-state actors. In *Laval* and *Viking*, the Court aimed at merging the two: the activities of the Swedish trade union left the workers hired out by a Latvian to a Swedish company to work on a building site in north Sweden in early December without electricity and thus without light and heating. The employers did not engage in equally effective ways of industrial action, and the facts of the case do not reveal whether they actually attempted to do so. A mediation meeting is mentioned, during which Laval could have signed a collective agreement with the effect of putting an immediate end to collective action, while the exact amount of wages to be paid to the Latvian workers would have been an issue under negotiation.[284] The employer decided instead for litigation (which was funded by the Swedish employers' association)[285] and applied for a court order that the industrial action should cease. Similarly, in *Viking* the employers preferred to use court proceedings over engaging in industrial action or collective bargaining, without attempting to achieve an agreement first. It is

283 Chapter 3, II, pp. 90–92.
284 Paragraph 36 of the judgment.
285 See above note 109 (p. 134).

open to doubt whether the specific actions by the specific trade unions constituted a restriction of the economic freedoms.

In *Laval*, the Court did not make any deliberations on this. It only referred to its former case law, according to which 'rules which are not public' must also be bound by the freedom to provide services if that right is not to be compromised,[286] and stated that the threat of collective action to convince an employer to sign a collective agreement is no different from the actual conclusion of such an agreement.[287] AG Mengozzi, by contrast, had allowed ten paragraphs to explore the question.[288] His decisive argument seemed to be that the Swedish company under siege by Swedish trade unions could only have avoided the consequences of sending the hired workers home by signing a collective agreement[289] and accordingly by an action which would have had the same economic effect as if the Member State, in this case Sweden, had imposed a statutory minimum wage on the hired-out workers.[290] Had the Court taken up this argument, this would have resulted in a contradictory judgment: after all, the Court found it particularly outrageous that the Swedish trade unions would not agree on a fixed minimum wage, but insisted on wages which varied with qualification and exposure to demanding working conditions.[291] Thus, in *Laval* there is no convincing explanation why the Court found the collective action had a restrictive effect on Laval. After all, Laval could have avoided all the negative effects had it accepted an agreement that required negotiating appropriate wages.

In *Viking*, the Court was a little more precise, stating that collective industrial action was capable of constituting an obstacle to freedom of establishment only if and in so far as it has to be seen as 'inextricably linked' to the conclusion of a collective agreement.[292] It is not clear whether the Court has thought this through fully. If the consequential collective agreement was really the source of the restriction, interesting constellations could emerge in Member States where the right to strike is granted independently from concluding a collective agreement or where collective agreements are not legally binding and thus no regulatory instruments.[293] Thus, were a trade union merely to threaten to strike any time the employer threatened transnational relocation,

---

286 Paragraph 98.
287 Paragraph 99.
288 Paragraphs 230–240.
289 Paragraph 235.
290 Paragraph 236, a rather loose link to previous case law (Dashwood, 2007–2008, p. 535).
291 Paragraphs 69, 70, 110.
292 Paragraph 36, 60.
293 This last argument is used by Dashwood, above note 290, in order to exempt the UK system from the *Viking* and *Laval* logic, although he is not optimistic.

while explicitly refusing to enter into negotiations for an agreement to alleviate the consequences of relocation, this would not constitute a restriction under this logic. However, possibly this is not what the Court meant to say. Neither the Court nor the AG considered what exactly established a restriction in the *Viking* case. The actions which induced Viking to refrain from relocating seem rather modest: the circulation of an e-mail by an international confederation of trade unions and the threat of the Finnish trade union to call for a strike. Of course it must be left to any employer as to whether it seeks conflict with the trade unions or prefers instead to steer a conciliatory course. However, it seems difficult to support the suggestion that these two acts qualify as 'private action that is capable of effectively restricting others from exercising their right to freedom of movement'.[294] Such a restriction might well have flowed from a collective agreement. However, an agreement is always the result of bargaining, a process during which both parties can make their influence felt.

Having found a restriction of the relevant economic freedom in both cases, the Court then proceeded to justification. As is well known, the Court did not hold collective action justifiable in any of these cases.[295] The human rights and democratic aspects of the cases are discussed below.[296]

The youngest case in the reference period revisited the horizontal effects of free movement of workers in the field of sports, now considering rules of a French sports association having been revised after the *Bosman* case.[297] The *Lyonnais* case, also known as the *Bernard* case,[298] concerns the fate of a young French footballer who migrated to the UK after finishing his initial three-year training contract with Olympique Lyonnais, who had offered him only a fixed-term contract of one year. Not content with the salary, he signed with Newcastle United, under a contract of undisclosed duration. Relying on the 'Charte du football professionnel' (Football Charter), his former employer sued Mr Bernard and Newcastle United for damages equivalent to a full annual salary. Under the Football Charter, Mr Bernard was prevented from working for another club for a full three years. However, his employer was not under any obligation to offer him employment for these three years. The Charter did not explicitly provide for damages, but the French labour court considered the claim as in principle justified under general rules of liability for breach of contract.

---

294 This is the threshold for a restriction by non-governmental actors established in AG Maduro's opinion to *Viking* at paragraph 43.

295 See below text between notes 443–450.

296 Parts II. 3, pp. 197–199 and III. 4. b), pp. 206–208.

297 Chapter 3, notes 31 (p. 84) and 69 (p. 90).

298 Case C-325/08 *Olympique Lyonnais v Bernard* [2010] ECR I-2177.

The Court considered the question of whether the rule in the Football Charter combined with the consequences regarding damages would infringe Article 45 TFEU. The Court first made clear that it treated this case as a horizontal case. It clarified very shortly that working conditions are frequently laid down by collective agreements or 'other acts concluded or adopted by private persons', and that thus Article 45 to be fully effective would have to have horizontal effect. The judgment and the opinion of AG Sharpstone mention that the Football Charter qualifies as a collective agreement under French law. It is, however, quite doubtful whether this qualification is correct.[299] The Court did not discuss these finer points, but proceeded immediately to the question of justification. Refining its *Bosman* ruling, it now held that the sports clubs' interest in receiving reimbursement for training costs is a legitimate one, which can in principle justify a restriction of free movement. However, the Court considered that the specific damages went over and above what was necessary to achieve this aim, and were thus not justified.

By their result, all three of these cases support employers' economic rights in horizontal relations – each time relying on the need to make economic freedoms efficient. Thus, the horizontal effect of economic freedoms was defended in order to reinforce the internal market, rather than to socially re-embed rights. This resulted in support for the position of employers and their associations – a position that is already characterised by relative strength, an imbalance which the institution of collective bargaining seeks to mitigate. Despite all effort to portray the trade unions as the only power decisive in industrial relations, these judgments cannot hide the fact that the social embedding of employees' rights via guarantees of rights to collective action is effectively dis-embedded in the name of transnational economic integration. In the first two cases, the requirements for establishing a restriction are lowered considerably. On the other hand, the last case revisited the practice of sports associations to issue unilateral conditions for employment contracts that leave players in the position of always being on a fixed-term position and also being restricted in international moves. Such practices are, after the initially courageous *Bosman* ruling in 1995, now relatively easy to justify.

(b) CONSUMER RIGHTS Finally, horizontal effects of EU consumer rights could contribute to socially embedded constitutionalism. Although usually created by directives, these ultimately aim to boost transnational consumption as a necessary corollary to free movement of goods and services – which is a pivotal element of the EU economic constitution. Horizontal effects of EU consumer rights can best be generated by regulations, such as Regulation

---

[299] See below pp. 205–206.

261/2004 establishing common rules on compensation and assistance to passengers in the event of denied boarding and of cancellation or long delay of flights. The International Air Transport Association (IATA) and European Low Fare Airline Association (ELFAA)[300] challenged this regulation, as they found compensation for flights cancelled with less than two weeks' notice and the provision of refreshments and accommodation in cases of excessive delays too costly. The Court upheld the regulation, in particular as it could not find disproportionate infringement of business rights by establishing these horizontal consumer rights.[301]

### e) Evaluation

From 2007, many authors have portrayed the Grand Chamber rulings in *Laval* and *Viking* as the ultimate evidence that the Court of Justice disrupts the social fabric of national societies[302] and has decoupled economic and social integration for good, making a social market economy impossible.[303] Some have added that these cases together with case law on free movement of companies signify a new phase, in which only liberal varieties of capitalism will gain the Court's approval.[304]

Looking at a wider variety of case law adjudicated by the Grand Chamber, the analysis above results in a more nuanced picture, where cases such as *Viking*, *Laval* and *Cartesio* leave strong impressions, but are not the only highlights. Over a number of socio-economic problems addressed several times, such as gambling and betting, taxation, organising the professions, health care, education and immigration and a broad spread of miscellaneous cases, we can observe some across-the-board tendencies but also quite a few contradictions, caused by cluster-specific developments as well as contradictions within clusters.

The strongest across-the-board tendency is the lowering of the threshold for the Court to find a restriction of any economic freedom. In a number of factual settings where it was quite difficult to recognise any transborder element,[305] the Court still found a restriction on the basis that the rule in question might hypothetically deter foreign providers from establishing or providing services.

---

300 Case C-344/04 *IATA and ELFAA* [2006] ECR I-403.

301 A Hungarian reference on the unfair terms of the directive's effect in horizontal relations (Case C-302/04 *Ynos kft* [2006]ECR I-371) was inadmissible because the conflict occurred before Hungary's accession.

302 E.g. Barnard, 2008, Joerges, 2011.

303 Scharpf, 2010.

304 Höpner and Schäfer, 2010.

305 See, for example, the cases *Blanco Pérez* (above note 60), *COM v Italy (Trailers)* (above note 38), *COM v Italy (motor insurance)* (above note 181) and *Gysbrecht* (above note 37).

The Court also merged non-discriminatory and discriminatory restrictions of economic freedom at times. In the *ČEZ* case[306] and the *Neukirchinger* case[307] it held that factual settings which usually would qualify as obstacles to transnational business activity also infringed the prohibition of nationality discrimination. While this may have been motivated by the fact that the Court found no economic freedom to be applicable, similar confusion occurred in tax cases, where some national rules were considered as obstacles to freedom of establishment on grounds of their discriminatory character.[308]

All this may indicate a future tendency to conflate economic freedoms and the prohibition of nationality discrimination into a general freedom to conduct one's business in the internal market.[309] If there is any new difficulty for Member States or societal actors in maintaining or establishing rules to support social integration, the danger emanates from this tendency, not from applying economic freedoms to collective agreements.[310]

The case law on the new freedom to conduct one's business in the internal market at will was contradictory in the range of justification allowed to Member States and the EU itself for restricting economic freedoms. Received wisdom held that only express derogations from economic freedoms are available for issuing discriminatory rules, while non-discriminatory obstacles trigger a wider range of justifications under the general public interest doctrine.[311] The rationale behind this is that discrimination between national economies combined into an internal market can only be tolerated if explicitly authorised, but that an internal market should not exclude diversity of national legal orders in order not to undermine competition between legal orders. This rationale is abandoned when the Grand Chamber allows Member States to rely on a general interest justification in relation to different treatment of resident and non-resident companies in the field of taxation,[312] but not in the field of labour law,[313] to name but one example.

More contradictions emerge in the breadth of discretion granted to different regulators and in different fields. First, under internal market rationales it may be defendable for the Court to allow a wider range of justification to the

---

[306] Above note 76.

[307] Above note 80.

[308] Case *Oy AA*, for example, above note 166.

[309] In line with this, the Court also derived a guarantee of the freedom of contract from the economic freedoms, see above p. 146 with note 183.

[310] Which also is not a new development at all, as shown in Chapter 3 (p. 90 with notes 68–71).

[311] See Chapter 3, pp. 85–86 with notes 41–43, for the rationale behind this.

[312] See above pp. 143–144 with notes 162–165 on the *Thin Cap Group Litigation*.

[313] See above. pp. 132–134 with notes 103–112 on the *Laval* case.

EU legislator[314] than to Member States. After all, EU legislation in favour of general interests does not distort the internal market, but rather creates equal conditions for all. However, if Member States are granted different levels of discretion in different socio-economic fields, this would be more difficult. Presently, no reason at all is offered for allowing a preference for professionalism of pharmacies (i.e. that pharmacies be headed by a professional pharmacist),[315] but not for outpatient dental clinics,[316] or for granting Member States wide discretion for legislation on road security,[317] taxation or gambling and betting monopolies,[318] but not in relation to consumer law[319] or planning of pharmacies.[320] This is less than convincing.

Intriguingly, the Court's case law on economic freedoms offers some support for socially embedded constitutionalism, albeit in unexpected ways.

While one usually expects horizontal effects of rights to work in favour of constitutionalising socio-economic spheres, the Court of Justice used the horizontal effects of economic freedoms to further strengthen the market position of actors who are already well able to fend for their own, over those whose market position can be considered structurally weaker. The *Viking, Laval* and *Bernard* rulings could thus support the view that the internal market gives preference to creating rights for international business rather than workers.

Interestingly, rights to receive social benefits and to profit from public social institutions effectively provided preconditions for non-possessing migrants to actually enjoy their free movement rights. The cases where the Court explicitly stated such positive duties partly even supported the mobility of poorer migrants and their children against fierce opposition from Member States.

Generally, this case law is also less contradictory, possibly due to the lower number of cases and fields: the Court retains an economic focus on EU citizenship in that the discretion of Member States is larger the farther a case on social rights moves away from the employment market or other markets. This also means that access to a social institution is less protected the farther this

---

314 See, for example, the *Natural Health Alliance* case (above note 27) and the *Schmelz* case (above note 93).

315 Cases *Apothekerkammer des Saarlandes* and *COM v Italy* (Pharmacies), above pp. 124–125 with notes 56, 57 and 59.

316 Case *Hartlauer*, above note 52.

317 Cases *COM v Italy (trailers)*, pp. 121–122 with notes 38–41 and *COM v Italy (motor insurance)* notes 181, 189.

318 Case *Markus Stoß*, above p. 139 with notes 137, 139, but see also case *Placania*, where no such discretion was allowed (note 135).

319 Case *Gysbrecht*, above note 37.

320 Case *Blanco Pérez*, above pp. 125–126 with note 60 (this case was decided in favour of the national rules, but on the basis of a strict proportionality test).

institution is moved away from the market. The Court has been selective in qualifying public services as services provided against remuneration: a state health care sector is a commercial service, but a state higher education sector is not. Accordingly, citizens can claim more rights in health care provision than in equal access to public universities.

## 2. Equality and non-discrimination before the Grand Chamber since 2004

### a) Notion and reach

The Court of Justice has promoted equality rights as 'part of the foundations'[321] of the EU from early on, partly referring to economic and social aims of European integration and partly to the human rights foundations of equal treatment and non-discrimination.

Equal treatment and non-discrimination as principles of the EU's judicial constitution thus straddle different fields of law. On the one hand, equality and non-discrimination are political missions characteristic for the EU not only in internal market law, but also in social law and policy.[322] This has been related to the fact that non-discrimination as a principle of social policy is best suited to a neo-liberal agenda[323] and to the necessity to combat national parochialism through EU legal integration.[324] On the other hand, they are elements of European human rights law. It is thus adequate to treat equality rights as a category in their own right, providing a bridge between economic freedoms and other human rights.

### b) Numerical overview

Although it can sometimes seem as if the EU is very much concerned with non-discrimination and equal treatment, the quantitative contribution of this field to recent case law has been relatively minor, constituting only 23 cases out of 173 (see Figure 4.2: equality and non-discrimination).

In contrast to all other fields, emanations of liberal constitutionalism are less frequent in this field than those of socially embedded constitutionalism. This mirrors the EU's commitment to combat discrimination in the market place, in particular the employment sphere. The EU has created a comprehensive body

---

321 This notion was used in *Defrenne II* paragraph 12, see above Chapter 3 (pp. 91–92 with notes 77–80).

322 See Chapter 3, pp. 94–97, with notes 93 and 116.

323 See Streeck, 1995, pp. 389, 400 and More, 1999 and, more recently, Somek, 2011.

324 This seems implicit in Weiler, 2003, pp. 22–23.

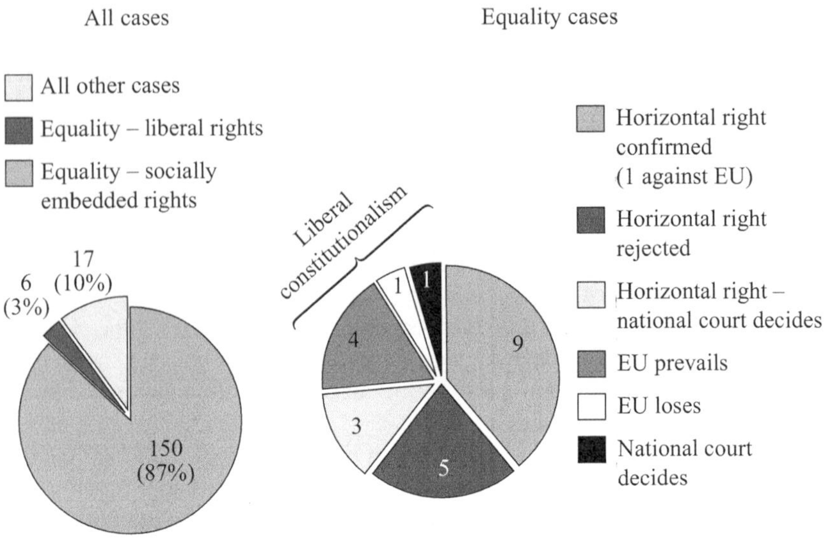


*Figure 4.2 Equality and non-discrimination*

of legislation for this purpose, first on sex discrimination, despite the lack of any explicit legal basis in the Treaties,[325] and from 2000 with legal bases to combat discrimination on grounds of sex, racial or ethnic origin, religion and belief, disability, age and sexual orientation (Articles 19 and 157 TFEU).[326] In academic writing, non-discrimination law is now partially seen as a wholly

325 Directive 75/117/EEC on equal pay and Directive 76/207/EEC on equal treatment of men and women (both now integrated in Directive 2006/54/EC) were the first of these, followed by Directive 79/7/EEC on equal treatment of women and men in social security and Directive 86/378/EEC on occupational pensions (now: 96/97/EC). Later on, there was only slow progress, with limited consideration of gender equality in the directives on maternity protection (Directive 92/85/EC) and parental leave (Directive 2010/18/EU based on the Social Policy Agreement) and on the burden of proof (Directive 97/80/EC). After a long break in legislative activity Directive 2004/113/EC provided for limited expansion of EU sex-discrimination law beyond employment into the field of provision of goods and services (see also Schiek, 2010a, pp. 475, 479).

326 Directive 2000/43/EC on race discrimination in employment and beyond, Directive 2000/78/EC on discrimination on grounds of disability, age, religion and belief and sexual orientation in employment. The plan to complement the latter directive by rules on the provision of goods and services has not been realised so far (see Schiek and Mulder, 2011; on the interrelation of all these discrimination grounds see Schiek, 2011a).

autonomous field,[327] while other authors stress the interrelation between internal market law on the one hand and EU social law and policy on the other.[328] The Court has referred to these directives as only specifying general (constitutional) principles of EU law, which seems a logical consequence of interpreting the equal pay principle (Article 157 TFEU, ex Article 141 EC) as a constitutional right with horizontal direct effect. Equality rights are frequently enforced in the employment sector as the main field where they apply horizontally. Even if litigation aims at obliging Member States or even the EU to change legislation or employment practices in order to conform to the requirements of non-discrimination law, it will also impact on horizontal relations, as the Court applies the same standards to public and private employers. Thus, most case law in this field, even if directed against public authorities, aimed at making equal treatment effective in horizontal relations.

### c) The perspective of liberal constitutionalism

As a liberal constitutional principle, equal treatment aims at consistency of the use of authority, and thus safeguards a basic principle of justice in the relations of public authority with citizens. It is a common tradition of most Western constitutions, which goes back far into pre-democratic times: usually Aristotle is quoted as its source.[329] In short, the traditional principle of equal treatment requires – in the words of the European Court of Justice – 'that comparable situations must not be treated differently and that different situations must not be treated in the same way unless such treatment is objectively justified.'[330] Due to the fact that it is rooted in pre-democratic times, this principle has been subjected to manifold criticism and in particular the second part of the formula (which requires treating non-equal facts and persons differently in proportion to the specific difference) has long been held to be incommensurable with the basic egalitarian principle at the base of true democracy.[331] Nevertheless, the

327 Bell, 2011.

328 Schiek, 2010a, pp. 477–478 with further references, see also Somek, 2011.

329 The main reference to arithmetical equality in Aristotelian terms can be found in the 'Politeia' and has been translated by Trevor Saunders as follows: 'Thus, for example, one takes right for equality, and it is, but equality only for equals, not for all. And thus one also takes inequality for right, and it is, but not for all, but only for unequals' (Aristotle, 'Politea', Trevor Saunders translation 1995, paragraph 1280a).

330 See, as an example from the reference period, case C-344/04 (above, note 300) paragraph 96.

331 Perels based this critique on his vision of substantive (as opposed to formal) democracy. In his view, substantive democracy would inevitably lead to measures which effectively reduce social inequalities. He feared that the second leg of the Aristotelian formula would be used to delegitimize such measures (Perels, 1979, p. 81; see also Schiek, 2002b).

Court has repeatedly confirmed this formula and the Grand Chamber has relied on it in no fewer than five cases since 2004. These cases expose an extremely formal[332] approach to equality.

For example, in the *IATA & ELFAA* case[333] discussed above the claimants had complained of being included in the contested regulation, because they derived a right to be treated differently from the fact that their business concept differs from that of the Star Alliance. They thus demanded to not be subjected to EU consumer law. The Court rejected the claim, stating that the EU legislator was obliged to treat consumers consistently who were in a comparable situation in cases of delay and cancellation irrespective of the airline. Similarly, in a claim by Nuova Agricast[334] challenging the Commission's decision not to interfere in the administration of a certain kind of regional aid in Italy, the technocratic structure of the Aristotelian principle is apparent: Nuova Agricast's application for one year had been rejected due to scarce funds and the business had waived the right to be automatically included in the next application round, intending to enhance its application. However, due to scarce funds, only businesses which had opted for automatic inclusion received aid in that year. Here, the Court could not find different treatment as well. It held that undertakings opting for automatic inclusion were not comparable with those having opted for resubmission, offering a long-winded argument that the preparedness to change an application indicated a lesser degree of need for the aid. Also, when Arcelor[335] challenged Directive 2003/87/EC establishing a greenhouse gas emission scheme on the grounds of covering installations in the steel sector, but not in the aluminium and plastics sector, the Court found that these sectors were comparable for the purposes of the directive, although their greenhouse emissions differed vastly, but that the different treatment was justified by the increased administrative difficulty that would have resulted from including the aluminium and plastic sector. Similarly, the *Horvath* case on implementation[336] of the EU obligation to maintain 'good agricultural and environmental conditions' (GAEC) of land no longer actively farmed under EU Regulation 1782/2003 in the UK turned partly on equal treatment: English farmers were under an obligation to maintain public rights of way as an element of the GAEC, while Welsh and Scottish farmers were not. The Court, applying the formal equal treatment principle, found that different implementation by different regional authorities does not necessarily constitute discrimination.[337]

---

332 Fredman, 2011, pp. 8–13.

333 C-344/04 *IATA and ELFAA* [2006] ECR I-403, paragraphs 93–100 (on other aspects of the case see text accompanying note 300).

334 Case C-390/06 *Nuova Agricast* [2008] ECR I-2577.

335 Case C-127/07 *Société Arcelor Atlantique* [2008] ECR I-9895.

336 Case C-428/07 *Horvath* [2009] ECR I-6355.

337 For an account from a national perspective see Cardwell and Hunt, 2010.

At times, applying the formal equality principle can have perverse effects. In the *Egenberger* case,[338] an agricultural producer challenged a set of regulations[339] protecting the UK's privileged position in marketing New Zealand butter which could be imported into the EU at reduced customs duties ('quota butter'). According to that regulation, anyone importing New Zealand quota butter had to provide an Inward Monitoring Agreement 1 Certificate, which could only be applied for in the UK. At first sight, this seemed a straightforward case of nationality discrimination that cannot possibly be compatible with the internal market. However, the Court decided the case on the basis of Article 40(2) TFEU prohibiting discrimination between consumers and producers, which in its view constitutes a specific expression of the general principle of equal treatment. The Court then discussed at length whether importers from different Member States were comparable, before finding that the regulations indeed were not compatible with EU law. It seems remarkable that discrimination on grounds of nationality was held to be justifiable at all, though.

Finally, the *Laserdisken* case[340] on the transposition of Directive 2001/29/EC on aspects on copyright and related rights in Denmark is illustrative. That directive contains the principle of exhaustion of copyright in the EU only. Accordingly, an undertaking trading in copyrighted works acquired outside the European Union would have to obtain the consent of the EU-resident copyright holder before trading these works within the EU. As has become apparent in earlier case law,[341] Scandinavian copyright law was traditionally based on international exhaustion.[342] Accordingly, before implementation, the acquisition of copyrighted works with the consent of an extra-EU right holder would enable the acquisitor to trade these works freely within the EU. Such trade was at the heart of Laserdisken's business: the sale of imported copies of cinematographic works, mostly special editions. Laserdisken thus challenged the validity of Directive 2001/29/EC and of implementing national

---

338 Case C-313/04 *Egenberger* [2006] ECR I-6331.

339 Council Regulation 1255/1999/EC was neutral in that respect, stating that import licences should be issued by any Member State to any applicant, irrespective of their place of establishment (Article 26(2)) and prohibiting any discrimination (Article 29). It also delegated further regulations to the EU Commission (Article 26(3)), which issued Regulation 2535/2001 containing the requirements referred to above (Articles 32, 34 and Annex XII).

340 Case C-479/04 *Laserdisken* [2006] ECR I-8089. The main relevance of the case lies in the relationship between copyright and freedom of expression (see below II. 3. c) (2) (p. 194)).

341 Case C-355/96 *Silhouette International* [1998] ECR I-4799.

342 For reference see the submission of the Swedish government, then only an EEA member, in paragraphs 20 and 21 of the *Silhouette* ruling.

legislation, among others on grounds of discrimination. It argued that copyright holders in non-EU countries were treated differently from those in EU countries.[343] The Court very shortly stated that these right holders were not in comparable situations and that thus EU law prohibits treating right holders from within and without the EU identically.

As a result, in four out of the five cases the acts of the EU legislator were held to not infringe the principle of equal treatment and in the one case on national legislation the decision was left to the national court. At times, the reasons expose weaknesses of the Aristotelian principle of equality. The *Laserdisken* case may be the most extreme example: The Scandinavian countries pursued a more cosmopolitan approach to intellectual property law, according to which citizens of this one world should in principle be treated equally. This principle is not even comprehensible either to the Court or to its Advocate General. Applying the Aristotelian formula, they both condemn Sweden to pursue inequality in favour of a 'fortress Europe' policy instead.

#### d) The perspective of socially embedded constitutionalism

From the perspective of socially embedded constitutionalism, equality rights are expanded beyond the relation between citizens and public authority into socio-economic spheres governed by market principles. EU law achieves this by specifying equality rights as prohibitions to discriminate on a finite list of grounds.[344] The general principle of equal treatment, with its obligation to treat all others consistently, easily clashes with traditional ideals of liberty and privacy underpinning a free market economy, which depends on individuals acting on individual preferences without any objective justification. What appears to narrow down the reach of equality rights on the face of it, in fact leads to widening the mission of EU non-discrimination law for the market place: it aims at overcoming specific socio-economic disadvantage and, at the same time, achieving social inclusion of those not enjoying equal recognition in social practice on grounds such as being racialised, categorised as female or considered disabled.

EU non-discrimination law aimed at the market place has been read as an attempt to achieve a new era of defining equality rights in a holistic way,[345]is seen as a success story of European integration,[346] and gives rise to a

343 This argument was obviously slightly misrepresented by the Court, as it stated the claimant as saying that these different classes of copyright holders were not in a comparable situation.

344 Above notes 325 and 326.

345 Bell, 2011, Schiek, 2002a.

346 See Witte, 2009.

respectable body of case law.[347] However, the limited extent to which the relevant case law truly transcends the narrow confines of the Aristotelian principle is a source of critique.[348] Grand Chamber rulings from 2004 highlight the potential for contradiction within this field of law: some expand equality law in the market sphere or widen its concepts, while others seem to revert to Aristotelian principles with potentially negative effects on the EU constitution of equality.

*(1) Expanding the scope of equality rights* Some Grand Chamber rulings have expanded the effects of EU non-discrimination laws in the market place by stressing the horizontal effects of provisions in the relevant directives due to their constitutional relevance.

The *Mangold* case of 2005[349] commenced this series of rulings. The claimant questioned whether the prohibition of age discrimination in employment (Directive 2000/78) rendered inapplicable German legislation which excluded workers older than the age of 52 from statutory protection against fixed-term contracts. Finding that such legislation constituted age discrimination was not difficult. This was a hard case because, on the one hand, the implementation period had not yet expired when Germany lowered the age threshold for protection from 58 to 52 years of age and, on the other hand, because this was a horizontal case, although, according to established wisdom, directives must not have any horizontal direct effect.[350] The Court relied on the fact that the 'principle underlying the prohibition of [...] discrimination [was to be] found [...] in various international instruments and the constitutional traditions common to the Member States [...] [and] must thus be regarded as a general principle of EU law'.[351] From this, it derived that the general principle of non-discrimination related to age, as specified in Directive 2000/78, had horizontal effect and was independent from being implemented by a directive. In the subsequent *Bartsch* case,[352] the Court clarified that Member States are not generally bound by the principle of non-discrimination on grounds of age. Rather, the case at hand must be within the scope of application of EU law.

The *Kücükdeveci* case[353] revisited the question of horizontal direct effects

---

347 See for a summary on sex-equality jurisprudence Castello and Davies, 2006. Among the other discrimination grounds, age has elicited most case law Schiek, 2011b.

348 Fredman, 2011, Hepple, 2004.

349 C-144/04 [2005] ECR I-9981.

350 See above note 282.

351 Paragraphs 74–75 of the judgment.

352 C-427/06 [2008] ECR I-7245.

353 Case C-555/07 [2010] ECR I-365.

of the prohibition of age discrimination. Again, in a horizontal case, a German statutory rule was questioned according to which the seniority of a worker acquired before turning 25 years of age would not count towards a progressive increase of the statutory notice period in cases of dismissal. Again, this was obviously age discrimination. The question was whether the prohibition of age discrimination applied in a horizontal case when the implementation of the directive had left the statutory rule untouched. The Court reaffirmed that the prohibition of age discrimination amounted to a general principle of EU law, now also relying on Article 21(1) of the Charter. As in Mangold, the Court held a non-discrimination principle to be directly effective in a horizontal situation in so far as the national court was barred from applying a specific discriminatory exception from a statutory provision. Thus, the horizontal effect was only exclusionary.

Finally in *Test-Achats* of March 2011,[354] the Court was asked to consider the validity of Directive 2004/113 in so far as that directive allowed for Member States to maintain rules legitimising the use of gender-specific actuarial data for determining insurance premiums. While the case related to the validity of EU legislation, the impact was clearly to be felt in the market place. The Court held that transition periods for applying sex equality on the insurance sector were adequate, but it found that allowing Member States to maintain an unlimited exception was unacceptable. As in Kücükdeveci, the Court relied on Article 21 of the Charter and also on Article 23, according to which equality between men and women must be ensured in all areas, and further mentioned Article 157 TFEU to underline the importance of sex equality as a principle of EU law. There was no argument whatsoever concerning the specific role of freedom of contract or other liberal market principles which might legitimate a restricted view on sex equality in the insurance industry.

The *Impact* case also should be mentioned here:[355] a trade union challenged rules in the Irish public service among others because they constituted pay discrimination of fixed-term workers contravening Article 4 of the social partner agreement on fixed-term contracts (Directive 1999/70). The Court held that the non-discrimination clause (in contrast to other provisions such as Article 5 which required more generally restricting fixed-term employment) was sufficiently clear to allow direct effect. This potentially would also strengthen the position of claimants in horizontal relationships.

These four decisions confirm that non-discrimination rights specified in directives retain their character as general principles of EU law (from December 2009 also included in the Charter). This leads the Court to

---

[354] Case C-236/09 *Association belge des Consommateurs Test-Achats ASBL (Test-Achats)* 1 March 2011 (nyr).

[355] Case C-268/06 *Impact* [2008] ECR I-1757.

acknowledging horizontal effects of EU non-discrimination directives, derived from their human rights quality. These cases thus support the aspiration of equality rights as constitutional principles to reach out into social reality.

Further, the Court sometimes interpreted the directives in expansive ways. It expanded the prohibition of sex discrimination to include not only a prohibition of discrimination on grounds of pregnancy, but also on grounds of undergoing a form of fertility treatment specific to women. Thus, an employer could evade the reach of maternity protection law, but not of sex discrimination law when dismissing a worker whose ova had been fertilised externally, but who had not (yet) managed to become pregnant.[356]

It also finally confronted discriminatory practices in the insurance industry, who collate sex-specific actuarial tables and price women's pensions and health care contributions higher than men's corresponding to 'actuarial risk'. To an insurance mathematician there is no discrimination in attributing risk to sex rather than unhealthy lifestyle, for example, as women and men are not comparable under their actuarial tables. The Court's Grand Chamber had first contradicted such views[357] in its *Lindorfer* ruling, concerning the use of sex-specific rates on transferring national pension entitlements to EU pension schemes. Relying on the human rights character of a prohibition of sex discrimination, the Court rejected any economic justification for sex-specific actuarial tables. The *Test-Achats* case[358] confirmed this position in its result, but with a weaker reasoning: among others, the Court considered whether the EU legislator could have explicitly allowed sex-specific actuarial tables as 'objective' justification for discrimination.

The Court also widened the notion of discrimination by acknowledging that discrimination by association is comprised under this heading. Thus, Ms Coleman[359] could rely on the EU ban of disability discrimination when she was harassed at her workplace after requesting flexible working times in order to be able to accommodate the special needs of her disabled child: while she was not disabled herself, she was discriminated against on grounds of the disability of another. This reading will be relevant to racial discrimination as well, and it would also question the Court's reluctance to accept discrimination on grounds

---

[356] Case C-506/06 *Mayr* [2008] ECR I-1017, on earlier positions to pregnancy discrimination see Chapter 3, II (p. 93 with notes 84–85).

[357] Which were also held by the General Court (case T-204/01 *Lindorfer* [2004] ECR II-361). The ECJ had been undecided in the past and had stated that an employer who is subjected to discriminatory insurance tariffs by private suppliers when contracting for occupational pensions for her employees may pay different tariffs, as long as women and men receive the same pensions for the same contributions as a result (Case C-200/91 *Coloroll* [1994] ECR I-4397, C-152/91 *Neath* [1993] ECR I-6935).

[358] Above note 354.

[359] Case C-303/06 *Coleman* [2008] ECR I-5603.

of the sex of one's spouse as sex discrimination rather than discrimination on grounds of sexual orientation.

So far, the Court has viewed the prohibition as discrimination against homosexual employees and their spouses (sexuality discrimination) as separate from sex discrimination. It has widened its practical relevance by supporting claims of homosexuals and/or their spouses to occupational pensions on a par with heterosexual married couples. In the *Maruko* case,[360] the surviving partner of a male homosexual couple domiciled in Germany claimed a survivor's pension under his partner's pension scheme, although the relevant collective agreement only provided for survivors' pensions for married couples. The *Römer* case[361] concerned the rule that public pensions for married persons are higher than for unmarried ones. Mr Römer wished to clarify that as a homosexual he could claim the same pension as a married heterosexual man. Both Maruko and Römer had entered into a registered partnership under German law, which was devised as an alternative to marriage for homosexuals. It did not provide the same rights, but was with time envisaged to approximate to marriage. As there were many unmarried heterosexual men who would, likewise, have been excluded from the benefits desired by Maruko and Römer, these cases should have been decided under indirect discrimination:[362] the rules did not distinguish on the grounds of sexual orientation, but on the grounds of not being married, which disproportionately worked to the disadvantage of homosexuals. To avoid the verdict of indirect discrimination, Germany would have had to objectively justify its rules. As those rules are informed by an outdated model of marriage, under which one spouse provides and the other keeps the common household, this might have been difficult. The Court, however, found that this was direct discrimination, if marriage and civil partnership were sufficiently comparable for the field of pensions.

The Grand Chamber also confirmed employees' rights in some cases on age discrimination. The *Kücükdeveci* case has been mentioned already,[363] where the Court substantively confirmed that non-discrimination rules prevent

---

360 C-267/06 *Maruko* [2008] ECR I-1757.

361 Case C-147/08 *Römer* 10 May 2011 (nyr).

362 As proposed by AG Ruiz Jarabo Colomer (paragraphs 97–102). In its case law on sex equality the Court had accordingly held that a distinction based on being subjected to compulsory military service only constituted indirect sex discrimination: the link between being male and being required to serve was not inextricably linked to sex (as in the case of pregnancy), but rather created by legislation (case C-79/99 *Schnorbus* [2000] ECR I-10997). Thus, when Ms Schnorbus raised a sex-discrimination case because she was rejected as a trainee lawyer, while male applicants with lower grades were accepted, she learned that this differentiation could be objectively justified by the men's special services to their country.

363 Above note 353.

employers and legislators from disregarding employees' seniority acquired at a young age. In the *Andersen* case,[364] the Court found unjustified age discrimination in a piece of legislation excluding employees over 50 years of age from statutory severance payments if they were able to claim an occupational pension at the time of their dismissal.

*(2) Narrow readings of non-discrimination law* In other cases, the Court defended narrow views of non-discrimination rights.

In the *Chacon Navas* case,[365] the Court used a restrictive definition of disability. A Spanish court referred the question of whether dismissal on grounds of longstanding illness should be treated as dismissal on grounds of disability. The Court based its reasoning on a medical definition of disability, according to which only those who are permanently impaired on grounds of a medical condition are disabled,[366] and stated that the concept of disability could not be read to include discrimination on another ground. This reasoning neglected the longstanding sociological debate according to which disability is the result of an interaction of a person with an impairment with society, and not an inherently medical condition.[367] The resulting 'social model of disability' is the basis of the World Health Organisation's definition of disability and has more recently informed the UN Convention on the Rights of Persons with Disabilities.[368] Accordingly, there is hope for the Court to correct its position in the future.[369]

The *Cadman* case[370] defined sex discrimination narrowly, reviewing the conditions under which, formerly, neutral promotion criteria were indirectly discriminatory. Seniority is one of the promotion criteria tending to have a detrimental effect on women, in particular in fields that have only recently become accessible to them. In 1990, the Court had not accepted the requirement for part-time employees to take longer to achieve seniority – in proportion to the reduction in their working time – if the employer could not prove that

---

364 Case C-499/08 *Ingeniørforenigen i Denmark acting on behalf of Ole Andersen v Region Syddanmark* 12 October 2010 (nyr).

365 Case C-13/05 [2006] ECR I-6467.

366 Paragraphs 43 and 45.

367 The social model of disability is usually credited to Colin Barnes (see, e.g., Barnes C., 1990 and and Mercer, 2003). For a critique of *Chacón Navas* on this base see Quinn, 2008, pp. 254–257.

368 The Convention is available on the UN website: http://www.un.org/disabilities/convention/conventionfull.shtml.

369 In the *Coleman* case (above note 359) the Court has already taken the first step towards distancing itself from an overly narrow interpretation of the notion of disability (paragraph 46).

370 Case C-17/05 *Cadman* [2006] ECR I-9583.

additional experience actually contributed to improved performance.[371] In the *Cadman* case, the Court reversed the burden of proof, stating that seniority usually contributes to better performance and that employees are the ones who must prove that this is not the case.[372]

*(3) Merging rationales of equality as consistency and non-discrimination law* Equality under the perspective of liberal constitutionalism pursues the aim of guaranteeing consistency of public policy. Instead, non-discrimination rights under the perspective of socially embedded constitutionalism pursue the aim of overcoming socio-economic disadvantage and promoting equal recognition of human beings with their differences. If based on the Aristotelian formula, equality as consistency clashes with the principles of socially embedded non-discrimination law. Equality rights under the Aristotelian formula are first of all contingent upon a person proving that they are comparable to another person and secondly any different treatment is always capable of being objectively justified, provided it is proportionate to some aim.[373] Accordingly, those suffering socio-economic disadvantage are required to prove that they are equally deserving, as a precondition for equal treatment and different treatment on grounds such as sex, race or disability is not prohibited in principle, but only as long as it cannot be justified. Despite these cleavages, the Court has merged non-discrimination law for socio-economic reality with the principles used for equality as consistency.

For example, in the *Test-Achats* case comparability of women and men was questioned[374] and in the *Maruko* and *Römer* cases, the Court required the national court to decide whether life partnerships for homosexuals are actually comparable with heterosexual marriage under the relevant national legislation. This opens the way for national legislators to avoid comparability, in order to shun the obligation to grant homosexuals equal pension rights.

If comparability is required as a precondition for equal treatment, non-discrimination will become a relative rather than an absolute principle – which contrasts with the approach the EU legislator has taken so far, except in the field of age discrimination:[375] a looser frame of protection applies here, allowing differentiation on grounds of age if this is 'objectively and reasonably justified by a legitimate aim, including legitimate employment policy [and] labour market [...] objectives' (Article 6(1) Directive 2000/78/EC). The Court

371 Case C-33/89 *Kowalska* [1990] ECR I-2591.
372 Paragraphs 35–40 of the *Cadman* judgment.
373 See above notes 329–331.
374 Above note 354 paragraph 29.
375 See on this in more detail Schiek, 2011b.

has used this to support general justifiability in a number of cases.[376] Two examples shall suffice to illustrate. In the *Palacios de la Villa* case,[377] the Court contradicted its finding in *Mangold*[378] where it had demanded strict scrutiny for justification of age discrimination under Article 6(1) Directive 2000/78/EC. In *Palacios*, the Court said that Member States generally have a wide discretion in discriminating on grounds of age and stressed that they could change their policies frequently, without adducing any evidence for their efficiency in order to justify compulsory retirement.[379] Similarly loose standards were applied in the *Wolf* case, where the Court had to decide on the legitimacy of a maximum recruitment age of 30 years of age for fire fighters in Hessen (Germany). It relied on the 'genuine occupational requirement' justification under Article 4, which is not specific to age discrimination. It accepted the argument that anyone past the age of 45 or 50 was no longer able to engage in active fire fighting due to the 'medically proven aging process',[380] arguably supporting the very stereotypes that seem to call for a prohibition of age discrimination. This shows that the loose standard of Article 6(1) Directive 2000/78/EC has the potential to spill over to other articles of the directive and to other 'forbidden grounds' as well.

### e) Evaluation

The Grand Chamber case law on equality and non-discrimination oscillates between a formal principle of equality as consistency applied to the EU and its Member States in public spheres and a substantive non-discrimination law aiming to transform socio-economic reality. Principles underlying both fields contradict each other. For that reason, the observation of spill-over from the realm of liberal constitutionalism (equality as consistency) to socially embedded constitutionalism (substantive non-discrimination) may indicate a turn to liberal constitutionalism. This may spell the end of the grand era of EU non-discrimination law aiming at transforming societies into becoming more inclusive while recognising diversity.

---

376 Case C-411/05 *Palacios de la Villa* [2007] ECR I-8531, Case C-229/08 *Wolf* [2010] ECR I-1, Case C-341/08 *Petersen* [2010] ECR I-47, Case C-45/09 *Rosenbladt* 12 October 2010 (nyr).

377 Case C-411/05 note 376.

378 Above note 349.

379 Paragraphs 68, 70 and 74 of the *Palacios* case (above note 376).

380 Paragraphs 34, 41 of the *Wolf* ruling (above note 376).

## 3. Human Rights before the Grand Chamber

### a) Notion and reach

As explained above, EU human rights adjudication developed on a different trajectory from human rights case law typical for nation states. Among others, this meant that EU liberal human rights constitutionalism was more relevant for reining in Member States than for controlling the EU institutions. Although the market-focus of EU law usually supports horizontal rights, this has not impacted on human rights adjudication yet. However, the Court had started to adjudicate conflict between human rights (as protected by Member States) and economic rights (as wielded by economic actors). These cases also have potentially horizontal aspects and may be expected to increase in number with the increase in socio-economic tensions.

### b) Numerical overview

The numerical overview shows that the allegedly underdeveloped field of human rights is more relevant than the established field of equality law – at least before the Grand Chamber from 2004. There are no fewer than 43 human rights cases altogether. As regards liberal constitutionalism, there are – compared to economic freedoms – more cases where rights are wielded against the EU itself (21 cases) and fewer where Member States are held to account (16 cases). However the EU is much more successful in defending itself against human rights claims than Member States. It prevails in 16 out of 21 cases, while Member States prevail in four out of 16 cases. The field of socially embedded constitutionalism is relatively weakly developed so far, as horizontal effects of EU human rights are not yet acknowledged and horizontal conflicts not even recognised (see Figure 4.3, on human rights).

### c) The perspective of liberal constitutionalism

*(1) Procedural rights* The relatively high number of 43 human rights cases includes 13 cases concerning procedural rights,[381] which are referred to as 'general principles of EU law' and supported by reference to the Charter from

---

[381] Such rights can ultimately be deduced from Article 6 ECHR ('In the determination of his civil rights and obligations or of any criminal charge against him, everyone is entitled to a fair and public hearing within a reasonable time by an independent and impartial tribunal established by law. Judgement shall be pronounced publicly by the press and public may be excluded from all or part of the trial in the interest of morals, public order or national security in a democratic society, where the interests of juveniles or the protection of the private life of the parties so require, or the extent strictly necessary in the opinion of the court in special circumstances where publicity would prejudice the interests of justice.').

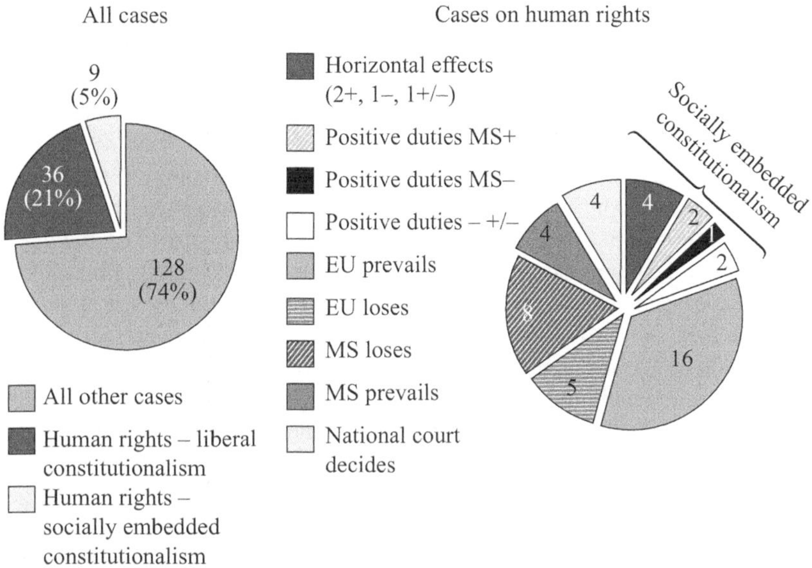


*Figure 4.3 Human rights*

December 2009. These rights include the cluster 'rights of the defence, legal certainty and protection of legitimate expectations'[382] and the right to effective judicial protection of EU rights (efficiency and equivalence).[383] Many of these[384] concerning EU competition law, agricultural law and conflicts between the Commission and its contractors, would qualify as administrative cases if brought before national courts. In eight of these cases the EU institutions or Member States institutions implementing EU law succeeded, although citizens relied on human rights[385] and in five cases the procedural rights of citizens were confirmed.[386]

382 Case C-455/06 *Heemskerk BV* [2008] ECR I-8763, paragraph 47, case C-285/09 *R* 7 December 2010 (nyr) paragraph 45.

383 Case C-432/05 *Unibet* [2007] ECR I-2271, on the question of whether a Member State had to provide for an 'actio popularis' for having national legislation declared as contravening the EU Treaty.

384 One case was a 'consumer-citizen case' concerning the validity of Annex 4 to Regulation 622/2003/EC specifying articles that cannot be brought on board an aircraft. The annex was declared invalid in so far as it aimed to create obligations of citizens because it was not published (case C-345/06 *Heinrich* [2009] ECR I-1659).

385 In cases C-303/05 *Advocaten voor de Wereld VZW* [2007] ECR I-3633, C-413/06 *Bertelsmann AG and Sony Cooperation at America v IMPALA and Commission* [2008] ECR I-4951, C-47/07 P *Masdar* [2008] ECR I-9761, C- 441/07 *Alrosa* [2010]

At times, it is difficult to see how the Court's use of human rights furthers justice. For example, in the *Bertelsmann* case,[387] an international association of independent music producers (IMPALA) challenged the decision of the Commission to declare the planned merger of the Bertelsmann and Sony music production enterprises as compatible with the internal market. IMPALA feared, given the transparency of the music market, that musicians would become unable to contract with them. The CFI[388] had allowed their claim, and the economic giants appealed. The case before the Court turned on the question whether the Commission could rightly rely on a market study financed by Bertelsmann and Sony in finding that there was indeed no transparency, although they had found before, based on their own evidence, that the market was sufficiently transparent to make retaliation for contracting with musicians who had contracted with the new giant enterprises a realistic possibility. Bertelsmann and Sony had produced their voluminous evidence at the last minute and the Commission complied under time constraints established by the merger regulation. Bertelsmann's and Sony's rights of defence and legal certainty turned the tables in their favour: the Commission decision to allow their merger without conditions was upheld, while the independent producers' right of having their legitimate expectations protected remained unmet.

Further, the validity of the Framework decision concerning a European Arrest Warrant was challenged through references by national courts as it violated the honoured principles of *nulla poene sine lege*[389] and *ne bis in idem*.[390] In both cases, the European Arrest Warrant was found to be above any challenge under these human rights.[391] Cases closer to traditional civil rights

---

ECR I-5945, C-352/09 P *Thyssen Krupp Nirosta* 29 March 2011 (nyr) and C-550/07 P *AKZO* 14 September 2010 (nyr) EU institutions prevailed over the claims of economic actors and a civic society organisation, while in cases C-432/05 *Unibet* [2007] ECR I-227 and C-285/09 R note 382 Member States' authorities prevailed.

386 In cases C-362/08 P *Internationaler Hilfsfond* [2010] ECR I-669, C-345/06 *Heinrich* (above note 384) and C-455/06 *Heemskerk* [2008] ECR I-8763 the EU institutions lost their case, while in Cases C-2/06 *Kempter* [2008] ECR I-411 and C-420/06 *Jager* [2008] ECR I-1315 national authorities lost their case against agricultural producers.

387 Case C-413/06 *IMPALA* note 385.

388 Since the Treaty of Lisbon, the former Court of First Instance is referred to as the General Court. Accordingly, in case law and other activities from before 1 December 2009 it will be referred to as the 'CFI', and relating to later developments, the new name, with the abbreviation GC, will be used.

389 No one shall be subjected to criminal responsibility for a behaviour that was not included in a clearly defined criminal offence at the time when it was committed, ultimately deduced from Article 7 ECHR, see also Article 49 Charter.

390 No one shall be punished twice for the same behaviour (see Article 4 of Protocol No 7 to the ECHR and Article 50 Charter).

391 Cases C-303/05 *Advocaten voor de Wereld* [2007] ECR I-3533, C-261/09 *Mantello* 10 November 2010 (nyr).

litigation concerned the lawyer's privilege not to betray information about his or her clients.[392] The litigation initiated by a number of Belgian professional lawyers' organisations aimed at partly invalidating Directive 91/308/EEC on the prevention of money laundering seems worthy of note, as this directive obliges lawyers to disclose the financial dealings of their clients. The Court found that this did not infringe the principles enshrined in Article 6 ECHR though.

Twenty-nine of the 43 human rights cases actually concerned substantive rights. Of these, the majority (21) can be categorised as falling within the category of liberal constitutionalism, i.e. protecting liberties against encroachment by public authorities.

*(2) Substantive rights* No fewer than nine of these cases related to Member States' legislation or administration relative to non-citizens, eight of which related to migration of EU citizens and third-country nationals – a field where the CJEU's protection of citizens who are foreigners within the EU seems especially necessary.[393]

In six of these cases[394] the citizen's rights were confirmed, in one case the decision was left to the national court[395] and in two cases the policies of Member States prevailed.[396] All these cases obviously concerned the right to move freely or to remain in a state of one's choosing,[397] partly also in

---

392 Cases C-305/05 *Ordre des barreaux francophones et germanophone et al.* [2007] ECR I-5305 and C-550/07 P *AKZO et al.* 14 September 2010 (nyr). The latter case had originally been initiated by European, international and national lawyers' associations questioning the Court's case law on the role of in-house lawyers in competition law cases. The Court upheld the principle to deny in-house lawyers of corporations a 'legal counsel privilege' in competition cases.

393 Chapter 3, II. (p. 102 with notes 144–147).

394 Cases C-241/05 *Bot* [2006] ECR I-9627, C-524/06 *Huber* [2008] ECR I-9705, C-357/09 PPU *Kadoev* [2009] ECR I-11189, C-188 and 189/10 *Melki and Abdel* [2010] ECR I-5665, C-57/I-109 and 201/09, B and D 9 November 2010 (nyr) and C-145/09 *Tsakouridis* 23 November 2010 (nyr).

395 Case C-465/07 *Elgafaji* [2009] ECR I-921.

396 Cases C-175/08 *Abdullah et al.* [2010] ECR I-1493, C-31/09 *Bolbol* [2010] ECR I-5537.

397 The right to free movement is guaranteed for EU citizens as human right in Article 45(1) Charter. This is not a general human right and accordingly Article 45(2) Charter states that it may (but does not have to) be granted to third-country nationals. Protocols to the ECHR guarantee the right to move freely within a state and to leave any state (Article 2 Protocol No 4 to the ECHR), the right not to be expelled collectively (Article 4 Protocol No 4, see also Article 19 Charter), the right not to be expelled by and to reenter at any time the state where one is a citizen (Article 5 Protocol No 4) and the right to procedural safeguards if expelled as an alien (Article 1 Protocol No 7 ECHR).

combination with the right to a family life[398] and rights relating to protection against expulsion.[399]

However, these rights were not mentioned in five cases, although the Court provided efficient protection.[400] The *Bot* case,[401] concerning the sensitive issue of travelling Romanian citizens being expelled by France (even before Romania's accession to the EU),[402] is one example. The Court was asked to interpret Articles 11(1) and 20(1) of the Convention Implementing the Schengen Agreement (CISA), allowing non-EU citizens to move within the EU Schengen countries on a travel visa for three months within any six-month period from the date of first entry. Mr Bot had altogether spent four months in France after his first entry into the Schengen area on 15 August 2002, on two separate visits, the second of which had commenced at the end of November 2002. He then left the area at the end of January 2003 but returned on a new travel visa from Hungary (not a Member State then), entering Germany or Austria by 20 February 2003. On 23 March he was stopped and questioned by French police and subsequently expelled on the grounds of overstaying his travel visa. On a literal interpretation of the CISA, his visit in France was still within the framework of the CISA on 23 March, as he had only reentered the Schengen area about a month earlier. The Commission and Finland suggested a purposive interpretation of the notion 'first entry', which would have the second six-month period start by the end of November 2002, rendering his stay in France illegal on 20 March 2003. The Court rejected this in favour of a literal interpretation, relying on legal certainty, but without ever referring to the fundamental rights of aliens to move freely.[403]

In four cases, human rights were explicitly referred to. Thus, for the interpretation of Article 12(1) Directive 2004/83, the Court relied on the Geneva

---

398 Article 8 ECHR and Article 7 Charter.

399 Article 45 (1) Charter for EU citizens, Article 1 Protocol 7 to the ECHR. The Charter also guarantees the right to asylum in line with the Geneva Convention and the protocol on the status of refugees (Article 18) and the right not be expelled to a state where there is a risk of being subjected to the death penalty, torture or inhuman and degrading treatment (Article 19(2)).

400 See cases *Bot*, *Kadoev* and *Melki* (above note 394), *Elgafajii* (above note 395) and *Abdullah* (above note 396).

401 C-241/05 above note 394.

402 In late spring 2011, France made headlines for returning to the practice of expelling Roma, who frequently had Romanian EU citizenship. The EU Commission offered some condemnation, without taking any legal steps. See Dawson and Muir, 2011.

403 Here under Article 45(2) Charter and Article 1 Protocol No 7 ECHR – the latter provision would have been an ideal support for the Court's line of reasoning.

Convention relating to the status of refugees,[404] although in the *B&D* case[405] it held that refusal of refugee status does not need to comply with principles of proportionality, while allowing Member States to grant asylum under national law where their constitution required such compliance. The *Tsakouridis* case confirmed that Member States are bound by human rights as general principles of EU law when relying on exceptions from rights granted to citizens by EU legislation. In this case, Germany was prevented once again from expelling a convicted drug user on the basis of generalisations concerning his ability to reintegrate into society without taking into account his rights to a family life.[406] In the *Huber* case, the Court stressed the necessity to interpret Directive 95/46 in line with the right to privacy, before holding that special retention of data on foreigners was not compatible with EU law.[407] However, the main principle on which the court relied was equal treatment of EU citizens rather than privacy rights. This seems to suggest that collecting and storing the same data in respect of third-country nationals would not be a problem.[408]

Eleven of the cases relating to protection of substantive rights against public authority concerned conflicts with the EU, and only in two of these were the citizens' rights confirmed.

One of these cases was the widely discussed *Kadi* case[409] where the Court partly invalidated Regulation 881/2002/EC implementing UN resolutions 1267 (1999), following EU Common Position 2002/402/CFSP. The UN resolution emerged in the aftermath of the bombing of the Twin Towers in New York on 11 September 2001. It obliged State parties to freeze assets of persons and organisations who were viewed as being connected to Osama bin Laden or to Al-Qaeda and the Taliban and had been included in a list compiled from

---

404 Case C-31/09 *Bolbol*, above note 396.

405 Case C-57, 101/09 *B&D* above note 394. This latter case seems to constitute another example of the perverse use of human rights by the Court: German authorities did not wish to deny a right to asylum or protection as refugee to a person who would normally be granted asylum or refugee status because that person was somehow affiliated to one of the numerous organisations listed in the Annex to EU Common Position 2001/931, implementing the 'post 9/11' UN Resolutions. The referring court asked whether Directive 2004/83 would oblige Member States to maintain the asylum status. The Court answered that Germany may grant asylum or refugee status, if stressing that this was not related to EU obligations.

406 Case C-145/09 above note 394, paragraph 52.

407 Case C-524/06 above note 394, paragraph 47 for the human rights base of the directive.

408 Paragraphs 70, 73–81.

409 Case C-402 and 415/05P *Kadi and Al Barakaat* [2008] ECR I- 6351, see also the more recent follow-up case GC T-85/09 *Yassin Abdullah Kadi v European Commission* 30 September 2010 (nyr).

information provided by states. The regulation made the Convention legally binding for the Member States. In Mr Kadi's and Mr Baykara's cases, this meant that they and their families could not access social benefits on which their families depended. Upon referral by a UK court, the Court held that the regulation restricted the right to property in disproportionate ways, partly because the persons affected had no right to be heard and the inclusion or non-inclusion of persons on the list seemed eclectic.[410] However, as has been widely noted in academic critique, the ECJ here usurped the authority to subject UN activities to scrutiny under the constitutional law of the EU, similar to the approach of the German Constitutional Court in its first 'Solange' decision.[411] Relying on primacy of EU law, the Court rejected the contestation that EU law can be subjected to a legality test based on national constitutional law. Yet, it subjected the adequacy of a UN resolution to scrutiny based on human rights guaranteed as general principles of EU law, thus asserting its own authority as a human rights court.[412] As a result, the ECJ safeguarded third-country nationals from being excluded from civil life by the relevant EU regulation implementing UN Resolution 1267 (1999), which has been criticised as based on irrational fears.[413] From a human rights perspective, this must be seen as a positive development.

In an evaluation of not only the spectacular cases but also all Grand Chamber decisions, the Court appears in a less positive light though. *Kadi* was not the first case where the Grand Chamber considered the said UN resolution. In the earlier case *Gestoras pro Amnistiia*,[414] the claimant, a human rights organisation active in the Basque country, had been included on a list containing terrorist organisations (as being part of the ETA) under Council Common Position 2001/931, which implemented UN Resolution 1373 (2001). As a consequence, it lost its legal personality and all its assets. The original claim before the CFI aimed at gaining information on the grounds for inclusion in the list. The Court held that no human rights problem whatsoever ensued from refusing Gestoras pro Amnistiia any information on why they were dissolved.[415] A more recent

---

410 Paragraphs 352–376 of the judgment.

411 BVerfGE 37, 271 Common Market Law Reports 1974 (2) 540–571.

412 See Isiksel, 2010, pp. 561–562, supplying numerous references while rejecting the parallel in the end. See, for a critique from an international law perspective, de Búrca, 2010. For a more conciliatory perspective see Sabel and Gerstenberg, 2010, pp. 529–530.

413 The UN resolutions have even been characterised as 'Texas law' (Eeckhout, 2009).

414 Case C-354/04P *Gestoras pro Amnistiia* [2007] ECR I-579.

415 Case C-355/04P *Segi* [2007] I-1579 was a parallel case from the French part of the Basque country.

case[416] concerned Regulation 2580/2001, another measure based on UN Resolution 1373 (2001). The German referring court questioned whether the criminalisation of individuals on the basis that they had paid contributions to a Kurdish political organisation (while enjoying political asylum from being prosecuted as Kurdish activists in Turkey) was in line with human rights standards. The German court found it problematic that the individuals were criminalised because their organisation had not submitted objections against being included on the relevant EU terrorist organisations list. The difference between this and the *Kadi* case, as the Court stresses, is that the individuals, E and F, were to be imprisoned rather than suffering a seizing of their assets. Also, the establishing of the 'terrorist list' under this regulation was in the hands of EU institutions. The Court found that E and F should not be imprisoned for paying contributions before June 2007 because they had no realistic chance of objecting to their organisation being included on the list. The Court found, though, their imprisonment from July 2007 did not violate any human rights. Thus, adjudication on drawing up of a list of terrorist organisations by EU institutions seems less coherent than in the *Kadi* ruling.

Another group of cases concerned data protection, including the disputed data retention directive.[417] In the *Schecke & Eifert* case, data protection rights of naturalised persons applying for agricultural aid were raised. While the Court acknowledged that the right to privacy was impinged upon, it also held that this interference was justified by the principle of transparency as a public interest.[418] By contrast, data protection in favour of economic actors was ranked highly in the cases *Technische Glaswerke Ilmenau (TGI)*[419] and *Bavarian Lager*.[420] In both cases, economic actors requested information underlying Commission Decisions with which they disagreed: TGI considered that state aid received by a competitor should have been proclaimed as infringing the internal market and Bavarian Lager wished to challenge the

416 C-550/09 *E & F* [2010] ECR I-6209.

417 On the problems in relation to protection of privacy in this directive see Kühling, 2010, p. 480. In March 2010, the German constitutional court held that the German implementation of that directive is invalid, as it violates the fundamental right to privacy (BVerfGE 125, 260, English summary available under http://www.bverfg.de/en/press/bvg10-011en.html). The constitutional court also stated that the directive itself was capable of being implemented in ways that do not violate the German constitution, though, thus avoiding a head-on collision with the EU legislator and any obligation to make its first reference to the Court of Justice. Before the Court, Ireland challenged the legality of the directive, but no human rights aspects were discussed in this action (Case C-301/06 *Ireland v EP and Council* [2009] ECR I-593).

418 Case C-92/09 *Schecke* 9 November 2010 (nyr) paragraph 68–72.

419 Case C-139/07 P *TGI* [2010] ECR I-5883.

420 Case C-28/08P *Bavarian Lager* [2010] ECR I-6051.

Commission's inactivity regarding an infringement of the free movement of goods by the UK. In both cases, the privacy rights of the competitors of these undertakings were successfully relied upon to maintain the secrecy the Commission wished to be attached to its actions.

More positively, the Court protected air passengers' privacy rights in a ruling on the EP's challenge of the Council's and the Commission's decision to make personal data of air passengers available to the US authorities.[421]

The two remaining cases in liberal constitutionalism concerned rights of economic actors. The *Laserdisken* case[422] concerned Directive 2001/29 on the harmonisation of certain aspects of copyright and its implementation in Denmark. As in all Nordic countries, the directive's principle of regional exhaustion of intellectual property rights clashed with the more internationally oriented Scandinavian tradition. Laserdisken claimed, inter alia, that increased difficulties in distributing films would also impinge on the freedom of expression of viewers. The Court held that the right of a copyright holder to withhold her consent to viewing did not impinge on their right to distribute their films (and thus their opinion). As regards the right to gain information, the Court found that any restriction was justified.[423] The *FIAMM* case[424] concerned a claim for damages by companies disadvantaged by the retaliation of the US, based on a WTO DSB ruling concerning the EU's regulations on the banana market. The companies claimed that their property rights and rights to conduct their business had been infringed. The Court stressed that these rights have long been protected, but were subject to restrictions in relation to their social functions. Going beyond former case law, it also considered that any restriction must be proportionate and should not infringe the very substance of the right in question. However, the Court rejected the claim on the basis of the negotiated nature of DSB decisions.

#### d) The perspective of socially embedded constitutionalism

From the perspective of socially embedded constitutionalism, public authorities should undertake to establish conditions enabling actual enjoyment of human rights, and human rights should also be guaranteed in horizontal relations. In the reference period, the Grand Chamber decided eight cases relating to such socially embedded views of human rights.

---

421 Case C-317/04 *EP v Council* [2005] ECR I-2457.

422 Case C-479/04 *Laserdisken* [2008] ECR I-6885; see above, under note 340 for the principle of equal treatment.

423 Paragraphs 62–65.

424 Case C-120/06P *FIAMM* [2008] ECR I-6513.

*(1) Promotion of human rights* An obligation of Member States to promote privacy flows from Directive 95/46/EC on protecting privacy while allowing the free flow of data through the internal market. In the reference period, the Grand Chamber specified those obligations in two cases. The *Tietosuojavaltuutettu* case[425] concerned a dispute between two Finnish data protection authorities over the question of whether transfer of personal data published in a newspaper to a daughter company of that same newspaper should be prohibited. The newspaper in question regularly publishes the identity of all Finnish residents earning an annual income exceeding a certain threshold, and wished to complement the print version by a text messaging service for subscribers, for which the data transfer was a technical requirement. The case turned on an interpretation of Article 9 of Directive 95/46, which in the Court's view aims at reconciling the two fundamental rights of freedom of expression and privacy.[426] The human rights lawyer might expect some reference to the positive obligation of states to promote human rights in ways minimising conflicts between rights and some deliberations of whether and in how far restrictions of privacy are necessary in order to maintain freedom of expression and freedom of the press. No such argument is offered. The Court merely ruled that Directive 95/46 does not prohibit processing and storing of data already available in the public domain for merely journalistic (as opposed to commercial) purposes. The Court left the decision on whether the purpose was merely journalistic to the national court.

An infringement action against Germany[427] concerned institutional aspects of the data protection directive. The German system of supervising data protection differentiates between the public and the private sector. For the public sector, representatives with sole responsibility towards parliament are established, while controllers for the private sector are integrated in the public administration and subject to hierarchical supervision. The Court held that the position of the controllers did not qualify as independent under Article 28 Directive 96/45/EC. The mentioning of the human rights furthered by the directive serves to enhance state obligations.

Two cases could have supported positive state obligations to promote the freedom of expression, information and the press by endeavouring to maintain media diversity. The *Régie Networks* case[428] concerned a scheme supporting local radio stations (and thus media diversity) in France, under which commercial actors had to pay a levy on any income derived from advertising on broadcasting. The Court held that the Commission's omission to challenge this

---

425 C-73/07 *Tietosuojavaltuutettu* [2008] ECR I-7075.
426 Paragraph 55.
427 Case C-518/07 *COM & EDPS v Germany* [2010] ECR I 1885.
428 Case C-333/07 *Société Régie Networks* [2008] ECR I-10807.

scheme violated the Treaty for lack of reasoning of its decision, without mentioning the human rights dimension, though. The *Mediaprint* case[429] concerned Austrian legislation prohibiting any commercial communication promising bonuses for consumers linked to periodicals and in particular linking participation in a competition or game of chance to the purchase of a periodical. This legislation among others aimed at furthering media diversity by limiting recourse to commercial practices only available to large media groups. The Court held that this legislation – as any rule restricting commercial practices – had the potential of restricting free movement of goods and needed to be justified by reference to overriding reasons in the general interests, such as promotion of human rights. Directive 2005/29/EC had fully harmonised legislation on unfair commercial practices. It deems as unfair 31 specific practices and requires Member States to make a case-by-case assessment for all other practices. Austrian legislation was not covered by the 31 grounds list. Thus, it could not be upheld, as it did not allow justification of the condemned practices in each individual case. The Court did not refer to the specific role of human rights in this case at all, which it had held in such high esteem in the *Schmidberger* and *Omega* cases referred to above.[430] It just declared that Austrian legislation infringed Directive 2005/29/EC and had to be changed. A further case concerned the protection of consumers against unfair terms in standard contracts and confirmed the obligation of national courts to enforce these from their own motion.[431]

*(2) Fundamental rights in horizontal relations and rights promotion* Horizontal effects of human rights can be an important element of socially embedded constitutionalism. However,[432] they may also enhance an already powerful position in social reality as well as create the preconditions for enjoying human rights. The Court's case law for considering human rights as defences against economic freedoms is especially interesting here because activities covered by the Treaties' economic freedoms may also be protected by human rights: for example, economic activities protected by the freedom to provide services or establish an enterprise transnationally may correspond to those activities protected by a right to conduct one's business. This right is not specifically protected by the ECHR, although it may partly overlap with the right to private life and to property.[433] It is protected in many European

429 Case C-540/08 *Mediaprint* 9 November 2010 (nyr).
430 Chapter 3, II, pp. 103–105.
431 Case 137/08 *VB Pénzügyi Lízing* 29 November 2010 (nyr).
432 Above pp. 164–168 with notes 279–294.
433 Article 8 ECHR and Article 1 of the first protocol to the ECHR.

constitutions, though[434] and also in the Charter (Article 16). Accordingly, the Court has long accepted a combined 'right to property and the freedom to pursue a trade or profession' as a general principle of EU law.[435] Thus, in cases such as *Schmidberger*, there is really a need for human rights of different citizens to be reconciled.[436]

This was also the situation in the *Promusicae* case:[437] Promusicae, an organisation of producers and publishers of musical and audiovisual recordings, asserted intellectual property rights of its members by requiring that Telefónica, a commercial company providing internet access, disclose the identity and behaviour of customers using a site for downloading and sharing music, while Telefónica instead sought to protect their customers' privacy. The competing human rights had been partly regulated in EU directives[438] and are protected by the Charter (Article 17 (2) and 8). The Court held that it was for the Member States to adequately balance conflicting human rights while implementing EU law and interpreting the relevant national law.

The cases *Laval* and *Viking* – beyond their relevance for economic freedoms[439] – also concerned horizontal human rights conflicts: the trade unions and workers in both cases relied on their rights of freedom of association and the right to take collective action, while the economic freedoms claimed by their employers corresponded to their human right to conduct a business. In both cases the Court attempted to recognise the right to collective action as a fundamental right.[440] Thus, it did not return to nineteenth-century doctrines of appraising collective action as a tort rather than a human right.[441] However, in its result the Court managed to subordinate workers' rights to collective action to business rights.

The first step towards this result was to categorise the right to strike as a social right (Article 28 Charter, Article 6 European Social Charter) and to

---

434 The Spanish, Portuguese and Italian constitution may be quoted as examples, and the German constitution contains the right to choose one's profession as well as the general freedom to act unencumbered by requirements for authorisation (Articles 12, 2 GG).

435 See Case C-120/06P *FIAMM* [2008] ECR I-6513, paragraph 183 with numerous references.

436 See on this Chapter 3, II. pp. 103–105 with notes 129–138.

437 Case C-274/06 *Productores de Música de España (Promusicae)* [2008] ECR I-271.

438 Directives 95/46/EC and 2000/58/EC on data protection and directives 2000/31/EC and 2001/19/EC on intellectual property rights.

439 See above pp. 164–168 with notes 280–295.

440 ECJ *Laval* para 90, ECJ *Viking* paragraph 43, the latter explicitly referring to Article 6 ESC.

441 See Jacobs, 2010 (1985).

conveniently overlook that it is rooted in the liberal right of freedom of assembly (Article 12 Charter, Article 11 ECHR). As liberties traditionally were protected more efficiently than so-called socio-economic rights, the de-recognition of the dual nature of collective labour rights[442] may well be the first step to their substantive devaluation. This shortcoming seems even more problematic in the light of recent case law by the ECtHR, according to which the right to association under Article 11 ECHR includes the right to bargain collectively and thus implicitly also to strike.[443]

Further, in both cases the Court deviated from the much-praised *Schmidberger* method: in *Schmidberger* it had appreciated that the right to free speech and assembly was in principle guaranteed irrespective of the aims pursued with a specific assembly. In *Viking* and *Laval*, the Court held that collective action 'restricting' economic freedoms could only be justified if it pursued specific aims that the Court found adequate, namely the 'protection of workers' against 'serious threat' of jobs or working conditions[444] in a manner that did not leave any insecurity on the employer's part about the results of negotiations[445] and did not require an employer deploying workers from one Member State to another to comply with wages and other conditions beyond the national minimum pay.[446] Accordingly, the Court did not accept the right to organise in trade unions and the derived right to take collective action as such, but only under the condition that this right was used to further very specific interests of workers.

As regards the 'balancing' of two opposing fundamental rights, the Court did not engage in any assessment of the question of whether the restriction of rights to association and the taking of collective action is balanced by a corresponding restriction of the right to conduct one's business. This seems the main weakness of these cases from a human rights perspective. Under all the international treaties to which the Court so aptly refers, restrictions of the right to association and collective action can only be justified if these restrictions are necessary in a democratic society in the interest of national security or public safety or for the protection of the rights and freedoms of others.[447] This means that the restriction of the right to association and to strike can only be justified in so far as it is necessary to safeguard any corresponding rights of

442 See Novitz, 2008.

443 ECtHR, App. Nr. 34503/97 *Demir v Baykara*, 48 EHRR 54 and App. 68959/01 *Enerji Yapi-Yol v Turkey*, 49 EHRR 108, on these see Ewing and Hendy, 2010.

444 *Viking* paragraphs 80 and 81.

445 *Laval* paragraph 102.

446 *Laval* paragraph 109.

447 See Article 11 ECHR as well as Article 31 European Social Charter.

the employers. The Court has, however, only considered whether the restriction of the employers' economic freedoms is justified and has not questioned the restriction of workers' rights. Accordingly, the required balancing of two opposing human rights has not taken place.

In contrast to the *Promusicae* case, where this balancing was left to the national court, the Court did not leave the national court any scope to decide in the *Laval* case.[448] In the *Viking* case the Court left some degree of assessment to the national court. However, it stated beyond doubt that a trade union must not pursue a 'flag of convenience' policy under any circumstances.[449]

While the weighing of human rights in these first two cases where the Court was confronted with transnational collective action was incomplete, there is some development in the less contentious case concerning the German 'Riester Rente'.[450] The Court stated that the aim of the parties to the collective agreement to protect the earnings of workers when invested in a pension scheme by designating reliable funds 'does not affect the essence of the right to bargain collectively'.[451] While one might expect more substantiation for such a statement, it must be acknowledged that the Court now considers limits to favouring the economic freedoms over the human right of freedom of association. While in *Viking* and *Laval* any balancing of fundamental rights of workers and fundamental freedoms (and thus implicitly of employers' human rights) was absent, the Court has now taken a first step towards such balancing. Regrettably, the Court still accorded a lower level of protection to human rights. While an economic freedom can only be restricted if that restriction is proportionate, the human right to bargain collectively can be restricted as long as its essence is not eliminated. As a result, the human right to bargain collectively as protected at national level 'loses the battle' against the economic freedoms, which were in this case enforced against a Member State.

#### e) Evaluation

The Court's human rights case law from 2004 shows a clear preference for the perspective of liberal constitutionalism. In this sphere, remarkable progress

---

[448] Paragraph 119 (*Laval*).

[449] Paragraph 75-90 (*Viking*).

[450] Case C-271/08, see also above p. 137 with note 122.

[451] Paragraph 49 of the *Laval* ruling. AG Trstenjak was more specific, stating: 'it must be determined whether [...] fundamental freedoms may justify a restriction on the fundamental right to bargain collectively and the fundamental right to autonomy in that process or, conversely, whether those fundamental rights demand that the scope of those fundamental freedoms and the secondary law based thereupon must be limited.' (paragraph 84) Her conclusion is the same as the Court's: she assumed that the collective agreement could have specified criteria for choosing a provider rather than specifying the provider (paragraphs 202–223).

has been achieved in applying the Charter and asserting the Court's authority as human rights adjudicator for the EU itself. The perspective of socially embedded constitutionalism is yet underdeveloped. The Court has difficulty in recognising horizontal human rights conflicts if they emerge as conflicts between economic freedoms and human rights, and also in adjudicating these adequately. However, cases such as *Promusicae* demonstrate that there is potential to refrain from taking one side in such conflicts. Also, there are some cautious steps towards acknowledging positive obligations to ensure the preconditions of human rights enjoyment.

## III. DEMOCRATIC/COLLECTIVE RULE-MAKING POST ENLARGEMENT

### 1. Notion and Reach

Democratic elements of the EU have been developed via Treaty reform. Case law is scarce and often the Court refers to issues such as the role of self-regulation in society, civil society and industrial relations in passing, without paying much attention to any theoretical issues involved or even its own assumptions. Case law in this section will thus consist of two different categories. On the one hand, there are cases that deal primarily with democratic organisation of the EU and/or its Member States or with democratic institutions within society. On the other hand, cases mainly based on rights protection will be mentioned here again if they reveal any visions/positioning on democracy within society or in public spheres. A new category of cases will be introduced where the Court addressed the remaining scope for organising the economy or society on grounds other than those of competitive markets.

### 2. Numerical Overview

Even under this rather wide radar, only 35 cases decided by the Grand Chamber post 2004 can be categorised as relating to this field. As in the field of equality, rulings concerning socially embedded constitutionalism constitute the majority here (26 cases) and the rulings concerning public regulation of markets (including establishing or maintaining public sectors) constitute the largest part (17 cases). (See Figure 4.4 on democratic/collective rule-making.)

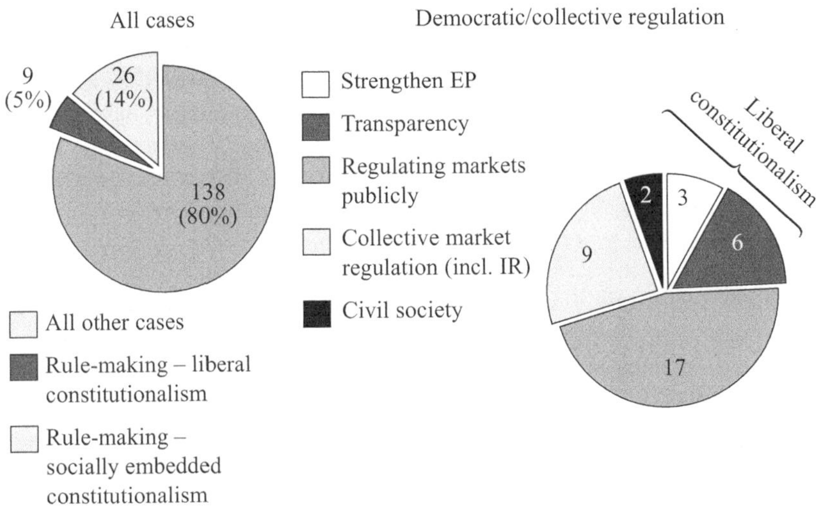


*Figure 4.4 Democratic/collective rule-making*

## 3. The Perspective of Liberal Constitutionalism

In the scarce case law concerning democratic rule in public spheres, the cases on transparency (Article 15 TFEU = ex Article 255 EC) abound. Partly, these have been discussed already as cases concerning privacy rights, as data protection of citizens may well conflict with transparency of EU decisions.

As it happened, transparency was deemed to outrank data protection and vice versa when this served to uphold decisions taken by the EU Commission.[452] The principle of transparency received a more favourable reception in three other cases, which were all initially raised by civil society organisations: one related to widespread protests against allowing an industrial plant to be erected in a nature reserve in Hamburg;[453] one raised by an individual citizen and MEP active among others in refugee issues related to draft EU legislation on asylum;[454] and one raised initially by API, defending journalists' rights to report on activities of the Court of Justice.[455] In the first two cases the Court held that the Commission and the Council had (partly) not

[452] See cases C-92/09 *Schecke*, C-28/08P *Bavarian Lager* and C-139/07 P *TGI* (above pp. 193–194 with notes 419–421).

[453] Case C-64/05 *Sweden v Council* [2007] ECR I-11389, originally raised by the Hamburg section of the International Foundation for Animal Welfare (IFAW), challenging the landfill of the 'Mühlenberger Loch', which destroyed the natural environment of rare species.

[454] Case C-39/05P *Sweden & Turco v Council* [2008] ECR I-4723.

[455] Case C-514/07 *Sweden et al. v API & Commission* 21 September 2010 (nyr).

complied with the requirements of transparency as specified by Regulation 1049/2001/EC, thus supporting the access to information about actions of the institutions, which again is a prerequisite of public scrutiny of these institutions. In the third case, however, the Court held that journalists have no right to access legal submissions made by the Commission in Court cases, as this might compromise its position in further litigation. One could say that the Court protected, against being made too public and thus subjected to political challenge, judicial procedures brought before it.

In relation to these cases it is worthwhile noticing that two of them were originally brought by civil society organisations, who attempted to sue the EU legal order to pursue their aims. Their involvement indicates that the Court is perceived as contributing to the Europeanisation of democracy, albeit mainly in public spheres.

There were also three cases relating to elections to and prerogatives of the European Parliament. Two concerned the EP's electorate and expanded the rights of Dutch citizens residing in former colonies as well as the prerogative of the UK to give the vote to non-EU citizens in line with their policy on national elections.[456] The third case confirmed the EP's prerogatives to be consulted for legislation on asylum and refugee policies.[457]

Overall, this case law seemed to support concepts of democracy and also confirmed the role of civil society organisations in the European democratic field. While the case law on transparency has weaknesses, in two out of six cases the transparency of national or EU procedures was actually enhanced.

## 4. The Perspective of Socially Embedded Constitutionalism

There is virtually no case where the Court explicitly addressed any necessity to maintain or establish democracy in socio-economic spheres, either by maintaining a public sector or a non-public sector not dominated by market principles or by supporting institutions for legitimate collective regulation in socio-economic spheres. Nevertheless, some case law impacts on the ability of Member States to maintain such elements of socially embedded constitutionalism or implicitly relate to the same phenomenon at EU level.

### a) Regulating markets

In line with the historic priority of the economic constitution, most cases related in this manner to democracy and collective rule-making in societal spheres concern public regulation of markets, mostly at Member States' levels.

---

456 Cases C-300/04 *Eman & Sevinger* [2006] ECR I-8055, C-145/04 *Spain v UK* [2006] ECR I-7917, on these Shaw, 2008.

457 Case C-133/06 *EP v Council* [2008] ECR I-3189.

Partly, case law already related under freedom to provide services and freedom of establishment also concerned public regulation of markets. It may be recalled that the Court accepted a planification regime for Spanish pharmacies[458] as well as the principle that Italian and German pharmacies must be headed by a professional pharmacist rather than organised commercially.[459] Also, some cases on the freedom to receive health care services confirmed the prerogative of Member States to effectively remove health care from market mechanisms: it may be recalled that the Commission lost cases against Spain and France, because the Court found the refusal of reimbursement of health care received abroad to be justified by the argument that a public health service needs to be maintained.[460] Similarly, the Commission lost a case against Germany because the Court in effect confirmed the prerogative of regional units to organise waste treatment as a public service without recourse to public tendering.[461] Similarly, the Court upheld that municipalities can treat parking fees as income derived from a public, rather than a market-based, activity, albeit in exceptional circumstances,[462] and the Court has also endorsed the Commission's decision not to challenge an under-price sale of a former French public undertaking for postal services, relying on the buyer's obligation to continue to offer services of general interest. Thus, there exists a certain leeway for Member States to maintain public sectors.

There were also cases in which the Court seemed implicitly to accept national price regulations. For example, where an international pharmaceutical concern was allowed to prevent parallel imports from states where prices for medicine were capped by public rule.[463] Also, the Court was reluctant to accept a tax regime favouring a specific region[464] or the maintenance of a publicly regulated energy market even for a transitional period after accession to the EU.[465]

Regarding EU-level regulating of markets, the Court implicitly endorsed maintaining planification in the agricultural sector by upholding a regime-planning production volume of cotton.[466] Also the decision on the stability and

---

458 Case C-570/07 *Blanco* (above, pp. 125–126 with note 60).

459 Cases C-171/07 *Apothekerkammer des Saarlandes* (above p. 124 with note 56) and C-531/06 *COM v Italy* (above, pp. 124–125 with note 57).

460 Cases C-211/08 *COM v Spain* (above, pp. 158–1159 with note 255) and C-512/08 *COM v France* (above p. 158 with note 254).

461 Case C-480/06 *COM v Germany* (above, p. 136 with note 119).

462 Case C-288/07 *Isle of Wight* [2008] ECR I-7203.

463 Case C-468/07 *Sot. Lélos kai Sia* [2008] ECR I-7139, see also Case C-439/08 *VEBIC* 7 December 2010 (nyr), which concerned the price of bread in the period after deregulation of bread prices in Belgium.

464 Case C-88/03 *Portugal v Council* [2006] ECR I-7115.

465 Case C-413/04 *EP v Council* [2006] ECR I-11221, C-414/04 *EP v Council* [2006] ECR I-11279 (relating to the Estonian and Slovenian energy market).

466 Case C-310/04 *Spain v Council* [2006] ECR I-7285.

growth pact at the occasion of French and German defaults could be considered here. In this case, the Council had decided not to proceed as the Commission had proposed, and to review its own decision on sanctioning France and Germany – not Greece – for defaulting the targets for state debt and inflation under the stability and growth pact.[467]

Three rulings referring to liberalisation of former public sectors are also relevant for the question of how far public or regulated sectors within the internal market can be maintained under EU constitutional law.

Two rulings on the telecommunication sector[468] deal with excessive payments of commercial providers for network licences and access to interoperability networks, and both strengthen as a result the position of the commercial provider. While it is intuitively convincing that a licensing fee of more than 5 million € is not equitable,[469] the second case concerned the question of how far former public providers that are still under an obligation to provide a universal service may continue to cross-subsidise some of their less profitable services by gains made in others.[470] The Court disallowed these cross-subsidies mainly because there was no clear definition of the universal service obligation,[471] assuming rather uncritically that the provision of a universal service will be taken care of by 'the forces of free markets'.[472] A case on postal services, the *Chronopost* case,[473] seemed to endorse a different logic. Here, a competitor of Chronopost claimed that the undertaking had received state aid, contrary to EU rules, when it acquired parts of the formerly publicly owned postal service at an under-market price. However, this was partly to compensate for the obligation to provide express postal services not only in profitable city areas, but also to more sparsely populated islands. The Court accepted this obligation as a sufficient and precisely described obligation to provide a service in the general economic interest and therefore rejected the competitor's claim.[474]

Price controls in the liberalised market were at stake in the *Federutility* case, concerning the internal market in natural gas.[475] Italy had, just before 1 July 2007, the date from which, according to Directive 2003/55/EC, the gas market should be liberalised, issued legislation providing for the administrative fixing

467 Case C-27/04 *COM v Council* [2004] ECR I-6649.

468 Case C-392,422/04 i-21 Germany [2006] ECR I-8559; Case C-152, 154/07 Arcor et al. [2008] ECR I-5959.

469 Case C-392/04 ibid.

470 Case C-152/07 ibid.

471 Paragraph 26.

472 Paragraph 27.

473 Case C-341/06 *Chronopost* [2008] ECR I-4777.

474 For more aspects of this decision see Vesterdorf, 2009.

475 Case C-265/08 *Federutility et al.* [2010] ECR I-3377.

of prices for gas delivery to domestic customers in particular circumstances of health or economic disadvantage. The claimants, Italian undertakings, maintained that, in a liberalised market, prices should be determined by supply and demand without state intervention. The directive was silent on a principle of supply and demand governing the gas market. It merely obliged Member States to ensure that consumers could choose their provider from the liberalisation date (Article 23(1), and generally to act 'with a view to achieving a competitive, secure and environmentally sustainable market in natural gas' (Article 3(1)). Its purpose was, inter alia, to ensure free movement of goods, freedom to provide services and freedom of establishment (Recital 4). Here, the Court derived from the term 'competitive, secure and environmentally sustainable market' that the gas market must be based on supply and demand in principle.[476] Accordingly, Member States have to justify any price control regime.[477] Because the price controls were limited to specific categories of customers and constituted exceptional measures, the Court found these measures to be justified.

### b) Self-regulation and democratisation of society

Socially embedded constitutionalism also requires democratisation of socio-economic spheres and the acceptance of institutions for collective regulation. Again, the Court did not refer to any of this explicitly. However, some case law relates to self-regulation of market by business and some to collective regulation of labour markets through industrial democracy.

It may be recalled that the *Olympique Lyonnais* case[478] concerned the validity of a charter for professional football which in effect restricted free movement rights of football players. This charter was issued under a statutory regime for sports in France by no fewer than four organisations. Of these, only one represented football players, two represented the employers and one coaches and trainers. Furthermore, some of these organisations were set up by statute, as was an obligation to establish the Football Charter.[479] Accordingly, employees are underrepresented and the Football Charter resembles a unilateral body of rules imposed on employees. The Court merely stated that this rulebook would qualify as a collective agreement under French law and thus held that it was a private contract linked to the free movement of workers under its horizontal effect.

---

476 Paragraph 18 of the decision.

477 Paragraph 25 of the decision.

478 Case C-325/08, see also above, pp. 168–170.

479 See Branco Martins, 2004, quoted from http://www.asser.nl/default.aspx?site_id=11&level1=13910&level2=13947&level3=&textid=36312 (public domain results of a Commission sponsored report), under 5.3.2.

It seems dubious whether this regime can qualify as legitimate self-regulation on markets because the players' interests seem underrepresented. Also, the mode of negotiation may or may not ensure a balanced approach to all interests involved. Thus, it is generally positive that the Court restricted some of the Football Charter's negative effects on players, such as excessive damages for 'breach of contract'.[480] However, in principle the Court accepted the Football Charter and its main rules on reimbursing the football club who first trained a promising player – without taking recourse to any legitimacy of the mode of regulation. Another case also concerning private agreements comes, naturally, from the realm of competition law. The *Cipolla* case[481] practically endorsed a fee regime established by the Italian bar, since it was made legally binding by the ministry of justice. The Court thus embraced a unilateral regulation by a professional body, without considering any issue of representation.

As regards collective labour agreements and the underlying processes of establishing them, the decisions that immediately come to mind are those relating to *Laval* and *Viking*. These cases have already been discussed in relation to the notion of horizontal effect of free movement rights[482] and of the role of human rights.[483] Clearly, these cases also allow some conclusions relating to the Court's view of industrial relations – although the matter of whether collective labour rights should generally be determinative for employment conditions in Member States is not addressed explicitly. However, there is another set of cases, already discussed in relation to EU equality law, where the Court likewise referred to collective bargaining and collective agreements. This set consists of the cases *Rosenbladt*,[484] *Impact*[485] and *Palacios de la Villa*.[486] Interestingly, the Court seemed to take quite different perspectives on industrial relations in both these groups of cases.

The cases *Laval* and *Viking* challenged the Court to relate a system of largely autonomous regulation of employment conditions to the rules on the internal market. As the facts have been summarised already,[487] a very short recap may suffice here: in both cases, employers sought to use labour deployed from a low-wage Member State (Latvia and Estonia respectively) to a high-wage Member State (Sweden and Finland respectively), relying on

---

480 See above pp. 168–169 with note 298.
481 Case 96/04 *Cipolla* (see above, note 21).
482 Above, pp. 132–134 with notes 101–112 and pp. 164–168, notes 280–297.
483 Above, pp. 197–199 with notes 439–450.
484 Above, note 376.
485 Above, note 355.
486 Above, note 376.
487 Above, pp. 133–134.

their EU right to freely provide their services or establish across borders. Trade unions opposed the low pay (but not the use of foreign labour as such) and initiated collective action, in both cases also relying on solidarity action, in order to convince the employer to engage in negotiations on adequate wages. In the *Laval* case the industrial action was sufficiently effective to cause the insolvency of one employer (but not the one taking the case to the Court of Justice); in *Viking* the threat of collective action was sufficient to induce the employer to refrain from using low-wage labour.

As has been stated, the Court recognised the human rights protection for collective bargaining and collective action. However, there is limited evidence of any recognition for the specific legitimising quality of employment conditions regulated collectively. As the term industrial democracy suggests, collective bargaining and collective agreements can be seen as a form of democratically legitimated regulation in society. One could even assume that such regulation is more legitimate than imposing protective legislation in favour of workers. Protective legislation always has a paternalistic element, while engaging in collective bargaining and collective action (or the threat of it) enables workers to operate on a level playing field with employers. This achieves a degree of emancipation not available under protective legislation.

The Court demonstrated some understanding of industrial relations, stating that 'collective action [...] may be the trade unions' last resort to ensure the success of their claim to regulate the work of [...] employees collectively' and 'must be considered as inextricably linked to the collective agreement'.[488] Nevertheless, it did not seem to see much of a difference between industrial democracy and protective legislation. This is most apparent in the *Laval* case, where the trade union is seen as the agent of the Member State (Sweden), which seeks to impose its wage law on a foreign service provider. The Court states that 'the national authorities in Sweden have entrusted management and labour with the task of setting, by way of collective negotiations, the wage rates which national undertakings are to pay their workers'[489] and repeatedly uses the term 'a Member State's trade union' or a 'trade union of a Member State'.[490] Disregarding the specific procedural legitimacy of autonomously negotiated collective agreements, the Court did not hesitate to restrict the autonomy of the bargaining process. It even assumed the competence to judge whether the aims pursued by trade unions were adequate. Thus, in the *Viking* case, the Court stated that only certain objectives could justify industrial action, which must aim to 'protect and improve [...] terms and conditions of

488 *Viking* case, Paragraph 36.

489 *Laval* case, paragraph 69.

490 Paragraphs 96, 99, 107 (specifying that it is the trade union of the host Member State).

employment'. In the Court's view, the ITF campaign against 'flags of convenience' cannot possibly fall into that category. Thus, it appears that trade unions should be restricted to participation in regulation of employment issues within national borders, and should not seek to impinge on employers' transnational economic interests. In the *COM v Germany (third pillar pension)* case,[491] the Court stated that the objectives pursued by a collective agreement are legitimate in so far as the level of pensions should be enhanced, but not in so far as security of investments and participation of workers in decisions made over the strategy of a pension fund should be achieved by choosing certain providers. The Court stated that the parties to the collective agreement should have agreed on a tendering process in which they laid down these aims as social criteria to be imposed on any successful tenderer.[492]

Accordingly, the Court did not accept the autonomy of the collective bargaining process, but rather found it legitimate for the judiciary to impose specific themes on trade unions and employers and their associations, if they want to avoid the collective bargaining process and any resulting industrial action being declared invalid on the grounds of violating EU economic freedoms. Were the Court to respect the collective bargaining process, it would have to restrict itself to content control of collective agreements, rather than control of the bargaining process. Further, it would only subject collective agreements to content control in such matters in which the process cannot be expected to represent all the interests at stake. This would, for example, justify controlling collective agreements for discriminatory rules. This is so, because the collective bargaining process mandates that employees and employers focus on the widest common denominator, which often leads to a low regard for minority interests.[493]

In the other group of cases relating to collective agreements, the Court had stressed a different aspect of industrial democracy: it positively endorsed the capacity of collective bargaining to provide flexibility of employment conditions. In the *Palacios de la Villa* case, the Court had to decide whether the following clause in a Spanish collective agreement violated the prohibition to discriminate on grounds of age: 'In the interest of promoting employment, it is agreed that the retirement age will be 65 years.' Discussing whether this exception from the prohibition of age discrimination was justified under Article 6(1) Directive 2000/78/EC, the Court, inter alia, relied on the fact that the derogation was contained in a collective agreement. It stated 'the relevant

---

491 Case C-271/08 *COM v Germany* above p. 137 with note 122.

492 Paragraphs 49 et seq. The Court's case law on public procurement has not been conducive to the assumption that such social criteria would actually be accepted (see for more detail on this Arrowsmith and Kunzlik, 2009).

493 Further on this see Schiek, 2012 (forthcoming), paragraphs 395–455.

national legislation allows the social partners to opt, by way of collective agreements – and therefore with considerable flexibility – for application of the compulsory retirement mechanism so that due account may be taken not only of the overall situation in the labour market concerned, but also of the specific features of the jobs in question'.[494] This reasoning was repeated nearly literally in the *Rosenbladt* case, also on compulsory dismissal at age 65 based on a collective agreement.[495] Thus, here the Court accepted the specific advantages of the collective bargaining process and was prepared to step back in its content control – unfortunately in such a field where the parties to collective agreements cannot be expected to represent interests adequately.

## 5. Evaluation

Democracy does not primarily develop before courts, but rather in social practices repeated over and over again in public and socio-economic spheres. However, in a constitutional democracy such as the EU, courts have a strong role in rights protection, within which they can respect or even promote these processes at times. Thus, it is no surprise that the rights-related rulings of the Court's Grand Chamber also touch upon democratic processes. It could be shown that it has supported elements of liberal constitutionalism related to transparency and the role of the European Parliament. Partly this support was selective, depending on whether the Court had to decide between transparency and data protection and could favour the secrecy of Commission politics at the same time. By contrast, the Court largely failed to recognise the relevance of industrial relations for a functioning transnational democracy with aspirations to integrate markets in rulings which remain the subject of ongoing research.[496] However, the Court of Justice of the European Union is no exception among other courts in Europe in that it has difficulties appraising the complexity of industrial action when first confronted with employers' claims against it. National courts had more than two hundred years to become accustomed to the reality of industrial democracy and, also, the ECtHR has developed its recently more progressive case law over a period of more than forty years. There may even be a beacon of hope in the Court's contradictory positioning towards industrial democracy and collective self-regulation: if it is able to recognise the potential of flexibility inherent in regulating the employment relationship by collective agreement, it may develop its very restrictive

494 Case C-411/05 *Palacios de la Villa*, paragraph 74.

495 Case C-45/09 *Rosenbladt*, paragraph 49. See also Opinion of AG Pedro Cruz Villalón of 19 May 2011 in case C-447/09 *Prigge*, paragraphs 78–85.

496 See Bücker and Warneck, 2010, announcing ongoing research for the next three years.

reasoning on transnational collective bargaining and collective action if they impact on the economic freedoms with increasing exposure to this subject.

## IV. CONCLUSION

This chapter has analysed the EU's judicial constitution's positioning between liberal constitutionalism and socially embedded constitutionalism,[497] based on Grand Chamber decisions post-Enlargement on substantive questions of EU constitutional law. As was to be expected from the trajectory of European constitutional law analysed in Chapter 3, these rulings mainly relate to the EU's 'economic constitution', which has a much longer tradition than its political, civil and social constitution.[498] Thus, the Chamber's docket provides ample opportunity to adjudicate individual rights of economic actors, but offers fewer opportunities to engage with constitutional law beyond mainly economic concerns, such as human rights and equal treatment beyond markets. The resulting focus on the internal market does not, however, necessitate that the EU's judicial constitution develop a 'neo-liberal bias',[499] or pushes the EU and its Member States towards a liberal market economy,[500] or enhances the European economic constitution over any nationally pursued social policy,[501] nor does it necessitate favouring liberal constitutionalism over socially embedded constitutionalism.

In supporting European integration through law, the Grand Chamber was 'biased' in favour of economic rights generally, whether this supported liberal or socially embedded constitutionalism. As regards a constitution of equality, human rights protection and questions of democracy, the rulings leaned towards liberal constitutionalism. Beyond this, the picture emerging from categorising and analysing 173 recent cases is simultaneously more nuanced and more uniform than at times expected.

Nuances, and a movement beyond the point to which the constitutional trajectory had come by 2004, emerge in very specific fields where the Grand Chamber had to deliver a large number of decisions. For example, relating to taxation, the Court has recently been more lenient towards Member States with comparatively strong economic performances protecting their tax base. It has achieved this doctrinally only by finding discriminatory legislation to

---

497 For the notions of liberal and socially embedded constitutionalism see Chapter 2, II.

498 For these notions see Chapter 3, p. 79.

499 See Smismans, 2010, p. 187.

500 Höpner and Schäfer, 2010, Scharpf, 2010.

501 Joerges and Roedl, 2009.

infringe economic freedoms.[502] This means that the Chamber has partly reversed the dynamic of negative integration in this field by softening the Dassonville formula – a development that had been seen as impossible.[503] Nuances distinguishing more recent case law from received wisdom can also be detected in the move to merge fundamental freedoms. Until 2003/2004 the Court maintained a distinction between free trade and factor mobility, the Court relinquished this distinction by considering service provision to be 'temporary' if ongoing for more than seven years, and more generally in the fields of gambling and betting, taxation and anything to do with industrial relations. While traditionally, Member States could in principle expect an entrepreneur establishing abroad to integrate into their national legal order, this expectation now needs specific justification.[504] This corresponds to the freedom to choose one's corporate domicile under free movement of companies, which has been confirmed, but not expanded recently.[505]

Similarly, rulings in the field of equality law[506] differ from earlier periods. Equality case law used to be a driver of a socially responsible internal market: the Court introduced the horizontal effect of the equal pay clause in the 1970s and of other discrimination principles in the early 2000s and it established principles of substantive equality by enforcing the prohibition of indirect discrimination and by allowing positive action (under strict preconditions). More recently, the Grand Chamber tends to stress equality as consistency over substantive equality though, even when deciding on directives aimed at promoting equality in socio-economic reality. As regards human rights protection, the post-2004 rulings show a surge towards perspectives of liberal constitutionalism, even if this leads to a curb on the EU's prerogatives. Further, contrasting the received wisdom that economic and social integration have been decoupled in the Court's case law,[507] the Grand Chamber frequently relates economic and social integration to each other.[508]

On the other hand, there is consistency with former case law in specifically conflictive fields. The Grand Chamber rulings in *Viking* and *Laval*, which have been portrayed as unexpected and deviating from anything known until 2007 in academic writing, are actually in most respects a continuation of former case law. They cut across the three fields of protecting economic freedoms, human rights and democracy, and at the same time illuminate potential clashes

502 See above, pp. 130–131, notes 82–93, pp. 140–146, notes 148–180.
503 Scharpf, 2010.
504 See Chapter 3, pp. 88–90, above pp. 122–126.
505 See Chapter 3, pp. 87–88, above pp. 126–128.
506 Above, pp. 173–185.
507 E.g. Scharpf, 2002, Joerges and Roedl, 2009, p. 3.
508 See above, pp. 148–149.

between liberal and socially embedded constitutionalism, which necessitates a separate evaluation here. Regarding protection of economic freedoms in horizontal relations, the Court had acknowledged horizontal effects of the freedom of establishment and the freedom to provide services from 1974,[509] and explicitly expanded this to collective labour agreements in 1999.[510] The *Viking* case takes this case law even further as it lowers the threshold for finding a restriction: not only a fully fledged collective agreement has been held as constituting a restriction, but also the mere circulation of an e-mail requiring trade unions to refrain from negotiating a collective agreement while another trade union is engaged in negotiations underpinned by a threat of strike action. The *Laval* case confirms that the demands of a trade union in negotiations – if underlined by strike actions – qualify as restriction, and not just the (legally binding) agreement signed after successful negotiations. These, not the fact that the Court subjects any collective agreement to the supremacy of economic freedoms, are novelties. As regards human rights protection, the Court remains within the concept of its pre-2000 case law: it does not acknowledge liberties to associate and take collective action, but rather categorises these human rights as just another mandatory requirement, which Member States can bring forward to justify restrictions.[511] The Court thus refused to expand its reasoning in *Schmidberger* (in favour of the freedom of assembly) to the right of freedom of association, from which the ECtHR derives rights to collective bargaining and collective action.[512] The Court also confirmed its case law from the 1990s, which already disregarded any intrinsic value of industrial democracy.[513] The main novelty of the *Viking* and *Laval* litigation lay in the vastly increased wage differentials between the poorest and the richest Member States after Eastern Enlargement.[514] Both cases originated from before 2004: the conflict in *Viking* had started in 2001 and the Swedish company Laval submitted its bid for a contract in Sweden in 2003. Obviously,

[509] Case *Walrave*, see Chapter 3, p. 90, note 68.

[510] Case *Fernandez Bobadilla*, see Chapter 3, p. 90, note 71.

[511] The case *COM v France* (Chapter 3, p. 91, note 74) already indicated potential challenges for national constitutional rights to collective action (Muylle, 1998, Orlandini, 2000). A specific regulation was issued aiming to protect freedom of association from overzealous enforcement of free movement of goods (Regulation 2679/98/EC of 7 December 1998).

[512] However, the *COM v Germany* ruling (above note 122) might indicate a moderate change.

[513] See Chapter 3, p. 110.

[514] In 2004, the median gross earnings in Finland were at 31 998 € p.a. and in Sweden 33 344 € p.a., but in Estonia and Latvia did not exceed 5 658 € p.a. and 3 806 € p.a. respectively. Hourly labour costs in Finland were at 25.34 €, in Sweden 31.08 €, in Estonia at 4.24 € and in Latvia at 2.77 € (source: Eurostat).

counsel for business in Finland and Sweden respectively had advised their clients to exploit the inner-EU gap in labour costs after Enlargement to their advantage. Their success was almost entirely predictable on the basis of former case law.

This nuanced picture still allows us to identify a few predominant tendencies. While it is true that the Grand Chamber at times supports principles associated with socially embedded constitutionalism, it is equally true that this occurs more frequently if it plays out in favour of EU policies (and thus pro-integration generally) or if working in favour of the so-called cosmopolitan elite of free movers: the students of the Erasmus generation (as long as they do not require state support for maintenance); the mobile worker (if not made to relocate by her employer in order to provide services while undercutting local wages); the free moving member of the 'liberal professions'. These socially embedded rights are stronger the closer they are to economic rights (as opposed to citizenship rights of not economically active people). The elite of free movers[515] may thus have an interest in increasing commercialisation of social services such as education and health care, as this eases their access to these. However, in exceptional cases, such as *Elchinov* or *Teixeira*, this form of social integration worked in favour of citizens from very poor states or just very poor citizens. From the perspective of the local population, the implicit commercialisation of public institutions may not be wholly positive though: services made available for those willing and able to move might deplete funds for local provision. Also, a slight bias in favour of economic freedoms emerges in the frequency with which economic freedoms prevail over either national policy or social integration aims. This seems particularly virulent when antagonistic interests are negotiated, such as conflicting human rights of business and labour, discord between migrating individuals and national welfare institutions or clashes between internal market imperatives and institutions providing (social) services of general interest.

While these trends exist as a factual development, it is open to doubt whether there is any collective intention of the Grand Chamber judges (or any programmatically minded avant-garde among them) to achieve this trend. These doubts are nourished by the extent to which case law is contradictory.[516] These contradictions are most frequent in cases relating to rights derived from economic freedoms, where there is the largest amount of cases and we can expect the highest level of professionalism. The inconsistencies are especially surprising as we have only covered case law by the Grand Chamber, with a relatively stable composition and a wide range of expertise. This inconsistency

---

515 On the EU's middle-class bias see Andreotti and Galès, 2011, and Fligstein, 2008.

516 See above, pp. 170–73, 185, 199–200, 209.

endangers the credibility of autonomous judicial discourse, whose doctrinal consistency is generally seen as a precondition for successful 'judicialized governance'.[517] However, it also indicates that there is presently scope to influence the European judiciary, who may still be finding their exact position after Eastern Enlargement and the recent global economic crisis.

This invites a different view on EU constitutional law, which contrasts to the factual development of Grand Chamber rulings with EU constitutional law in the Treaties as they stand after the Treaty of Lisbon. The next, and final, chapter is dedicated to discussing these new provisions from a hermeneutic perspective, focusing on the potential of eliminating contradictions between different elements of EU constitutional law through case law, harmonising legislation and rules created by societal actors. It will emphasise the positioning of Treaty law between liberal and socially embedded constitutionalism as well as between economic and social integration.

517 Stone Sweet, 2011, pp. 129–131, with further references.

# 5. Economic and social integration under the EU's normative constitution

## I. INTRODUCTION

Having established the thrust of the EU's judicial constitution as evident in Grand Chamber cases from 2004 (Chapter 4), based on the trajectory of the EU's substantive constitutional law in promoting economic freedoms, furthering equality rights, protecting human rights and relating to democracy (Chapter 3), this chapter first investigates how two other elements of EU constitutional law are positioned between liberal and socially embedded constitutionalism, and thus how they are ordained to meet the challenges of economic and social integration. First, it considers the values, objectives and general orientations announced by the EU's written constitution as established by the Treaties (II). It then discusses the distribution of competences between the EU and its Member States and regional bodies as well as the role of societal actors within EU governance and as transnational norm builders (III). Finally, it discusses whether these three elements of the EU constitution are in harmony as regards economic and social integration (IV). Finding that there is a gap, deliberations are made as to how it can be closed. The idea of an EU constitution of social governance is explored to this end (V).

## II. THE EU'S VALUES, OBJECTIVES AND GENERAL ORIENTATION

### 1. Relevance of Values and Objectives

Explicit values are a relatively young element of EU constitutional law,[1] which was only introduced with the Treaty of Lisbon. Its predecessors had restricted themselves merely to tasks (which are now grown into objectives). However, these tasks were also based on unwritten values. The tasks of the EEC from the beginning elaborated the wider policy aims the Community

---

[1] See above Chapter 2, IV, pp. 69–71.

hoped to achieve with its main pragmatic intention, the establishment of the Common Market. Also, programmatic norms have always been scattered over the Treaties, spelling out general orientations to be pursued in specific policy fields framed by each of the Treaty chapters. Such programmatic clauses are not just interesting from a discursive analysis. According to the Court, they are also legally binding.[2] Even if they do not specify explicit rights or obligations, they must still be relied upon when interpreting (preferably widening) the scope of application of directly effective provisions of EU law.[3] They are thus truly constitutional norms. As such, their relation to liberal and socially embedded constitutionalism is worth investigating in order to fully grasp the EU constitution.

## 2. Values and Objectives before the Treaty of Lisbon

The EU's normative base has long conveyed the ideal of interrelated economic and social integration.[4] The Treaty founding the European Economic Community specified a combination of economic, social and political objectives that the Community would have as its task, which it would fulfil by establishing a Common Market, in its Article 2:

> The Community shall have as its task, by establishing a Common Market and progressively approximating the economic policies of the Member States, to promote throughout the Community a harmonious development of economic activities, a continuous and balanced expansion, an increase in stability, an accelerated raising of the standard of living and closer relations between the States belonging to it.

---

[2] Under 'Schmittian' concepts of constitutional law, which have been influential in a number of Member States, programmatic provisions can never be legally binding (Koutnatzis, 2005, pp. 85–87 and – criticising this perspective – Schiek, 2001, pp. 35–46 (paragraphs 46–67). The ECJ has rejected this approach, however, and held that the EU's own social progression clause is not deprived of legal effect by its programmatic character (ECJ case 126/86 *Zaera* [1987] ECR 3698, paragraph 14).

[3] The Court had derived from Article 117 EEC (now 155 TFEU) the principle that unequal pay for women and men in violation of Article 119 EEC (now 157 TFEU) must be remedied by raising women's pay to that of men (case 43/75 *Defrenne II* [1976] ECR 455) and that the notion of undertaking in the directive on transfer of undertakings must be read widely in order to secure maximum protection of workers (case C-449/93 *Rockfon* [1995] ECR I-4291). More recently it has relied on Article 2 EC in stating that rights derived from the economic freedoms "must be balanced against the objectives pursued by social policy" (Case C-438/05 *Viking* [2007] ECR I-I-10779, paragraph 79, Case C-341/05 *Laval* [2007] ECR I-11767, paragraph 105).

[4] For more detail on this see Schiek, 2008.

Accordingly, the common market and coordination of national economic policies were only ever means to other ends. The EEC Treaty breathed the belief of embedded liberalism[5] by stating that its socio-economic aims would be achieved on the back of the common market, possibly supported by national policies. This was also expressed in Article 117 EEC, the initial provision of the social policy chapter. It defined the goal of the EEC social policy as promoting 'improved working conditions and an improved standard of living for workers, so as to make possible their harmonisation while the improvement is being maintained.' The next subsection stated that all this would be achieved through the functioning of the Common Market and through approximating national social policies. Subsequent Treaty changes by the Treaties of Maastricht (1992/93) and Amsterdam (1997/99)[6] confirmed the instrumental position of the internal market and the programmatic interrelation of social and economic integration, while expanding the Treaty aims considerably.

The Treaty of Maastricht added as goals for the Community to promote a 'high degree of convergence of economic performance, a high level of employment and social protection (…) and economic and social cohesion and solidarity among the Member States.' (Article 2 EC) It also modified the merely expansive orientation of the EEC, by replacing 'harmonious development of economic activities' by 'harmonious and balanced development of economic activities', 'continuous and balanced expansion' by 'sustainable and non-inflationary growth respecting the environment' and the 'accelerated raising of living standards' by 'raising of living standards and quality of life'. These modifications embrace the then new concept of sustainability. The newly founded EU aimed to 'promote economic and social progress which is balanced and sustainable', (Article 2 EU pre Lisbon) indicating that the confidence in limitless growth had been lost.[7] The Treaty of Maastricht also dedicated the new 'close coordination of Member States' economic policies' not only to the internal market, but also to the 'principle of an open market economy with free competition' (Article 3a EC). Further, the lords of the Treaties now decreed that the wider Treaty aims should be achieved 'by establishing a common market and an economic and monetary union and by implementing the common policies and activities referred to in Articles 3 and 3a'. This meant that EU-level policy making was seen as a precondition for achieving any of the socio-economic aims to which the EU had committed itself. Normatively, the time of embedded liberalism had already gone by in 1993.[8]

---

5 See Chapter 1, p. 18 with note 74.

6 The dual dates indicate the year of adopting the Treaty text and the year of its coming into force after ratification by all Member States.

7 On a recent perspective with historical references see Nikolaïdis, 2010.

8 In a similar vein from a social policy perspective Ferrera, 2010, pp. 49–50.

The Treaty of Amsterdam only added a few new aims for the Community and the Union, including equality between women and men and improving the quality of the environment. More importantly, it specified the commitments towards active EU policies for the revised social policy chapter. The new Article 136 EC transformed social policy into a common task of the EU and its Member States, embracing social policy aims beyond improving working conditions and raising living standards, such as adequate social protection, dialogue between management and labour, development of human resources with a view to high levels of employment and combating social exclusion. The Treaty of Amsterdam also complemented the Treaty title on economic policy by a title on employment, with its own specific objective: employment should be promoted by changing the workforce into an adaptive, skilled and trained one, and by making labour markets responsive to economic change (Article 125 EC, now Article 145 TFEU, substantively unchanged). Thus, workers were to adapt to the demands of the changing economy, while the employers were relieved from any obligation to adapt to new developments in order to achieve a high level of employment. Thus, before the Treaty of Lisbon, the EU's objectives hinted at a normative socio-economic model interlinking economic and social integration.

The EU did not have explicit values though. The Treaty of Maastricht had, however, established principles of the EU, to which any acceding state must agree. These comprised liberty, democracy, respect for human rights and fundamental freedoms. Clearly, these principles embraced central categories of classical liberal constitutionalism, but remained silent as to any socially embedding of these. Thus, while the EU had given itself a proactive task, it also acclaimed principles of a non-proactive, liberal state. The values and objectives, as far as they were specified in the Treaties, were thus clearly contradictory.

## 3. Values and Objectives after the Treaty of Lisbon

After the Treaty of Lisbon, the Treaties for the first time assert values common to the EU and its Member States (Article 2 TEU) that have to be read in connection with the EU's objectives (Article 3 TEU). Having values common to the EU and its Member States implies the potential for creating a shared constitutional space consisting of national and EU law. While the Treaty only modestly impacted on substantive EU law,[9] its elaborated values, objectives and general orientation have been read as re-balancing the Treaty in favour of

---

[9] Beneyto, 2008, states that there was insufficient agreement in relation to economic policy as well as 'fields of explicit interest to citizens, such as social policy' (pp. 15, 17).

social values.[10] The EU's normative base thus needs to be reassessed considering the paradigms of liberal and socially embedded constitutionalism and gauging their potential to contribute towards reconciling economic and social integration.

### a) Objectives and values

The objectives of the EU are now comprised in Article 3 EU, which merges the former Article 2 EU and Articles 2, 3 EC. The new Article 2 EU adds considerable substance to the former objectives by elevating the principles of the Treaty of Maastricht to values, and to complement liberty, democracy, respect for human rights and fundamental freedoms by human dignity and the rights of persons belonging to a minority. According to Article 2, 2nd sentence, 'these values are common to the Member States in a society in which pluralism, non-discrimination, tolerance, justice, solidarity and equality between women and men prevail'. The 2nd sentence values have been qualified as those having a more social orientation.[11] The Treaty text is slightly ambiguous. On the one hand, the wording of Article 2 might suggest that only the more social values mentioned in the second sentence are to be pursued by the Member States within societies, while the values more akin to liberal constitutionalism are the true EU values. This would stress the values of liberal constitutionalism, and leave any social embedding to the Member States. On the other hand, both sentences might be intended to be read together, which would again indicate that the social values in the second sentence are also part of the EU value base.[12]

The main argument in favour of the second interpretation is that the innovation of Article 2 would be very limited if only the values relating to liberal constitutionalism were true EU values. Further support can be drawn from Article 3 TEU, which names the EU's objectives, and includes for the first time the objective of social justice. If the EU is to promote social justice, it certainly must also be based on the value of solidarity. Solidarity, however, is only mentioned in Article 2, 2nd sentence, EU. From this, we can deduce that the values specified in this sentence are also values of the EU. This interpretation is further supported by the fact that Article 2, 2nd sentence, phrases society in the singular. A provision that only addressed the Member States would have to speak of a plurality of national societies. A purposive, grammatical and systemic interpretation of Articles 2, 3 EU thus demonstrates that all the values

---

10 Craig, 2010, pp. 329–330.

11 Craig, 2010, p. 312.

12 This position is maintained, but not supported by any reasoning, by Armstrong, 2010, p. 242; Dawson and de Witte, 2012 (forthcoming); Piris, 2010, p. 310.

of Article 2, including those mentioned in the 2nd sentence, are values of the EU.

As regards the objectives of the EU, Article 3 paragraphs 3 and 4 TEU specify the socio-economic aims. They read:

> 3. The Union shall establish an internal market. It shall work for the sustainable development of Europe based on balanced economic growth and price stability, a highly competitive social market economy, aiming at full employment and social progress, and a high level of protection and improvement of the quality of the environment. It shall promote scientific and technological advance.
>
> It shall combat social exclusion and discrimination, and shall promote social justice and protection, equality between women and men, solidarity between the generations and protection of the rights of the child.
>
> It shall promote economic, social and territorial cohesion, and solidarity among the Member States.
>
> It shall respect its rich cultural and linguistic diversity, and shall ensure that Europe's cultural heritage is safeguarded and enhanced.
>
> 4. The Union shall establish an economic and monetary union whose currency is the euro.

On the one hand, the Treaty of Lisbon has strengthened the values and objectives related to economic integration. Going a step beyond the Treaty of Maastricht, the establishment of the internal market and of economic and monetary union are now no longer a means to an end, but veritable Treaty objectives in their own right. This seems to strengthen the economic freedoms, which after all constitute the internal market (Article 26 TFEU): they are now underlined by Treaty objectives. One could say that the Treaty has grown into the judicial constitution that has always considered the economic freedoms as constitutional values on their own.

On the other hand, the specific internal market aim is immediately followed by more social objectives. In the same subparagraph the EU is committed to a highly competitive social market economy, full employment and social progress. Historically, the social market economy was instrumental in post-war Germany in establishing an ordo-liberal consensus.[13] However, this is not necessarily the case for the EU. It is more likely that those insisting on this term during the negotiations on the convention meant to anchor a compromise between merely economic and social objectives into the EU constitution of the

13 See only Joerges and Roedl, 2009, pp. 3–5, with more references to their own works.

internal market.[14] Thus, the internal market is now reined in by competitiveness and price stability on the one hand, representing neo-liberal values, and full employment and social progress, and the social in the market economy on the other hand, representing social values.

Furthermore, Article 3 paragraph 3, third sentence TEU reinforces the combat against social exclusion and discrimination, and the promotion of gender equality, but introduces as new objectives social justice and protection as well as solidarity between the generations. The Treaty of Lisbon is the first Treaty ever to even mention social justice. Although this aim is not made very explicit, and is not underscored by specific competences, this step should not be underestimated. Social justice cannot be achieved by establishing derivative social policies. It rather refers to the heart of (national) social policy in its own right. However weakly the Treaty specifies social justice, by including it at all it seems to indicate that achieving social justice must not be left to the Member States, but rather constitutes a task to be pursued at the European level. The least one must expect of the EU after the Treaty of Lisbon is that it takes positive steps towards enhancing social justice as a European concept. This clearly goes beyond 'just' refraining from compromising national and regional policies promoting social justice through restrictive case law or overly neo-liberal legislation.[15] Its new values and objectives commit the European Union to reconciling economic and social integration as a constitutional mandate.

The contradictions seem to abound when considering values in specific Treaty chapters. First, the economic policy chapter seems to abandon the mission of a social market economy, when it stresses that the EU and the Member States pursue economic policy 'in accordance with the principle of an open market economy with free competition' (Article 119 TFEU). This wording, which was already established with the Treaty of Maastricht, seems to exclude striving for a social market economy. This contrasts with Article 151 TFEU, which faithfully copies ex Article 136 EC: in its view the EU shall strive for enhancing working and living conditions and other social policy aims, and take an active regulatory role in this. Also, Article 145 TFEU copies Article 125 EC, demanding that Member States promote adaptation of workers rather than of capital to a changing economy.

---

14 See Armstrong, 2010, p. 244; with further references see also implicitly Scharpf, 2010. See also Azoulaï, 2008, who reads the installation of the social market economy as a step towards substantive constitutionalisation in favour of balancing economic integration and social policy.

15 As could be derived from the EC Treaty before Lisbon, see Schiek, 2008, pp. 50–51.

The EU remains a contradictory polity, based on conflicting values, rather than only on economic integration and liberal constitutionalism. The Treaty of Lisbon has enhanced the EU's commitment to social integration, with a new emphasis on solidarity[16] and social justice. However, as this goes along with a strengthening of the internal market, which is now a Treaty objective in its own right, the Treaty of Lisbon also calls for a true reconciliation of economic and social integration. It neither allows reliance on economic integration at EU levels and delegation of creating preconditions for social integration to national levels, nor does it give social integration priority over economic integration, as the old Treaties had. The Treaties as reformed by the Treaty of Lisbon commit the EU to reconciling economic and social dimensions of European integration at the EU level and thus also within the Member States.

### b) 'Horizontal clauses' in the TFEU

This reconciliation is further supported by a number of horizontal clauses provided for in the Treaty on the Functioning of the European Union. Horizontal clauses were first introduced in the Treaty of Amsterdam, where they referred to gender equality (ex Article 3(2) EC) and to environmental protection (ex Article 6 EC), i.e. to policy fields sitting on the fringes of social policy in a wide sense. After the Treaty of Lisbon, the TFEU contains no fewer than six horizontal clauses (Articles 7–12).

First of all, under Article 7 TFEU the Union shall ensure consistency between all its policies, and always take account of all its objectives. As the provision also stresses the principle of conferral, this can be read as a hint that all policy objectives, also those which have not been complemented by specific competences, must be considered while action is taken in such policy fields where the EU has competences. Thus, for example, objectives such as the promotion of social justice should be mainstreamed in any policy, including those aimed at enhancing the internal market.

Articles 8 and 11 TFEU maintain the existing horizontal clauses on gender mainstreaming (ex Article 3(2) EC) and environmental protection (ex Article 6 EC). Article 9 has been hailed as the 'horizontal social clause'.[17] It obliges the Union to take five social policy fields into account in all its policies: promoting employment, social protection, fighting social exclusion, a high level of education and training and the protection of human health. This clause, on the one hand, mirrors a classical approach to national welfare states[18] in focusing on (re)distribution (social protection, fighting social

---

16 Ross, 2010.

17 Ferrera, 2010, pp. 57–58, Dawson and de Witte, 2012 (forthcoming); on the evolution of the clause see Piris, 2010, p. 310.

18 See on this Chapter 1, IV, pp. 34–35.

exclusion). Corresponding to the tradition in EU social policy, it also encompasses market annexed social policies:[19] furthering employment at EU level also furthers factor mobility, an inherently economic aim, and a high level of education and training is a necessary contribution to competitive markets in the global knowledge economy. Finally, health has been proven to be a veritable market in the EU by now, so that promoting human health can also be a market expansion strategy. Regulatory social policy, so far the thrust of EU social policy,[20] is conspicuously absent from the clause. Article 10 complements the gender mainstreaming clause by a non-discrimination mainstreaming clause. Its wording seems to indicate that beyond gender equality the EU is only committed to banning discrimination rather than establishing positive preconditions for equality in fact. Article 12 bolsters the position of EU consumer law by obliging the EU to take its demands into account in all its policies.

### c) The human rights agenda and social values

While the EU's new human rights agenda after the Treaty of Lisbon has already been covered,[21] it seems worthwhile to take a second look from the perspective of rights relevant for social integration. In this respect, the new human rights agenda also exposes some contradictions. Some aspects are clearly supportive of socially embedded constitutionalism. This applies also to the Charter in so far as its solidarity and equality chapters can be read as retrospectively underpinning much EU legislation in the social policy field with a constitutional base. Also, the explicit reference to the European Social Charter in Article 151 TFEU underpins the relevance of so-called socio-economic rights for EU constitutional law. On the other hand the Charter partly endorses the concepts of liberal constitutionalism, e.g. in that it only applies to public actors (the EU and its Member States).[22] Further, the unfortunate division between rights and principles may well lead to weakening social rights.[23] Some suggest that the plan for the EU to accede to the ECHR, but not the ESC, also contributes to widening the gap between social and liberal human rights.[24] However, this rather seems to reflect the different weight these two instruments are given within the Council of Europe.[25] The EU had no alternative to expanding the Charter for remedying an inadequate neglect of social rights.

---

19 See Chapter 1, IV, p. 41.
20 See Chapter 1, IV, pp. 42–44.
21 See Chapter 3, II. pp. 98–100, Chapter 4, II, pp. 186–199.
22 de Witte, 2009.
23 See above, Chapter 3, II, pp. 102–103.
24 de Witte, 2005.
25 Armstrong, 2010, p. 246.

### 4. Reconciling Social and Economic Integration as Constitutional Demand

The analysis above has shown that the EU's values and objectives after the Treaty of Lisbon, taken together with horizontal clauses and its renewed human rights agenda, establish new constitutional demands towards economic and social integration. On the one hand, the Treaties still promote the internal market, now as a Treaty aim in itself, on the basis of largely unchanged substantive law. This economic constitution is now complemented by a human rights constitution, whose liberal elements have already informed the Court's case law to a large degree. It is also complemented by an enhanced body of values and objectives, accompanied by the more progressive elements of the new human rights constitution, which, overall, demand that economic integration should be embedded with social aims, or social integration in the terminology of this book. Normatively, the Treaty thus endorses both liberal and socially embedded constitutionalism.

## III. CONSTITUTION OF COMPETENCES

As has been discussed in Chapter 2, social embedding of liberal constitutionalism does not usually result from the free flow of market forces. Political activity is needed to conciliate economic and social integration. The EU as a multilevel polity allocates competences for such activities at different levels. The constitution of competences decides whether the EU or its Member States or both in cooperation or coordination can take such action.

### 1. General Layout

It is no secret that the Treaty of Lisbon endeavoured to clarify the EU's multilevel constitution by specifying the EU's exact competences. Articles 2–6 TFEU are aimed at fulfilling this task, endowing the Union with exclusive, shared and supporting and coordinative competences. For economic and employment policies the competence regime is not fully clarified, as a mix between coordination and broad guidelines as established by the Treaty of Maastricht is transposed to the TFEU without clarifying this hybrid construct (Article 5 TFEU). This curious mix of mere coordination and ensuring that the coordination is adhered to is the basis for the Open Method of Coordination in wide realms of social policy.

As regards economic and social integration, it is easy to observe that the EU has a few exclusive and some shared competences relating to economic integration, but only shared and coordinative competences relating to social integration. Exclusive EU competences (Article 3 TFEU) prevail for establishing the customs union, the competition rules, monetary policy for Member States whose currency is the euro, and the common commercial policy. Shared competences (Article 4 TFEU) prevail in relation to all other aspects of the internal market, social policy, economic and social cohesion, consumer protection and common safety concerns in public health matters. These shared competences are specified in relation to social policy and public health by the addition 'for the aspects defined in this Treaty'. The relevant Treaty chapters specify that the EU has no competences for pay, the right of association, and the right of industrial warfare (Article 153(5) TFEU), and that the Member States retain the responsibility for managing health services and medical care and for allocating the resources assigned to them (Article 168(7) TFEU). Further, the EU has coordinative and supportive competences (Article 6 TFEU) in the field of protection and improvement of human health as well as education.

The EU competence regime must be seen against the background of the enhanced relevance of the principles of conferral and subsidiarity (Article 5 TEU), which safeguard national competences. As an additional procedural safety belt, the Treaty of Lisbon has empowered national parliaments to ensure that no competence creep on the part of the EU institutions occurs (Article 12 EU).

## 2. Legislative Competences – and Their Limits

Thus, in furthering economic integration, the EU has a range of regulatory competences at its disposal. It can support the mobility of labour as a factor by social security coordination and other means (Articles 46, 47 TFEU), harmonise company law (Article 50 TFEU) and recognition of qualifications (Article 53 TFEU), liberalise the service economy (Articles 59 TFEU), ease direct investment from and to third countries (Article 64 TFEU) and international transport (Article 91 TFEU), give effect to competition rules (Article 103 TFEU) and state aid principles (Article 109 TFEU), harmonise indirect taxes (Article 113 TFEU), create European intellectual property rights (Article 118 TFEU) and approximate any national laws, regulations and administrative practices if this is necessary to establish the internal market or maintain its functioning (Article 114 TFEU).

In relation to social policy, the EU can create minimum requirements in the fields of working environment, working conditions (including those of third-country nationals), social security and social protection of workers, information and consultation of workers, representation and defence of collective interest of workers and employers. However, this only applies if coordinative action is not sufficient and if development of small and medium enterprises is not affected (Article 153 TFEU). It can also create a common vocational training policy (Article 166 TFEU) and legislate to protect public health in strictly limited fields (Article 168(4) TFEU, introduced by the Treaty of Lisbon). The Treaty of Lisbon also created a new, if somewhat complex, legislative competence for services of general interest. Article 14 TFEU obliges Member States and the EU 'each within their respective powers' to ensure that such services operate adequately. The provision also stresses that services of general economic interest occupy a place in the shared values of the Union and its Member States. Both these sentences also imply that there should be a European dimension to SGEI. This is underlined by the last sentence, which gives the EU a legislative competence in the matter. This competence can be used in order to establish European level SGEI, including their funding.[26]

In fields cutting across economic and social policy, the EU can create environmental legislation (Article 191 TFEU), create legislation to combat discrimination (Article 19 TFEU), create immigration law (Articles 78, 79 TFEU), and legislate in favour of mutual recognition of judicial decisions (Article 82 TFEU) and criminal prosecution (Article 83 TFEU).

While it may seem that EU legislation is rather limited in the field of social policy, this is partly mitigated by the breadth of the general 'internal market competence' (Article 114 TFEU), which has also been interpreted generously by the Court. For example, the ruling in *Natural Health Alliance*[27] also concerned the EU's competence to regulate in favour of restricting trade in certain 'health foods' under that provision. Expanding on the line of cases starting with Germany's challenge to a directive restricting tobacco advertisements,[28] the Court reaffirmed the wide scope of Article 114 TFEU: this competence is triggered when it is merely 'likely' that obstacles to trade emerge because Member States 'are about to' take divergent measures in a certain field. While mere divergence is said to be insufficient,[29] the threat of different national rules which could be wielded against imports under the protection of public health was sufficient in the Court's view to create the presumption that divergence with the potential to impinge on the internal

---

26 Accordingly, the Economic and Social Council demands the establishment of EU-level SGEI's in order to bolster citizens' identification with the EU (ESCS own initiative report 'Services of general economic interest: how should responsibilities be divided up between the EU and the Member States' [2010] OJ C 128/65, paragraphs 4.1–4.12, see also Taylor, 2008; more generally on the new provision, see Fiedziuk, 2011.

27 C-154 and 155/04 [2005] ECR I-6451; on the substance Chapter 4, II, p. 120.

28 C-397/98 *Germany v Parliament and Council* [2000] ECR I 8419, C-434/02 *Arnold André* [2004] ECR I 11825, C-210/03 *Swedish Match* [2004] ECR I-11893 and C-491/01 *British American Tobacco* [2002] ECR I-11453.

29 Case C-154/04 *Natural Health Alliance*, paragraph 28.

market would emerge. It was then irrelevant that the internal market was not the main motive of the directive, which rather aimed to protect human health.[30] Thus, there is some potential to use the internal market clause for social policy legislation, should the EU institutions agree that such legislation is needed. Beyond Article 114 TFEU, the EU can also legislate in any field that 'directly affects' the functioning of the internal market (Article 115 TFEU), and if it is necessary to attain another policy objective (Article 352 TFEU). The latter competence is restricted in so far as it is clearly subsidiary to specific legislative competences. This is now (after the Treaty of Lisbon) stressed in Article 352(2) TFEU. Further, it is now clarified that Article 352 cannot be relied upon in fields where harmonisation of laws is excluded (Article 352(3)).

The limits of legislative competences are exacerbated by the increasing difficulty in achieving any consent to legislate. This is not only the case in the many fields where EU legislation requires unanimity in the Council – as in many social policy fields and if using the broad competences of Articles 115 and 352 TFEU – but even where only a qualified majority is needed. The time-consuming nature of EU regulation is the basis of Scharpf's assertion that the EU cannot become a social market economy.[31] Realistically he assumes that a small interest group is sufficient in order to create a line of case law, but enormous effort is required in order to counteract the negative integration achieved in this way by EU legislation.

## 3. Judicial Competences

Scharpf's argument illuminates the fact that the competences for EU legislation must be seen in context with the competence of the EU judiciary. These competences are far less constrained than the legislative competences – mainly due to the Court's own case law. The Court has already established for the legal framework before the Treaty of Lisbon that competence norms only restrict EU legislation, but not to the applicability of the EU Treaties at large. As demonstrated in Chapter 4 in relation to taxation, health care and industrial relations,[32] the Court has established a standing formula according to which Member States are bound to observe EU law even in fields where the EU has no competence at all, or where the EU has not (yet) used a shared competence. It is not to be expected that this changes with the mere specification of competences.

---

30 Case C-167/05 *COM v Sweden* [2008] ECR I-2127, paragraphs 32, 30.
31 Scharpf, 2010.
32 For more detail see Chapter 4, pp. 130–133, 156–160.

Thus, there is a model for ensuring obeisance with constitutionally binding norms without using EU competences for legislating in their favour: Member States have long been held to be bound by the relevant constitutional norms nevertheless. In practice, this has mainly reinforced the elements of the EU economic constitution – with limited exceptions in the field of competition law. Thus, the Court has held that the economic freedoms must be complied with by any national regulation of the health care sector and by the action of any trade union.[33] However, it has exempted certain classes of collective agreements from the scrutiny of the EU competition authorities.[34]

In order to properly assess the constitution of competences, judicial competences need to be considered.

## 4. Coordinative and Budget Competences

Legislation is not the only way for the EU to impact on economic and social integration. In fields as important as economic policy and combating of poverty, the EU relies traditionally on coordination, partly supported by common guidelines.

The EU can further generate impact by spending funds on certain policies. The European social funds (Articles 162–164 TFEU), agricultural policies (Article 39, 40, 43 TFEU) and the EU research funding (Article 182 TFEU) are examples of budgetary competences that can have redistributive consequences. Despite the relatively modest EU budget in comparison with national budgets, such policies do have an impact.

## 5. Evaluating the Constitution of Competences

With all these nuances, it still appears that the distribution of competences across different levels of the EU polity has partly remained at the stage of embedded liberalism. While the EU level has command over competences to regulate in most economic policy fields – with the notable exception of economic policy as such – their competences in social policy fields are limited. This lack of competences can be partly mitigated by using overarching competences in favour of social integration. However, further frictions are caused by the ever-increasing difficulty of achieving an EU-wide consensus on any social policy measure and the relative ease with which strategic litigants can make use of the wide judicial competences, flowing from the unlimited applicability of directly enforceable Treaty norms.

---

[33] For more detail see Chapter 4, pp. 124–126, 156–160 (health), 136–137, 164–169 (industrial relations).

[34] For more detail see Chapter 3, pp. 91–92.

# IV. FRICTIONS AND CLOSING GAPS

It appears that there are frictions between the new constitutional framework of values and objectives established by the Treaty of Lisbon on the one hand and the established frame for EU competences, including judicial competences, on the other hand. The values and objectives demand the pursuit of social justice, which is specified by a number of further values aligned to the ideals of socially embedded constitutionalism. The EU competences still seem reminiscent of the times when liberal constitutionalism held sway: EU regulation in central social policy fields is excluded in favour of coordination and recommendations, while the direct application of economic liberties within Member States is continuously enforced by a judiciary enjoying a wider competence than the EU legislator. In the last seven years, this judiciary has continued to demonstrate a tendency to exacerbate said economic liberties – interjected with lines of case law where either national autonomy or genuine social rights enforcement has been endorsed.

## 1. Challenges Ahead

The question is how these frictions can be overcome. So far, academic critique has frequently seen the interaction of the judicial constitution on the one hand and the cumbersome EU legislative process on the other hand as a vicious circle in which any move towards integrating economic and social objectives is doomed to fail.[35] Others have proposed new modes of governance instead of legislation, and especially so for the muddy waters of social policies,[36] or to leave those muddy waters for the Member State to navigate.[37] Any more constructive proposals have been very cautious, proposing a new logic surpassing dichotomies of national or EU-level public regulation by other means.[38]

By contrast, our purposive interpretation of the EU's new values and objectives demands attributing responsibility for economic and social integration across levels of the EU multilevel policy without a competence divide between the economic and the social. Also the use of different modes of governance will have to be combined – neither adjudication nor legislation nor policy coordination will be sufficient to positively enhance social justice in the EU. Finally, it is open to doubt whether governance by Member States and the

---

35 Scharpf, 2010, Joerges and Roedl, 2009.

36 Armstrong, 2010.

37 Joerges and Roedl, 2009.

38 For recent overviews see Falkner, 2010, Azoulaï, 2008, and the contributions in Marlier and Natali (eds), 2010.

EU institutions through adjudication, legislation and policy coordination is sufficient to mould societal processes towards enhancing social justice. This suggests considering active contributions of civil society and socio-economic action at national as well as transnational levels as part of the solution.

The remainder of this chapter offers some deliberations towards a cautiously optimistic approach from a legal-normative perspective. It questions the apparent determination of EU constitutional law and proposes alternatives departing from the constitutional value base. Whether these alternatives are used in practice is of course a question of political stamina.

## 2. Economic and Social Integration – at EU or National Level

As shown in Chapters 1 and 3, the history of European integration began with a preference for EU-level economic integration and reluctance to allow social integration to proceed beyond national levels. This corresponded with the ordo-liberal creed that economic governance should not be moulded by political initiative, but rather left to the spontaneous order of competitive markets (apart from establishing the preconditions for markets to function on the basis of meritorious competition). Social policy, even if not going beyond (re)distribution of funds, was seen as highly political and requiring democratic legitimacy. It was thus left to the national levels. In contrast to this ideological starting point, the EU's predecessors were also given explicit competences to (re)distribute public moneys, not least in the field of agricultural policy.[39] Nevertheless, the perception of that phase is one of relegating economic and social integration to different levels. The EU's predecessors proceeded beyond that initial stage by allocating competences for some regulatory social policies to the European level, but maintained the sole competence of Member States for redistributive policies – beyond the European Social and Regional Funds and agricultural policy.

The underlying model of embedded liberalism has since lost its viability, as has been shown by many authors.[40] Usually this is attributed to the incremental encroachment of directly effective economic freedoms and competition law on national welfare systems and, to a lesser degree, employment legislation. These developments intensified regulatory competition between Member States on the one hand, and served as a justification for reducing non-marketised welfare payments on the other hand. Also, the Member States whose currency is the euro have lost any opportunity of counteracting economic

---

[39] See above Chapter 1, p. 39.

[40] See e.g. Giubboni, 2006, pp. 56–93.

crises through other means than austerity policy in a regulatory environment heavily leaning towards fiscal discipline.[41]

Above all, the extreme increase in differentials between Member States with the latest enlargement round has enhanced the visibility of dynamics that had been established much earlier. Revisiting the factual settings of some of the cases discussed in Chapters 3 and 4 serves to illustrate the point: when Mrs Müller-Fauré preferred to be treated by her familiar German dentist rather than a Dutch one, the respective transfers of funds occurred between systems of roughly comparable financial soundness.[42] When Mr Elchinov had his eye saved in Berlin by a treatment that was not available in his native Bulgaria, the transferring health fund had at their disposal about one-tenth of the equity per member in comparison to any health fund in Germany. When Mr Guiot paid his workers from a third country under French rather than under Belgian collective agreements, the difference between those payments amounted to less than 5%. When Viking ferries sued trade unions in order to overcome established industrial relations which had governed their economic activities for decades, they expected to achieve a reduction of wages to about 30% of what they were paying before.[43]

Once this divergence is combined with a global economic crisis impacting on the 'Eurozone', the demand for more national autonomy in matters related to redistributive payments, employment regulation and wages can only be perceived as a beggar-my-neighbour policy: Member States with traditionally high export surpluses demand that those dependent on internal consumption for any economic development revert to austerity measures, thus smothering what little economic activity is left.[44] This may seem drastic language, but it reflects sound empirical findings made by social scientists.

Recent, heated debates on case law relating to collective action against low-wage competition have ultimately shirked the question of how to negotiate different wage levels in an increasingly diverse EU. Those arguing in favour of retaining national competences[45] or the unfettered autonomy of trade

---

[41] See Chapter 1, pp. 27–28.

[42] For a more elaborate description of these health cases see Chapter 4 (pp. 156–159, note 241 (*Müller-Fauré*) and note 97 (*Guiot*).

[43] For a more elaborate treatment of posting of workers see Chapter 4 (pp. 131–132).

[44] Liddle and Diamond, 2010, pp. 86–88.

[45] Joerges and Roedl (2009, p. 18) consider autonomous bargaining processes in the Scandinavian tradition as a national 'welfare state position'. In going beyond single national models, Jacobs has proposed for Member States from the Rhineland and Scandinavia to use the instrument of closer cooperation to protect higher wage levels (Jacobs, 2009, pp. 124–125), agreeing on deleting Article 151(5) TFEU for their cooperation. A "third strategy" for balancing industrial relations and economic freedoms neither through adjudication nor by EU level legislation to ensure that "the right to

unions and employers' associations from high wage countries effectively seem to defend retaining these high-wage sectors. While empirical data on wage competition is scarce, it does not seem likely that defending those high-wage packets will contribute towards establishing a living wage throughout the EU. Conversely, lowering wages in Sweden will also not help Romanians earn a living wage, though. Thus, more intelligent strategies will have to be found.

The increasing demand to safeguard national autonomy for social protection, industrial relations and social services of general interest may be a viable strategy for the richer pre-2004 Member States, whose economic stability is backed up by a strong, export-oriented economy, and whose social stability is secured by a well-developed and balanced social settlement of diverging class interests and other cleavages that may be important nationally (e.g. post-colonial immigration streams and resulting diversity). These exceptional economies may be able to sustain a 'reversed ordo-liberalism'[46] according to which any direct effect of internal market law should not be applied to social realms within their borders. For the poorer economies, and in particular for the former socialist countries, such national egotism is not likely to result in maintaining adequate social standards within. National social policy closure is increasingly unsustainable if the EU is to achieve enhanced social justice throughout. Member States and national societies need to become embedded in EU-level social policy, aiming, e.g., to make sustainable transfers from poorer to richer countries without restricting the free movement of the citizens of those countries.[47] Last but not least the recent impact of the global economic crisis upon less export-oriented economies at the fringes of the Eurozone demonstrates that the persistent existence of the EU monetary and economic union depends on establishing reliable transnational and EU-wide solidarity structures. National closure and immunisation is certainly no longer sufficient.[48]

All this can be better established by social sciences other than law, whose scholars have thus been referenced above. However, if the EU has a viable constitutional mandate to pursue social justice, real-life factors will have to

---

strike is protected in accordance with national law" (Monti, 2010, 71). It, too, relegates any industrial relations model to national levels.

[46] See Giubboni, 2010, p. 254, see also, with less drastic language, Kilpatrick, 2009, p. 864.

[47] From the perspective of traditional redistributive policies, Ferrera demands the establishment of supra-national sharing schemes that cushion export and import of benefits (2010, pp. 52–54). Ferrera prefers the term nesting over embedding.

[48] Recent research comparing the emergence of social integration in the EU and the US shows an interesting contrast: while social embedding of markets in the founding phase of the US relied on federal action, the founding phase of the EU excluded action by the Community. This research seems to indicate that there are at least historical models of developing a social policy from a higher level – albeit against the background of a very low level of social protection (see Finkin, 2011, Moses, 2011).

impact upon the interpretation and application of its EU constitutional law. The normative orientation required by socially embedded constitutionalism demands that the likely bearing of legislation and non-legislation on social justice is assessed and addressed at national and EU levels.

## 3. Different Modes of Governance

The competences available to the EU for furthering economic and social integration differ, and these differences correspond to a range of governance modes the EU may pursue. The impact of EU constitutional law, and particular the EU's new value base on EU policy making, will differ for different modes of governance. Using a contested term such as governance, a short explanation of its use here is required. Subsequently, the potential implementation of the new constitutional requirements, across four forms of governance that are of practical relevance in the EU, are being explored.

The term 'governance' derives from government but relates to the interaction of those governing and those governed, to overcoming command-and-control structures by more interactive ways of achieving a certain goal, and finally to the increasing rule under participation by private parties.[49] It mainly refers to mixed forms of rule-making and regulation: there can be governance by or with governments, or governance without government,[50] as well as unilateral governance (e.g. by multinational companies) or participatory governance. In the EU, the distinction between governing and governance is not always upheld, though, as strictly hierarchical modes of governing are still referred to as governance.[51] Without attempting to solve any theoretical conflict here, the term governance is used pragmatically[52] to indicate any form of governing in the EU. It is also used in a rather limited way, as it relates to the modes of governance established by EU law. Thus, the manifold nuances of experimental governance are not all touched upon, as law is less imaginative as governance in practice.

Thus, hierarchical governance refers to the strict rule of law. In the EU, this mode of governance is engendered where EU law is directly applicable, and its primacy over national law accepted unquestioningly. Hierarchical governance occurs when the Commission issues decisions and regulations, as it does in the competition law field (including state aid), and when the Court issues a judgment which is then implemented by national courts.

49 Scott, 2002, pp. 60–61, de Búrca and Scott, 2006, pp. 2–3.
50 Kooiman, 2003, pp. 77–131.
51 See Armstrong, 2010, pp. 46–47.
52 As by de Búrca and Scott, 2006.

Where the EU only harmonises national legislation, it frequently uses directives, whose implementation always allows some latitude for Member States as long as the aim of the legislation is achieved (Article 288 TFEU). In these cases hierarchical governance is modified, in that those governed (the Member States) contribute to and are involved in the establishment of binding rules. Especially in the field of social policy, the EU also initiates hybrid forms of governance, in that it allows for the Member States to entrust the two sides of industry with the implementation of EU directives (Article 153(3) TFEU). Beyond this, the EU has developed a wide variety of even more hybrid forms of governance, while, for example, utilising private norm-setting institutions for specifying technical standards.[53] All this operates against the background of 'hard law', as directives are legally binding. Thus, hierarchical governance and governance by participation are mixed (or hybrid), in different measure.

Further, governance by negotiation (i.e. the so-called new forms of governance) has been established at EU level in the realm of the Open Method of Coordination.[54] In this form of governance, legally binding measures are wholly absent, while policies are coordinated through a system of targets and reports, which Article 5 TFEU now specifies as guidelines. Negotiations on guidelines predominantly take place between governments at EU and national levels, but the development of targets and their specific measurements offers ample scope for including civil society and experts into the governance realm.

Through these forms of governance, a declining degree of legal obligation is observed. This does not necessarily coincide with a declining degree of efficiency of Europeanisation though.[55] Partly, combinations of different forms of governance are seen as the most efficient way to implement any policy that seeks to shape society.[56] A common feature is the more-or-less dominant role of public actors – this is definitely governance with or even by government, or governance by judges.

In the EU there is also the potential for governance by private actors. Frequently, this form of governance is of dubious legitimacy, for example when industry is left to regulate for itself.[57] However, as established in more detail earlier,[58] collaborative self-regulation based on negotiation of diverging interests under conditions of factually comparable bargaining power is

---

53 Schepel, 2005.

54 See on this Armstrong, 2010, Ashiagbor, 2005, Smismans, 2004.

55 For empirical evidence of the OMC's relative efficiency see Heidenreich and Zeitlin, 2009.

56 de Búrca, 2006.

57 See Héritier and Eckert, 2008.

58 Chapter 2, p. 58.

capable of imbuing the resulting regulation with more democratic legitimacy than distant state rule. This is the model of industrial democracy, which at least theoretically could be transposed to other realms as well.

## 4. Potential Impact of the EU's Constitutional Value Base

If substantive constitutional principles typical for socially embedded constitutionalism are taken seriously, they must be seen as a normative guide for governing the entity to which they apply. Accordingly, the Treaty of Lisbon's constitutional demand to reconcile economic and social integration must impact on the development of the EU polity. This impact will differ by modes of governance, though.

### a) Hierarchical governance: the EU's judicial constitution

The most hierarchical form of governance in the EU relies on the direct effect and primacy of Treaty law enforced judicially. Governance by judges depends in its efficiency on the continued acceptance of the Court's rulings, which of course is an empirical problem beyond the scope of this book. From the perspective of EU constitutional law, it is assumed that governance by judges is efficient, as the Court is considered as its highest authority.

As we have seen throughout the book, directly binding Treaty norms are more typical for the realm of economic integration than the realm of social integration. While four economic freedoms, and two competition rules for private actors and the state aid rules, support economic integration, only the equal pay clause and free movement and equality rights for citizens can be relied upon for partly supporting the EU social constitution. Complying with the new constitutional demand for reconciling economic and social integration will be a particular challenge if directly effective norms of the economic constitution collide with other norms that aim to socially embed economic integration or liberal constitutionalism. Under the new constitutional law of the EU, the directly effective norms should, in this situation, not take unqualified precedence. Rather, they should be reconciled with their socially embedded counterpart.

Under the new constitutional demands of reconciling economic and social integration, the EU institutions themselves must be held to be bound to observe the EU's social values when acting in the field of economic integration as well. This includes the Court of Justice, which increasingly becomes the final arbiter of directly effective Treaty norms and their interaction with national policies. Thus, the Court will have to activate the new constitutional demand for social justice.

There are relatively easy ways to achieve this in a traditional doctrinal way, which should appeal to the Court. As we have seen in Chapter 4, in cases of clashes of interest the Court tends to treat any economic freedom as the rule, and any social value as the exception. While this allows Member States to justify policies embodying social values, the EU is under no obligation to justify the intrusion in national policies and the rejection of the complementary social values in the name of economic freedoms. This structural imbalance justifies the critique that the balancing of values before the Court is balanced only in name, not in substance.[59]

As already demanded by AG Trstenjak in her opinion to *COM v Germany*,[60] a second step needs to be reintroduced into the balancing act. Before policies, actions or legislation promoting human rights or social values are squashed in the name of economic freedoms, the Court must investigate whether a less intrusive way of maintaining the substance of the economic freedom is available. In other words, human rights and social values must not only be used in defensive ways, but the economic freedoms should also have to defend themselves against the moral imperative of those. This would constitute a true balancing act, giving both the economic freedoms and competing values equal status.

This also differs from granting Member States a margin of appreciation for protecting any values they prefer nationally. This strategy may be adequate for negotiating the competence spheres of different public actors.[61] It does not negotiate a different value base of economic and social integration substantively – Member States could also prefer a neo-liberal constitution, after all. Establishing a practice of balancing economic and social integration substantively could achieve a social embedding of economic constitutionalism in cases where its demands are openly competing with social values or human rights.

### b) Modified hierarchical governance: harmonisation

Where the EU legislates and in the process leaves scope for Member States to adapt the implementation to their national requirements, it has every opportunity to take into account the needs of social integration when legislating for the internal market and of economic integration when legislating in the field of social policy. In recent years, legislation has at times been too exuberant and reinforced a dominance of economic integration aims and an internal market ideology that did not actively embrace social values. For example, the services

---

59 Barnard, 2008.

60 C-271/08 *COM v Germany* ('Riester Rente'), discussed in Chapter 4, pp. 137 and 197.

61 For an approach basing such balancing on deliberative democracy and overlapping consensus see Sabel and Gerstenberg, 2010.

directive[62] has deprived Member States of the possibility of justifying public policy aims, including those derived from social policy, without establishing a European floor of rights.[63] Legislation in the field of consumer law has been accused of a similar tendency.[64] In the future, any piece of legislation must take the constitutional demand for reconciling economic and social integration into account. This is first and foremost an argument to be used in the political process leading to legislation. The Commission, in its legislative proposals, frequently relies on the requirements of economic freedoms and competition rules in order to limit their social ambition. In the future, it will have to rely on the EU's values and objectives as constitutional norms counterbalancing any overreliance on liberal constitutionalism. Again, the Court may well become the final arbiter in cases where EU legislation is challenged by economic actors. So far, it has been lenient towards the EU, and accepting of its policy making.[65]

### c) Negotiated governance: the open method of coordination

Where the EU coordinates, or coordinates and ensures, it might seem at first sight that there is less need for any constitutional control. However, it is a mistake to consider that OMC processes do not effectively impact on societies in Member States because they are not legally binding. While there are vastly different assessments of OMC processes as applied to social integration, critique of an overly neo-liberal touch of these abounds.[66] These critiques mainly remain at a political level. However, the constitutional demands of paying heed to social values in all economic policies can be mobilised to underpin political arguments. While the EU is a community of law, such legal arguments should also open access to the Court of Justice. Of course, this form of juridification is relatively weak.

The EU cannot, in the fields discussed, create binding regulation. It is thus inhibited from creating a protective floor of rights, or establishing minimum standards. Under the new constitutional demands, an expansive reading of those competence norms that allow such regulation might be attempted.[67] If the new constitutional demands are taken seriously, the divergence of national

---

62 Directive 2006/123 [2006] OJ L376/36.

63 See for a critique Schiek, 2008.

64 Micklitz and Reich, 2009.

65 See cases C-154/04 *Alliance for Natural Health*, discussed in Chapter 4 with note 27, C-58/08 Vodafone, discussed in Chapter 4 with note 193, C-344/04 IATA, discussed in Chapter 4 with note 300.

66 See e.g. Ashiagbor, 2005, Smismans, 2010, Frazer and Marlier, 2010.

67 See above III. 2, pp. 226–227.

rules under the influence of regulatory competition[68] would often justify the presumption of a race to the bottom for certain social values. Because economic integration must now be better embedded within social values, this would bring about the EU's competence to regulate in order to create a higher floor of social rights than would otherwise emerge without intervention.

**d) Transnational social governance**

The constitutional demands in favour of reconciling economic and social integration thus find a constitutional anchor in relation to hierarchical, modified and negotiated governance. The debate on whether any ensuing juridification of EU social integration is desirable, or even realistic, is not the theme of this book. What we have shown is that there is the potential for EU constitutional law to rise to the challenge of economic and social integration. All this is, however, only relevant where the EU has a competence, however slight, and uses it.

Nevertheless, the EU constitution of competences seems incomplete in its explicit response to the challenges of social integration. As we have seen, important fields such as wages are not open to EU activity at all. In other fields such as social inclusion, education and culture the EU has merely the competence to coordinate national orders. What is more, these restrictions are based on good reasons. For one, they correspond to the principle in a number of Member States of leaving the setting of wages to the two sides of industry, partly on the basis of a constitutional guarantee of collective bargaining and the autonomy of collective agreements. In addition, attempting to capture all deficiencies of social integration by public action, or even the rather cumbersome processes of EU legislation, might well have a smothering effect on transnational societal exchange, which is the practical precondition for enhancing EU social integration.

Thus, instead of relying only on governance modes in which the EU and its Member States participate, European governance should also embrace private norm-setting as an element of socially embedded constitutionalism. Of course, this can only apply if norm-setting by economic actors does not result in undue dominance of already powerful economic actors. Such private governance would counteract social justice rather than support it. However, there are numerous options for legitimate governance by actors other than states and the EU. Beyond the established model of industrial relations, these include actions of charitable organisations, associations pursuing social integration from their own motion, insurance funds and mutual societies engaged in health care or

---

[68] See on this concept above Chapter 3, II, pp. 86–90, Chapter 4, II, pp. 126–128.

care for the elderly, or even autonomous or semi-autonomous local municipalities concerned to maintain basic social services. Any of those actors could either combine to form a transnational or even European level organisation, or they could cooperate in European networks. The EU competence regime would no longer seem incomplete if policies established by these (potential) European or transnational civil society organisations were to be accepted as part of European social governance. In accepting a constitution of social governance, the EU and its Courts could perhaps solve some of the dilemmas of governing for social justice. Also, accepting governance beyond EU-induced deliberations, the EU would also allow for transnational social integration to emerge from below.

While the detailed development of advocacy arguments defending the constitution of social governance in practice has the potential to fill its own book, a few consequences of what has been developed above should be outlined.

First, some imagination is needed for a future practice of European social governance. Some (perhaps utopian) examples could include the following:

- Trade unions from several Member States take measures to prevent a deadly wage competition between workers from different Member States by agreeing to prevent their members from competing with each other, especially while some trade unions are engaged in collective action.[69]
- A European university league may agree on a system providing for equitable contributions to universities in states where many students from other universities want to study, in order to create a sustainable system of exchange that does not deplete funds of those universities which depend on high fees for studying there.
- Health care funds might create an agreement under which they ensure that members from poorer states pay contributions in line with the national wage level at their place of residence but still can profit from expensive treatments in richer states without depleting their health fund's resources.
- Mutual housing associations from different Member States may establish a points-based system that enables their members who wish to move abroad to use each other's subsidised housing.[70]

---

[69] This is actually the least utopian example: as a reaction of the ECJ's *Laval* and *Viking* rulings, plans to develop sustainable cooperative structures between trade unions are actually underway (Bücker and Warneck, 2010, p. 139).

[70] Two cases concerning the question in how far social housing may be subsidised by Member States are pending before the Court at the time of writing (cases C-203/11 – nv All Projects and Developments, a reference by a Belgian court, and C-133/12 P – Stichting Woonlinie). Their outcome may well further restrict the scope of transnational activities of subsidised housing associations.

In all these fields, the EU has no regulatory competence. Wages and industrial action are excluded from EU legislation altogether (Article 153(5) TFEU).[71] In the field of education, the EU may only coordinate (Articles 165–166 TFEU), and the same applies for combating social exclusion and modernising social protection systems beyond social protection of workers (Article 153(1) letter j and k, (2)(a) TFEU). For this reason, sectors such as social housing or health care may seem beyond the EU competence presently – the question of whether this has changed through Article 14 TFEU, which explicitly empowers the EU to create EU-level Services of General Economic Interest, is beyond the scope of this book. Even if the EU now has a competence in this matter, it may not be easy to find the political consensus to use it. Isolated national policies, on the other hand, are not suitable for solving the transnational problems indicated above. Several Member States could engage in cooperation outside or even within the EU legal framework[72] and achieve a level of European social integration that way. However, it is more likely that Member States would be unable to agree. Thus, European social integration from below may well step into fill a gap left by competence norms and political realities.

Such activity may well, however, conflict with economic freedoms or competition law if the relevant EU Treaty rules are interpreted without any flexibility, relying on individualist values exclusively. Following the argument developed above for hierarchical governance, an alternative seems feasible. Given that cooperation between trade unions is the most likely strategy, it may be feasible to outline a potential counter-argument in this field.

Mitigating dominance in markets is the main purpose of establishing or at least legalising industrial relations and workers' freedom of association. As has recently been established by the ECtHR,[73] the actual enjoyment of this

---

[71] The most recent version of a proposal for a "Monti II regulation" (COM (2012) 130 final of 21 March 2012) recommends creating EU level "general principles and rules … with respect to the exercise of the fundamental right to take collective action within the context of (economic freedoms)" (Article 1). The proposed legal base is Article 352 TFEU, whose paragraph 3 explicitly prohibits to recur to Article 352 in fields where other Treaty articles exclude approximation of law (Article 153 (5) TFEU for industrial action). Partly the Regulation confirms existing rights of management and labour (Article 3(2)), when it stresses that they maintain the competence to establish arbitration for disputes on transborder collective industrial action by EU level collective agreement. However, the Commission also suggests requiring Member States to warn foreign employers about trade union plans for transborder conflict (Article 4). This seems problematic in the light of autonomy of collective bargaining and also exceeds the EU's competence.

[72] See again Jacobs, as quoted above (note 45).

[73] *Demir v Turkey* App. No 34503/97 12 November 2008, 48 E.H.R.R. 54, *Enerji Yapi Yol Sen v Turkey*, App. No 68959/01, 21 April 2009 49 E.H.R.R. 108, see also Chapter 4, p. 198.

guarantee from the arsenal of human liberties (not mere social rights) requires that state parties acknowledge a right to collective bargaining and to collective action. In an internal market, trade unions might agree to support each other's national collective action by solidarity action, asking their members not to be posted or hired out to an employer whose work force is engaged in industrial action. Imagine that HUMANPOWER, a temporary works agency domiciled in one Member State and active across a variety of Member States, as a consequence, is repeatedly unable to fulfil its contracts on cross-border hiring out of services and has to pay contractual penalties. It claims damages against the trade unions. Imagine further that national legislation and case law restricts these damages because exorbitant claims would render the exercise of workers' freedom to associate impractical. The claim of HUMANPOWER is rejected before the national court. HUMANPOWER then succeeds in having its case referred to the Court, which is called to decide whether Member State Y infringed freedom to provide services by allowing its court to protect freedom of association in this way. Were the Court to follow the logic it applied in *Viking*,[74] *Laval*[75] and *COM v Germany*,[76] HUMANPOWER would be in a good position. The Court would find that the risk of subjection to industrial action resulting from conflicts to which HUMANPOWER is no party makes providing services across borders more risky, which is sufficient to establish an obstacle. Accordingly, the damages regime needs justification. If the Court were to take the constitutional demand to safeguard social justice seriously, it would have to take a different approach. There would be several options for ensuring that the right to take collective action is given a position equal with the economic freedom to provide services across a border. First, the Court could qualify the risk to be subjected to industrial action as a normal risk of business operating in a democratic country which respects human rights. Thus, it could just say that being subjected to industrial action once in a while as such does not constitute any obstacle to business freedom in Europe. This would still leave the Court the option to intervene if a strike is driven by xenophobic motives that conflict with free movement of workers, e.g. if strikers use slogans such as 'British Jobs for British Workers!',[77] under the concept of abuse of rights. Alternatively, the Court would have to ask not only whether the reduction of damages is necessary

---

[74] Case C-438/05 [2007] ECR I-10779, see Chapter 4 with notes 280, 440.

[75] Case C-341/05 [2007] ECR I-11767, see Chapter 4 with notes 101, 280, 293, 313, 440–446, 490.

[76] Case C-271/08 15 July 2010, see Chapter 4 with note 122, 492, and above note 60.

[77] This slogan was used by striking workers protesting against employment of Italians at a British refinery (see on this Barnard, 2009). As here, supporting a residual oversight of industrial action by the Court, Kilpatrick, 2009, p. 864.

to protect industrial relations, as it would usually do under the *Viking* and *Laval* test. Further, it would also have to ask whether demanding exorbitant damages from trade unions is actually necessary to maintain HUMANPOWER'S freedom to provide services.

Under the constitutional demand of reconciling economic and social integration, it is difficult to see how the judges would be unable to respond to such demands. They may be unwilling, and they may lack the opportunity for some time. After all, such claims require that citizens decide to take their cases to the Court, and that they trust the Court to defend their human rights as well as any economic freedoms. However, it is certainly not impossible for EU judges to support a constitution of social governance in adjudicating those conflicts.

## V. CONCLUSION: TOWARDS A CONSTITUTION OF SOCIAL GOVERNANCE

It has been shown that the constitutional demands for social justice, which are now part of the EU's constitutional law, are not easy to fulfil in practice.

As EU constitutional law now requires developing social justice at European levels, national closure of socially embedded constitutionalism should be a phenomenon of the past. Demanding the isolation of national social policies from EU intervention was never a promising strategy, in that it would not engender social justice throughout the EU. With increasing diversity among Member States and increasingly efficient economic integration, it is less and less a practical option to provide for social justice nationally. Thus, the European-level pursuit of social justice is an inevitable step for the EU in order to maintain any prospect of socially embedded constitutionalism. This step has been taken with the Treaty of Lisbon.

While EU constitutional law now places the values of social justice and solidarity at the same level as the objective to achieve the internal market, substantive EU law caters for the requirements of liberal constitutionalism and socially embedded constitutionalism to different degrees. Substantive EU law contains many more provisions for safeguarding economic integration than for furthering social integration. Also, the EU competences are more pronounced in the field of economic integration: while the EU has some social policy competences, it also lacks competences in decisive social policy fields.

In order to overcome this tension, EU constitutional law can be read as a constitution of social governance, which relies on actions by states, the EU, and by the citizens themselves in order to realise economic and social integration in their interrelation. The practical establishment of the constitution of social governance will not be easy though.

EU policies furthering social justice sustainably are not only deficient because the EU does not have adequate legislative competences. Frequently, political agreement to use existing competences cannot be achieved. Should societal actors step into the void left by a lack of competences, this would not necessarily lead to unfettered development of socially embedded constitutionalism. Rather, judicial campaigners may attempt to address the Court for striking down not only national policies enforcing closure, but also transnational social regulations, which can qualify as social integration from below. For reasons expanded convincingly in academic writing,[78] any conflicts with economic actors emanating from transnational social integration from below will most likely be brought before the Court of Justice as the final arbiter. Placing social rights into the hands of the judiciary may be a 'dangerous game'.[79] However, there is no alternative to this. The Court will thus have the responsibility to refine its doctrines in order to integrate the 2009 values and objectives of the EU into its readings of economic freedoms, competition rules and competence norms. It is possible for the Court to do so in ways that can command the respect of European lawyers. The Court thus has a high level of responsibility to activate the 2009 EU constitutional demand to socially embed economic integration. It is to be hoped that Europe's judges can face this responsibility before the European project loses the trust of Europe's less privileged citizens.

78 Kelemen, 2011, Scharpf, 2010.
79 Wedderburn, 2007, p. 421.

# Bibliography


Ahmed, T. and I. de Jesus Butler (2006), 'The European Union and human rights: an international law perspective', *European Journal of International Law,* 17(4), 771–801.

Alber, J. (2010), 'What the European and American welfare states have in common and where they differ: facts and fiction in comparisons of the European Social Model and the United States', *Journal of European Social Policy,* 20(2), 102–125.

Alber, J., T. Fahey and C. Saraceno (2008a), *Handbook of Quality of Life in the Enlarged European Union*, Abingdon and New York: Routledge.

Alber, J., T. Fahey and C. Saraceno (2008b), 'Introduction: EU enlargement and quality of life', in J. Alber, T. Fahey and C. Saraceno (eds), *Handbook of Quality of Life in the Enlarged European Union*, Abingdon and New York: Routledge, pp. 1–24.

Ales, E. (2009), 'Transnational collective bargaining in Europe: the case for legislative action at EU level', *International Labour Review,* 148(1–2), 149–162.

Ales, E., S. Engblom, T. Jaspers, S. Laulom, S. Sciarra and A. Sobczak (2006), *Transnational Collective Bargaining: Past, Present, Future*, Brussels: European Commission.

Alexander, J.C. (2005), '"Globalisation" as collective representation: the new dream of a cosmopolitan civic sphere', *International Journal of Politics, Culture and Society,* 19(1–2), 81–90.

Alkoby, A. (2010), 'Three images of "global community": theorizing law and community in a multicultural world', *International Community Law Review,* 12(1), 35–79.

Alter, K. (2006), 'Private litigants and the new international courts, *Comparative Political Studies,* 39(1), 22–49.

Alter, K. (2009), *The European Court's Political Power,* Oxford: Oxford University Press.

Alter, K. and J. Vargas (2000), 'Explaining variation in the use of European litigation strategies: European Community law and British gender equality policy', *Comparative Political Studies,* 33(4), 316–346.

Anderson, G.W. (2005), *Constitutional Rights after Globalization*, Oxford and Portland: Hart.

Andreotti, A. and P. Le Galès, (2011), 'Elites, middle classes and cities', in A. Favell and V. Guiraudon (eds), *Sociology of the European Union,* Basingstoke: Palgrave Macmillan, pp.76–99.

Aristotle (1995), *Politea* (T. Saunders, translation 1995 edn), Oxford: Clarendon Press.

Armstrong, K.A. (2010), *Governing Social Inclusion. Europeanization through Policy Coordination,* Oxford: Oxford University Press.

Arnull, A. (2008), 'The Americanization of EU Law Scholarship', in A. Arnull, P. Eeckhout and T. Tridimas (eds), *Continuity and Change in EU Law – Essays in Honour of Sir Francis Jacobs*, Oxford: Oxford University Press, pp.415–431.

Arrowsmith, S. and P. Kunzlik (2009), *Social and Environmental Policies in EC Procurement Law*, Cambridge: Cambridge University Press.

Ashiagbor, D. (2005), *The European Employment Strategy*, Oxford: Oxford University Press.

Athanassiou, P. (2009), *Withdrawal and Expulsion from the EU and EMU – Some Reflections*, Frankfurt: European Central Bank.

Avdagic, S., M. Rhodes and J. Visser (2011), *Social Pacts in Europe. Emergence, Evolution and Industrialization*, Oxford: Oxford University Press.

Azoulaï, L. (2008), The Court of Justice and the social market economy, *CMLR,* 45(5), 1335–1346.

Balassa, B. (1961), *The Theory of Economic Integration*, Homewood, IL: R.D. Irwin.

Baldwin, R. and C. Wyplosz (2009), *The Economics of European Integration* (3rd edn), London: McGraw Hill.

Banks, K. (2008), 'The application of the fundamental freedoms to Member State tax measures: guarding against protectionism or second-guessing national choices?', *ELR* 33(4), 482–506.

Baquero Cruz, J. (2002), *Between Competition and Free Movement, the Economic Constitutional Law of the European Union*, Oxford and Portland: Hart.

Baquero Cruz, J. (2008), The legacy of the Maastricht-Urteil and the Pluralist Movement, *ELJ* 14(4), 389–422.

Baquero Cruz, J. (2011), 'The Case Law of the European Court of Justice on the Mobility of Patients – an Assessment', in J.W. Gronden, E. Szyszczak, U. Neergaard and M. Krajewski (eds.), *Health Care and EU Law*, The Hague: T.M.C. Asser Press, pp.79–102.

Bar, Clive, E. von, and H. Schulte-Nölke (2009), *Principles, Definitions, Model Rules of European Private Law. Draft Common Frame of Reference,* Munich: Sellier Publishers.

Barbier, C. (2010), *De Lisbonne à Europe 2020: une nouvelle direction pour*

*la stratégie économique de l'Union européenne?*, Brussels: Observatoire Social Européen.
Barnard, C. (2008), 'Social dumping or dumping socialism?', *Cambridge Law Journal,* 67(2), 262–264.
Barnard, C. (2009a), 'British jobs for British workers: the Lindsey Oil Refinery dispute and the future of local labour clauses in an integrated EU market', *Industrial Law Journal,* 38(2), 245–277.
Barnard, C. (2009b), 'Trailing a new approach to free movement of goods?, *Cambridge Law Journal* 68(2), 288–290.
Barnard, C. (2010a), *EU Employment Law* (3rd edn), Oxford: Oxford University Press.
Barnard, C. (2010b), *The Substantive Law of the EU – the Four Freedoms* (3rd edn), Oxford: Oxford University Press.
Barnes, C. (1990), *The Cabbage Syndrome: the Social Construction of Dependence*, London, New York and Philadelphia: Falmer Press.
Barnes, I. and C. Mercer (2003), *Disability,* Malden, MA: Polity Press.
Bauman, Z. (2004), *Europe: an Unfinished Adventure*, Cambridge: Polity Press.
Beckfield, J. (2006), 'European integration and income inequality', *American Sociological Review,* 71(6), 964–985.
Begg, I., J. Craxler and J. Mortensen (2008), *Is Social Europe Fit for Globalisation?,* Brussels: European Commission.
Behrens, K., C. Gaigné, G.I. Ottaviano and J.F. Thisse (2007), 'Countries, regions and trade: on the welfare impacts of economic integration', *European Economic Review* 51(5), 1277–1301.
Bell, J. (2010), 'The Role of the European Judges in an Era of Uncertainty', in P. Birkinshaw and M. Varney (eds), *The European Union Legal Order after Lisbon*, Alphen aan den Rijn: Kluwer International, pp. 277–290.
Bell, M. (2008), EU anti-racism policy – the leader of the pack?, in H. Meenan (ed.), *Equality Law in an Enlarged European Union*, Cambridge: Cambridge University Press, pp.178–201.
Bell, M. (2011), 'The Principle of Equal Treatment: Widening and Deepening', in G. de Búrca and P. Craig (eds), *The Evolution of EU Law*, Oxford: Oxford University Press, pp.611–641.
Bellamy, R. (2006), 'The European Constitution is dead, long live European constitutionalism', *Constellations*, pp.181–189.
Beneyto, J.M. (2008), 'From Nice to the Constitutional Treaty: Eight Theses on the (Future) Constitutionalisation of Europe', in S. Griller and J. Ziller, *The Lisbon Treaty. EU Constitutionalism without a Constitutional Treaty?,* Vienna: Springer, pp.1–21.
Benhabib, S. (2006), 'The Philosophical Foundations of Cosmopolitan Norms', in S. Benhabib, *Another Cosmopolitanism*, Oxford: Oxford University Press, pp.13–44.

Bercusson, B. (2009), *European Labour Law* (2nd edn) (after Bercusson's death prepared for publication by K. D. Ewing, ed.), Cambridge: Cambridge University Press.

Besselink, L.F. (2009), 'The Notion and Nature of the European Constitution after the Treaty of Lisbon', in J. Wouters, L. Verhey and P. Kiiver, *European Constitutionalism beyond Lisbon*, Antwerp: Intersentia, pp.261–281.

Biermeyer, T. (2011), 'European company regulation between economic and social integration', in D. Schiek, U. Liebert and H. Schneider (eds), *European Economic and Social Constitutionalism after the Treaty of Lisbon*, Cambridge: Cambridge University Press, pp.148–173.

Blanpain, R. (2010), 'The European Union and Employment Law', in R. Blanpain (ed.), *Comparative Labour Law and Industrial Relations in Industrialised Market Economies* (10th revised edn), The Hague: Kluwer International, pp.169–194.

Blanpain, R. and J. Baker (2004), *Comparative Labour Law and Industrial Relations in Industrialised Market Economies*, The Hague: Kluwer.

Boeri, T. and H. Brücker (2005), 'Migration, co-ordination failures and EU Enlargement', IZA Discussion Paper, 1600 (May).

Bogdandy, A. von (2010), 'Founding Principles', in A. von Bogdandy and J. Bast (eds), *Principles of European Constitutional Law* (2nd edn), Munich and Portland, OR: Beck and Hart, pp.11–54.

Bogdandy, A. von and J. Bast (eds) (2010), *Principles of European Constitutional Law* (2nd edn), Munich and Portland: Beck and Hart.

Böhnke, P. (2008), 'Patterns of social integration and exclusion', in J. Alber, T. Fahey and C. Saraceno (eds), *Handbook of Quality of Life in the Enlarged European Union*, Abingdon and New York: Routledge, pp.304–327.

Borgmann-Prebil, J. and M. Ross (2010), 'Promoting European Solidarity: between Rhetoric and Reality?', in J. Borgmann-Prebil and M. Ross (eds), *Promoting Solidarity in the European Union*, Oxford: Oxford University Press, pp.1–22.

Borlotti, B. and D. Siniscalo (2004), *The Challenges of Privatization,* Oxford: Oxford University Press.

Börzel, T. (2002), 'Pace-setting, foot-dragging and fence-sitting: Member State responses to Europeanization', *JCMS* 40(2), 193–214.

Börzel, T. (2005), 'Europeanization: How the European Union Interacts with Its Member States', in S. Bulmer and Ch. Lequesne (eds), *The Member States of the European Union*, Oxford: Oxford University Press, pp.45–69.

Branco Martins, R. (2004), 'A European legal football match heading for extra time: social dialogue in the European professional football sector', *The International Sports Law Journal,* 2004(3–4), 17–29.

Bříza, P. (2009), 'The Czech Republic. The Constitutional Court on the Lisbon Treaty. Decision of 28 November 2008', *European Constitutional Law Review* 5(1), 143–164.

Browne, J., S.F. Deakin and F. Wilkinson (2002), *Capabilities, Social Rights and European Market Integration*, University of Cambridge CBR WP, 253 (December).

Brunkhorst, H. (2010), 'Constitutionalism and Democracy in the World Society', in P. Dobner and M. Loughlin (eds), *The Twilight of Constitutionalism?*, Oxford: Oxford University Press, pp.179–199.

Bücker, A. and W. Warneck (2010), *Viking – Laval – Rüffert: Consequences and Policy Perspectives,* Brussels: European Trade Union Institute.

Budge, I., I. Crewe and D. McKay (2001), *The New British Politics* (2nd edn), Harlow: Longman.

Busemeyer, M.R. and R. Nikolai (2010), 'Education', in F.G. Castles, S. Leibfried, J. Lewis, H. Obinger and C. Pierson (eds), *The Oxford Handbook of the Welfare State*, Oxford: Oxford University Press, pp.494–508.

Cafruny, A.W. and J.M. Ryner (2009), 'Critical Political Economy, in A. Wiener, A. and T. Diez (eds), *European Integration Theory*, Oxford: Oxford University Press, pp.221–240.

Calhoun, C. (2005), 'Constitutional patriotism and the public sphere: interest, identity, and solidarity in the integration of Europe', *International Journal of Politics, Culture and Society,* 18(3–4), 257–280.

Caparoso, J. and S. Tarrow (2009), 'Polanyi in Brussels: supranational institutions and the transnational embedding of markets', *International Organization* 63(4), 593–620.

Cappelletti, M., M. Seccombe and J. Weiler (1985), *Integration through Law: Europe and the American Federal Experience* (vol. 1), Berlin and New York: Walter de Gruyter.

Cardwell, M., and J. Hunt (2010), 'Public rights of way and level playing fields', *Environmental Law Review,* 12(4), 291–300.

Carrera, S. (2009), *In Search of the Perfect Citizen? The Intersection between Integration, Immigration and Nationality in the EU*, Leiden and Boston: Martinus Nijhoff Publishers.

Carruba, C.J., M. Gabel and C. Hankla (2008), 'Judicial behavior under political constraints: evidence from the European Court of Justice', *American Political Science Review,* 102(4), 435–452.

Cartabia, M. (2009), 'Europe and rights: taking dialogue seriously', *European Constitutional Law Review,* 5(1), 5–31.

Castello, C., and G. Davies (2006), 'The case law of the Court of Justice in the field of sex equality since 2000', *CMLR 43*(3), 1547–1612.

Castillo de la Torre, F. (2005), 'Tribunal Constitucional (Spanish Constitutional Court), Opinion 1/2004 of 13 December 2004, on the Treaty establishing a Constitution for Europe', *CMLR* 42(4), 1169–1202.

Castles, F.G., S. Leibfried, J. Lewis, H. Obinger and C. Pierson (eds) (2010), *The Oxford Handbook of the Welfare State,* Oxford: Oxford University Press.

Cerami, A (2011), 'Social mechanisms in the establishment of the European Economic and Monetary Union', *Politics and Policy,* 39(3) 345–371.

Chalmers, D., G. Davies and M. Giorgio (2010), *European Union Law* (2nd edn), Cambridge: Cambridge University Press.

Checkel, J.T. (1999), 'Social construction and integration', *Journal of European Public Policy,* 6(4), 545–560.

Chen, M.X. (2009), 'Regional economic integration and geographic concentration of multinational firms', *European Economic Review,* 53(3), 335.

Choudhry, S. (2008), *Constitutional Design for Divided Societies*, Oxford: Oxford University Press.

Christiansen, T., K.E. Jørgensen and A. Wiener (1999), *The Social Construction of Europe*, London: Sage.

Chryssochoou, D.N. (2009), *Theorizing European Integration* (2nd edn), London and New York: Routledge.

Cichowski, R. (2006), Courts, rights and democratic participation, *Comparative Political Studies,* 39(1), 50–75.

Cichowski, R. (2007), *The European Courts and Civil Society. Litigation, Mobilization and Governance,* Cambridge: Cambridge University Press.

Comité Intergouvernemental créé par la conférence de Messine (1956), *Rapport des chefs de délégation aux ministres des affaires étrangères* (Spaak Report), Brussels: Conférence Intergouvernementale.

Conant, L. (2006), Individuals, courts and the development of European social rights. *Comparative Political Studies,* 39(1), 70–100.

Coppel, J. and A. O'Neill (1992), 'The European Court of Justice: taking rights seriously?', *Legal Studies,* 12(2), 227–239.

Court of Justice of the European Union (2010), *Discussion Document of the Court of Justice of the European Union on Certain Aspects of the Accession of the European Union to the European Convention for the Protector of Human Rights and Fundamental Freedoms*, Luxembourg: Court of Justice.

Court of Justice (2011), *Annual Report 2010*, Luxembourg: Publications Office of the European Union.

Craig, P. (2010), *The Lisbon Treaty. Law, Politics and Treaty Reform,* Oxford: Oxford University Press.

Craig, P. (2011), Integration, Democracy and Legitimacy, in P. Craig and G. de Búrca (eds), *The Evolution of EU Law* (2nd edn), Oxford: Oxford University Press, pp.13–40.

Craig, P. and G. de Búrca (2011), *EU Law* (5th edn), Oxford: Oxford University Press.

Creighton, B. (2010), 'Freedom of Association', in R. Blanpain (ed.),

*Comparative Labour Law and Industrial Relations in Industrialized Market Economies* (10th edn), Alphen aan den Rijn: Kluwer, pp.285–337.

Curtin, D. (2006), European Legal Integration: Paradise Lost?', in D. Curtin (ed.), *European Integration and Law,* Antwerp and Oxford: Intersentia, pp.1–54.

Cutler, C. (2003), *Private Power and Global Authority: Transnational Merchant Law and the Global Political Economy*, Cambridge: Cambridge University Press.

Daly, M. (2006), 'EU social policy after Lisbon', *JCMS,* 44(3), 461–483.

Daly, M. (2008), 'Whither EU social policy? An account and assessment of developments in the Lisbon social inclusion process', *Journal of Social Policy* 37(1), 1–19.

Damjanovic, D. and B. de Witte (2009), 'Welfare Integration through EU Law: the Overall Picture in the Light of the Lisbon Treaty', in U. Neergaard, R. Nielsen and L. M. Roseberry (eds), *Integrating Welfare Functions into EU Law*, Copenhagen: DJØF, pp.33–94.

Damsgaard Hansen, E. (2001), *European Economic History*, Copenhagen: Copenhagen Business School Press.

Dashwood, A. (2007–2008), 'Viking and Laval: Issues of Direct Effect', *Cambridge Yearbook of European Legal Studies,* 10, 525–540.

Däubler, W. (1997), *Der Kampf um einen weltweiten Tarifvertrag,* Baden-Baden: Nomos.

Davies, P. (1997), 'Posted workers: single market or protection of national labour law systems?', *CMLR* 24(4), 571–602.

Davis, D. (2008), 'Socioeconomic rights: do they deliver the goods?', *I-CON* 6(4), 687–711.

Dawson, M. (2009), 'The ambiguity of social Europe in the open method of coordination', *ELR* 34(1), 55–79.

Dawson, M. and B. de Witte (2012 (forthcoming)), 'The EU Legal Framework of Social Inclusion and Social Protection: Between the Lisbon Strategy and the Lisbon Treaty', in B. Cantillon, P. Ploscar and H. Verschuren (eds), *Social Inclusion and Social Protection: Interactions between Law and Policy,* Antwerp: Intersentia.

Dawson, M., and E. Muir (2011), 'Individual, institutional and collective vigilance in protecting fundamental rights in the EU: lessons from the Roma', *CMLR* 48(3), 751–775.

Deakin, S. (2005), '"Capability" Concept and the Evolution of European Social Policy', in M. Dougan and E. Spaventa (eds), *Social Welfare and EU Law*, Oxford and Portland: Hart, pp. 3–24.

Deakin, S. (2006), 'Legal diversity and regulatory competition: which model for Europe?', *ELJ,* 12(4), 440–454.

Deakin, S. and A. Supiot (2009), *Capacitas*, Oxford: Oxford University Press.

Deakin, S. (2007–2008), 'Regulatory competition after *Laval*', *Cambridge Yearbook of European Legal Studies,* 10, 581–609.

de Búrca, G. (2005), 'Rethinking law in neofunctionalist theory', *Journal of European Public Policy,* 12(2), 310–323.

de Búrca, G. (2006), 'EU Race Discrimination Law: a Hybrid Model?', in G. de Búrca and J. Scott (eds), *Law and New Governance in the EU and the US*, Oxford and Portland, OR: Hart, pp.97–119.

de Búrca, G. (2008), 'Developing democracy beyond the state', *Columbia Journal of Transnational Law,* 46(2), 221–278.

de Búrca, G. (2010), 'The European Court of Justice and the international legal order after Kadi', *Harvard International Law Journal,* 51(1), 1–49.

de Búrca, G. and J. Scott (2006), 'Introduction', in G. de Búrca and J. Scott (eds), *Law and New Governance in the EU and the US*, Oxford and Portland: Hart, pp.1–12.

de Búrca, G. (2011), 'The Evolution of EU Human Rights Law', in P. Craig and G. de Búrca (eds), *The Evolution of EU Law* (2nd edn), Oxford: Oxford University Press, pp.465–497.

Dehousse, R. (2003), 'Beyond representative democracy: constitutionalism in a polycentric polity', in J. Weiler and M. Wind (eds), *European Constitutionalism beyond the State*, Cambridge: Cambridge University Press, pp.135–156.

Delanty, G. (2009), *The Cosmopolitan Imagination*, Cambridge: Cambridge University Press.

Delhey, J. (2004), European Social Integration: From convergence of countries to transnational relations between people, *WZB Discussion Papers,* 201 (February).

de Schutter, O. and S. Deakin (2005), *Social Rights and Market Forces: Is the Open Coordination of Employment and Social Policies the Future of Social Europe?,* Bruxelles: Bruylant.

de Sousa Santos, B. (2005), 'Beyond Neoliberal Governance: the World Social Forum as Subaltern Cosmopolitan Politics and Legality', in B. de Sousa Santos and C.A. Rodriguez-Garavito (eds), *Law and Globalisation from Below*, Cambridge: Cambridge University Press, pp.29–63.

de Sousa Santos, B., and C.A. Rodriguez-Garavito (2005), 'Law, Politics, and the Subaltern in Counter-Hegemonic Globalization', in B. de Sousa Santos and C.A. Rodriguez-Garavito (eds), *Law and Globalization from Below: Towards a Cosmopolitan Legality*, Cambridge: Cambridge University Press, pp.1–26.

Deutsch, K.W. (1971), *The Analysis of International Relations*, Englewood Cliffs, NJ: Prentice Hall.

de Witte, B. (1991), 'Community law and national constitutional values', *Legal Issues of Economic Integration,* 18(1), 1–25.

de Witte, B. (2005), 'The Trajectory of Fundamental Social Rights in Europe', in G. de Búrca and B. de Witte (eds), *Social Rights in Europe*, Oxford: Oxford University Press, pp.153–168.

de Witte, B. (2009), 'The crumbling public/private divide: horizontality in European anti-discrimination law', *Citizenship Studies,* 13(5), 515–525.

de Witte, B. (2011), 'Direct Effect, Supremacy and the Nature of the Legal Order', in P. Craig and G. de Búrca (eds), *The Evolution of EU Law*, Oxford: Oxford University Press, pp.323–362.

DG ECFIN (1996), *European Economy – Reports and Studies – Economic Evaluation of the Internal Market* (vol. 4), Luxemburg: Office for Official Publications of the European Communities.

Dilling, O., M. Herberg and G. Winter (2008), *Responsible Business – Self-Governance and Law in Transnational Economic Transactions*, Oxford and Portland: Hart.

Dobner, P. and M. Loughlin (eds) (2010), *The Twilight of Constitutionalism*? Oxford: Oxford University Press.

Dølvik, J.E. (1999), *Die Spitze des Eisbergs. Der EGB und die Entwicklung des Euro-Korporatismus*, Münster: Westphälisches Dampfboot.

Douglas-Scott, S. (2006), 'A tale of two courts: Luxembourg, Strasbourg and the growing European human rights acquis', *CMLR,* 43(3), 629–665.

Doukas, D. (2009), 'The verdict of the German Federal Constitutional Court on the Lisbon Treaty: not guilty, but don't do it again', *ELR* 34(4), 866–888.

Drexl, J. (2010), 'Competition Law and Part of the European Constitution', in A. von Bogdandy and J. Bast (eds), *Principles of European Constitutional Law*, Munich and Portland: Beck and Hart, pp.659–697.

Dukes, R. (2008), 'Constitutionalizing employment relations: Sinzheimer, Kahn-Freund, and the role of labour law', *Journal of Law and Society,* 35(3), 341–363.

Dummet, A. (1994), 'The starting line: a proposal for a draft Council Directive concerning the elimination of racial discrimination', *New Community,* 20(3), 530–534.

Dunhoff, J.L. and J.P. Trachtman (eds) (2009a), 'A functional approach to international constitutionalization', in J.L. Dunhoff and J.P. Trachtman (eds), *Ruling the World? Constitutionalism, International Law and Global Governance*, Cambridge: Cambridge University Press, pp.3–25.

Dunoff, J.L. and J.P. Trachtman (eds) (2009b), *Ruling the World? Constitutionalism, International Law and Global Governance*, Cambridge: Cambridge University Press.

Dworkin, R. (1996), *Freedom's Law: the Moral Reading of the American Constitution*, Oxford: Oxford University Press.

Edström, Ö. (2008), 'The free movement of services and the right to industrial action in Swedish law – in the light of the *Laval* case', in M. Rönnmar (ed.), *EU Industrial Relations v National Industrial Relations,* Kluwer International, pp.169–191.

Eeckhout, P. (2009), 'Kadi and Al Barakaat: Luxembourg is not Texas – or Washington', *European Journal of International Law – Talk*, 25 February.

Egger, P., M. Larch and M. Pfaffermayr (2006), 'On the welfare effects of trade and investment liberalisation', *European Economic Review,* 51(3), 669.

Eichengreen, B. (2007), *The European Economy since 1945 – Coordinated Capitalism and Beyond*, Princeton and Oxford: Princeton University Press.

Elhauge, E. and D. Geradin (2007), *Global Competition Law and Economics,* Oxford and Portland: Hart.

Ely, J.H. (1980), *Democracy and Distrust. A Constitutional Theory of Judicial Review*, Harvard: Harvard University Press.

Eriksen, E.O. (2009*), The Unfinished Democratisation of Deliberation. The European Case*, Oslo: Arena (www.arena.uio.no).

Esping-Andersen, G. (1990), *The Three Worlds of Welfare Capitalism,* Cambridge: Polity Press.

Esping-Andersen, G. (1999), *Social Foundations of Post-Industrial Economies*, Oxford: Oxford University Press.

European Commission (2010a), *The Social Situation in the European Union 2009*, Luxemburg: Publication Office of the European Union.

European Commission (2005), *Working Together for Growth and Jobs: a New Start for the Lisbon Strategy*, Brussels: European Commission.

European Commission (2010b), *Europe 2020. A Strategy for Smart, Sustainable and Inclusive Growth*, Brussels: European Commission.

European Commission (2010c), *Europe in Figures – Eurostat Yearbook 2010,* Brussels: European Commission (Eurostat).

European Foundation for the Improvement of Working and Living Conditions (2007), *Employment and Working Conditions for Foreign Workers,* Dublin: European Foundation for the Improvement of Working and Living Conditions.

European Integration Consortium (2009), *Labour Mobility within the EU in the Context of Enlargement and the Functioning of the Transitional Arrangements*, Brussels: European Commission.

Evans Case, R., and T.E. Givens (2010), 'Re-engineering legal opportunity structures in the European Union? The starting line group and the politics of the racial equality directive', *JCMS* 48(2), 221–241.

Evans, A.C. (1982), 'European citizenship', *Modern Law Review*, 45(3), 497–515.

Everson, M., and J. Eisner (2007), *The Making of a European Constitution: Judges and Law beyond Constitutive Power,* Abingdon and New York: Routledge.

Ewing, K., and J. Hendy (2010), 'The dramatic implications of *Demir* and *Baykara'*, *Industrial Law Journal,* 39(1), 2–51.

Falkner, G. (2010), 'European Union', in F.G. Castles, S. Leibfried, J. Lewis, H. Obinger and C. Pierson (eds), *The Oxford Handbook of the Welfare State*, Oxford: Oxford University Press, pp.292–305.

Favell, A. and V. Guiraudon (2011), *The Sociology of the European Union*, London: Palgrave Macmillan.

Favell, A and V. Guiraudon (2009), 'The sociology of the European Union: an agenda', *European Union Politics,* 10(4), 550–576.

Ferrera, M. (2009), 'The JCMS Annual Lecture: national welfare states and European integration: in search of 'virtuous nesting', *JCMS,* 47(2), 219–233.

Ferrera, M. (2010), 'Mapping the Components of Social EU: a Critical Analysis of the Current Institutional Patchwork', in E. Marlier and D. Natali (eds), *Europe 2020: Towards a More Social EU?*, Brussels: Peter Lang, pp.45–67.

Fiedziuk, N. (2011), 'Services of general economic interest and the Treaty of Lisbon: opening doors to a whole new approach or maintaining the status quo?', *ELR,* 36(2), 226–242.

Finkin, M. (2011), 'The states as labour law laboratories: a US-EU comparison', *CEPR – The Role of Experiments for the Advancement of Effective Labour Legislation*, Workshop Paper, pp.1–25.

Fitzpatrick, B. (2000), 'Converse Pyramids and the EU Social Constitution', in J. Shaw (ed.), *Social Law and Policy in an Evolving European Union,* Oxford and Portland: Hart, pp.303–324.

Fligstein, N. (2008), *Euroclash. The EU, European Identity and the Future of Europe,* Oxford: Oxford University Press.

Fligstein, N. (2011), 'Markets and Firms', in A. Favell and V. Guiraudon (eds), *Sociology of the European Union*, Basingstoke: Palgrave Macmillan, pp.100–124.

Fossum, J.E. (2010), 'The Future of the European Order', in P.V. Birkinshaw, *The European Union Legal Order after Lisbon*, Alphen aan den Rijn: Kluwer, pp.32–56.

Fossum, J.E. and A.J. Menéndez (2010), 'The Theory of Constitutional Synthesis: a Constitutional Theory for a Democratic European Union', Oslo: *RECON Online Working Papers.*

Fossum, J.E. and H.-J. Trenz (2006), 'The EU's fledgling society: from deafening silence to critical voice in European constitution making', *Journal of Civil Society* 2(1), 57–77.

Fox, E.M. (2008), 'Competition Law', in A. F. Lowenfels (ed.), *International Economic Law* (2nd edn), Oxford: Oxford University Press, pp.417–464.

Fraisse, L. (2005), 'The third sector and the policy process in France: the centralised horizontal third sector community faced with the reconfiguration of the state-centred republican model', *Third Sector European Policy Papers,* 7 (October).

Franzen, M. (2010), 'Conflict of Laws in Employment Contracts and Industrial Relations', in R. Blanpain (ed.), *Comparative Labour Law and Industrial Relations in Industrialized Market Economies*, Kluwer International, pp.221–241.

Fredman, S. (2011), *Discrimination Law* (2nd edn), Oxford: Oxford University Press.

Fredman, S. (2008), *Human Rights Transformed*, Oxford: Oxford University Press.

Freeman, R. (2006), *People Flows in Globalisation, NBER Working Paper*, 12315 (June).

Gallie, D. and S. Paugam (2002), *Social Precarity and Social Integration*, Brussels: European Commission.

Gerber, D.J. (1994), 'Constitutionalizing the economy: German neoliberalism, competition law and the "new" Europe', *American Journal of Comparative Law,* 42(1), 25–84.

Gerber, D.J. (1998), *Law and Competition in Twentieth Century Europe: Protecting Prometheus*, Oxford: Clarendon Press.

Giddens, A. (2000), *The Third Way and Its Critics,* Cambridge: Polity.

Giddens, A. (2006), 'A Social Model for Europe?', in A. Giddens, P. Diamond and R. Liddle (eds), *Global Europe, Social Europe*, Cambridge: Polity, pp.14–35.

Gill, S. (1995), 'Globalization, market civilization and disciplinary neoliberalism. Millennium', *Journal of International Studies,* 24(3), 39–95.

Ginsburg, T. (2003), *Judicial Review in New Democracies*, Cambridge: Cambridge University Press.

Giubboni, S. (2006), *Social Rights and Market Freedom in the European Constitution. A Labour Law Perspective,* Cambridge: Cambridge University Press.

Giubboni, S. (2010), 'Social Rights and Market Freedom in the European Constitution: a Reappraisal', in K. Tuori and S. Sankari (eds), *The Many Constitutions of Europe*, Farnham: Ashgate, pp.241–261.

Glennester, H. (2010), 'Sustainability of Western welfare states', in F.G. Castles, S. Leibfried, J. Lewis, H. Obinger and C. Pierson (eds), *The Oxford Handbook of the Welfare State*, Oxford: Oxford University Press, pp.689–702.

Gormley, L. (2009), *EU Law of Free Movement of Goods and Customs Union,* Oxford: Oxford University Press.

de Graaff, J. (1958), *Theoretical Welfare Economics*, Cambridge: Cambridge University Press.

Graetz, M.J. and A.C. Warren (2007), 'Dividend taxation in Europe: when the ECJ makes tax policy', *CMLR,* 44(6), 1577–1623.

Graser, A. (2006), 'Approaching the 'Social Union?', in E.O. Eriksen, C. Joerges and F. Roedl (eds), *Law and Democracy in the Postnational Union*, Oslo: ARENA, pp.259–287.

Graziadei, M. (2006), 'Comparative Law as the Study of Transplants and Receptions', in M. Reimann and R. Zimmermann (eds), *The Oxford Handbook of Comparative Law,* Oxford: Oxford University Press, pp.441–475.

Griller, S. (2008), 'Is This a Constitution? Remarks on a Contested Concept', in S. Griller and J. Ziller (eds), *The Lisbon Treaty. EU Constitutionalism without a Constitutional Treaty*?, Wien: Springer, pp.21–56.

Grimm, D. (2005), 'Integration by Constitution', *I-CON* 3(2–3), 193–208.

Grimm, D. (2010), 'The Achievement of Constitutionalism and Its Prospects in a Changed World' in P. Dobner and M. Loughlin, *The Twilight of Constitutionalism?*, Oxford: Oxford University Press, pp.3–22.

Grimmel, A. (2010), 'Judicial Interpretation or Judicial Activism?: the Legacy of Rationalism in the Studies of the European Court of Justice', *Centre for European Studies Working Paper*, 176 (July).

Haas, E. (2004), 'Introduction: Institutionalism or Constructivism', in E.B. Haas and D. Dinan (eds), *The Uniting of Europe: Political, Social and Economic Forces 1950–1957,* Indiana: University of Notre Dame Press, pp. i–xxix.

Habermas, J. (1996), *Between Facts and Norms,* Cambridge: Polity Press.

Habermas, J. (1996), *Citizenship and National Identity* (Appendix II), in *Between Facts and Norms* (English, translated by William Regh, ed.). Cambridge: Polity Press, pp.491–515.

Halberstamm, D. (2009), 'Constitutional Heterarchy: the Centrality of Conflict in the European Union and the United States', in J.L. Dunoff and J.P. Trachtman (eds), *Ruling the World? Constitutionalism, International Law and Global Governance*, Cambridge: Cambridge University Press, pp.326–355.

Hall, P. A. and D. Soskice (2001), 'An Introduction to Varieties of Capitalism', in P. Hall and D. Soskice (eds), *Varieties of Capitalism. The Institutional Foundations of Comparative Advantage,* Oxford: Oxford University Press, pp.1–68.

Haltern, U. (2004), 'Integration through Law', in A. Wiener and T. Diez (eds), *European Integration Theory* (1st edn), Oxford: Oxford University Press, pp.177–196.

Hänninen, S. (2010), 'Social Constitution in Historical Perspective: Hugo Sinzheimer in the Weimar Context', in K. Tuori and S. Sanskari (eds), *The Many Constitutions of Europe,* Farnham and Burlington: Ashgate, pp. 219–239.

Hardin, G. (1968), 'The Tragedy of the Commons', *Science* 162 (December), 1243–1248.

Harpaz, G. (2009), 'The European Court of Justice and its relations with the European Court of Human Rights: the quest for enhanced reliance, coherence and legitimacy', *CMLR,* 46(1), 105–141.

Hartley, T.C. (2004), *EU Law in a Global Context,* Cambridge: Cambridge University Press.

Harvey, D. (2005), *A Brief History of Neo-liberalism*, Oxford: Oxford University Press.

Hatje, A. (2010), 'The Economic Constitution within the Internal Market', in A. von Bogdandy and J. Bast (eds), *Principles of European Constitutional Law*, Munich and Portland: Beck and Hart, pp.589–622.

Hatzopoulos, V. (2002), 'Killing national health and insurance systems but healing patients?', *CMLR,* 39(4), 683–729.

Heckscher, E.F. (1919), 'Utrikeshandelns verkan pa inkomsverdelnigen', *Ekonomisk Tidskrift,* 21(2), 1–32.

Heidenreich, M. and C. Wunder (2008), 'Patterns of regional inequality in the enlarged European Union', *European Sociological Review* 24(1), 19–36.

Heidenreich, M. and J. Zeitlin (eds) (2009), *The Open Method of Coordination and National Social and Employment Policy Reforms: Influences, Mechanisms and Effects,* London: Routledge.

Heller, H. (1971a), Rechtsstaat oder Diktatur (1930), in H. Heller (ed.), *Gesammelte Schriften*, Leiden: Mohr, pp.443–462.

Heller, H. (1971b), Politische Demokratie und Soziale Homogeneität (1928), in H. Heller (ed.), *Gesammelte Schriften* (vol. 2, pp. 421–442), Leiden: Mohr.

Heller, H. (2000), 'Political Democracy and Social Homogeneity', in A.J. Jacobsen and B. Schlink (eds), *Weimar: a Jurisprudence of Crisis*, Berkeley and London: University of California Press, pp.256–265.

Hepple, B. (2004), 'Race and law in Fortress Europe', *Modern Law Review* 67(1), 1–15.

Hepple, B. (2005), *Labour Law and Global Trade,* Oxford and Portland, OR: Hart.

Héritier, A. and S. Eckert (2008), 'New modes of governance in the shadow of hierarchy: self-regulation by industry in Europe', *Journal of Public Policy* 28(1), 113–138.

Hiebert, J.L. (2010), 'Governing Like Judges', in T. Campbell, K. D. Ewing and A. Tomkins (eds), *The Legal Protection of Human Rights*, Oxford: Oxford University Press, pp.40–65.

Hinrichs, O. (2001). *Kündigungsschutz und Arbeitnehmerbeteiligung bei Massenentlassungen – Europarechtliche Aspekte und Impulse* (1st edn), Baden-Baden: Nomos.

Hirschl, R. (2004), *Towards Juristocracy. The Origins and Consequences of the New Constitutionalism*, Harvard: Harvard University Press.

Hix, S., A.G. Noury and G. Roland (2007), *Democratic Politics in the European Parliament*. Cambridge: Cambridge University Press.

Hoekman, B.M. and M.M. Kostecki (2009), *The Political Economy of the World Trade System* (3rd edn), Oxford: Oxford University Press.

Höpner, M. and A. Schäfer (2010), 'A new phase of European integration: organised capitalism in post-Ricardian Europe', *West European Politics* 33(2), 344–368.

Hoskyns, C. (1996), *Integrating Gender: Women, Law and Politics in the European Union*, London: Verso.

Hurrelmann, A. (2004), 'European Constitutionalism and Social Integration', *The Federal Trust Online Papers*, 13 (July).

Isiksel, N.T. (2010), 'Fundamental rights in the EU after Kadi and Al Barakaat', *ELJ* 16(5), 551–577.

Jabko, N. (2011), *Which Economic Governance for the European Union?*, Stockholm: Swedish Institute for European Policy Studies

Jachtenfuchs, M., and B. Kohler-Koch (2004), 'Multi-Level Governance', in A. Wiener and T. Dietz (eds), *European Integration Theory* (1st edn), Oxford: Oxford University Press, pp.97–115.

Jacobs, A. (2009a), 'Collective Labour Relations', in B. Hepple, and B. Veneziani (eds), *The Transformation of Labour Law in Europe*, Oxford and Portland, OR: Hart, pp.201–231.

Jacobs, A. (2009b), 'The Social Janus Head of the European Union: the Social Market Economy versus Ultraliberal Policies', in J. Wouters, L. Verhey and P. Kiiver (eds), *European Constitutionalism beyond Lisbon*, Antwerp: Intersentia, pp.111–128.

Jacobs, A. (2010 [1985]), 'Collective Self-Regulation', in B. Hepple (ed.), *The Making of Labour Law in Europe: a Comparative Study of Nine Countries up to 1945* (2nd edn (reprint)), Oxford and Portland, OR: Hart, pp.139–145.

Jacobs, F. (2008), 'The state of international economic law: re-thinking sovereignty in Europe', *European Journal of International Economic Law,* 11(1), 5–41.

Jacqué, J. P. (2011), 'The accession of the European Union to the European Convention on Human Rights and Fundamental Freedoms', *CMLR,* 48(2), 995–1023.

Jiménez García-Herrera, T. (2010), *Social Integration, Statement on Behalf of the EU,* New York: European Union, Spanish Presidency.

Joerges, C. (2004), 'What is left of the European Economic Constitution?', *EUI Working Papers,* 113 (November).

Joerges, C. (2007), 'Rethinking European Law's Supremacy: a Plea for a Supranational Conflict of Laws', in B. Kohler-Koch and B. Rittberger (eds), *Debating the Democratic Legitimacy of the European Union*, Lanham, MD: Rowman and Littlefield, pp.311–328.

Joerges, C. (2010), *The Idea of a Three-Dimensional Conflicts of Law as Constitutional Form, RECON Online Working Papers*, 5 (May), 1–37.

Joerges, C. (2011), 'Will the welfare state survive European integration?', *European Journal of Social Law,* 1(1), 4–19.

Joerges, C. and J. Falke (eds) (2010), *The Social Embeddedness of Transnational Markets*, Bremen: ZERP.

Joerges, C. and F. Roedl (2009), 'Informal politics, formalised law and the "social deficit" of European integration: reflections after the judgments of the ECJ', in *Viking* and *Laval, ELJ,* 15(1), 1–19.

Jones, C. (2005), *Applied Welfare Economics*, Oxford: Oxford University Press.

Kelemen, R.D. (2011), *Eurolegalism. The Transformation of Law and Regulation in the European Union,* Cambridge, MA: Harvard University Press.

Kenner, J. (2003), 'Economic and Social Rights in the EU Legal Order: the Mirage of Indivisibility', in T. Hervey and J. Kenner (eds), *Economic and Social Rights under the EU Charter of Fundamental Rights – A Legal Perspective*, Oxford and Portland, OR: Hart, pp.1–26.

Kilpatrick, C. (2009), '*Laval*'s regulatory conundrum: collective standard setting and the Court's new approach to posted workers', *ELR*, 36(2), 844–865.

Kingreen, T. (2010), 'Fundamental Freedoms', in A. von Bogdandy and J. Bast (eds), *Principles of European Constitutional Law*, Munich and Portland: Beck and Hart, pp.515–549.

Kirchhof, P. (2010), 'The European Union of States', in A. von Bogdandy and J. Bast (eds), *Principles of European Constitutional Law* (2nd edn), Munich and Portland, OR: Beck and Hart, pp.735–762.

Kohler-Koch, B. (2010), 'Civil society and EU democracy: "astroturf" representation?', *Journal of European Public Policy*, 17(1), 100–116.

Kohli, M., K. Hank and H. Kühnern (2009), 'The social connectedness of older Europeans: patterns, dynamics and contexts', *Journal of European Social Policy*, 19(4), 327–340.

Komárek, J. (2009), 'The Czech Constitutional Court's Second Decision on the Lisbon Treaty of 3 November 2009', *European Constitutional Law Review,* 5(3), 345–352.

Kooiman, J. (2003), *Governing and Governance,* London: Sage.

Kostakopoulou, D. (2008), 'The evolution of European Union citizenship', *European Political Science*, 7(3), 285–295.

Koutnatzis, S.-I. (2005), 'Social rights as constitutional compromise: lessons from comparative experience', *Columbia Journal of Transnational Law,* 44(1), 74–133.

Krisch, N. (2010), *Beyond Constitutionalism*, Oxford: Oxford University Press.

Kühling, J. (2010), 'Fundamental Rights', in A. von Bogdandy and J. Bast (eds), *Principles of EU Constitutional Law*, Munich and Portland: Beck and Hart, pp.479–515.

Lamping, W. (2010), 'Mission Impossible? Limits and Perils of Institutionalising Post-National Social Policy', in M. Ross and Y. Borgmann-Prebil (eds), *Promoting Solidarity in the European Union*, Oxford: Oxford University Press, pp.46–72.

Laursen, F. (2003), *Comparative Regional Integration*, Aldershot: Ashgate.

Leibfried, S. (2010), 'Social Policy. Left to the Judges and the Markets?', in H. Wallace, M. A. Pollack and A. R. Young (eds), *Policy Making in the European Union* (6th edn), Oxford: Oxford University Press, pp.253–281.

Lennaerts, K. (2003), 'Interlocking legal orders in the European Union and comparative law', *International and Comparative Law Quarterly,* 52(4), 873–906.

Levi, M., E. Ostrom and J.E. Alt (1999), 'Conclusion', in J.E. Alt, M. Levi and E. Ostrom (eds), *Competition and Cooperation*, New York: Russell Sage Foundation, pp.331–337.

Liddle, R. and P. Diamond (2010), 'The Coming Social Crisis in the EU and What Is to Be Done', in E. Marlier and D. Natali (eds), *Europe 2020: Towards a More Social EU?*, Brussels: Peter Lang, pp.69–92.

Liebert, U. (2007), 'The Politics of Social Europe and the Lisbon Process', in B. Stråth and L. Magnusson (eds), *European Social Solidarities – Tensions and Contentions of a Concept*, Brussels: Peter Lang, pp.285–288.

Little, I.M. (2002), *A Critique of Welfare Economics*, Oxford: Oxford University Press.

Littoz-Monnet, A. (2010), 'Dynamic Multi-Level Governance – Bringing the Study of Multi-Level Interactions into the Theorising of European Integration', *European Integration Online Papers,* 14 (April), 01.

Lodge, M. (2008), 'Regulation, the regulatory state and European politics', *West European Politics,* 31(1), 289–301.

Longo, M. (2006), *Constitutionalising Europe. Processes and Practices,* Farnham, UK and Burlington, US: Ashgate.

Lord, C. (1998), *Democracy in the European Union*, Sheffield: Sheffield University Press.

Loughlin, M. (2010), 'What Is Constitutionalisation?', in P. Dobner and M. Loughlin (eds), *The Twilight of Constitutionalism*?, Oxford: Oxford University Press, pp.47–71.

Lowenfeld, A.F. (2008), *International Economic Law* (2nd edn), Oxford: Oxford University Press.

Macaulay, S. (2008), 'A new legal realism: elegant modes and the messy law

in action', *New Legal Realism*, 2 (http://www.newlegalrealism.org/workingpapers).
MacCormick, N. (1993), 'Beyond the sovereign state', *Modern Law Review,* 56(1), 1–18.
MacCormick, N. (1995), 'The Maastricht-Urteil: sovereignty now', *ELJ,* 1(3), 259–266.
Magnette, P. (2007), 'How can one be European? Reflections on the pillars of European identity', *ELJ,* 13(5), 664–679.
Magnusson, L. (2010), *After Lisbon – Social Europe at the Crossroads?,* Brussels: European Trade Union Institute.
Maher, I. (2011), 'Competition Law Modernization: an Evolutionary Tale?', in P. Craig and G. de Búrca (eds), *The Evolution of EU Law* (2nd edn), Oxford: Oxford University Press, pp.717–741.
Mahoney, J. (2007), *The Challenge of Human Rights: Origin, Development, and Significance*, Malden, MA: Blackwell.
Maio, M.D. (2008), 'Uncertainty, trade integration and the optimal level of protection in a Ricardian model with a continuum of goods', *Structural Change and Economic Dynamics,* 19 (August), 315–329.
Majone, G. (1999), 'The regulatory state and its legitimacy problem, *West European Politics,* 22(1), 1–24.
Majone, G. (2005), *Dilemmas of European Integration – Ambiguities and Pitfalls of Integration by Stealth*, Oxford: Oxford University Press.
Majone, G. (2006), 'The common sense of European integration', *Journal of European Public Policy,* 13(5), 607–626.
Malmberg, J. (2010), 'Posting Post *Laval.* International and National Responses', *Uppsala Center for Labor Studies Working Papers* 5 (June), 1–26.
Marenco, G. (1987), 'Competition between national economies and competition between businesses – a response to Judge Pescatore', *Fordham International Law Journal* 10(3), 420–443.
Marlier, E. and D. Natali (eds) (2010), *Europe 2020. Towards a More Social EU?,* Brussels: Peter Lang.
Mattei, U., and F.G. Nicola (2007), 'A "social dimension" on European private law? The call for setting a progressive agenda', *Global Jurist,* 7(1), 1–55.
Maydell, B. von, K. Borchardt, K.-D. Henke, R. Leitner, R. Muffels, M. Quante et al. (2006), *Enabling Social Europe*, Heidelberg: Springer.
Mayer, F.C. (2010), 'Multilevel Constitutional Jurisdiction', in A. von Bogdandy and J. Bast (eds), *Principles of European Constitutional Law* (2nd ed.), pp. 399–439. Munich and Portland, OR: Beck and Hart.
Mayes, D.G. and Z. Mustaffa (2010), 'Social Models in the Enlarged EU', *RECON Online Working Papers*, 20 (October), 1–29.
Menéndez, A.J. (2009), 'The Unencumbered European Taxpayer as the

Product of the Transformation of Personal Taxes by the Judicial Empowerment of "Market Forces"', in R. Letelier and A.J. Menéndez (eds), *The Sinews of European Peace. Reconstituting the Democratic Legitimacy of the Socio-Economic Constitution of the European Union*, Oslo: Arena, pp.157–267.

Menéndez, A.J. (2010), 'Governance and Constitutionalism in the European Order', in P. Birkinshaw and M. Varney, *The European Union Legal Order after Lisbon*, Alphen aan den Rijn: Kluwer, pp.65–90.

Menéndez, A.J. (2011), *United They Diverge? From Conflicts of Law to Constitutional Theory? On Christian Joerges' Theory*, Oslo: ARENA Working Paper 02/2011.

Meyers, J.B. (2010), 'Rethinking "constitutional design" and the integration/accomodation dichotomy', *Modern Law Review,* 73(4), 656–678.

Micklitz, H.-W. and B. de Witte (2012), *The European Court of Justice and the Autonomy of the Member States,* Antwerp: Intersentia.

Molle, W. (2003), *Global Economic Institutions*, London: Routledge.

Molle, W. (2006), *The Economics of European Integration* (5th edn), Aldershot: Ashgate.

Möller, K. (2009), 'Two conceptions of positive liberty: towards an autonomy-based theory of constitutional rights', *Oxford Journal of Legal Studies*, 29(4), 757–786.

Möllers, C. (2010), 'Pouvoir Constituant – Constitution – Constitutionalism', in A. von Bogdandy and J. Bast (eds), *Principles of European Constitutional Law* (2nd edn), Munich and Portland, OR: Beck and Hart, pp.169–204.

Monnet, J. (1976), *Memoires*, Paris: Fayard.

Monti, G. (2007), *EC Competition Law*, Cambridge: Cambridge University Press.

Monti, M. (2010), *A New Strategy for the Internal Market*, Brussels: European Commission.

Morano-Foadi, S. and S. Andreadakis (2011), 'Reflections on the architecture of the EU after the Treaty of Lisbon: the European judicial approach to fundamental rights', *ELJ,* 47(5), 596–610.

Moravcsik, A. (2002), 'In defence of the "democratic deficit": reassessing legitimacy in the European Union', *JCMS*, 40(4), 603–624.

Moravcsik, A. (2004), 'Is there a democratic deficit in world politics? A framework for analysis', *Government and Opposition,* 39(2), 336–363.

Moravcsik, A. and F. Schimmelfennig (2009), 'Liberal Intergovernmentalism', in A. Wiener and T. Diez (eds), *European Integration Theory* (2nd edn), Oxford: Oxford University Press, pp.67–87.

More, G. (1992), 'Reflections on pregnancy discrimination under European Community law', *Journal of Social Welfare and Family Law,* 14(1), 48–56.

More, G. (1999), 'The Principle of Equal Treatment: from Market Unifier to Fundamental Right?', in P. Craig and G. de Búrca (eds), *The Evolution of EU Law*, Oxford: Oxford University Press, pp.517–553.

Moreau, M.-A. (2007), 'The Originality of Transnational Social Norms as a Response to Globalisation', in B. Bercusson and C. Estlund (eds), *Regulating Labour in the Wake of Globalisation*, Oxford and Portland: Hart, pp.254–269.

Moses, J. (2011), 'Is constitutional symmetry enough? Social models and market integration in the US and Europe', *JMCS,* 49(4), 823–843.

Mossialos, E., G. Permanand, R. Baeten and T.K. Hervey (2010), *Health Systems Governance in Europe, the Role of European Union Law and Policy*, Cambridge: Cambridge University Press.

Münch, R. (2008), 'Constructing a European society by jurisdiction', *ELJ,* 14(5), 519–541.

Mundlak, G. (2002), 'The Limits of Labour Law in a Fungible Community', in J. Conaghan, R.M. Fischl and K. Klare (eds), *Labour Law in An Era of Globalization*, Oxford: Oxford University Press, pp.279–298.

Mundlak, G. (2009), 'De-territorializing labour law', *Law and Ethics of Human Rights,* 3(2), 188–222.

Murphy, C. (2010), 'The concept of integration in the jurisprudence of the European Court of Human Rights', *European Journal of Migration and the Law* 12(1), 23–43.

Muylle, K. (1998), 'Angry farmers and passive policemen: private conduct and the free movement of goods', *ELR,* 23(5), 467–474.

Neergard, U., R. Nielsen and L. Roseberry (2008), *The Services Directive – Consequences for the Welfare State and the European Social Model,* Copenhagen: DJØF Publishing.

Nergelius, J. (2008), 'Between Collectivism and Constitutionalism: the Nordic Countries and Constitutionalism', in J. Nergelius (ed.), *Constitutionalism: New Challenges,* Leiden and Boston: Martinus Nijhoff, pp.119–154.

Neumann, F. (1967), *Demokratischer und Autoritärer Staat* (H. Marcuse, ed.), Vienna: Europäische Verlagsanstalt.

Nic Shuibhne, N. (2010), 'The resilience of EU market citizenship', *CMLR* 47(6), 1597–1628.

Nicol, D. (2010), *The Constitutional Protection of Capitalism*, Oxford and Portland: Hart.

Niemann, A., and P. Schmitter (2009), 'Neofunctionalism', in A. Wiener and T. Diez (eds), *European Integration Theory* (2nd edn), Oxford: Oxford University Press, pp.45–66.

Nikolaïdis, K. (2010), 'Sustainable integration: towards EU 2.0?', *JCMS* 48(1), 21–54.

Nolte, G. (2005), *European and US Constitutionalism,* Cambridge: Cambridge University Press.

Noonan, C. (2008), *The Emerging Principles of International Competition Law,* Oxford: Oxford University Press.

Nourse, V., and G. Shaffer (2010), 'Varieties of new legal realism: can a new world order prompt a new legal theory?', *Cornell Law Review,* 95(1), 61–138.

Novitz, T. (2008), 'A human rights analysis of the *Viking* and *Laval* judgments', *Cambridge Yearbook of European Legal Studies,* 16, 540–561.

Nussbaum, M. (2001), *Women and Human Development*, Cambridge: Cambridge University Press.

O'Brien, C. (2011), 'Case analysis *Ibrahim* and *Teixeira'*, *CMLR,* 48(1), 203–225.

OECD (1998), *Harmful Tax Competition – an Emerging Global Issue*, Paris: OECD.

OECD (2006), *The OECD's Project on Harmful Tax Competition – 2006 Update on Progress in Member Countries,* Paris: OECD.

Oeter, S. (2010), 'Federalism and Democracy', in A. von Bodgandy, and J. Bast (eds), *Principles of European Constitutional Law* (2nd edn), Munich, Oxford and Portland, OR: Beck and Hart, pp.55–82.

Ohlin, B. (1933), *Interregional and International Trade*, Cambridge, MA: Harvard University Press.

Ohlin, B. (1956), 'Social aspects of European economic co-operation', *International Labour Review*, 74(1–2), 99–123.

O'Leary, S. (2002), *Employment Law at the European Court of Justice: Judicial Structures, Policies and Processes*, Oxford: Hart.

O'Leary, S. (2011), 'Free Movement of Persons and Services', in P. Craig and G. de Búrca (eds), *The Evolution of EU Law*, Oxford: Oxford University Press, pp.499–545.

Oliver, P. (1999), 'Some further reflections on the scope of Articles 28–30 (Ex 30–36) EC', *CMLR,* 36(4), 783–806.

Orlandini, G. (2000), 'The free movement of goods as a possible 'community' limitation on industrial conflict', *ELJ,* 6(4), 341–362.

Ostrom, E. (2010), 'Beyond markets and states: polycentric governance for complex economic systems', *American Economic Review,* 100(3), 641–672.

Outhwaite, W. (2008), *European Society*, Oxford: Oxford University Press.

Pareto, V. (1966), *Manuel d'économie politique* (first published 1909) (with a Preface by R. Dehem), Genève: Droz.

Parker, O. (2008), 'Challenging "new constitutionalism" in the EU: French resistance, "social Europe" and "soft" governance', *New Political Economy,* 13(4), 397–417.

Perels, J. (1979), 'Der Gleichheitssatz zwischen Hierarchie und Demokratie', in J. Perels (ed.), *Grundrechte als Fundament der Demokratie*, Frankfurt: Suhrkamp, pp.69–95.

Peters, A. (2006), 'Compensatory constitutionalism: the function and potential of international law norm and structures', *Leiden Journal of International Law,* 19(3), 579–610.

Petersmann, E.-U. (2006), 'Multilevel Trade Governance in the WTO Requires Multi-Level Constitutionalism', in E.-U. Petersmann and C. Joerges, *Constitutionalism, Multilevel Trade Governance and Social Regulation*, Oxford and Portland: Hart, pp.5–58.

Petersmann, E.-U. (2008), 'Human rights, international economic law and 'constitutional justice', *European Journal of International Law,* 19(4), 769–798.

Pigou, A.C. (1920), *Economics of Welfare*, London: Macmillan.

Piris, J.-C. (2010), *The Lisbon Treaty. A Legal and Political Analysis,* Cambridge: Cambridge University Press.

Plender, R. (1976), 'An incipient form of European citizenship, in F. Jacobs (ed.), *European Law and the Individual,* New York: North-Holland Publishers, pp.39–55.

Poaires Maduro, M. (1998), *We the Court. The European Court of Justice and the European Economic Constitution*, Oxford and Portland: Hart.

Poiares Maduro, M. (1999), 'Striking the Elusive Balance between Economic Freedom and Social Rights in the EU' in P. Alston (ed.), *The EU and Human Rights* (pp. 449–469), Oxford: Oxford University Press, pp.449–469.

Poiares Maduro, M. (2009), 'Courts and Pluralism: Essay on a Theory of Judicial Adjudication in the Context of Legal and Constitutional Pluralism', in J.L. Dunoff and J.P. Trachtman, *Ruling the World? Constitutionalism, International Law and Global Governance*, Cambridge: Cambridge University Press, pp.356–379.

Poiares Maduro, M. (1997), 'Reforming the market or the state? Article 30 and the European Constitution: economic freedoms and political rights', *ELJ,* 3(1), 55–82.

Polanyi, K. (1957 [1944]), *The Great Transformation*, Boston: Beacon Press.

Preuß, U. K. (2010), 'Disconnecting Constitutions from Statehood: Is Global Constitutionalism a Viable Concept?', in P. Dobner, and M. Loughlin (eds), *The Twilight of Constitutionalism?*, Oxford: Oxford University Press, pp.23–46.

Quinn, G. (2008), 'Disability Discrimination Law in the European Union', in H. Meenan (ed.), *Equality Law in an Enlarged European Union*, Cambridge: Cambridge University Press, pp.231–277.

Rawls, J. (1999), *The Law of Peoples*, Cambridge, MA: Harvard University Press.

Reh, C. (2008), 'The convention on the future of Europe and the development of integration theory: a lasting impact?', *Journal of European Public Policy,* 15(1), 781–794.

Rehder, B. (2007), 'What Is Political about Jurisprudence? Courts, Politics and Political Science in Europe and the United States', *MPifG Discussion Paper*, 7(5).

Reich, N. (1994), 'The "November Revolution" of the European Court of Justice: Keck, Meng and Audi revisited', *CMLR,* 31(3), 459–492.

Reich, N., and H.-W. Micklitz (2009), 'Crónica de una muerte anunciada: the Commission proposal for a "Directive on Consumer Rights"', *CMLR,* 46(3), 471–519.

Ricardo, D. (1817), *On the Principles of Political Economy and Taxation*, London: John Murray.

Ringe, W.-G. (2010), 'Company law and free movement of capital: nothing escapes the ECJ?', *Cambridge Law Journal,* 69(2), 378–409.

Risse, T. (2009), 'Social Constructivism and European Integration', in A. Wiener and T. Diez (eds), *European Integration Theory*, Oxford: Oxford University Press, pp.144–161.

Risse, T. (2010), *A Community of Europeans? Transnational Identities and Public Spheres* (2nd edn), Ithaca and London: Cornell University Press.

Rogowski, R. (2008), *The European Social Model and Transitional Labour Markets: Law and Policy*, Aldershot: Ashgate.

Rosenfeld, M. (2008), 'Rethinking constitutional ordering in an era of legal and ideological pluralism', *I-CON* 6(3 and 4), 415–455.

Ross, M. (2010), 'Solidarity – A New Constitutional Paradigm for the EU?', in M. Ross and Y. Borgmann-Prebil (eds), *Promoting Solidarity in the European Union*, Oxford: Oxford University Press, pp. 23–45.

Ruggie, J. (1982), 'International regimes, transactions, and change: embedded liberalism in the postwar economic order', *International Organization,* 36(2), 379–415.

Rüthers, B. (2005), *Die unbegrenzte Auslegung* (5th edn), Tübingen: Mohr.

Ruzza, C. and V. della Sala (2007), *Governance and Civil Society in the European Union: Normative Perspectives*, Manchester: Manchester University Press.

Sabel, C.F. and O. Gerstenberg (2010), 'Constitutionalising an overlapping consensus: the ECJ and the emergence of a coordinate constitutional order', *ELJ,* 16(5), 511–550.

Sacco, R. (1991), 'Legal formants. A dynamic approach to comparative law', *American Journal of Comparative Law,* 39(1–2), 1–34.

Sadurski, W. (2008), '"Solange Chapter 3": constitutional courts in Central Europe – democracy – European Union', *ELJ,* 14(1), 1–35.

Sanders, A.L. (1985). 'Players and process: the evolution of employment law in the EC', *Comparative Labor Law,* 7(1), 1–31.

Sauter, W., and H. Schepel (2009), *State and Market in European Union Law,* Cambridge: Cambridge University Press.

Schaal, G.S. (2000), *Integration durch Verfassung und Verfassungsrechtsprechung?,* Berlin: Duncker and Humblot.

Schaal, G.S. (2001), 'Integration durch Verfassung und Verfassungsrechtssprechung?', *ÖZP* 30(2), 221–232.

Scharpf, F. (1999), *Governing Europe – Effective and Democratic?*, Oxford: Oxford University Press.

Scharpf, F. (2010), 'The asymmetry of European integration, or why the EU cannot be a "social market economy"', *Socio-Economic Review,* 8(2), 211–250.

Scharpf, F.W. (2002), 'The European social model: coping with the challenges of diversity', *JCMS,* 40(4), 645–670.

Scharpf, F.W. (2009), 'Legitimacy in the multilevel European polity', *European Political Science Review,* 1(2), 173–204.

Schepel, H. (2005), *The Constitution of Private Governance,* Oxford and Portland: Hart.

Schiek, D. (2001), Artikel 20 Abs. 1–3 V: Sozialstaat, in E. Denninger, W. Hoffman-Riem, H.-P. Schneider and E. Stein (eds), *Alternativkommentar zum Grundgesetz* (Vol. 2), Neuwied: Luchterhand.

Schiek, D. (2002a), 'Elements of a new framework for the principle of equal treatment of persons in EC Law Directives 2000/43/EC, 2000/78/EC and 2002/73/EC changing Directive 76/207/EEC in context', *ELJ,* 8(2), 290–314.

Schiek, D. (2002b), 'Torn between arithmetic and substantive equality? Perspectives on equality in German labour law', *International Journal for Comparative Labour Law and Industrial Relations,* 18(2), 137–157.

Schiek, D. (2005), 'Autonomous collective agreements as a regulatory device in European labour law: how to read Articles 139 EC', *Industrial Law Journal,* 34, 23–56.

Schiek, D. (2007), 'Implementing non-discrimination directives – typologies for legal transplanting', *Internationaal Colloquium Europees Verzekeringsrecht – Colloques Internationaux de droit européen de assurance,* 7, 47–83.

Schiek, D. (2008a), 'The European Social Model and the Services Directive', in U. Neergaard, R. Nielsen and L. Roseberry (eds), *The Services Directive – Consequences for the European Social Model and the Welfare State,* Copenhagen: DJØF.

Schiek, D. (2008b), 'Transnational Collective Labour Agreements in Europe and at European Level – Further Readings of Article 139 EC', in M. Rönnmar (ed.), *EU Industrial Relations v National Industrial Relations,* Wolters Kluwer, pp.83–104.

Schiek, D. (2010a), 'EU non-discrimination law and policy: gender in the maze of multidimensional equalities', in C. Hohmann-Dennhardt, M.

Körner and R. Zimmer (eds), *Geschlechtergerechtigkeit. Liber Amicorum Heide Pfarr*, Baden-Baden: Nomos, pp.472–488.

Schiek, D. (2010b), 'Is There a Social Ideal of the European Court of Justice?', in U. Neergaard, R. Nielsen and L. Roseberry (eds), *The Role of the Courts in Developing a European Social Model – Theoretical and Methodological Perspective,* Copenhagen: DJØF, pp. 63–96.

Schiek, D. (2010c), 'Comparative law and European harmonisation – a match made in heaven or uneasy bedfellows?', *European Business Law Review*, 21(2), 203–255.

Schiek, D. (2010d), 'Europe's socio-economic constitution after the Treaty of Lisbon', in T. Dieterich, M. Le Friant, L. Nogler, K. Katsutoshi and H. Pfarr (eds), *Individuelle und kollektive Freiheit im Arbeitsrecht. Gedächtnisschrift für Ulrich Zachert*, Baden-Baden: Nomos, pp.162–178.

Schiek, D. (2011a), 'Organising EU Equality Law around the Nodes of "Race", Gender and Disability', in D. Schiek and A. Lawson (eds), *EU Non-Discrimination Law and Intersectionality: Investigating the Triangle of Racial, Gender and Disability Discrimination*, Farnham: Ashgate, pp.11–27.

Schiek, D. (2011b), 'Age discrimination before the ECJ – conceptual and theoretical issues', *CMLR,* 48(3), 777–799.

Schiek, D. (2012), 'ECJ Fundamental Rights Case Law, Member States' Prerogative and Citizens' Autonomy', in H.-W. Micklitz and B. de Witte (eds), *The ECJ and the Autonomy of Member States,* Antwerp: Intersentia, pp. 219–258.

Schiek, D. (2012, forthcoming), 'Tarifvertrag und anders legitimiertes Recht', in W. Däubler (ed.), *Tarifvertragsgesetz,* Baden-Baden: Nomos.

Schiek, D. and V. Chege (eds) (2009), *European Union Non-Discrimination Law – Comparative Perspectives on Multidimensional Equality Law*, London and New York: Routledge.

Schiek, D. and J. Mulder (2011), 'Intersectionality in EU law: a Critical Re-appraisal', in D. Schiek and A. Lawson (eds), *EU Non-discrimination Law and Intersectionality*, Farnham and Burlington, VA: Ashgate, pp.259–273.

Schiek, D., U. Liebert and H. Schneider (2011), *European Economic and Social Constitutionalism after the Treaty of Lisbon,* Cambridge: Cambridge University Press.

Schiek, D., L. Waddington and M. Bell (eds) (2007), *Cases, Materials and Text on National, Supranational and International Non-Discrimination Law,* Oxford and Portland: Hart.

Schmitter, P.C. (2000), 'An Excursus on Constitutionalism', *ConWeb,* 2000(3).

Sciarra, S. (2001), *Labour Law in the Courts: National Judges and the European Court of Justice*, Oxford and Portland: Hart.

Scott, C. (2002), 'The governance of the European Union: potential of multi-level control', *ELJ*, 8(1), 59–79.
Sen, A. and M. Nussbaum (1993), *The Quality of Life*, Oxford: Clarendon Press.
Senior Nello, S. (2008), *The European Union. Economics, Policies and History* (2nd edn), Maidenhead: McGraw Hill.
Shanks, M. (1977), 'Introductory article: the social policy of the European Communities', *CMLR*, 14(3), 375–383.
Shaw, J. (1995), 'Introduction', in J. Shaw and G. More (eds), *New Legal Dynamics of the European Union* (pp. 1–32), Oxford: Clarendon Press.
Shaw, J. (2008), 'The political representation of Europe's citizens (case note)', *European Constitutional Law Review*, 4(1), 162–186.
Siebert, H. (1991), 'The integration of Germany: real economic adjustment', *European Economic Review*, 35(2–3), 591–602.
Silver, H. (2010), 'The social integration of Germany since unification', *German Politics and Society*, 28(1), 165–188.
Simpson, G. (1994), 'Imagined Consent: Democratic Liberalism in International Legal Theory', *Australian Yearbook of International Law* 15, 103–128.
Smend, R. (1968), Verfassungslehre und Verfassungsrecht (1928), in R. Smend (ed.), *Gesammelte Schriften*, Berlin: Duncker and Humblot.
Smismans, S. (2004), *Law, Legitimacy and European Governance. Functional Participation in Social Regulation*, Oxford: Oxford University Press.
Smismans, S. (2010), 'European Constitutionalism and the Democratic Design of European Governance: Rethinking Directly Deliberative Polyarchy and Reflexive Constitutionalism', in K. Tuori and S. Sankari (eds), *The Many Constitutions of Europe*, Farnham: Ashgate, pp.169–193.
Smith, A. (1776), *The Wealth of Nations*, London: W. Strahan and T. Cadell.
Snell, J. (2007), 'Non-discriminatory tax obstacles in Community law', *International and Comparative Law Quarterly*, 56(2), 339–370.
Snyder, F. (2011), 'EMU – Integration and Differentiation: Metaphor for the European Union', in P. Craig and G de Búrca (eds), *The Evolution of EU Law* (2nd edn), Oxford: Oxford University Press, pp.687–716.
Somek, A. (2006), 'Weak Social Policy', in E.O. Eriksen, C. Joerges and F. Roedl (eds), *Law and Democracy in the Postnational Union* (1st edn), Oslo: Arena, pp.317–331.
Somek, A. (2011), *Engineering Equality: an Essay on European Anti-Discrimination Law*, Oxford: Oxford University Press.
Spaventa, E. (2000), 'On discrimination and the theory of mandatory requirements', *Cambridge Yearbook of European Legal Studies* 3, 457–473.
Spaventa, E. (2007), *Free Movement of Persons in the European Union: Barriers to Movement in Their Constitutional Context*, Alphen aan den Rijn: Kluwer.

Statistisches Bundesamt (2011), *Öffentliche Sozialleistungen – Statistik zum Elterngeld,* Wiesbaden: Statistisches Bundesamt.

Stein, E. (1981), Lawyers, judges and the making of a transnational constitution, *American Journal of International Law,* 75(1), 1–55.

Stein, E. (2001), Artikel 20 Abs. 1–3 III – Demokratie, in E. Denninger, W. Hoffmann-Riem, H.-P. Schneider and S. Ekkehart (eds), *Alternativkommentar Grundgesetz*, Neuwied: Luchterhand, pp.1–30.

Stiglitz, J. (2002), *Globalization and Its Discontents*, St Ives: Penguin Books.

Stone Sweet, A. (2011), 'The European Court of Justice', in P. Craig and G. de Búrca (eds), *The Evolution of EU Law*, Oxford: Oxford University Press, pp.121–153.

Stone Sweet, A., and W. Sandelholtz (1998), 'Integration, Supranational Governance and Institutionalization of the European Polity', in A. Stone Sweet and W. Sandelholtz (eds), *European Integration and Supranational Governance*, Oxford: Oxford University Press, pp.1–26.

Streeck, W. (1995), 'From Market Making to State Building? Reflections on the Political Economy of European Social Policy', in S. Leibfried and P. Pierson, *European Social Policy between Fragmentation and Integration*, Washington: The Brookings Institution, pp.389–431.

Streit, M., and W. Mussler (1995), 'The economic constitution of the European Community', *ELJ,* 1(1), 5–30.

Supiot, A. (2010), 'A legal perspective on the economic crisis of 2008', *International Labour Review,* 149(2), 151–162.

Syrpis, P. (2007), *EU Intervention in Domestic Labour Law*, Oxford: Oxford University Press.

Tagourias, N. (2007), *Transnational Constitutionalism. International and European Models*, Cambridge: Cambridge University Press.

Taylor, M.D. (2006), *International Competition Law – a New Dimension for the WTO?,* Cambridge: Cambridge University Press.

Taylor, P. (2008), *The End of European Integration: anti-Europeanism Examined,* London: Routledge.

Tettinger, P.J. (2010), Art. 28, in H. von Mangoldt, F. Klein and C. Starck, *Kommentar zum Grundgesetz* (6th edn), Munich: Vahlen.

Teubner, G. (2010), 'Fragmented Foundations: Societal Constitutionalism beyond the State', in P. Dobner and M. Loughlin (eds), *The Twilight of Constitutionalism?,* Oxford: Oxford University Press, pp.327–341.

Thatcher, M., and D. Coen (2008), 'Reshaping European regulatory space: an evolutionary analysis', *West European Politics,* 31(1), 806–836.

Thorelli, H.B. (1958/59), 'Antitrust in Europe: national policies after 1945', *University of Chicago Law Review,* 26(2), 222–236.

Threlfall, M. (2007), 'Advancing integration and the social dimension of the EU', *Global Social Policy,* 7(3), 271–293.

Threlfall, M. (2003), 'European social integration: harmonization, convergence and single social areas', *Journal of European Social Policy,* 13(2), 121–139.

Tinsbergen, J. (1954), *International Economic Integration*, Amsterdam: Elsevier.

Tobler, C. (2005), *Indirect Discrimination. A Case Study into the Development of the Legal Concept of Indirect Discrimination under EC Law,* Antwerp: Intersentia.

Trenz, H.-J. (2008), Elements of a Sociology of European Integration, *ARENA Working Paper* 11 (May).

Trenz, H.-J., and K. Eder (2004), 'The democratising dynamics of a European public sphere', *European Journal of Social Theory,* 7(1), 5–25.

Trenz, H.-J., N. Bernhard and E. Jentges (2009), 'Civil Society and EU Constitution-Making', *RECON Online Working Papers,* 7 (June).

Trstenjak, V. and E. Beysen (2011), 'European consumer protection law: curia semper davit remedium?, *CMLR,* 48(1), 95–124.

Tsebelis, G. (2008), 'Thinking about the recent past and the future of the EU', *JCMS* 46(2), 265–292.

Tully, J. (2007), 'The imperialism of modern constitutional democracy', in M. Loughlin and N. Walker (eds), *The Paradox of Constitutionalism,* Oxford: Oxford University Press, pp.315–338.

Tuori, K. (2010), 'The Many Constitutions of Europe', in K. Tuori and S. Sankari (eds), *The Many Constitutions of Europe*, Farnham and Burlington: Ashgate, pp.3–30.

United Nations Commission for Social Development (2010), *Promoting Social Integration, Resolution*, Geneva: United Nations, Chairman of the Commission Leslie Kojo Christian.

United Nations Research Institute for Social Development (1994), *Social Integration: Approaches and Issues,* Geneva: United Nations.

United Nations Secretary-General (2009), *Promoting Social Integration, Report*, Geneva: United Nations, Economic and Social Council.

Vandamme, J. (1983), 'De la Politique Sociale à l'Espace Social Européen?', *Revue du Marché Commune*, 26(272), 562–565.

van den Bergh, R., and P.D. Camesasca (2006), *European Competition Law and Economics: a Comparative Perspective*, London: Sweet and Maxwell.

van den Bossche, P. (2008), *The Law and Policy of the World Trade Organization. Text, Cases and Materials* (2nd edn), Cambridge: Cambridge University Press.

van den Bossche, P. (2009), *The Law and Policy of the World Trade Organization* (2nd edn), Cambridge: Cambridge University Press.

van der Eyden, T. (2003), *Public Management of Society. Rediscovering French Institutional Engineering in the European Context*, Amsterdam: IOS Press.

van der Mei, A.P., and G. Essers (2009), Case C-352/06, *Brigitte Bosmann*, *CMLR*, 49(3), 959–972.

van Hoek, A. (2007), 'Private international law aspects of collective actions – comparative report', in F. Dorssemont, T. Jaspers and A. van Hoek (eds), *Cross-border Collective Actions in Europe: a Legal Challenge,* Antwerp: Intersentia, pp.425–468.

Vasileva, K. (2010), *Population and Social Conditions*, Brussels: Eurostat (European Commission).

Vauchez, A. (2010), 'The transnational politics of judicialization. Van Gend en Loos and the making of EU polity', *ELJ*, 16(1), 1–28.

Vaughan-Whitehead, D. (2003), *EU Enlargement versus Social Europe? The Uncertain Future of the European Social Model*, Cheltenham, UK and Northampton, MA, USA: Edward Elgar.

Velluti, S. (2010), *New Governance and the European Employment Strategy*, Abingdon and New York: Routledge.

Verloren van Themaat, P. (1960), *Speech before the Conference on the Legal Problems of the European Economic Community and the European Free Trade Association*, London: EEC Commission.

Vesterdorf, P. (2009), 'Case Note ECJ C-431/06 Chronopost', *CMLR* 46(4), 1305–1326.

Vincent-Jones, P. and D. Hughes (2008), 'Schisms in the church: NHS systems and institutional divergence in England and Wales', *Journal of Health and Social Behaviour,* 49(4), 400–416.

Visser, J. (2008), 'Extension through dilution? European integration, enlargement and labour institutions', in J. Alber, T. Fahey and C. Saraceno (eds.), *Handbook of Quality of Life in the Enlarged European Union*, London and New York: Routledge, pp.175–197.

Walker, N. (2010), 'Constitutionalism and Pluralism in a Global Context', *RECON Online Working Papers*, 3 (May).

Walker, N. (2010), 'Constitutionalism and the incompleteness of democracy: an iterative relationship', *University of Edinburgh School of Law Working Paper Series,* 25 (July).

Walker, N. (2010), 'Multilevel Constitutionalism: Looking beyond the German debate', in K. Tuori and S. Sankari, *The Many Constitutions of Europe,* Farnham and Burlington: Ashgate, pp.143–169.

Wallace, C. (2000), 'Community Sex Discrimination Law in National Law Courts', in J. Shaw, *Social Law and Policy in an Evolving European Union*, Oxford and Portland, OR: Hart, pp.119–133.

Ward, I. (2009), *A Critical Introduction to European Law* (3rd edn), Cambridge: Cambridge University Press.

Weber, M. (1980 (1922)), *Wirtschaft und Gesellschaft* (J. Winckelmann, ed.), Tübingen: Mohr Siebeck.

Wedderburn, B. (2007), 'Labour Law 2008: 40 years on', *Industrial Law Journal* 38(4), 397–424.

Weiler, J.H. (2003), 'In Defence of the Status Quo: Europe's Constitutional Sonderweg', in J.H. Weiler and M. Wind (eds), *European Constitutionalism beyond the State*, Cambridge: Cambridge University Press, pp.7–23.

Weiler, J.H. and N. Lockhart (1995), 'Taking rights seriously: the European Court of Justice and its fundamental rights jurisprudence', *CMLR*, 32 (1 (part I), 2 (part II), 51–94 (part I); 579–627 (part II).

Weiler, J.H. and M. Wind (2003), *European Constitutionalism beyond the State*, Cambridge: Cambridge University Press.

Wendt, I. and A. Gideon (2011), 'Services of general interest provision through the third sector under EU competition law constraints: the example of organising healthcare in England, Wales and the Netherlands', in D. Schiek, U. Liebert and H. Schneider (eds), *European Economic and Social Constitutionalism after the Treaty of Lisbon*, Cambridge: Cambridge University Press, pp.251–276.

White, R.C. (2010), 'The new European social security regulations in context', *Journal of Social Security Law,* 17(3), 144–163.

Wiener, A. (2005), 'Soft Institutions' (discontinued in the 2nd edition 2010), in A. von Bogdandy and J. Bast (eds), *Principles of European Constitutional Law,* Oxford and Portland, OR: Hart, pp.419–451.

Wiener, A. and T. Diez (2009), 'Introducing the Mosaic of Integration Theory', in A. Wiener and T. Diez (eds), *European Integration Theory* (2nd edn), Oxford: Oxford University Press, pp.1–22.

Wiener, A. and T. Diez (2009), 'Taking Stock of Integration Theory', in A. Wiener and T. Diez, *European Integration Theory*, Oxford: Oxford University Press, pp.241–252.

Wilkinson, R. and K. Picket (2009), *The Spirit Level. Why Equality Is Better for Everyone,* London: Penguin.

Williamson, O.E. (1985), *The Economic Institutions of Capitalism,* New York: The Free Press.

Williamson, O.E. (2010), Transaction cost economics: the natural progression, *American Economic Review,* 100(3), 673–690.

Wincott, D. (2003), 'Beyond social regulation? New instruments and/or a new agenda for social policy at Lisbon?', *Public Administration,* 81(3), 533–553.

Wind, M. (2003), 'The European Union as polycentric polity: returning to a neo-medieval Europe?', in M. Wind and J.H. Weiler (eds), *European Constitutionalism beyond the State*, Cambridge: Cambridge University Press, pp.103–131.

Wind, M., D. Sindbjerg Martinsen and G. Pons Rotger (2009), 'The uneven

legal push for Europe: questioning variation when national courts go to Europe' *European Union Politics,* 10(1), 63–88.
Wollenschläger, F. (2011), 'A new fundamental freedom beyond market integration: Union citizenship and its dynamics for shifting the economic paradigm of European integration', *ELJ,* 12(1), 1–34.
Wollmann, H. (2010), 'Das deutsche Kommunalsystem im europäischen Vergleich – Zwischen kommunaler Autonomie und 'Verstaatlichung?', in J. Bogumil and S. Kuhlmann, *Kommunale Aufgabenwahrnehmung im Wandel*, Wiesbaden: VS Verlag, pp.323–353.
Woolfson, C. and J. Sommers (2006), 'European Mobility in Construction', *European Journal of Industrial Relations*, 12(1), 12–68.
Wouters, J., L. Verhey and P. Kiiver (2009), *European Constitutionalism beyond Lisbon*, Antwerp: Intersentia.
Zeno-Zencovich, V. and N. Vardi (2008), 'European Union Law as a Legal System in a Comparative Perspective', *European Business Law Review*, 19(2), 243–265.
Zürn, M., S. Wälti and H. Enderlein (2010), 'Introduction', in H. Enderlein, S. Wälti and M. Zürn (eds), *Handbook to Multilevel Governance*, Cheltenham, UK, and Northampton, MA, USA: Edward Elgar, pp.1–23.

# APPENDIX: DOCUMENTATION OF CASE LAW ANALYSIS

These three tables document in schematic form the result of the case law analysis whose results are presented in Chapter 4, in accordance with the scheme presented in the last sub-chapter of Chapter 2. As announced in Chapters 3 and 4, the main divider is the differentiation between rights protection (left column) and providing institutions for democratic/collective legislation and rule-making. A third table contains the cases that were not analysed. In the two substantive tables, **+** indicates that the relevant position was upheld in the end, – indicates that it is not, and **+/–** is used if positions are partly protected or the decision is left to the national court. * indicates involvement of civil society actors at national or European level (mostly because a civil society organisation brought a case or intervened).

*Table A.1 Rights protection*

| Case number and parties (abbreviated) | Liberal constitutionalism: guaranteeing rights in 'public spheres', safeguarding spheres where private rule prevails | | | | | | Socially embedded constitutionalism: guaranteeing rights in social reality | | | | | |
|---|---|---|---|---|---|---|---|---|---|---|---|---|
| | Protecting rights (against public actors) | | | | | | Protecting rights horizontally | | | Positive duties/enjoyment of rights | | |
| | Liberty, human rights | | Equality | | Economic freedom | | Liberty, human rights | Equality | Economic freedom | Liberty, human rights | Equality | Economic freedom |
| | EU | MS | EU | MS | EU | MS | | | | | | |
| C-47/08 *COM v Belgium* | | | | | | + | | | | | | |
| C-50/08 *COM v France* | | | | | | + | | | | | | |
| C-51/08 *COM v Luxembourg* | | | | | | + | | | | | | |
| C-53/08 *COM v Austria* | | | | | | + | | | | | | |
| C-54/08 *COM v Germany* | | | | | | + | | | | | | |
| C-61/08 *COM v Greece* | | | | | | + | | | | | | |
| C-147/08 *Roemer* | | | | | | | | +/– | | | | |
| C-119/09 *Société fiduciaire nationale d'expertise comptable* | | | | | | + | | | | | | |
| C-424/09 *Toki* | | | | | | **a) –** | | | | | | |

| | | | | | | | | | | | | |
|---|---|---|---|---|---|---|---|---|---|---|---|---|
| Joined cases C-201/09 P and C-216/09 P *Arcelors* | – | | | | | | | | | | | |
| C-352/09P *Thyssen Krupp Nirosta v COM* | –<br>– | | | | | | | | | | | |
| C-565/08 *COM v Italy* | | | | | | – | | | | | | |
| C-29/10 *Koelzsch* | | | | | | a) – | | | | | | |
| C-34/09 *Ruiz Zambrano* | | | | | | a) + | | | | | | |
| C-236/09 *Test-Achats* | | | | | | | | + | | | | |
| C-382/08 *Neukirchinge* | | | | | | a) + | | | | | | |
| C-285/09 *R.* | | – | | | | | | | | | | |
| C-145/09 *Tsakouridis* | | +/– | | | | | | | | | | |
| C-261/09 *Mantello* | – | | | | | | | | | | | |
| C-101/09, C-57/09 *B & D* | | + | | | | | | | | | | |
| C-137/08 *VB Pénzügyi Lízing* | | | | | | | | | | a) + | | |
| C-540/08 *Mediaprint* | | | | | | | | | | a) – | | |
| C-92/09, C-93/09 Sch*ecke* | – | | | | | | | | | | | |
| C-97/09 *Schmelz* | | | | | – | | | | | | | |
| C-499/08 Andersen | | | | | | | | + | | | | |
| C-45/09 *Rosenbladt* | | | | | | | | a) – | | | | |
| C-512/08 *COM v France* (health care) | | | | | | | | | | | | a) – |
| C-173/09 *Elchinov* | | | | | | | | | | | | a) + |
| C-550/07 P AKZO | – | | | | | | | | | | | |
| C-46/08 *Carmen Media Group* | | | | | | +/– | | | | | | |

*Table A.1 Continued*

| Case number and parties (abbreviated) | Liberal constitutionalism: guaranteeing rights in 'public spheres', safeguarding spheres where private rule prevails | | | | | | Socially embedded constitutionalism: guaranteeing rights in social reality | | | | | |
|---|---|---|---|---|---|---|---|---|---|---|---|---|
| | Protecting rights (against public actors) | | | | | | Protecting rights horizontally | | | Positive duties/enjoyment of rights | | |
| | Liberty, human rights | | Equality | | Economic freedom | | Liberty, human rights | Equality | Economic freedom | Liberty, human rights | Equality | Economic freedom |
| | EU | MS | EU | MS | EU | MS | | | | | | |
| C316,358,360,409, and 410/07 *Stoß* | | | | | | +/– | | | | | | |
| C-409/06 *Winner Wetten* | | | | | | + | | | | | | |
| C-271/08 *COM v Germany* (Riester) | | | | | | + | – | | | | | |
| C-550/09 *E & F* | – | | | | | | | | | | | |
| C-441/07 P *Alrosa* | – | | | | | | | | | | | |
| C-28/08 P *Bavarian Lager* | – | | | | | | | | | | | |
| C-139/07 P *Technische Glaswerke Ilmenau* (TGI) | – | | | | | | | | | | | |
| C188-9/10 *Melki* | | + | | | | | | | | | | |
| C-31/09 *Bolbol* | | – | | | | | | | | | | |
| C-211/08 *COM v Spain (health)* | | | | | | | | | | | | **a) –** |

| | | | | | | | | | | | | |
|---|---|---|---|---|---|---|---|---|---|---|---|---|
| C-58/08 *Vodafone* | | | | | – | | | | | | | |
| C570-571/07 *Blanco Pérez* | | | | | | – | | | | | | |
| C-91/08 *Wall* | | | | | | – | | | | | | |
| C-73/08 *Bressol* | | | | | | a) + | | | | | | |
| C-325/08 *Olympique Lyonnais* | | | | | | | | | – | | | |
| C-518/07 *COM v Germany* | | | | | | | | | | + | | |
| C175, 176, 178, 179/08 *Salahadin Abdulla* | | – | | | | | | | | | | |
| C-135/08 *Rottmann* | | | | | | +/–a) | | | | | | |
| C-480/08 *Teixera* | | | | | | a) + | | | | | | |
| C-310/08 *Ibrahim* | | | | | | a) + | | | | | | |
| C-362/08 *Internationaler Hilfsfond v COM* | + | | | | | | | | | | | |
| C-555/07 *Kücükdeveci* | | | | | | | | a) + | | | | |
| C-341/08 *Petersen* | | | | | | | | a) +/– | | | | |
| C-229/08 *Wolf* | | | | | | | | a) – | | | | |
| C-357/09 PPU *Kadzoev* | | + | | | | | | | | | | |
| C-169/08 *Presidente del Consiglio dei Ministri* | | | | | | + | | | | | | |
| C-115/08 *ČEZ* | | | | | | + | | | | | | |

*Table A.1 Continued*

| Case number and parties (abbreviated) | Liberal constitutionalism: guaranteeing rights in 'public spheres', safeguarding spheres where private rule prevails | | | | | | Socially embedded constitutionalism: guaranteeing rights in social reality | | | | | |
|---|---|---|---|---|---|---|---|---|---|---|---|---|
| | Protecting rights (against public actors) | | | | | | Protecting rights horizontally | | | Positive duties/enjoyment of rights | | |
| | Liberty, human rights | | Equality | | Economic freedom | | Liberty, human rights | Equality | Economic freedom | Liberty, human rights | Equality | Economic freedom |
| | EU | MS | EU | MS | EU | MS | | | | | | |
| C-428/07 *Horvath* | | | | +/- | | | | | | | | |
| C-123/08 *Wolzenburg* | | | | | | **a) +** | | | | | | |
| C-42/07 *Liga Portuguesa de Futebol Profissional* | | | | | | **–** | | | | | | |
| C-480/06 *COM v Germany* | | | | | | **–** | | | | | | |
| C-171/07 *Apothekerkammer des Saarlandes and others* | | | | | | **–*** | | | | | | |
| C-531/06 *COM v Italy* | | | | | | **–*** | | | | | | |
| C-518/06 *COM v Italy* | | | | | | **–** | | | | | | |
| C-169/07 *Hartlauer* | | | | | | **+/–** | | | | | | |
| C-345/06 *Heinrich* | **+** | | | | | | | | | | | |
| C-465/07 *Elgataji* | | **+/–** | | | | | | | | | | |
| C-110/05 *COM v Italy* | | | | | | **–** | | | | | | |

| | | | | | | | | | | | | |
|---|---|---|---|---|---|---|---|---|---|---|---|---|
| C-301/06 *Ireland v Parliament and Council* | – | | | | | | | | | | | |
| C-318/07 *Persche* | | | | | | + | | | | | | |
| C-350, 520/06 *Schultz-Hoff* | | | | | | | | | + a) | | | |
| C-333/07 *Régie Networks* | | | | | | | | | | +/– | | |
| C-127/07 *Arcelor Atlantique* | | – | | | | | | | | | | |
| C-205/07 *Gysbrechts* | | | | | | +a) | | | | | | |
| C-210/06 *Cartesio* | | | | | | – | | | | | | |
| C-213/07 *EAR v Karatzoglou* | | | | | | – | | | | | | |
| C-47/07 P *Masdar* | – | | | | | | | | | | | |
| C-524/06 *Huber* | | + | | | | | | | | | | |
| C-73/07 *Tietosuojavaltuutettu* | | +/– | | | | | | | | +/– | | |
| C-455/06 *Heemskerk and Schaap* | + | | | | | | | | | | | |
| C-158/07 *Förster* | | | | | | –a) | | | | | | |
| C-353/06 *Grunkin and Paul* | | | | | | a) + | | | | | | |
| C-427/06 *Bartsch* | | | | | | | | – | | | | |
| C-120/06 P *FIAMM* | – | | | | | | + | | | | | |
| C-402/05 P *Kadi* | + | | | | | | | | | | | |
| C-127/08 *Metock* | | | | | | a) + | | | | | | |
| C-303/06 *Coleman* | | | | | | | | + | | | | |

*Table A.1 Continued*

| Case number and parties (abbreviated) | Liberal constitutionalism: guaranteeing rights in 'public spheres', safeguarding spheres where private rule prevails | | | | | | Socially embedded constitutionalism: guaranteeing rights in social reality | | | | | |
|---|---|---|---|---|---|---|---|---|---|---|---|---|
| | Protecting rights (against public actors) | | | | | | Protecting rights horizontally | | | Positive duties/enjoyment of rights | | |
| | Liberty, human rights | | Equality | | Economic freedom | | Liberty, human rights | Equality | Economic freedom | Liberty, human rights | Equality | Economic freedom |
| | EU | MS | EU | MS | EU | MS | | | | | | |
| C-66/08 *Kozlowski* | | | | | | **a) –** | | | | | | |
| C-413/06 P *Bertelsmann* | + | | | | | | | | | | | |
| C-49/07 *MOTOE* | | | | | | + | | | | | | |
| C-188/07 *Commune de Mesquer* | | | | | | – | | | | | | |
| C-194/06 *Orange European Smallcap Fund* | | | | | | + | | | | | | |
| C-352/06 *Bosmann* | | | | | | **a) –/+** | | | | | | |
| C-268/06 *Impact* | | | | + | | | | + | | | | |
| C-390/06 *Nuova Agricast* | | | – | | | | | | | | | |
| C-167/05 *COM v Sweden* | | | | | | – | | | | | | |
| C-337/05 *COM v Italy* | | | | | | + | | | | | | |

| | | | | | | | | | | | | |
|---|---|---|---|---|---|---|---|---|---|---|---|---|
| C-212/06 *Gouvernement de la Communauté française and Gouvernement Wallon* | | | | | | a) + | | | | | | |
| C-267/06 *Maruko* | | | | | | | | a) + | | | | |
| C-420/06 *Jager* | | + | | | | | | | | | | |
| C-506/06 *Mayr* | | | | | | | | a) + | | | | |
| C-2/06 *Kempter* | | + | | | | + | | | | | | |
| C-275/06 *Promusicae* | | | | | | | +/– | | | | | |
| C-101/05 *Skatteverket* | | | | | | – | | | | | | |
| C-341/05 *Laval* | | – | | | | + | – | | + | | | |
| C-396/05 *Habelt* | | | | | | a) + | | | | | | |
| C-291/05 *Eind* | | | | | | a) + | | | | | | |
| C-438/05 *ITTF and FSU (Viking)* | | | | | | | – | | + | | | |
| C-11/06 *Morgan* | | | | | | | | | | | | a) + |
| C-112/05 *COM v Germany* | | | | | | + | | | | | | |
| C-411/05 *Palacios de la Villa* | | | | | | | | – | | | | |
| C-227/04 P *Lindorfer* | | | + | | | | | + | | | | |
| C-287/05 *Hendrix* | | | | | | a) + | | | | | | |
| C-318/05 *COM v Germany* | | | | | | a) + | | | | | | |
| C-431/05 *Merck Genéricos* | | | | | | + | | | | | | |
| C-76/05 *Schwarz and Gootjes-Schwarz* | | | | | | a) + | | | | | | |

*Table A.1 Continued*

| Case number and parties (abbreviated) | Liberal constitutionalism: guaranteeing rights in 'public spheres', safeguarding spheres where private rule prevails | | | | | | Socially embedded constitutionalism: guaranteeing rights in social reality | | | | | |
|---|---|---|---|---|---|---|---|---|---|---|---|---|
| | Protecting rights (against public actors) | | | | | | Protecting rights horizontally | | | Positive duties/enjoyment of rights | | |
| | Liberty, human rights | | Equality | | Economic freedom | | Liberty, human rights | Equality | Economic freedom | Liberty, human rights | Equality | Economic freedom |
| | EU | MS | EU | MS | EU | MS | | | | | | |
| C-212/05 *Hartmann* | | | | | | **a) +** | | | | | | **a) +** |
| C-213/05 *Geven* | | | | | | **a) –** | | | | | | **a) –** |
| C-231/05 *Oy AA* | | | | | | **–** | | | | | | |
| C-305/05 *Ordre des barreaux francophones and germanophones and others* | **–*** | | | | | | | | | | | |
| C-170/04 *Rosengren and others* | | | | | | **a) +** | | | | | | |
| C-303/05 *Advocaten voor de wereld* | **–*** | | | | | | | | | | | |
| C-523/04 *COM v Netherlands* | | | | | | **+** | | | | | | |
| C-432/05 *Unibet* | | **+/–** | | | | | | | | | | |
| C-524/04 *Test Claimants in the Thin Cap Group Litigation* | | | | | | **+/–*** | | | | | | |

| | | | | | | | | | | | | |
|---|---|---|---|---|---|---|---|---|---|---|---|---|
| C-292/04 *Meilicke and others* | | | | | | + | | | | | | |
| C-338/04 *Placanica* | | | | | | + | | | | | | |
| C-354/04 P *Gestoras Pro Amnistía* | – | | | | | | | | | | | |
| C-355/04 P *Segi* | – | | | | | | | | | | | |
| C-150/04 *COM v Denmark* | | | | | | **a) +** | | | | | | |
| C-265/05 *Perez Naranjo* | | | | | | **a) –** | | | | | | |
| C-1/05 *Jia* | | | | | | **a) +** | | | | | | |
| C-374/04 *Test Claimants in Class IV of the ACT Group Litigation* | | | | | | –* | | | | | | |
| C-446/04 *Test Claimants in the FII Group Litigation* | | | | | | +* | | | | | | |
| C-513/04 *Kerckhart and Morres* | | | | | | – | | | | | | |
| C-17/05 *Cadman* | | | | | | | | **a) +/–** | | | | |
| C-241/05 *Bot* | | + | | | | | | | | | | |
| C-290/04 FKP *Scorpio* | | | | | | –/+ | | | | | | |
| C-452/04 *Fidium Finanz* | | | | | | – | | | | | | |
| C-193/05 *COM v Luxembourg* | | | | | | + | | | | | | |
| C-506/04 *Wilson* | | | | | | + | | | | | | |
| C-196/04 *Cadbury Schweppes* | | | | | | + | | | | | | |

*Table A.1 Continued*

| Case number and parties (abbreviated) | Liberal constitutionalism: guaranteeing rights in 'public spheres', safeguarding spheres where private rule prevails | | | | | | Socially embedded constitutionalism: guaranteeing rights in social reality | | | | | |
|---|---|---|---|---|---|---|---|---|---|---|---|---|
| | Protecting rights (against public actors) | | | | | | Protecting rights horizontally | | | Positive duties/enjoyment of rights | | |
| | Liberty, human rights | | Equality | | Economic freedom | | Liberty, human rights | Equality | Economic freedom | Liberty, human rights | Equality | Economic freedom |
| | EU | MS | EU | MS | EU | MS | | | | | | |
| C-479/04 *Laser-disken* | – | | – | | | | | | | | | |
| C-406/04 *De Cuyper* | | | | | | **a) –** | | | | | | |
| C-13/05 *Chacón Navas* | | | | | | | | **a) –** | | | | |
| C-313/04 *Egenberger* | | | + | | | | | | | | | |
| C-212/04 *Adeneler* | | | | | | | | | | | | **a) +** |
| C-317/04 & 318/04 *Parliament v Council* | + | | | | | | | | | | | |
| C-372/04 *Watts* | | | | | | **a) –** | | | | | | **a) –** |
| C-302/04 *Ynos* | | | – | | | | | | **a) –** | | | |
| C-344/04 *IATA and ELFAA* | | | | | | | | | **a) +** | | | |
| C-144/04 *Mangold* | | | | | | | | + | | | | |
| C-154 & 155/04 *Alliance for Natural Health* | | | | | – | | | | | | | |

| | | | | | | | | | | | | |
|---|---|---|---|---|---|---|---|---|---|---|---|---|
| C-27/04 *COM v Council* | | | | | | | | | + | | | |

*Note:* In this table, the letter a) is used to indicate an individual citizen has profited from rights protection, rather than a (corporate) economic actor, indicating citizens', consumers' or employees' rights.

*Table A.2 European fields of democratic/collective rule-making*

| Case number and parties (abbreviated) | Liberal constitutionalism: guaranteeing democracy in public spheres (EU level) | | Socially embedded constitutionalism: expanding democracy to socio-economic spheres, alternatives to market rule, self-regulation | | | | | |
|---|---|---|---|---|---|---|---|---|
| | Parliamentary democracy | Transparency | Market regulation | | | | Civil society involved | |
| | | | public | | collective (ind .democracy: a)) | | | |
| | | | MS | EU | MS | EU | MS | EU |
| C-439/08 *VEBIC* | | | + | | | | | |
| C-92/09, C-93/09 *Volker and Markus Schecke* | | + | | | | | | |
| C-45/09 *Rosenbladt* | | | | | **+ a)** | | | |
| C-512/08 *COM v France* | | | + | | | | | |
| C-514/07 P, C-528/07 P and C-532/07 P *Sweden and others v API and COM* | | +/– | | | | | | |
| C-271/08 *COM v Germany (pension scheme)* | | | | | **– a)** | | | |
| C-28/08 P *COM v Bavarian Lager* | | – | | | | | | |
| C-139/07 P *COM v TGI* | | – | | | | | | |
| C-570-1/07 *Blanco Pérez* | | | + | | | | | |
| C-265/08 *Federutility* | | | + | | | | | |
| C-325/08 *Olympique Lyonnais* | | | | + | | | | |

| | | | | | | | | |
|---|---|---|---|---|---|---|---|---|
| C-480/06 *COM v Germany (waste)* | | | | | + | | | |
| C-171/07 *Apothekerkammer des Saarlandes and others* | | | + | | | | | |
| C-531/06 *COM v Italy (Pharmacies)* | | | + | | | | | |
| C-288/07 *Isle of Wiight Council and others* | | | –/+ | | | | | |
| C-468/06 *Sot. Lélos kai Sia* | | | – | | | | | |
| C-152/07 *Arcor* | | | – | | | | | |
| C-341/06 P *Chronopost* | | | + | | | | | |
| C-39/05 and 52/05 P *Sweden & Turco v Council* | | + | | | | | | |
| C-133/06 *EP v Council* | + | | | | | | | |
| C-268/06 *Impact* | | | | | | + | | |
| C-341/05 *Laval* | | | | | –a) | | | |
| C-64/05 P *Sweden v Council* | | + | | | | | | * |
| C-438/05 ITTF *and FSU (Viking)* | | | | | – a) | | | |
| C-112/05 *COM v Germany (Golden Shares)* | | | | | – a) | | | |
| C-411/05 *Palacios de la Villa* | | | | | + a) | | | |
| C-94 and 202/04 *Cipolla* | | | | | + | | | |
| C-413/04 *EP v Council (energy market Estonia)* | | | – | | | | | |
| C-414/04 *EP v Council (energy market Slovenia)* | | | – | | | | | |
| C-392/04 *i-21 Germany* | | | +/– | | | | | |

*Table A.2 Continued*

| Case number and parties (abbreviated) | Liberal constitutionalism: guaranteeing democracy in public spheres (EU level) | | Socially embedded constitutionalism: expanding democracy to socio-economic spheres, alternatives to market rule, self-regulation | | | | | |
|---|---|---|---|---|---|---|---|---|
| | Parliamentary democracy | Transparency | Market regulation | | | | Civil society involved | |
| | | | public | | collective (ind .democracy: a)) | | | |
| | | | MS | EU | MS | EU | MS | EU |
| C-145/04 *Spain v UK* | + | | | | | | | |
| C-300/04 *Eman & Sevinger* | a)+ | | | | | | | |
| C-310/04 *Spain v Council (cotton market)* | | | | + | | | | |
| C-88/03 *Portugal v COM (tax regime Azores)* | | | – | | | | | |
| C-27/04 *COM v Council (stability and growth pact)* | | | | – | | | | |

*Table A.3 Cases deemed not relevant (71 cases)*

| Case number | Parties | Why this case is not relevant |
|---|---|---|
| C-83/09P<br>9 June 2011 (nyr) | *COM v Kronoply and Kronotex* | The Commission's appeal in this case only relates to standing of 'upstream market participants' in state aid cases. The fundamental relevance of the case lies in its expansion on the Plaumann principles. The Court follows the more generous approach of the General Court here, stating that economic actors that are not immediate competitors of a recipient of state aid, but only affected by market developments in the immediately relevant market because their production uses raw materials from those markets, can also challenge a decision not to initiate an investigation of state aid. |
| C-375/09<br>3 May 2011 (nyr) | *Tele 2 Polska* | This action concerns the relation of national competition authorities and the Commission/the Court in enforcing EU competition law. The question is whether a national competition authority is competent to take a negative decision. The Court constructs the national competence narrowly. |
| C-235/09<br>12 April 2011 (nyr) | *DHL Express France* | This case relates to the Community trade mark. DHL challenges the use of the sign 'webshipping' by Chronopost, the former French state monopolist, before French courts. The question before the ECJ is whether these are competent to give a definite judgment. |
| C-96/09P<br>29 March 2011 (nyr) | *Anheuser-Busch v Budějovický Budvar* | Whether the geographical denomination 'bud' (relating to Budvar) may be used by a US firm. This is decided under the legal framework of the Community Trademark. |
| C-240/09<br>8 March 2011 (nyr) | *Lesoochranarske zoskupenie* | Hunters try to defend their rights to hunt the Brown Bear in the Slovak Republic and the standing of environmental organisations before national courts in any proceedings relating to the hunters applying for an exception from national legislation protecting a rare species. The organisations rely on the Aarhus Convention, to which the EU is a party. The EU has not yet implemented the Convention fully. The question before the ECJ is whether Article 9 (3) of the Convention is directly effective. The Court holds that the Convention has no direct effect, but that MS courts are under an obligation deriving from EU law to interpret their national law in line with the Convention as far as possible. |

*Table A.3 Continued*

| Case number | Parties | Why this case is not relevant |
|---|---|---|
| C-585/08 and C-144/09 7 December 2010 (nyr) | *Pammer and Hotel Alpenhof* | This case concerns the jurisdiction of national courts in consumer cases. |
| C-482/08 26 October 2010 (nyr) | *UK v Council* | This is an action by the United Kingdom versus the Council, by which the UK strives to participate in common rules on VISA in the Schengen area. While these rules may have negative effects on human rights in their application, such aspects were not pleaded in the case, because they are irrelevant to the competence question. |
| C-48/09 14 September 2010 (nyr) | *Lego Juris v OHIM* | This case concerns the Community Trademark regulation and the question whether the shape of the 'Lego bloc' can be registered as a trade mark. |
| C-428/08 [2010] ECR I-6764 | *Monsanto Technology* | This case relates to intellectual property in biological matter. The claimant holds a European patent on an enzyme making plants resistant against a herbicide, which is not protected in Argentina. The case turns on the question whether a re-imported soy meal which has been produced from plants containing the same enzyme in Argentina must not be traded in the EU to maintain the protection of this patent. |
| C-526/08 [2010] ECR I-6147 | *Commission v Luxembourg* | There is no relevance to rights or democracy, although the Court here grants a fundamental right (*ne bis in idem*) to a state. |
| C-533/08 [2009] ECR I-73 | *TNT Express Nederland* | Again this relates to matters of jurisdiction in civil matters (see C-585/08 and C-144/09 *Pammer and Hotel Alpenhof*). |
| C-246/07 [2010] ECR I-3317 | *Commission v Sweden* | Whether Sweden may uphold stricter environmental standards than the EU. Not relevant here. |
| Joined Cases C-236 to 238/08 [2010] ECR I-2417 | *Google France and Google* | Specific issue relating to trade mark rights. |
| Joined Cases C-379/08 and C-380/08 [2010] ECR I-2007 | *ERG and others* | This is a case concerning application of Directive 2004/35/EC including its 'polluter pays' principle to Italian companies, whose projects endangering the marine environment had been approved long before this directive was implemented. Also, the directive requires Member States to enter into a dialogue with enterprises being subjected to such obligations. While MS may change their assessment, they need to engage in this dialogue. |
| C-378/08 [2009] | *ERG and others* | This is a parallel case to the one above under the same name. |

| | | |
|---|---|---|
| ECR I-7533 | | |
| C-118/08 [2010] ECR I-635 | *Transportes Urbanos y Servicios Generales* | Liability of Member State for incorrect implementation of VAT directive – this substantive issue was already decided in 2002. In substance, this case belongs to a series of cases clarifying (once again) the relation between national (constitutional) courts and the Court of Justice. |
| C-461/05 [2009] ECR I-11887 | *COM v Denmark* | This group of cases concerns disputes between the Commission and Member States about the classification of imports relating to military equipment for the purpose of calculating the EU's 'own resources'. More specifically, these Member States have since the 1970s claimed a right to withhold information in this sensitive area and the Commission has since suspected that this serves the purpose to reduce the 'own resource' source of income for the EU. |
| C-409/05 [2009] ECRI-11859 | *COM v Greece* | |
| C-387/05 [2009] ECR I-11831 | *COM v Italy* | |
| C-372/05 [2009] ECR I-11801 | *COM v Germany* | |
| C-294/05 [2009] ECR I-11777 | *COM v Sweden* | |
| C-284/05 [2009] ECR I-11705 | *COM v Finland* | |
| C-239/06 [2009] ECR I-11913 | *COM v Italy* | |
| C-89/08 P [2009] ECR I-11245 | *COM v Ireland and others* | This is a state aid case where the appeal only relates to the question whether the Commission should have lost its case before the CFI due to insufficient reasoning. |
| C-358/08 [2009] ECR I-11305 | *Aventis Pasteur* | Specific issues relating to product liability. |

*Table A.3 Continued*

| Case number | Parties | Why this case is not relevant |
|---|---|---|
| Opinion 1/08 [2009] ECR I-11129 | Opinion of the Court | This opinion concerns the adaptation of agreements relating to the GATS in reaction to EU enlargement. This is an external trade issue entirely. |
| C-133/08 [2009] ECR I-9687 | *ICF* | This relates to coordination of national legal orders (conflicts of law). |
| C-478/07 [2009] ECR I-7721 | *Budějovický Budvar* | Whether 'bud' is a protected geographical denomination for beer from a certain region in the Czech Republic. |
| C-411/06 [2009] ECR I-7585 | *COM v Parliament and Council* | Relating to EU competences to regulate shipment of waste. |
| C-420/07 [2009] ECR I-3571 | *Apostolides* | This case relates to the conflict between Cyprus and Greece and its aftermath. When Greek Cypriots had to leave the Turkish part of the island, their property fell to the Turkish authorities and was sold to third parties, in this case to a UK citizen as a holiday resort. The question is whether UK courts are called to enforce a judgment by a Court sitting in the Greek part of Cyprus concerning a plot of land situated in the part where the EU does not have factual power. |
| C-205/06 [2009] ECR I-1301 | *COM v Austria* | These cases relate to the question whether Member States may maintain foreign direct investment agreements with third countries into which they entered prior to accession. |
| C-249/06 [2009] ECR I-1335 | *COM v Sweden* | |
| C-185/07 [2009] ECR I-663 | *Allianz (formerly Riunione Adriatica di Sicurtà)* | This case relates to the question whether courts of a Member State may refuse to enforce foreign arbitral awards – concerns regulation 44/2001. Not relevant (coordination of jurisdictions). |
| C-240/07 [2009] ECR I-263 | *Sony Music Entertainment* | Specific issues of IP law, not constitutionally relevant. |
| C-121/07 [2008] ECR I-9159 | *COM v France* | Concerns a penalty payment for failure to implement a judgment (C-419/03). |
| C-442/07 [2008] ECR I-8763 | *Verein Radetzky-Orden* | Two Austrian organisations of war veterans clash about the right of using a trade mark related to General Radetzky. The Court holds that EU trademark law does not apply to this issue, as these organisations do not have any economic purpose – on specific interpretation of trade mark law. |

| | | |
|---|---|---|
| C-455/06[2008] ECR I-8763 | *Danske Slagterij* | Follow up action by Danish pig breeders from a decision according to which Germany had violated a package of EU directives aiming to prevent pork from exuding a 'distinct sexual odour' by insisting on a very specific method to achieve that aim, which was customary in Germany but not in Denmark. The Court held that, as the directives were a concrete expression of free movement of goods, this also constituted a violation of that economic freedom and in principle gave the Danish farmers a state liability claim against Germany. However, the Court allowed finer points of German tort law to prevent this claim, under the principle of national procedural autonomy. |
| C-200/07 [2008] ECR I-7929 | *Marra* | Whether an MEP can claim immunity if insulting victims of fascism in a leaflet. |
| C-132/06 [2008] ECR I-5457 | *COM v Italy* | Whether a general tax amnesty in Italy is compatible with the sixth VAT directive. |
| C-308/06 [2008] ECR I-4057 | *Intertanko and others* | Concerns the legality of Directive 2005/35/EC under UN law. While it is interesting that the ECJ considers itself competent to adjudicate this, it does not raise issues of inner-EU constitutionalism – not relevant here. |
| C-91/05 [2008] ECR I-3651 | *COM v Council* | Conflict of competences regarding external policy, which is no longer relevant. |
| C-14 & 295/06 [2008] ECR I-1649 | *Parliament & Denmark v Commission* | Concerns a very specific interpretation of Directive 2002/95 and a Commission decision based upon it, according to which a certain substance was not banned from use, although it was environmentally detrimental. This is a merely administrative case, although related to environmental protection. |
| C-408/04 P [2008] ECR I-2767 | *COM v Salzgitter* | This is an appeal against a case still decided under the ECSC – no longer relevant. |
| C-132/05 [2008] ECR I-957 | *COM v Germany* | Whether German traders may use the notion 'parmesan' for cheese that is not from the Parmigiano reggio in Italy. No constitutional relevance. |

*Table A.3 Continued*

| Case number | Parties | Why this case is not relevant |
|---|---|---|
| C-199/06 [2008] ECR I-469 | *CELF and Ministre de la Culture et de la Communication* | Case results from litigation in the 1990s, concerning state aid rules for a French company promoting French language books abroad and thus enabling bookshops and publishers to respond to small-scale orders. While the substantive issue is interesting in that it relates to public regulation of markets (the Court held that the aid is justified under the cultural clause), it was, however, decided long before the reference period. In this case, the remaining question was whether France must require repayment of that aid for eriods when it had not (yet) been declared compatible with the Internal Market. The decision is left to the national court. |
| C-137/05 [2007] ECR I-11593 | *UK v Council* | Whether the UK can be excluded from legislation concerning the Schengen area, relating to biometric passports. Obviously, there is a fundamental rights relevance, but this argument was not raised. |
| C-77/05 [2007] ECR I-11459 | *UK v Council* | Whether the UK can be excluded from legislative activity within the Schengen area. This time, the issue is whether they must be allowed to decide on the establishment of an Agency dedicated to facilitate cooperation of the Schengen countries with the abstaining Member States UK and Ireland. This is a purely organisational matter, which (unlike the issue on the biometrical passport decided in case C-137/05 *UK v Council*) has no relevance for fundamental rights in particular. |
| C-161/06 [2007] ECR I-10841 | *Skoma Lux* | Concerning the use of languages after Enlargement. |
| C-280/06 [2007] ECR I-10893 | *ETI and others* | Italian competition law refers to Article 81 EC (now: 101 TFEU) and requires national law to be read in line with it. No EU relevance. |
| C-435/06 [2007] ECR I-10141 | *C* | A conflict about custody over children – a jurisdictional case. |
| C-273/04 [2007] ECR I-8925 | *Poland v Council* | Conflict relating to agricultural policy after the accession of Poland. Equal treatment of Member States. |

| | | |
|---|---|---|
| C-403/05 [2007] ECR I-9045 | *Parliament v Commission* | Concerns competences in external policies. |
| C-440/05 [2007] ECR I-9097 | *Commission v Council* | Concerns competences in criminal matters. |
| C-17/06 [2007] ECR I-7041 | *Céline* | Case turns on specific interpretation of the First Directive 89/104/EC on trademarks, which is not of constitutional relevance. |
| C-431/05 [2007] ECR I-7001 | *Merck Genéricos Produtos Farmacêuticos* | Merck Genéricos was sued by M & Co and MSL for violating their patent on a pharmaceutical product. Merck Genéricos relies on the fact that Portuguese legislation only protects patents for 15 years, whereas M & Co and MSL rely on Article 33 TRIPS, which provides protection for 20 years. The question before the Court concerns direct applicability of TRIPS in Member States. An answer is evaded by the Court, and the Court finds no violation of EU law (thus indirectly denying TRIPS direct effect in EU law). |
| C-119/05 [2007] ECR I-6199 | *Lucchini* | Concerns state aid under the ECSC Treaty. |
| C-284/04 [2007] ECR I-5189 | *T Mobile Austria and others* | Whether state activities in allocating frequency rights to mobile phone companies constitute economic activity attracting VAT. No constitutional relevance. |
| C-369/04 [2007] ECR I-5247 | *Hutchinson 3G and others* | |
| C-29/05 P [2007] ECR I-2213 | *OHIM v Kaul* | Relates mainly to procedural rights in reviewing decisions of the OHIM. |
| C-292/05 [2007] ECR I-1519 | *Lechouritou and others* | Relates to jurisdictional questions during proceedings by the descendants of victims of war crimes against Germany. |
| C-199/05 [2006] ECR I-10485 | *European Community* | Whether the EU is taxable in Belgium – not of interest. |
| C-356/04 [2006] ECR I-8501 | *Lidl Belgium* | Details on the interpretation of Directive 84/450/EEC and 97/55/EC on misleading advertising. |
| C-123/04 [2006] ECR I-7861 | *Industrias Nucleares do Brasil and Siemens* | A case on external economic relations under the EAC Treaty. Not relevant. |

*Table A.3 Continued*

| Case number | Parties | Why this case is not relevant |
|---|---|---|
| C-119/04 [2006] ECR I-6885 | *COM v Italy* | While the Court held in the 1990s that Italian universities unjustifiably restricted the access of foreign language lecturers to standard employment contracts, Italy did not adjust the legislation. This was held to be a violation of the Treaty upon an infringement action (Case C-212/99 *Commission* v *Italy*), but no action ensued. The Court held that Italy had again omitted to fulfil its Treaty obligation, but considered that a penalty payment was not justified. |
| C-432/04 [2006] ECR I-6387 | *COM v Cresson* | Pension rights of former commissioner who left her office as a result of fraud. Not of interest here. |
| C-217/04 [2006] ECR I-3771 | *UK v Parliament and Council* | Challenge on establishing an agency on E-commerce. |
| C-341/04 ECR I-3813 | *Eurofood IFSC* | Detail on interpretation of Regulation 1346/2000/EC on the question whether insolvency proceedings should be acknowledged transnationally. |
| C-417/04 P [2006] ECR I-3881 | *Region Sciliana v Commission* | Whether regions have standing before the ECJ (no). |
| C-177/04 [2006] ECR I-2461 | *COM v France* | Proceedings following failure of France to implement a judgment (C-52/00 *Commission* v *France*) on incorrect implementation of the product liability directive. |
| C-66/04 [2005] ECR I-10553 | *UK v Parliament and Council* | On validity of Regulation EC 2065/2003 concerning smoke flavouring, based on Article 95. Apparently a case under the ‘anti-regulation’ logic. Not interesting. |

Note: In addition to the short explanation in the introduction to Chapter 4, this table gives a little more detail why individual cases were not evaluated.

# Index